Imagination in an Age of Crisis

Imagination in an Age of Crisis

—— *Soundings from the Arts and Theology* ——

EDITED BY
Jason Goroncy
AND
Rod Pattenden

FOREWORD BY
Ben Quash

◆PICKWICK *Publications* · Eugene, Oregon

IMAGINATION IN AN AGE OF CRISIS
Soundings from the Arts and Theology

Copyright © 2022 Wipf and Stock Publishers. All rights reserved. Except for brief quotations in critical publications or reviews, no part of this book may be reproduced in any manner without prior written permission from the publisher. Write: Permissions, Wipf and Stock Publishers, 199 W. 8th Ave., Suite 3, Eugene, OR 97401.

Pickwick Publications
An Imprint of Wipf and Stock Publishers
199 W. 8th Ave., Suite 3
Eugene, OR 97401

www.wipfandstock.com

PAPERBACK ISBN: 978-1-6667-0688-8
HARDCOVER ISBN: 978-1-6667-0689-5
EBOOK ISBN: 978-1-6667-0690-1

Cataloguing-in-Publication data:

Names: Goroncy, Jason [editor] | Pattenden, Rod [editor] | Quash, Ben [foreword writer]

Title: Imagination in an age of crisis : soundings from the arts and theology / edited by Jason Goroncy and Rod Pattenden ; foreword by Ben Quash.

Description: Eugene, OR: Pickwick Publications, 2022 | Includes bibliographical references and index.

Identifiers: ISBN 978-1-6667-0688-8 (paperback) | ISBN 978-1-6667-0689-5 (hardcover) | ISBN 978-1-6667-0690-1 (ebook)

Subjects: LCSH: Imagination—Religious aspects—Christianity | Christianity and art | Aesthetics—Religious aspects—Christianity | Criticism, interpretation, etc. | Imagination | Theology in literature

Classification: BR115.A8 G67 2022 (print) | BR115.A8 (ebook)

05/11/22

Selections from *God Is Waiting in the World's Yard*, 2019, by M. T. C. Cronin. Reproduced with permission of the author.

Selections from *Human Looking*, 2021, by Andy Jackson. Reproduced with permission of the author and Giramondo Publishing.

Selections from *Ismene's Survivable Resistance*, 2021, by Claire Gaskin. Reproduced with permission of the author.

Selections from *This Shuttered Eye*, 2021, by Rose Lucas. Reproduced with permission of the author.

Selections from *Two Green Parrots*, 2019, by Anne M. Carson. Reproduced with permission of the author.

Unless otherwise stated, scripture quotations are from the New Revised Standard Version Bible, copyright © 1989 National Council of the Churches of Christ in the United States of America. Used by permission. All rights reserved worldwide.

> *To raise new questions, new possibilities, to regard old problems from a new angle, requires creative imagination and marks real advance in science.*
>
> —Albert Einstein and Leopold Infeld,
> *The Evolution of Physics*

> *The reserves of imagination at any given period in a society are finite.*
>
> —George Steiner, *Extraterritorial*

> *If there are angels,*
> *they must, I hope,*
> *find this convincing,*
> *this merriment dangling from terror,*
> *not even crying Save me Save me*
> *since all of this takes place in silence.*
>
> *I can even imagine*
> *that they clap their wings*
> *and tears run from their eyes*
> *from laughter, if nothing else.*
>
> —Wisława Szymborska, "Slapstick"

Contents

Contributors | xi

Illustrations | xxi

Foreword | xxv
—Ben Quash

Acknowledgments | xxix

Daring Imagination | 1
—Jason Goroncy

1. The Cloud of Unknowing | 27
   —Jordie Albiston

2. Yolŋu Scriptures and Hermeneutics: *Mäna/Buḻ'manydji* | 30
   —Maratja Dhamarrandji, with Jione Havea

3. Having Eyes to See: An Interview with Emmanuel Garibay | 44
   —Emmanuel Garibay, with Rod Pattenden

4. Why Imagination Matters | 48
   —Trevor Hart

5. Painting: A Contemplative Action in the Time of Pandemic | 68
   —Douglas Purnell

6. The Objects of Our Loyalties and the Power of Inanimate Objects | 72
   —Robin Jensen

7. The Shadow of the Cross | 83
   —Robert Cording

8. "If I Say...": Poetry "after God" in Times of Eco-social and Ecclesial Trauma | 85
   —Anne Elvey

9. Timpani | 107
   —Julie Perrin

10. Hope at the End of History | 109
    —Scott Kirkland

11. Home | 124
    —Petra White

12. Every Life Can Sing | 127
    —Trish Watts

13. "I Am Making Everything New!": Textless Music and the Expansion of the Christian Imaginary in Times of Disruption | 131
    —Jennifer Wakeling

14. Journal de l'Année de la Peste | 146
    —Kevin Hart

15. Setting the Record *Straight*: The Prophetic Art of Ai Weiwei | 148
    —Adrienne Dengerink Chaplin

16. What Do I Paint Now? | 170
    —Alfonse Borysewicz

17. Imagination and the Sacred: Contemporary Australian Fictions of Hybridity | 174
    —Lyn McCredden

18. Process Sequence | 195
    —Paul Mitchell

19. "It'll Take You Way Down to the Wilderness": Theology in Conversation with the Films of Rolf de Heer and David Gulpilil | 198
    —Katherine Rainger

20. Grass Cloak | 217
    —Penny Dunstan

21. "My Past Has Thrown Me Out": Reading Samuel Beckett's Plays in an Age of Trauma | 220
    —Jason Goroncy

22. Fellowship | 251
    —Christian Wiman

23. Do You Believe in God? | 252
    —Pádraig Ó Tuama

24. Imagined Conversations and Real Letters during COVID-Times | 254
    —Naomi Wolfe

25. Circular Repetition | 268
    —Karly Michelle Edgar

26. Ida Nangala Granites | 275
    —Steve Bevis

27. George Gittoes: The Artist as Prophet and Mystic | 278
    —Rod Pattenden

28. The Portable Church | 296
    —John Foulcher

29. Who Is an Artist, and Who Cares Anyway? | 297
    —Libby Byrne

30. Compelling Stories | 310
    —Glenn Loughrey

31. Figure Held in Water | 313
    —Michael Symmons Roberts

32. "Goin' to the City": African American Folk Ritual for Communal Healing | 318
    —Amina McIntyre

33. What to Make of This, What to Make | 334
    —Scott Cairns

Contributors

Jordie Albiston

Jordie Albiston published thirteen poetry collections and a handbook on poetic form. Two of her books have been treated for music-theatre, both enjoying seasons at the Sydney Opera House. Albiston's work has been recognized by prizes including the Mary Gilmore Award, the New South Wales Premier's Prize, and the 2019 Patrick White Literary Award. The sequence in this volume, "The Cloud of Unknowing," is loosely drawn from the first six chapters of the late fourteenth-century Christian mystic treatise of the same title. Jordie died on March 1, 2022.

Steve Bevis

Steve Bevis is the Director of the Masters of Transformational Development at Eastern College, a former Minister of the John Flynn Uniting Church in Alice Springs, and a current Director of the Alice Springs Meeting Place Foundation. He is also a singer-songwriter. www.stevebevis.com.

Alfonse Borysewicz

Alfonse Borysewicz, born and raised in Detroit, is a Brooklyn-based painter who after completing his seminary studies took up painting in Boston before moving to New York City over forty years ago. He exhibits widely, with his painting constructions revealing, as one art dealer recently noted, "a fortitude of a deep spiritual path." www.alfonseborysewicz.com.

Libby Byrne

Libby Byrne works as an artist, art therapist, and theologian following the invitation and discovery of art into new ways of being with people in liminal spaces, extending the way we think, perceive, and respond to questions of meaning and existence. Having worked as an art therapist in palliative care and trauma recovery, her current research addresses the nature and significance of art, both made and received, in the process of healing that is required for human beings to flourish and live well with illness and in health. Libby is a Senior Lecturer teaching into the Master of Art Therapy Program at La Trobe University whilst developing a growing body of research in the emerging field of practice-led theological inquiry. She works as an Adjunct Lecturer and Honorary Research Associate with the University of Divinity. www.libbybyrne.com.au.

Scott Cairns

Scott Cairns is the author of nine books of poetry, including *Idiot Psalms*, *Slow Pilgrim: The Collected Poems*, and his latest, *Anaphora: New Poems*. His work has appeared in *The Atlantic*, *The Paris Review*, *The New Republic*, *Poetry*, and elsewhere, and has been anthologized in *Best Spiritual Writing* and *Best American Spiritual Writing*. Cairns has also written a spiritual memoir, *Short Trip to the Edge*, and a book-length theological meditation, *The End of Suffering*. He currently serves as Professor of English and Director of the low-residency MFA in Creative Writing at Seattle Pacific University.

Adrienne Dengerink Chaplin

Born and raised in the Netherlands, Adrienne Dengerink Chaplin is a Visiting Research Fellow at King's College London, and Research Associate at the Margaret Beaufort Institute in Cambridge, UK. She works at the interface of philosophical and theological aesthetics, and served as the co-president of the Canadian Society for Aesthetics. She is the co-author of *Art and Soul: Signposts for Christians in the Arts*, and the author of *The Philosophy of Susanne Langer: Embodied Meaning in Logic, Art and Feeling*. Adrienne is the founding director and curator of the travelling exhibition "Art, Conflict and Remembering: The Murals of the Bogside Artists" (www.bogsideartistsexhibition.org) which seeks to increase British understanding of the causes and the legacy of the Troubles in Northern Ireland.

Robert Cording

Robert Cording taught English and creative writing at the College of the Holy Cross for thirty-eight years, and worked as a poetry mentor in the Seattle Pacific University MFA program. He has published nine collections of poems, the latest of which is *Without My Asking,* and a volume of essays on poetry and religion titled *Finding the World's Fullness.*

Maratja Dhamarra<u>n</u>dji

Maratja Dhamarra<u>n</u>dji is a Djambarrpuyŋu Yolŋu (indigenous elder) from Galiwin'ku (Elcho Island, East Arnhem Land) and an ordained minister of the Uniting Church in Australia. He undertook theological studies at Yalga Binbi Institute (Townsville) and Nungalinya College (Darwin), and worked for over twenty years as the chief Yolŋu Bible translator. He contributed to *Indigenous Australia and the Unfinished Business of Theology: Cross-cultural Engagement*, and regularly delivers cross-cultural training.

Penny Dunstan

Penny Dunstan is a Newcastle-based artist and agronomist/soil scientist with a specific interest in the decisions we make about land management and open-cut coal mine rehabilitation. In her art practice she invites the land to represent itself through various techniques, including working with farmed topsoils and their plants; long exposure, limited interference analogue plant-scape photography; and a writing practice that acknowledges the old ways on Wonnaura Country. www.pennydunstan.com.

Karly Michelle Edgar

Karly Michelle Edgar is a mixed media artist and PhD candidate researching the use of biography in palliative care, and is interested in story, spirituality, and reflective artwork. She has an BCA in theatre and an MA in Church Practice. She lives with fibromyalgia, on Wurundjeri land. www.karlymichelle.com.

Anne Elvey

Anne Elvey is a poet, editor, and researcher living on Boonwurrung Country in bayside Melbourne. She is an honorary research associate at Trinity College Theological School, University of Divinity, and an adjunct research fellow, School of Languages, Literatures, Cultures, and Linguistics, Monash University. Recent publications include: *Obligations of Voice*, and *Reading the Magnificat in Australia: Unsettling Engagements.*

John Foulcher

John Foulcher has published twelve books of poetry, the most recent being *Dancing with Stephen Hawking* (Pitt Street Poetry, 2021). His poetry has been published in national magazines, newspapers, and anthologies, and studied in Australian schools for over thirty years. In 2010, he was the Literature Board's resident at the Keesing Studio in Paris, and in 2019 he won the ACU Poetry Prize.

Emmanuel Garibay

Emmanuel Garibay is a visual artist from the Philippines who is known for his expressionist figurative style and the keen socio-political content of many of his works. He believes art can help awaken people's consciousness so they can pull themselves out of their despondency and bring about empowered change. Aside from being a prolific and internationally-established painter, he is also an active cultural organizer who has headed various art and cultural organizations since his student days. He is currently chairperson of Artletics, an artist-led organization that empowers communities through art education. Artletics runs the Linangan Art Residency Program in Alfonso, Cavite, which hones artistic and leadership skills in young talents through mentored studio practice, art classes, and immersion in community-building projects.

Jason Goroncy

Jason Goroncy lives on unceded Yalukit Willam country. He is Associate Professor of Theology in the University of Divinity, Australia, and has published widely in the areas of public theology, theology and the arts, and theological ethics. He is the author of *Hallowed be Thy Name: The Sanctification of All in the Soteriology of P. T. Forsyth*, and has edited *Descending on Humanity and Intervening in History: Notes from the Pulpit Ministry of P. T. Forsyth*, and *Tikkun Olam—To Mend the World: A Confluence of Theology and the Arts*. www.jasongoroncy.com.

Kevin Hart

Kevin Hart is Edwin B. Kyle Professor of Christian Theology at the University of Virginia, USA, where he also holds Professorships of English and French. His most recent publications are *Contemplation and Kingdom* and *L'Image vulnérble: Sur l'image de Dieu chez S. Augustin*. He is currently completing *Lands of Likeness*, which represents his Gifford Lectures at the University of Glasgow. His most recent collections of poetry are *Barefoot* and *Wild Track: New and Selected Poems*.

Trevor Hart

Trevor Hart is Rector of Saint Andrew's Episcopal Church, St. Andrews, former Professor of Divinity in the University of St. Andrews, and Canon Theologian of St. Ninian's Cathedral, Perth. He has lectured internationally and published widely on aspects of Christian theology, has a special interest in bringing theology into constructive conversation with artistry and other facets of human imagination, and was founding Director of the Institute for Theology, Imagination, and the Arts in the University of St. Andrews. Among his recent publications are *Making Good: Creation, Creativity and Artistry*, *In Him Was Life: The Person and Work of Christ*, and *Confession as Performance: The Apostles' Creed and the Drama of Human Life* (forthcoming). www.trevorahart.com.

Jione Havea

Jione Havea is co-parent for a seven-year-old, migrant to the unceded Wurundjeri lands and waters, native pastor (Methodist Church in Tonga), and research fellow with Trinity Methodist Theological College (Aotearoa New Zealand) and with Centre for Public and Contextual Theology, Charles Sturt University (Australia). Jione authored *Losing Ground: Reading Ruth in the Pacific*, and edited *Theologies from the Pacific*.

Robin Jensen

Robin M. Jensen is the Patrick O'Brien Professor of Theology at the University of Notre Dame (USA) where she also holds faculty positions in Art History and Classics. Her research focuses on the intersections of early Christian theology, ritual practices, and material culture. Among her published books are *Understanding Early Christian Art*, *Face to Face: Portraits of the Divine in Early Christianity*, *The Substance of Things Seen: Art, Faith, and the Christian Community*, *Living Water: Images, Symbols, and Settings of Early Christian Baptism*, *Christianity in Roman Africa: The Development of Its Practices and Beliefs*, and *The Cross: History, Art, and Controversy*.

Scott Kirkland

Scott A. Kirkland is the John and Jeanne Stockdale Lecturer in Practical Theology and Ethics at Trinity College Theological School, University of Divinity, Australia. He is the author of *Into the Far Country: Karl Barth and the Modern Subject*, as well as a forthcoming monograph on the demise of the end of history thesis in conversation with Giorgio Agamben and Franz Kafka.

Glenn Loughrey

Glenn Loughrey is an Australian artist who tells ancient stories from the heart of country through contemporary art. He identifies as Wiradjuri and his approach utilizes lines, dots, and color to make patterns that create their own stories within the primary art piece. While Glenn's practice arises out of his Aboriginality, he does not describe his practice as Aboriginal art. Instead, he considers it a fusion of styles and the exploration of story within a story. Earning national recognition in recent years, he has been selected as a finalist in the Moran Portrait Prize (2017), the Mandoorla Prize (2020), the Paddington Art Prize (2020), and the Blake Art Prize (2020), as well as semi-finalist in the Moran Portrait Prize in 2018. He has held exhibitions in major cities, including Melbourne and Brisbane, as well as in various regional locations across Australia, such as Healesville and Newcastle. Additionally, he contributes to several publications and regularly takes commissions to assist in the visual sharing of stories as part of educational pieces, which utilize his particular art practice. www.glennloughrey.com.

Amina McIntyre

Amina S. McIntyre is a PhD student at Vanderbilt University. She has earned a BA in Anthropology (Colby College), an MA in African American and African Diaspora Studies (Indiana University), an MFA in Playwriting (Spalding University), and Master of Theological Studies (Candler School of Theology at Emory University). Amina is an Atlanta regional playwright with production credits at Actor's Express, Atlanta History Museum, Out of Hand Theatre, Oakland Cemetery, and Vanguard Repertory Theatre. She is also an Elder in Full Connection with the Christian Methodist Episcopal Church, and a Co-Founder of Hush Harbor Lab. www.ladylovesherpen.com.

Lyn McCredden

Lyn McCredden is Professor of Australian Literature at Deakin University, Melbourne. She is the author of numerous literary critical works, including *The Fiction of Tim Winton: Earthed and Sacred*, *Luminous Moments: The Contemporary Sacred*, *Intimate Horizons: The Sacred in Australian Literature* (with Bill Ashcroft and Frances Devlin Glass), *Bridgings: Reading Australian Women's Poetry* (with Rose Lucas), and a volume of poetry, *Wanting Only*. Lyn is Director of the research network *Religion, Society, and Culture* at Deakin University; and is an active member of Churches of Christ in Australia.

Paul Mitchell

Paul Mitchell has published six books, including fiction, poetry, and non-fiction. His latest is a collection of personal essays, *Matters of Life and Faith*. He teaches writing at Whitley College and his work has been published widely over the past twenty-five years. www.paul-mitchell.com.au.

Pádraig Ó Tuama

Pádraig Ó Tuama is a poet and theologian from Ireland. His poems have been published in the *Harvard Review*, *Gutter*, *Poetry Ireland*, and elsewhere, as well as being featured on national broadcasters in Ireland, the UK, Australia, and New Zealand. He presents the podcast Poetry Unbound from On Being Studios. His books include *Readings from the Book of Exile*, *Sorry for your Troubles*, and *In the Shelter*. *Poetry Unbound*, a book from the series of the same name, is forthcoming from Canongate Books in 2022. www.padraigotuama.com.

Rod Pattenden

Rod Pattenden has written widely on the creative arts, spirituality, and religion in Australia, and has curated numerous exhibitions on Australian art, including the recent *George Gittoes: On Being There*. He was Minister of Adamstown Uniting Church in Newcastle where he developed Adamstown Arts, a community-based program in visual and performing arts, and is adjunct fellow with the Australian Centre for Christianity and Culture. He is co-founder of InterPlay Australia and former Chairperson of the Blake Prize for Religious Art. www.rodpattenden.id.au.

Julie Perrin

Julie Perrin is an oral storyteller and writer of short prayers and non-fiction stories. Her work has been published in Australian newspapers and magazines. Julie is the author of two collections, *Tender: Stories That Lean into Kindness*, and *A Prayer, a Plea, a Bird*, both published by MediaCom Education. Julie is currently serving as a chaplain in a major public hospital in Melbourne. www.tellingwords.com.au.

Douglas Purnell

Douglas Purnell is living a second life as a fulltime artist and curator. In his first life he was a minister in the Uniting Church in Australia, a pastoral theologian, author, family therapist, and group facilitator. Now he works in his studio every day seeking to create works that are not of some-recognizable thing, but that are poetic, and that call the viewers to be open to the mysteries of life. Doug has been an artist in residence at the Henry Luce III Centre for Arts and Religion in Washington DC, and has exhibited widely in the United States and Australia. www.dougpurnellart.com.

Ben Quash

Ben Quash is Professor of Christianity & the Arts at King's College London. He directs a major ten-year project to create an online Visual Commentary on Scripture (TheVCS.org). He runs an MA in Christianity & the Arts in association with the National Gallery, London, and broadcasts frequently on BBC Radio. He is a Trustee of Art + Christianity, and Canon Theologian of both Coventry and Bradford Cathedrals. His publications include *Abiding: The Archbishop of Canterbury's Lent Book 2013* (Bloomsbury, 2012) and *Found Theology: History, Imagination and the Holy Spirit* (T&T Clark, 2014), and he has written catalogue essays for exhibitions at Ben Uri Gallery, London, the Inigo Rooms in Somerset House, and the Vatican Pavilion at the Venice Biennale 2015.

Katherine Rainger

Katherine Rainger is the Senior Chaplain at Radford College in Canberra, Australia. Her research interests include Australian film and theology, the Book of Lamentations, and Palestinian theology.

Michael Symmons Roberts

Michael Symmons Roberts was born in Lancashire and his eight collections of poetry—including *Drysalter* and *Corpus*—have received accolades, including the Forward Prize, the Costa Poetry Prize, and the Whitbread Poetry Award, and have been shortlisted for the Griffin International Poetry Prize. He is a Fellow of the Royal Society of Literature, and Professor of Poetry at Manchester Metropolitan University. His latest collection—*Ransom*—was published by Cape in March 2021. www.symmonsroberts.com.

Jennifer Wakeling

Jennifer Wakeling is a musician, educator, and researcher whose special interests lie in the fields of music, theology, and music in Christian worship. Jennifer has been involved in church music and worship ministry for most of her life. She is passionate about exploring ways for worshippers to engage deeply and imaginatively with the qualitative and feeling dimensions of Christian meaning-generation through the use of textless music in worship.

Trish Watts

Trish Watts is a singer/songwriter, a registered voice movement therapy practitioner, a performing artist, educator, and community choir director. Believing that "every life deserves the opportunity to sing," she specializes in voicing who we truly are. Her life work is anchored in the bedrock of "play" and she celebrates thirty years as co-founder of InterPlay® Australia, a community arts practice. She was Music Director for the Sydney and Cambodia Threshold Choirs and the Phnom Penh Community Choir. Trish has worked as an artist, teacher, performer, and facilitator in Australia, Europe, India, South Africa, Cambodia, and the United States. www.trishwatts.com.

Petra White

Petra White lives in Berlin. Her most recent book is *Cities* (Vagabond Press, 2021).

Christian Wiman

Christian Wiman is the author and editor of numerous books, including *Hammer Is the Prayer: Selected Poems*, and *My Bright Abyss: Meditation of a Modern Believer*. He teaches religion and literature at Yale Divinity School, USA.

Naomi Wolfe

Naomi Wolfe is a trawloolway woman, connected to the northeast of Tasmania, with Jewish–German and Irish ancestry. Her dad was trawloolway Aboriginal and her mum was non-Indigenous. Both parents have passed away with Dad dying suddenly after a misdiagnosis. Naomi is a proud daughter, sister, and aunty, and was born, as her dad said, "askin' questions." She was previously the Academic Co-ordinator of Jim-baa-yer Indigenous Unit at Australian Catholic University, before university restructuring, but is now a lecturer within the School of Arts. Naomi is also the First Peoples Co-ordinator at the University of Divinity, Australia. She teaches Aboriginal and Torres Strait Islander and world Indigenous histories, along with other ancient civilizations such as Ancient Rome. She co-teaches theology with NAIITS: An Indigenous Learning Community, an international community of Indigenous and non-Indigenous peoples, who deliver Indigenous designed, Indigenous led, and Indigenous delivered theological education.

Illustrations

2.1 *Mäna / Buḻ'manydji*, date and materials unknown. Photo by Michelle Cook. Reproduced by permission of the Dhamarraṉdji Djambarrpuyŋu clan.

2.2 Maratja at his ceremony of certification in the 1970s. Photo by Kevin Inman. Reproduced by permission.

2.3 Justin at his Dhäbi initiation ceremony in 1995. Photo provided by Maratja Dhamarraṉdji. Reproduced by permission.

3.1 Emmanuel Garibay, *Selda (Prison Cell)*, 2020. Oil on canvas, 122 x 152.5 cm. Artist's collection.

5.1 Douglas Purnell, *C-V 27*, 2020. Acrylic on canvas, 122 x 91 cm. Artist's collection.

6.1 *The Three Hebrew Youths in the Fiery Furnace, from the Catacomb of Priscilla*, in Giuseppe Wilpert, *Roma Sotterranea: Le Pitture della Catacombe Romane,* vol. 2 (Rome: Desclée Lefebure and Co., 1903), Table 78.

6.2 *The Trial of the Three Hebrew Youths*. Left portion of a lid from the sarcophagus of St. Gilles, fourth century. Photo by Robin Jensen. Used with permission of the Museum of Saint-Gilles-du-Gard, France.

6.3 Cover of sheet music for the song *Shadrack (Shadrach)*, written and composed by Robert MacGimsey, 1931. Ink on paper, 30.48 x 22.86 cm. National Museum of American History, Washington, DC, USA. Used with permission of the Smithsonian Institution's National Museum of American History, Behring Center.

10.1   Colin McCahon, *Parihaka Triptych*, 1972. Acrylic on canvas, 175.4 x 437.0 cm. Gift of the artist, 1973. Held by the Govett-Brewster Art Gallery, New Plymouth, Aotearoa New Zealand, for the people of Parihaka. He tākoha nā te ringatoi, 1973. E tautiaki ana te whare whakairi toi o Govett-Brewster mā te iwi o Parihaka. Reproduced by permission.

12.1   Youth School EYC (Empowering Youth Cambodia) in partnership with Cambodia Sings, Phnom Penh. Photo supplied by Trish Watts.

15.1   Middle School, Sichuan earthquake, 2009. Photo by Xieyouding. Used with permission.

15.2   Ai Weiwei, *Sunflower Seeds*, 2008–10. Handcrafted porcelain. Tate Modern, London, England. Photo taken May 17, 2011. Photo in public domain.

15.3   Ai Weiwei, *Straight*, 2008–12. Steel. Royal Academy of Arts, London, England. Photo taken September 15, 2015. Photo by Malcolm Park editorial. Used with permission of Alamy.

16.1   Alfonse Borysewicz, *Road to Emmaus*, 2017–20. Oil and wax on linen, 45.72 x 35.56 cm. Artist's collection.

16.2   Alfonse Borysewicz, *NEOWISE COMET*, 2017–20. Oil and wax on linen, 45.72 x 35.56 cm. Artist's collection.

17.1   Sidney Nolan, *Book jacket design for Patrick White's novel* Voss, *1957*, 1957. Ink, wash, wax crayon, pen, and ink on card, 8.9 x 13.9 cm. Mitchell Library, State Library of New South Wales and courtesy of The Trustees of the Sidney Nolan Trust, ML 743, Sydney, Australia.

19.1   Ramingining artists and Djon Mundine, conceptual creator and artist, Bandjalung people, *The Aboriginal Memorial*, 1987–88. Natural earth pigments and binder on eucalyptus wood, 327 (H) cm (height irregular). National Gallery of Australia, Canberra, Australia. Purchased with the assistance of funds from National Gallery admission charges and commissioned in 1987, 1987.2240.1-200. Reproduced by permission of National Gallery of Australia.

19.2   Rolf de Heer and David Gulpilil on the set of *The Tracker*. Photo by Matthew Nettheim. Reproduced by permission of Rolf de Heer.

19.3 Screenshot from *Ten Canoes*. Photo by James Geurts. Reproduced by permission of Rolf de Heer.

19.4 Screenshot of David Gulpilil in *The Tracker*. Photo by Matthew Nettheim. Reproduced by permission of Rolf de Heer.

19.5 Screenshot of Grant Page, Damon Gameau, Gary Sweet, and David Gulpilil in *The Tracker*. Photo by Matthew Nettheim. Reproduced by permission of Rolf de Heer.

20.1 Penny Dunstan, *Grass Cloak*, 2020. Local harvest *Microlaena stipoides*, embroidery cotton, steel, and forest redgum (*Eucalyptus tereticornis*), 160 x 120 x 25cm. Artist's collection.

21.1 Scene from *Waiting for Godot in Fukushima*, directed by Yuta Hagiwara. Featuring Honami Shimizu, Shintaro Yokote, and Ichiro Matsubara. Near Futatsunuma Park, Fukushima, 2011. Photo by Takashi Fujii. Reproduced by permission.

21.2 Scene from *Krapp's Last Tape*, directed by Dominic Hill. Featuring Gerard Murphy as Krapp. Citizens Theatre, Glasgow, 2012. Photo by Tommy Ga-Ken Wan. Reproduced by permission.

21.3 Scene from *Come and Go*, directed by Marc Atkinson Borrull and Nicholas Johnson. Set by Colm McNally. Costumes by Liadain Kaminska Ní Bhraonáin. Featuring Siobhán Cullen, Ellen Flynn, and Ellen Patterson. Samuel Beckett Theatre, Dublin, 2012. Photo by Colm McNally. Reproduced by permission.

21.4 Scene from *Endgame*, directed by Dominic Hill. Featuring Peter Kelly as Nagg, David Neilson as Hamm, and Chris Gascoyne as Clov. Citizens Theatre, Glasgow, 2016. Photo by Tim Morozzo. Reproduced by permission.

21.5 Scene from *Happy Days*, directed by Yuta Hagiwara. Featuring Honami Shimizu as Winnie and Shin Ito as Willie. Keio University, Tokyo, 2018. Photo by Rakutaro Ogiwara. Reproduced by permission.

21.6 Scene from *Happy Days*, directed by Caitríona McLaughlin. Featuring Siobhán McSweeney as Winnie and Marty Rea as Willie. Olympia Theatre, Dublin, 2021. Produced by Landmark Productions. Photo by Patrick Redmond. Reproduced by permission.

21.7 Scene from *Happy Days*, directed by Michael Hurst. Featuring Robyn Malcolm as Winnie and Cameron Rhodes as Willie. Silo Theatre, Auckland, 2010. Photo by Andrew Malmo. Reproduced by permission.

21.8 Scene from *Krapp's Last Tape*, directed by Patty Gallagher. Featuring Paul Whitworth as Krapp. Jewel Theatre Company, Santa Cruz, 2011. Photo by Steve DiBartolomeo. Reproduced by permission.

24.1 Boat Harbour Beach, December 2020. Photo by Naomi Wolfe. Reproduced by permission.

25.1 Karly Michelle Edgar, *Repetition 1*, 2020. Ink pen on paper, 76 x 56 cm. Artist's collection.

26.1 Ida Nangala Granites, *Mina Mina*, 2020. Acrylic on canvas, 105 x 70 cm. The Binet Collection. Reproduced by permission of Ida Nangala Granites and Marcus Binet.

27.1 George Gittoes, *The Preacher*, 1995. Oil on linen, 181 x 250 cm. Collection of National Gallery of Australia, Canberra, Australia. Used with permission.

27.2 George Gittoes, *Security*, 2020. Oil on linen, 168 x 244 cm. Artist's collection.

27.3 George Gittoes, Diary entry, May 30, 2011. Kabul, Afghanistan. Used with permission.

29.1 Libby Byrne, *Draw Near in Faith, and . . .* , 2020. 19 pages. Graphite, gouache, and oil pastel on paper, 48 x 21 cm. Brooklyn Art Library, New York, USA. Used with permission.

29.2 Libby Byrne, "Who is an artist, and who cares anyway?," in *Draw Near in Faith, and . . .* , 2020, 2–7. Graphite, gouache, and oil pastel on paper, 48 x 21 cm. Brooklyn Art Library, New York, USA. Used with permission.

30.1 Glenn Loughrey, *Kurrajong Dreaming*, 2020. Acrylic on canvas, 122 x 182 cm. Collection of The Community of the Holy Name, Melbourne, Australia. Used with permission.

Foreword

Ben Quash

IN THE PROLOGUE TO his collection of essays *On Christian Theology*,[1] Rowan Williams describes three modes in which theology can be pursued. Each has its own particular rigor and style; its distinctive domains of concern and measures of success. The three modes he lays out are the *celebratory*, the *communicative*, and the *critical*.

Celebratory theology, according to Williams, corresponds loosely with what the nineteenth-century German theologian Friedrich Schleiermacher called "poetic" theology.[2] It is often undertaken in the mode of praise. Its ways of moving and persuading people work not so much through argument as through enticement: the conjuring of a vision of God and the world in its relation to God. It is unapologetic in its weaving of words, themes, and images in and out of one another in order to evoke a fullness of vision in Christian terms.

Communicative theology corresponds loosely with what Schleiermacher called "rhetorical" theology.[3] By contrast with the celebratory mode, apologetics *is* one of its main concerns. Rather than conjuring ever more possibilities from what has become Christianity's "native speech," it explores how Christian commitments (practical as well as intellectual) might be capable of expression in other "languages"—those of what Williams calls Christianity's "uncommitted environment."[4] It sees whether the categories of other worldviews and the shapes of other thought patterns can bear the weight of (perhaps even add something to) Christianity's articulation of itself. It converses.

---

1. Williams, *On Christian Theology*, xii–xvi.
2. See Schleiermacher, *The Christian Faith*, 78–85.
3. See Schleiermacher, *The Christian Faith*, 78–86.
4. Williams, *On Christian Theology*, xiv.

Critical theology corresponds loosely with what Schleiermacher called "scientific" theology.[5] The emphasis here is on rigorous interrogation by theology of its own presuppositions, norms, and language. It is theology at its most stringently self-reflexive: eliminating lazy or complacent thought and action; purifying its discourse. As Williams points out, radical forms of critical theology can lead to a heightened sense that relationship with God involves an experience of dispossession and something like darkness: some "atheous"[6] theologies of the twentieth century seem to emerge from it, although so do the apophatic strands of theology, many of them closely aligned with (and informed by) mystical experience, with its insistence that illumination is indexed to purgation.

Williams argues persuasively that these three modes of theology can correct each other in key ways. For example, a celebratory theology that ends up talking to itself—bogged down in its own internal networks of signs, or locked in its own private language (however joyously doxological)—needs to discover how impenetrable that can be for those listening (or looking) in from outside. Communicative theology turns the discourse outwards, and (like all good conversation, where there is give and take) can lead not only to a greater theological accountability to the world whose flourishing all Christian discourse seeks to serve, but also to theology's own enrichment, as it is spoken and re-spoken in new terms. It can find (rather than lose) itself in translation.

But, in turn, there is a risk here of dissipation. Moments may come when it seems that theology's center cannot hold; or, alternatively, that its center is no longer discernible. Multiple redescriptions of theology's claims can float free of any normativity.[7] The status of public truth, shared ethics, and mutual delight are all endangered when the quest for normativity is abandoned. Asking what we can have in common is a question that sinks easily in an ever-expanding sea of proliferating (and frequently conflicting) descriptions. So critical questioning is needed to reassert the claims of righteousness, peace, and joy, which Saint Paul highlights as marks of the kingdom of God (see Rom 14:17). The justice "that rolls down like waters" (Amos 5:24), the peace "that passes all understanding" (Phil 4:6), and the "inexpressible and glorious" joy "that no one can take away" (John 16:22; 1 Pet 1:8) are safeguarded best when critical theology takes its place alongside communicative and celebratory modes.

---

5. See Schleiermacher, *The Christian Faith*, 48, 81, 84–85, 116.

6. Williams, *On Christian Theology*, xv.

7. This need not be the same as "hegemony," though today it is often mistakenly supposed that norms must inevitably be coercive.

What has this to do with the arts? I think, everything.[8] And I think this book helps to show why.

It is tempting to suppose that the arts, when they are at work in the service of theology, belong very squarely in the celebratory domain of Williams's scheme. Indeed, Williams himself implies this to some extent. It is when giving examples of celebratory theology that he cites as examples hymnody, poetry, Byzantine iconography, and modern choruses. Jason Goroncy chooses an apt quotation from W. H. Auden to underscore the link between the arts and the untrammeled spirit of play that enables the human creature to rejoice before its maker: "*Homo Laborans* is also *Homo Ludens.*" But (as Goroncy's quotation shows) Auden was far from supposing that play's effects are restricted to initiates—those "inside the game." He discerned that to play—perhaps especially in our modern, technocratic, market-driven era—is a form of challenging political witness to those in one's surrounding environment. Making art is intrinsically a political act insofar as it resists the tendency of what Auden calls "Management" to define human beings only by their service of more or less anonymous systems of production. Insofar as this is "witness," it is communicative (while also being celebratory). And insofar as this is "challenging," it is critical (while also being celebratory *and* communicative).

This collection of essays and artistic interventions is of its time and place. While the collection has a global reach, many of its writers have deep roots in Australian contexts, which gives a grounded and specific edge to their voices. This in turn equips them to speak with persuasive and enlightening authenticity to those further afield, in ways that are bound to open fresh perspectives for them too. The contents of this volume are also marked in multiple places by the pervasive effects of the global coronavirus pandemic of 2020 and 2021.

Particularities of time and place are the scaffolding of all worthwhile artistic utterance, as of all theological utterance. To speak with a long reach requires one to speak meaningfully, and to speak meaningfully requires one to speak from somewhere. The celebratory aspects of this volume—in its advocacy of artistic making as a sign and a conduit of grace at work in the world, for the sake of liberation and joy—are by the same token essays in

---

8. This is what motivates the Visual Commentary on Scripture (TheVCS.org), which I edit. Like premodern collections of hymnody, prayer, homiletics, exegesis, and doctrinal definition, its bold, curated juxtapositions of visual artworks with biblical texts and commentary generate a form of visual theology that combines scholarly rigor with aesthetic delight, held within an ethos of conversational openness. It tries to sustain a context for the shared pursuit of truth and goodness, as well as (and along with) the shared enjoyment of beauty.

conversation and witness that seek touching points and answering responses from those who may have no formal religious faith but are fellow travelers in troubled times, and engines of critique of a world whose injustices are rank, and whose visions need purgation if they are to be fit for illumination. Joy marks the kingdom only when righteousness and peace are also present. These essays call for justice, wise speech, and attentive listening, precisely as they invite us to dance before the ark of God's covenant.

They are an appropriate embodiment, then, of Rowan Williams's insistence that celebratory, communicative, and critical modes of theology do not simply sit alongside each other (as mere alternative options), but rather exist in a circular relationship in which each one always has the others on either side of it. It is only hand in hand that we encounter them, and that (to adapt Michael Symmons Roberts's words towards the end of this volume) they offer us "a line to live by."

Bibliography

Schleiermacher, Friedrich. *The Christian Faith*. Edited by H. R. Mackintosh and J. S. Stewart. Translated by D. M. Baillie et al. London: T. & T. Clark, 1999.

Williams, Rowan. *On Christian Theology*. Oxford: Blackwell, 2000.

Acknowledgments

THIS PROJECT BEGAN IN the midst of a decision to cancel, due to COVID-19-related travel restrictions, a planned arts and theology event that was to be held in Naarm/Melbourne in July 2020. The Editors thank Christina Rowntree for her contribution to the imagined scope of the original event, and for her creative ideas and support in developing this current project. This continues our shared vision to deepen conversations between the arts, theology, and contemporary culture.

We acknowledge the assistance of the Australian Research Theology Foundation Inc. for a grant to support this publication.

Aboriginal and Torres Strait Islander readers are advised that this book contains the names and images of people who have died.

Daring Imagination

Jason Goroncy

What Time Is It?

It's difficult to think about art during an apocalypse.[1]

WHAT KIND OF TIME is this? Natural disasters, a global pandemic, nationalism, and widespread political demagoguery are among the highlights of the "blood-dimmed tide"[2] that is on the move. None of these are new threats, of course, although the first, at least, are now occurring at a frequency and magnitude once unimaginable. Despite reasoned calls to read the world through less apocalyptic lenses,[3] many, particularly those of the world's working and burgeoning middle classes, live with a growing recognition of unsettling contingency, the gnawing of dis-ease, the erosion of old certainties, and the despoliation of hope.[4] Many live too with growing desires for the re-enchantment of the places in which we find ourselves, places disenchanted and de-animated by modernity, and, in many parts of the world, by the ugly behemoth of settler colonialism. It is a difficult time. It is a time for undertaking responsible work. It is time to imagine that things might be otherwise. We imagine or we perish.[5]

1. Grady, "Why Art Matters at the End of the World," line 1.
2. Yeats, "The Second Coming," 189.
3. See, for example, Pinker, *Enlightenment Now*; Rosling et al., *Factfulness*.
4. See, for example, Case and Deaton, *Deaths of Despair*; Graham, *Happiness for All?*
5. Recent decades have seen debate among archaeologists about whether it is imagination, as a cultural reality, the belief in other possibilities, and not brain size, that allowed *Homo sapiens* to outperform and outlive their older human cousins, *Homo sapiens neanderthalensis*. See, for example, Mithen, *The Prehistory of the Mind*; Mithen, "The Evolution of Imagination," 28–54; Mithen, *The Singing Neanderthals*; Mithen, "Seven Steps in the Evolution of the Human Imagination," 3–29; Whiten and Suddendorf, "Great Ape Cognition and the Evolutionary Roots of Human Imagination," 31–59; Coolidge and Wynn, "An Introduction to Cognitive Archaeology," 386–92; Hodgson, "Costly Signalling," 446–65; Seghers, "A Tale of Two Species," 83–102.

Hope dares to imagine that "some revelation is at hand."[6] But revelation rarely appears as revelation. Revelation, epiphany, usually means only more disruption. Many of us, artists included, welcome such disruptive moments, although rarely for the disruption itself. The welcome is associated with the ways revelation—fresh vision—pushes to the surface a series of inescapable questions: existential questions, political questions, questions about the illusory character of economic and racial justice, questions about the vulnerable character of life's threatened systems, questions about our regular habits, deepest fears, and meaningful commitments, and questions about our responsibilities.

Of course, responding to such questions is no easy task. To that end, some have turned to art. Art can, no doubt, assist us to reckon with the world, but can art rescue us from its most horrid and brute facts? In his book *Why Only Art Can Save Us: Aesthetics and the Absence of Emergency*, the philosopher and cultural critic Santiago Zabala offers a sanguine response to that question. He argues that art can indeed save us from the greater demons of our nature, including neoliberal democracy, militarism, and global capitalism, and from arrangements where such forces alone, as a way to legitimize themselves, define what any real "emergency" is. Art, he suggests, has the capacity to save us from such nightmares precisely by attending to the work of disrupting the status quo—disrupting, for example, "capitalism's indefinite reproduction" and "realism's metaphysical impositions."[7] Zabala proposes that art provides the necessary aesthetic force "to shake us out of our tendency to ignore the 'social paradoxes' generated by the political, financial, and technological frames that contain us; the 'urban discharge' of slums and plastic and electronic wastes; the 'environmental calls' caused by global warming, ocean pollution, and deforestation; and the 'historical accounts' of invisible, ignored, and denied events."[8] Art's proper function is, therefore, to "thrust us into" actual emergencies; that is, to save us from discrimination, forgetfulness, and annihilation. Instead of being "points of arrival for consumers' identification, contemplation, and realization of beauty, works of art are points of departure to change the world, a world that needs new interpretations instead of better descriptions."[9]

Zabala's contribution to an aesthetic theory of ethics is laudable, and his assessment of the predicament we face—his own "description" of

---

6. Yeats, "The Second Coming," 189. This close association between imagination and revelation has deep roots in the Christian tradition. See Guite, *Faith, Hope, and Poetry*, 14; Hart, *Between the Image and the Word*, 229–49.

7. Zabala, *Why Only Art Can Save Us*, Introduction.

8. Zabala, *Why Only Art Can Save Us*, Introduction.

9. Zabala, *Why Only Art Can Save Us*, Introduction.

the problem—is as impressive as it is compelling. His suggested antidote, however, represents a mode of the poison of "aesthetic exceptionalism" unsupported by the facts.[10] There can be no question that art cannot save us from that which we are "too far gone to feel."[11] While art might be—and indeed is—a *part* of such work, neither the arts nor any other human activity represent a brake on our most demonic instincts; still less are they a kind of messianic fix. There can be no question about arts' complicity in, for example, the depravity of unbridled capitalism, or the propaganda that celebrates empire and champions the causes of autocrats, or the demise of a truly public commons. The Nazis loved their Wagner; Mirós and Pollocks sell for hundreds of millions of dollars in the same cities where people, including artists, die of starvation. It is a cruel lie to think of art as a way of escape from such horrors, despite artists', consumers', and critics' own claims and aspirations to the contrary. It is equally dishonest to deploy art to grace barbarism.[12]

Conversely, "the structure of responsible action involves both *willingness to become guilty [Bereitschaft zur Schuldübernahme] and freedom*."[13] Thus the responsible artist works not only with an acute awareness of the world being dislocated but also with a marked sense of personal complicity in that fact. From that place, artists, like theologians and other endangered species, are called to "adopt a 'position,'" to "make an *option* about reality, to be committed to a 'direction' (not an explanation . . .) of and in the world,"[14] to speak responsibly to that dislocation, to speak with fidelity to time and

---

10. Here see De Boever, *Against Aesthetic Exceptionalism*; De Boever, "Art and Exceptionalism," 161–81. De Boever takes the phrase "aesthetic exceptionalism" from Robson, "Against Aesthetic Exceptionalism," 213–29.

11. Forsyth, *The Work of Christ*, 18.

12. I take this point from Steiner, "A Note on Absolute Tragedy," 151–52: "On the level of decorum, of tact of spirit and of heart, it can be, indeed it has been, argued that the sheer dimensions of the inhuman as we have in recent history enacted and experienced it, that the anonymous, mechanistic functionality of modern mass-sadism and oppression, impose silence. The point is that even where they originate in humane outrage and in hope of enlightenment, art, eloquence, controlled shape, inevitably adorn. Should art run the risk of gracing barbarism? The inchoate scream out of the blackened mouth in the Beckett parable may be the only sort of response whose patent inadequacy does not trivialize (in contrast to the theatrical scream in Picasso's 'Guernica')."

13. Bonhoeffer, *Ethics*, 275. Cf. Bonhoeffer, *Ethics*, 282: "Those who in acting responsibly take on guilt—which is inescapable for any responsible person—place this guilt on themselves, not on someone else; they stand up for it and take responsibility for it. They do so not out of a sacrilegious and reckless belief in their own power, but in the knowledge of being forced into this freedom and of their dependence on grace in its exercise."

14. Williams, "Poetic and Religious Imagination," 179.

to eternity, and to acknowledge the meaningful relation of both (time and eternity) to being human in the world and, in so doing, dignify—but not justify or redeem—the human condition. Of course, there are no guarantees that artists—and those who patronize their work—will in fact take up this vocation to be other than co-conspirators of Wormwood.[15] (The structural racism, colonial bias, and invisibility, or token visibility, of artists reflected in gallery and museum exhibition spaces today provide little reason to think otherwise.) Indeed, art is inescapably part of the conspiracy that must be overcome. There is simply no getting around that fact. But art, among other human activities, might well provide a point of departure, a way to not simply bandage the wounds of victims beneath the wheels of injustice, but rather to drive a lance or to even throw oneself into the spokes of the wheel itself.[16] To such an end, imagination is certainly indispensable.

Writing in early April 2020, and within a week of India's first COVID-related lockdown, the Indian novelist Arundhati Roy asked: "What is this thing that has happened to us? It's a virus, yes. . . . But it is definitely more than a virus." She proceeds:

> Whatever it is, coronavirus has made the mighty kneel and brought the world to a halt like nothing else could. Our minds are still racing back and forth, longing for a return to "normality," trying to stitch our future to our past and refusing to acknowledge the rupture. But the rupture exists. And in the midst of this terrible despair, it offers us a chance to rethink the doomsday machine we have built for ourselves. Nothing could be worse than a return to normality.
>
> Historically, pandemics have forced humans to break with the past and imagine their world anew. This one is no different. It is a portal, a gateway between one world and the next.
>
> We can choose to walk through it, dragging the carcasses of our prejudice and hatred, our avarice, our data banks and dead ideas, our dead rivers and smoky skies behind us. Or we can walk through lightly, with little luggage, ready to imagine another world. And ready to fight for it.[17]

Roy suggests that to try to carry on with business as usual, however tempting and well-intentioned such efforts might be, would be to forego an

---

15. A reference to the delightful character in C. S. Lewis's *The Screwtape Letters*.

16. So Bonhoeffer, "Die Kirche vor der Judenfrage," 353: "Die *dritte* Möglichkeit besteht darin, nicht nur die Opfer unter dem Rad zu verbinden, sondern dem Rad selbst in die Speichen zu fallen."

17. Roy, "The Pandemic Is a Portal," lines 227–43.

unwonted opportunity to reimagine and re-embody alternative modes of our living and being together. She is not alone here.

Others are turning to a great variety of creative endeavors. Others still—including artists—are asking whether now is really the time to make art, to do imagination work, at all.[18] In the same month that Roy was speaking about this moment as "a gateway between one world and the next," the Australian musician Nick Cave responded to a series of questions about his own plans for the time during the COVID-19 pandemic. "My response to a crisis has always been to create," he writes. And to the question "Why is this the time to get creative?" he replied:

> Together we have stepped into history and are now living inside an event unprecedented in our lifetime. Every day the news provides us with dizzying information that a few weeks before would have been unthinkable. What deranged and divided us a month ago seems, at best, an embarrassment from an idle and privileged time. We have become eyewitnesses to a catastrophe that we are seeing unfold from the inside out. We are forced to isolate—to be vigilant, to be quiet, to watch and contemplate the possible implosion of our civilisation in real time. . . .
>
> As an artist, it feels inapt to miss this extraordinary moment. Suddenly, the acts of writing a novel, or a screenplay or a series of songs seem like indulgences from a bygone era. For me, this is not a time to be buried in the business of creating. It is a time to take a backseat and use this opportunity to reflect on exactly what our function is—what we, as artists, are *for*.[19]

---

18. In an essay published in *The Monthly* in March 2020, the music critic Anwen Crawford noted: "In a situation where the global spread of COVID-19 underlines, once again, that an economic system based entirely on profit-making and commodity production will quickly spiral into crisis when things cannot be bought and sold, art matters precisely because the value it creates is never wholly measurable in terms of profit. Art matters now because it demonstrates, as it always has, that there are ways of being in the world, and things we can make in the world, that might be an alternative to commodity production. Meanwhile, we live inside of capitalism—this enormous global commodity system, its parts intermeshed—which means that arts workers, along with everyone else, have got to sell something to survive: their labour or art, or both. And all of a sudden there is precious little to sell. May this crisis make us think more deeply, more urgently, about the need to organise together; about the fact that when workers, including arts workers, bear all the risk in a labour market, we are all acutely vulnerable when the risks multiply. This vulnerability is not inevitable, just the way things are; it is the result of politics. I think again of Bertolt Brecht, and the motto he appended to a section of his Svendborg Poems cycle, in 1939: 'In the dark times/Will there also be singing?/Yes, there will also be singing./About the dark times.'" Crawford, "Coronavirus," lines 125–45. See also Summers, *The Spirit of This Place*.

19. Cave, "What Are Your Plans for the Corona Pandemic?" lines 2, 30–51. Ten

Of course, we've been here—or at least somewhere like here—before. This is hardly the first time, even in recent history, that such questions have been asked. In the aftermath of the Second World War, for example, when the dominating backdrop was clearly otherwise than it is today, the German philosopher and social critic Theodor Adorno raised the question of whether our emotional responses to magnitudinous horrors ought to outweigh all our attempts to explain them.[20] It was this query too that led Adorno to state famously that "to write poetry after Auschwitz is barbaric," and that "the task of art today is to bring chaos into order;"[21] he later revised these positions. The line between explanation and intelligibility has been severed. In the wake of such, we are left with the possibility of Adorno's "negative theodicy," a kind of theodicy in which the old intellectual and philosophical distance is impossible. If we are to make any headway at all in recognizing how the Nazi death camps succeeded in the destruction of biographical life, and reorientate our thinking and action in response, we must learn how to regard such detention centers as the culmination of a trajectory embedded in the history of western culture in the wake of the Enlightenment—as, namely, the barbaric fruit of Europe's cultural, religious, artistic, scientific, technical, philosophical, and intellectual sophistication.[22] In other words, there can be no genuine acknowledgement

---

months later, Cave addressed the question of whether in the world as it is, shitty art is still worth making. In his response, Cave turned to the Bible's opening story. See Cave, "This World Is Shit."

20. Adorno was asking specifically whether the traumas of Auschwitz mean that "we cannot say any more that the immutable is truth, and that the mobile, transitory is appearance." Adorno, *Negative Dialectics*, 361. It is not, he insisted, a case of an impossibility of distinguishing between eternal truth and temporary appearances (Plato and Hegel had already shown us how that could be done); it is just that one cannot do so post-Auschwitz without making a sheer mockery of the fact: "After Auschwitz, our feelings resist any claim of the positivity of existence as sanctimonious, as wronging the victims: they balk at squeezing any kind of sense, however bleached, out of the victims' fate. And these feelings do have an objective side after events that make a mockery of the construction of immanence as endowed with a meaning radiated by an affirmatively posited transcendence." Adorno, *Negative Dialectics*, 361.

21. Adorno, "Art, Culture, and Society," 34.

22. See Adorno, *Negative Dialectics*, 366–67: "Auschwitz demonstrated irrefutably that culture has failed. That this could happen in the midst of the traditions of philosophy, of art, and of the enlightening sciences says more than that these traditions and their spirit lacked the power to take hold of [people] and work a change in them. There is untruth in those fields themselves, in the autarky that is emphatically claimed for them. All post-Auschwitz culture, including its urgent critique, is garbage. In restoring itself after the things that happened without resistance in its own countryside, culture has turned entirely into the ideology it had been potentially—had been ever since it presumed, in opposition to material existence, to inspire that existence with the

of the Shoah that does not begin with the realization that "we did it."[23] The possibility of any future that is anything other than barbaric—of "working our way out of barbarism"[24]—lies not in any appeal to alleged universal reason (Kant's *Vernunft*, for example) or in a renewed confidence born of human progress[25] or creative activity, and certainly not in capitalism—"a culture that reduces human beings to mere receptive apparatuses, to nodal points of conditioned reflexes, and by doing so paves the way for a situation of blind domination and a new barbarism"[26]—but rather in the confession of our own incurable failure. Similar "revelations" might be noted in regard to the coronavirus pandemic—in the privileges granted to rich nations[27] and in the disproportionately higher death rates among minority and poor populations,[28] realities that further expose the absolute evil of colonization, the corrosive poison of individualism,[29] and the "cult of selfishness"[30] that birth so many horrors *in* and *towards* our world. According to Adorno,

---

light denied it by the separation of the mind from manual labor. Whoever pleads for the maintenance of this radically culpable and shabby culture becomes its accomplice, while the [person] who says no to culture is directly furthering the barbarism which our culture showed itself to be."

23. While beyond the scope of this essay, it would be interesting to examine the link between the death camps, which were a fruit of human agency and of human imagination—and so also a location of human resistance—and the death and chaos caused by a global pandemic which is without a clear enemy, a fact that lies behind attempts to create an enemy, of which anti-Asian racism and the vitriol directed towards the anti-vaccination movement would be examples.

24. Adorno, "Marginalia to Theory and Praxis," 268.

25. This was a view shared also by Max Horkheimer, Adorno's colleague in the Frankfurt School, who warned that "after a period of progress, development of human powers, and emancipation for the individual, after an enormous extension of human control over nature, it finally hinders further development and drives humanity into a new barbarism." Horkheimer, "Traditional and Critical Theory," 227.

26. Adorno, "The Artist as Deputy," 106.

27. See, for example, Alaran et al., "Uneven Power Dynamics," e1–e3; Bump et al., "Political Economy of COVID-19"; Fidler, "Vaccine Nationalism's Politics," 749; Lomazzi et al., "Equitable Access to COVID-19 Vaccination," 1039–40. Cf. Yamada, "Poverty, Wealth, and Access," 1129–31; Masters et al., "Vaccination Timeliness and Delay," 2790–805.

28. See, for example, Evans, "COVID's Color Line," 408–10; Millán-Guerrero et al., "Poverty and Survival from COVID-19 in Mexico"; Millett et al., "Assessing Differential Impacts of COVID-19 on Black Communities," 37–44; Price-Haywood et al., "Hospitalization and Mortality," 2534–43; Wang et al., "Asian-Americans and Pacific Islanders in COVID-19," 3685–88; Williamson et al., "Factors Associated with COVID-19-Related Death," 430–36; Macchia et al., "COVID-19 among the Inhabitants of the Slums in the City of Buenos Aires."

29. See Bazzi et al., "Rugged Individualism."

30. Krugman, "The Cult of Selfishness is Killing America," 24.

"There is no way out of [such] entanglement. The only responsible course is to deny oneself the ideological misuse of one's own existence, and for the rest to conduct oneself in private as modestly, unobtrusively and unpretentiously as is required, no longer by good upbringing, but by the shame of still having air to breathe, in hell."[31]

Does this mean that art should risk doing away with itself? This matter was raised by the Canadian pianist Glenn Gould who, in February 1974, interviewed himself for the journal *High Fidelity*. In the context of a discussion on censorship, Gould's "interviewer," g.g., says: "You do realize, of course, that you're beginning to talk like a character out of Orwell?" To which the answering Gould responds: "Oh, the Orwellian world holds no particular terrors for me. . . . It's the post-Renaissance tradition that has brought the Western world to the brink of destruction. You know, this odd attachment to freedom of movement, freedom of speech, and so on is a peculiarly Occidental phenomenon. It's all part of the Occidental notion that one can successfully separate word and deed." Gould continues:

> It's only cultures that, by accident or good management, bypassed the Renaissance which see art for the menace it really is. . . . I feel that art should be given the chance to phase itself out. I think that we must accept the fact that art is not inevitably benign, that it is potentially destructive. We should analyze the areas where it tends to do least harm, use them as a guideline, and build into art a component that will enable it to preside over its own obsolescence— . . . because, you know, the present position, or positions, of art . . . are not without analogy to the ban-the-bomb movement of hallowed memory.[32]

Cave, Gould, and Adorno challenge us to pause and to examine what exactly art and artists are for—and to take up "other forms of engagement"[33] that such uncertain and time-altering times render morally unavoidable. It is certainly a time to consider our responsibility to and involvement in all kinds of violence, for example. To go on with business as usual in the aftermath of a century marked by war, genocide, growing economic inequality, and (other) climate-related crises would not only be an affront to the victims, human and other, but would also "conceal the full extent of our inhumanity and to suppose, absurdly, that we could make amends,"[34] given time and resources. Whatever else we might attempt to say about the

---

31. Adorno, *Minima Moralia*, 27–28.
32. Gould, "Interlude," 323, 324–25.
33. Cave, "What Are Your Plans for the Corona Pandemic?" line 52.
34. Rae, "Building from the Rubble," 137.

horrors of our time, we cannot and must not bypass the brute fact that we are responsible. But is this the only or final word on the matter? And if responsible, then responsible for what, and to what? Returning to Adorno and his book *Minima Moralia: Reflections on a Damaged Life*, we read:

> The only philosophy which can be responsibly practised in face of despair is the attempt to contemplate all things as they would present themselves from the standpoint of redemption. Knowledge has no light but that shed on the world by redemption: all else is reconstruction, mere technique. Perspectives must be fashioned that displace and estrange the world, reveal it to be, with its rifts and crevices, as indigent and distorted as it will appear one day in the messianic light. To gain such perspectives without velleity or violence, entirely from felt contact with its objects—this alone is the task of thought.[35]

Is what might be true for "philosophy" and "thought" also true for art? Redemption, the "messianic light," exposes the incongruity between the world as it appears now and the world *as it might be*. Human poiesis (and theology too, for that matter) can be—and in this world arguably often ought to be—a form of protest "against the world that is, in the name of the world that is not yet but ought to be."[36] It can be like recognizing oneself right in the midst of a broken world—akin to the way that the cellist Vedran Smailović placed himself in Sarajevo's partially-bombed National Library in 1992—and refusing to accept that the way things appear is the way that things must or will be. That exposure—birthed and sustained by profound and counterintuitive hope, hope born not of trust in markets or in a change of conditions but which is a wholly unanticipated gift from a stranger—serves as both a judgement upon all that threatens and overcomes life, and as a promise that there is a love that is stronger than death. If, as Virginia Woolf suggests, we insist on living, even if "only in moments of emergency,"[37] then such exposure is best thought of as precisely such a gift.[38]

---

35. Adorno, *Minima Moralia*, 247.
36. Sacks, *To Heal a Fractured World*, 27.
37. Woolf, *The Waves*, 96: "Only in moments of emergency, at a crossing, at a kerb, the wish to preserve my body springs out and seizes me and stops me, here, before this omnibus. We insist, it seems, on living. Then again, indifference descends."
38. In the wake of his son's tragic death, the South African theologian John de Gruchy suggests that "intense human experiences that transcend the ordinary conditions of life are loop-holes through which we glimpse mystery"; and this, he argues, requires at least an act of the imagination. To be sure, "being led into mystery is not irrational and undoubtedly requires more than an act of the imagination. But," he reminds us, "the journey is impossible without it, and reason, essential as it is, inevitably lags behind." De

That exposure also brings new possibilities for artists—in their freedom—to find their mandolins, their pens, their brushes, their shoes, their voices, their humanity, and their vocations as political actors. So W. H. Auden:

> In our age, the mere making of a work of art is itself a political act. So long as artists exist, making what they please and think they ought to make, even if it is not terribly good, even if it appeals to only a handful of people, they remind the Management of something managers need to be reminded of, namely, that the managed are people with faces, not anonymous members, that *Homo Laborans* is also *Homo Ludens*.[39]

This volume represents such a wager. It represents an effort, however broken and incomplete, to think about art's—and theology's—possibilities, purposes, limits, and ends. It represents an effort to tell the truth about our dislocation in and with and for the world. It represents an effort to pay attention.

Paying Attention

> The artist deals with what cannot be said in words. The artist whose medium is fiction does this *in words*. The novelist says in words what cannot be said in words.[40]

In his poem "In Memory of W. B. Yeats," W. H. Auden suggests that among the artist's gifts—offered from "ranches of isolation" and "busy griefs"—is a proclivity to bear witness to how things are with the world. Such a proclivity involves a commitment to attend to those largely untampered-with and

---

Gruchy, *Led Into Mystery*, 24, 25. Rejecting any suggestion that imagination is "the fanciful creation of absent meaning, a thumb-sucking exercise," de Gruchy, citing David Hogue, defines imagination as the "distinctively human capacity to envision multiple alternative realities, scenarios, and outcomes." De Gruchy, *Led into Mystery*, 27–28; Hogue, *Remembering the Future*, 44. And insofar as imagination so gifts us, it "frees us from the tyranny of the present, of the logical, of the 'real', . . . from the constraints of the now; as it pictures what events were like in the historic past or what they might become in the future." Hogue, *Remembering the Future*, 45. De Gruchy is here concerned to give voice to Christian faith's claims about creation being in suspense—living, as it were, with both an eschatological orientation and horizon—and also about the notion that although life is charged with the same brand of mystery that makes Franz Kafka's *The Trial* or Stieg Larsson's *The Girl with the Dragon Tattoo* a compelling read, life is not always as satisfying as a good mystery novel.

39. Auden, "The Poet & The City," 88.
40. Le Guin, "Introduction to *The Left Hand of Darkness*," 154.

untraversed spaces of our world, about what is present but underexposed or disregarded. It may even, Auden hints, involve leading with "unconstraining voice" the way toward healing, and toward a renewed sense of enchantment, freedom, responsibility, and praise beyond the pedestrian and clamorous.[41] But it cannot begin there, and it ought not set out with such a course already in mind.

Reflecting on literature produced by Sophocles and William Shakespeare, the Scottish philosopher Donald MacKinnon avers that "even if we are tempted to write them off as works of imagination, the imagination displayed in them is one powerful in the disclosure of what is; it is not the servant of idealist fantasy in the way in which we must surely judge that the comfortable musings of theologians and metaphysicians often are."[42] Such disclosure-work exhibits the hard-won habits of paying attention, which is "the rarest and purest form of generosity."[43] To recall a point made by W. G. (Max) Sebald in his 1977 Zürich lectures on the literature and air raids of the Second World War—about "people's ability to forget what they do not want to know, to overlook what is before their eyes,"[44]—paying attention involves the determined work of keeping alive what people and societies willingly choose to forget, or ignore, or deny, or bury. In this way, an artist can be "like a *passeur* who gets contraband across a frontier."[45] But "comfortable musings," whether those offered by theologians, philosophers, or artists—whose work is otherwise indispensable to the task—are of no help here. When the bombs are falling is not the time for "sitting out on . . . balconies drinking coffee."[46]

---

41. Auden, "In Memory of W. B. Yeats," 82, 83.

42. MacKinnon, "Atonement and Tragedy," 101.

43. Simone Weil, Letter to Joë Bousquet, April 13, 1942. Cited in Pétrement, *Simone Weil*, 462. She continues: "It is given to very few minds to notice that things and beings exist. Since my childhood I have not wanted anything else but to receive the complete revelation of this before dying." Weil also suggests, elsewhere, that "attention, taken to its highest degree, is the same thing as prayer," highlighting in the same breath that such attention "presupposes faith and love." Weil, in fact, recognizes a strong bond between paying attention, human artistry, and religion. See, for example, Weil, *Gravity and Grace*, 117: "Extreme attention is what constitutes the creative faculty in [human beings] and the only extreme attention is religious. The amount of creative genius in any period is strictly in proportion to the amount of extreme attention and thus of authentic religion at that period."

44. Sebald, *On the Natural History of Destruction*, Part 1.

45. Swinton and Lerner, *The Seasons in Quincy*. Berger was specifically describing the task of storytellers, but the description applies to other forms of art too.

46. Sebald, *On the Natural History of Destruction*, Part 1.

Mark Rothko once observed how the romantics "failed to realize that, though the transcendental must involve the strange and unfamiliar, not everything strange or unfamiliar is transcendental."[47] He accepted that such a move would face misunderstanding and hostility from a wider public precisely because it challenges the kind of familiarity and reliability upon which our senses of community and security depend. But such is the unavoidable path, he argued, for any who seek experience with transcendental matters. To this end, Rothko conceived of his painting as a series of "dramas,"[48] and the shapes therein as performers who move in ways that cannot be anticipated or described in advance—"move with internal freedom, and without need to conform with or to violate what is probable in the familiar world."[49] In times past, Rothko avers, such drama required the artist to employ a kind of authorized canon of familiar objects that would be declared in advance as referents to things transcendent. To that end, even the most creative and virtuous artists fashioned pantheons of "intermediaries, monsters, hybrids, gods, and demigods."[50] But today, in a kind of Jansenist move, Rothko insists, we ought to abandon the sanctioned associations between mediators and signs and things signified lest we side with the spirit of idolatry. The true witness, as some theologians have insisted, is always a witness *in cognito*, the true sign always a sign in disguise. Therefore, "the familiar identity of things has to be pulverized in order to destroy the finite associations with which our society increasingly enshrouds every aspect of our environment."[51] It is precisely Rothko's invitation to reject the domestication of the transcendent by way of its familiar associations, while at the same time confessing the inescapability of the demand for "monsters and gods"[52] and other signs in order to properly enact the human drama, which, he believes, also bespeaks art's—and the artist's—greatest frustration, paving the way for melancholy—and, we might add, for the possibility of collateral surprise, even beauty and joy.

Responsibility and Meaning

When we become intolerably oppressed by the mystery of human existence and by what seems the utter impotence of God

---

47. Rothko, "The Romantics Were Prompted, 1947," 58.
48. Rothko, "The Romantics Were Prompted, 1947," 58.
49. Rothko, "The Romantics Were Prompted, 1947," 59.
50. Rothko, "The Romantics Were Prompted, 1947," 59.
51. Rothko, "The Romantics Were Prompted, 1947," 59.
52. Rothko, "The Romantics Were Prompted, 1947," 58–59.

to do or even care anything about human suffering, we enter the stage of [T. S.] Eliot's "word in the desert," and hear all the rhetoric of ideologues, expurgating, revising, setting straight, rationalizing, proclaiming the time of renovation. After that, perhaps, the terrifying and welcome voice may begin, annihilating everything we thought we knew, and restoring everything we have never lost.[53]

Rothko's summons to reject any authorized canon of familiar objects in order to attend to, and understand more responsibly, matters both transcendent and sublunary represents a call to resist, among other things, the nirvana of thoughtlessness that characterizes so much of life. Such resistance also concerns in no small measure imaginative undertakings.

With her characteristic astuteness, Hannah Arendt identified not only that there is a "strange interdependence of thoughtlessness and evil,"[54] but also that imagination is "the prerequisite of understanding."[55] It is the coupling between thinking and judging. In her undergraduate seminar on "Contemporary Issues," offered at the University of California in the Spring of 1955, and that served as the foundation for her further work on the pandemics of loneliness and isolation that characterize much of modern life, Arendt explored the ways that commitment to human community calls forth a responsibility to attend to the important relationship between understanding and imagination. While understanding always demands undisturbed attention to the concrete particularities under investigation, it also takes for granted "a wider horizon of things" and necessitates locating such on a map of shared meaning. Indeed, imagination is indispensable for achieving the possibility of any shared meaning at all, for such meaning is predicated upon a commitment and a capability to imagine the world from

---

53. Frye, *Words with Power*, 265. Cf. Adorno, *Aesthetic Theory*, 52–53: "All that art can do is grieve for the sacrifice it makes, which, in its powerlessness, art itself is. Beauty not only speaks like a messenger of death—as does Wagner's Valkyrie to Siegmund—but in its own process it assimilates itself to death. The course toward the artwork's integration, identical with the development of its autonomy, is the death of the particular elements in the whole. What compels the artwork to go beyond itself, beyond its own particularity, seeks its own demise, the quintessence of which is the totality of the work. If the idea of artworks is eternal life, they can attain this only by annihilating everything living within their domain: This too inheres in their expression. It is the expression of the demise of the whole, just as the whole speaks of the demise of expression. In the impulse of every particular element of an artwork toward integration, the disintegrative impulse of nature secretly manifests itself. The more integrated artworks are, the more what constitutes them disintegrates in them. To this extent their success is their decomposition and that lends them their fathomlessness."

54. Arendt, *Eichmann in Jerusalem*, 288.

55. Arendt, "Contemporary Issues."

the other's perspective. Apart from such, human community—as community—remains an impossibility. Only as such can a "private experience," such as death or disease or loneliness or incarceration, be also a shared or common "political experience."[56] The alternative—and it is an ever-real one—is to abandon responsibility to cherish and cultivate the imagination and so shrink one's world and risk having one's life narrowed by ideology, whose tendencies always promote restriction and serve the gods of death. So Arendt, again: "Without imagination, understanding is possible only as long as customs (general rules of behavior) rule everything."[57]

Notwithstanding observations made above about suspicions regarding arts' capabilities and limits for rebuilding communities made broken through human or other actions, without imagination there can be no future in which human life flourishes. Without imagination, there can be no new reality. "We are the products of our imagination."[58] In the Christian faith, discourse about future things takes place under the umbrella of eschatology. Eschatology is not only about the hope of future unveilings; it is also about resisting premature ones, and about the imagination's learning to cultivate and grow into the deep mysteries of hope, which are as inscrutable as are the presence of evil and love.

---

56. Arendt, "Contemporary Issues."

57. Arendt, *Denktagebuch*, 1:315. Or as she would express it elsewhere: "The man-made world of things, the human artifice erected by *homo faber*, becomes a home for mortal [humans], whose stability will endure and outlast the ever-changing movement of their lives and actions, only insomuch as it transcends both the sheer functionalism of things produced for consumption and the sheer utility of objects produced for use. Life in its non-biological sense, the span of time each [human] has between birth and death, manifests itself in action and speech, both of which share with life its essential futility. The 'doing of great deeds and the speaking of great words' will leave no trace, no product that might endure after the moment of action and the spoken word has passed. If the *animal laborans* needs the help of *homo faber* to ease [their] labor and remove [their] pain, and if mortals need [their] help to erect a home on earth, acting and speaking [people] need the help of *homo faber* in [their] highest capacity, that is, the help of the artist, of poets and historiographers, of monument-builders or writers, because without them the only product of their activity, the story they enact and tell, would not survive at all. In order to be what the world is always meant to be, a home for [people] during their life on earth, the human artifice must be a place fit for action and speech, for activities not only entirely useless for the necessities of life but of an entirely different nature from the manifold activities of fabrication by which the world itself and all things in it are produced. We need not choose here between Plato and Protagoras, or decide whether [humanity] or a god should be the measure of all things; what is certain is that the measure can be neither the driving necessity of biological life and labor nor the utilitarian instrumentalism of fabrication and usage." Arendt, *The Human Condition*, 173–74.

58. Anishinaabe proverb, cited in LaDuke and Smith, "Ecology and Spirituality," 41.

Risking Hope

> If we don't change directions, we're going to end up where we're headed.[59]

When John Steinbeck wrote "The dawn came, but no day" and of dusk slipping "back toward darkness," he was bearing witness to the cruel reality that hope is goddamn hard work, and delayed hope is risky ground.[60] Steinbeck knew too that making art is always risky business. But more tragic than the loss of security is the loss of "the capability to imagine the totality as something that could be completely different."[61] Proximity to our various utopias can do this. Others also have borne witness to art's inescapably dangerous, political, and subversive work.[62]

Certainly, as already noted, imagination is required to make sense of—to bring order to, to remember, to orientate, to re-construct, to make one aware of, to story, to appraise—our past and our present.[63] The observation that we tell ourselves stories, and that we live by the stories we tell ourselves, is frequently made. But there is more. To imagine can be to engage in a commitment to the future, to possibilities yet unmade, to what is "otherwise absent."[64] It can also be to hope. Of course, hope, as I have argued, is inescapably marked with risk, with self-deception, and with the possibility of self-destruction.[65] Perhaps hope is not so far from love and faith after all.

---

59. Reuben Snake, cited in Cousineau, *A Seat at the Table*, vii.

60. Steinbeck, *The Grapes of Wrath*, 8.

61. Theodor Adorno, in Bloch, "Something's Missing," 3–4. See also Bloch, "Etwas fehlt," 353.

62. See, for example, Camus, *Resistance, Rebellion, and Death*, 251: "To create today is to create dangerously. Any publication is an act, and that act exposes one to the passions of an age that forgives nothing. Hence the question is not to find out if this is or is not prejudicial to art. The question, for all those who cannot live without art and what it signifies, is merely to find out how, among the police forces of so many ideologies (how many churches, what solitude!), the strange liberty of creation is possible." Also Tsuruta, "In Dialogue to Define Aesthetics," 213–14; Murdoch, "Salvation by Words," 235–42.

63. See Warnock, *Imagination*; Warnock, *Imagination and Time*.

64. Hart, *Between the Image and the Word*, 233. See Bloch, *The Principle of Hope*; Steiner, *Real Presences*, 56. Immanuel Kant famously suggested that of all the concerns that might occupy a person's mind, there are in fact only three questions worth thinking about: "1. What can I know? 2. What should I do? 3. What may I hope? [Was darf ich hoffen?]." Kant, *Critique of Pure Reason*, 677.

65. So Garrett Green's warning: "The modernist hermeneutics of suspicion, in its various forms, relied on a dualism of imagination and reality to cast doubt on religion as a form of imagination. In postmodern relativism, on the other hand, imagination has triumphed, but only at the price of losing its purchase on reality." Green, *Theology, Hermeneutics, and Imagination*, 199.

Some have suggested that hope may even be the ground of love and faith. So Charles Péguy:

> It is she [i.e., Hope], this little one, who carries everything.
> For Faith only sees what is.
> But Hope, she sees what will be.
> Charity only loves what is.
> But Hope, she loves what will be.
>
> Faith sees that which is.
> In Time and in Eternity.
> Hope see that which will be.
> In Time and for all Eternity.[66]

If this is true, imagining possible futures—futures beyond the age of the Anthropocene, for example—has, undoubtedly so, a "necessary and transformative reflexive impact upon our ways of being in the present."[67] So Václav Havel:

> The kind of hope I often think about (especially in situations that are particularly hopeless, such as prison) I understand above all as a state of mind, not a state of the world. Either we have hope within us or we don't; it is a dimension of the soul, and it's not essentially dependent on some particular observation of the world or estimate of the situation. Hope is not prognostication. It is an orientation of the spirit, an orientation of the heart; it transcends the world that is immediately experienced, and is anchored somewhere beyond its horizons. . . . Hope, in this deep and powerful sense, is not the same as joy that things are going well, or willingness to invest in enterprises that are obviously headed for early success, but, rather, an ability to work for something because it is good, not just because it stands a chance to succeed. The more unpropitious the situation in which we demonstrate hope, the deeper that hope is. Hope is definitely not the same thing as optimism. It is not the conviction that something will turn out well, but the certainty that something makes sense, regardless of how it turns out. In short, I think that the deepest and most important form of hope, the only one that can keep us above water and urge us to good works, and the only true source of the breathtaking dimension of the human spirit and its efforts, is something we get, as it were, from "elsewhere."

66. Péguy, "Le Porche du mystère de la deuxième vertu," 277–78.
67. Hart, *Between the Image and the Word*, 234.

It is also this hope, above all, which gives us the strength to live and continually to try new things, even in conditions that seem as hopeless as ours do, here and now.[68]

There is art that seems to ground us, and there is art that seems to take the ground from under us. With the latter, we are graced with the fact that the world being exposed, or at least that which the artist is seeking to expose, remains one that is finally untameable and unrepresentable. It is work that denies human mastery, shattering our confidence in what we name as "normal." To attend to this work, as Georges Didi-Huberman has argued, is to run the risk of not-knowing. "But this risk," he says, "will be suicidal only to [one] for whom knowledge is the whole of life." Didi-Huberman is here particularly concerned with the ways that images work, or can work. However, the same might be equally observed about other forms of art. What he calls "the unintelligible exuberance of a visual event"[69] makes imaginable—although by no means certain—the possibility of a more truthful self-discovery, that which is as much about knowing as it is about "not-knowing."[70] And here at this point, he suggests:

> We find ourselves . . . in the situation of the alienating choice. Let's give it a radical, if not exaggerated formulation: *to know without seeing* or *to see without knowing*. There is loss in either case. He [or she] who chooses only *to know* will have gained, of course, the unity of the synthesis and the self-evidence of simple reason; but he [or she] will lose the real of the object, in the symbolic closure of the discourse that reinvents the object in its own image, or rather in its own representation. By contrast, he [or she] who desires *to see*, or rather to look, will lose the unity of an enclosed world to find himself [or herself] in the uncomfortable opening of a universe henceforth suspended, subject to all the winds of meaning; it is here that synthesis will become fragile to the point of collapse; and that the object of sight, eventually touched by a bit of the real, will dismantle the subject of knowledge, dooming simple reason to something like a rend.[71]

Here the arts *can* connect with other activities of life, sabotaging our proclivity for mastery and management, removing the ground from under our feet. The arts can unmoor us. Like the furnaces wherein hope is forged,

---

68. Havel, *Disturbing the Peace*, 181–82.

69. Didi-Huberman, *Confronting Images*, 228. I am grateful to Ben Quash for drawing my attention to this aspect of Didi-Huberman's work. Quash, "Imaginative Hope."

70. Didi-Huberman, *Confronting Images*, 228.

71. Didi-Huberman, *Confronting Images*, 140.

the arts can disrupt the worlds we assume and open up possibilities for futures we hardly dare imagine, futures that *may* be—very often despite all evidence to the contrary. This is the gift that the arts offer, or *can* offer. Not certainty. Not rescue. But this other kind of gift.

The contributions that follow here represent just such an effort, and risk.

Essays

The collection of work here explores the vital role of the imagination in today's complex climates—social, cultural, environmental, political, racial, religious, spiritual, intellectual, etc. It asks: What contribution do the arts make in a world facing the impacts of, for example, globalism, colonialism, capitalism, militarism, climate change, pandemics, and the evolutions, often violent, of culture? What wisdom and insight, and orientation for birthing hope and action in the world, do the arts offer to Christian faith and to theological reflection?

The compendium here of poems, artworks, short reflections, and essays, offerings from art practitioners and academics from a diversity of cultural and religious traditions, demonstrates the complex intercultural and interdisciplinary nature of this conversation. There is examination here of critical questions in dialogue with various art forms and practices, offering a way of understanding a little more how the human imagination is formed, sustained, employed, and expanded.

Regarding the longer pieces, perhaps a précis of each can assist the reader to follow the main argument, as well as to make decisions about which they may wish to prioritize reading.

Maratja Dhamarra̱ndji and Jione Havea offer a reflection around an "Indigenous artwork," evidencing how this physical, tangible work is only one form of Yolŋu scriptures. Their essay, titled "Yolŋu Scriptures and Hermeneutics: *Mä̱na / Buḻ'manydji*," articulates how for the First Peoples of the (is)lands now known as Australia, "sacred texts" or "scriptures" come via a network of forms—material (drawings, paintings), oral (stories, legends), and ritual (lores, practices). It is not respectful, therefore, to read an artwork without also reading the connected dreaming stories and rituals. They offer an insight into how this approach works with a reading of *Mä̱na / Buḻ'manydji* (wounded shark). In this work, the network of forms requires, and opens toward, each other; in this regard, a sacred text or scripture is always more than the material text (that has been scripted). With this understanding of what counts as "scripture," they propose as characteristics of Yolŋu hermeneutics the openness to, and willingness to connect with, other forms and other scriptures.

In circumstances demanding the best and most serious responses of which we are humanly capable, the presumption that our capacity for acts of an identifiably imaginative sort should even be considered, let alone relied upon, is one likely to meet with significant resistance. A generous dose of "reason," we tend typically to suppose, is what is called for. In his essay "Why Imagination Matters," Trevor Hart argues the opposite. Imagination, he insists, not only matters but is our only hope. To set it in apposition and seek to subordinate it to "reason" is a mistake with a very long pedigree. But imagination furnishes the basic conditions necessary for acts of reasoning and many other skills by which humans have survived and triumphed over adversity to succeed. Indeed, without it we would not even be able to recognize a crisis were it right in our face.

In her essay "The Objects of Our Loyalties and the Power of Inanimate Objects," Robin Jensen recounts the biblical tale of the three Hebrew youths—Shadrach, Meshach, and Abednego—which, although set in the time of the Babylonian captivity of Israel around the sixth century BCE, was probably composed during the time when Jews were suffering from persecution under Hellenistic colonizers some four hundred years later. Afterwards, the three heroes were likened to Christian martyrs facing death, prison, or exile for refusing to renounce their religious beliefs. Through history and into modern times, the story of the three boys has been recounted as an exemplary instance of courageous resistance to oppressive regimes, heroic loyalty to the truth, and fortitude in the face of bigotry and injustice. Jensen draws attention to some more contemporary situations where the tale of Shadrach, Meshach, and Abednego finds curious resonance.

Anne Elvey's essay focuses on poetry that responds to contemporary and concurrent eco-social and ecclesial traumas. Two interrelated tropes—the material sacred and creative witness—form interpretative keys for considering contemporary poetry as an uncertain answer to this crucial time, disturbing received images of the divine. Settler poetry by Rose Lucas, Andy Jackson, M. T. C. Cronin, Claire Gaskin, and Anne Carson guide the exploration of poetry's relation to breath and wound. Elvey's essay centers on the wound "after God." Poiesis does not substitute for theology, but courageously inhabits a place of tension between the material sacred and the failures of institutions, including religious ones.

While it may seem that we are facing multiple apocalypses, there is an important sense in which these are in fact the return of older forms of settler colonial extraction and exploitation. This is the concern of Scott Kirkland's essay—"Hope at the End of History." Kirkland suggests that the moment of the collapse of the supposed smooth functioning of the globalized order so soon after its establishment is indicative of the fissures that have been forever present in the logics of capitalist settler colonial confiscation. To this end, he reads the story of non-violent resistance at Parihaka, in Aotearoa, as parabolic of possibilities lost, and of possibilities that remain should settler colonial forms of sovereignty be disestablished.

Jennifer Wakeling argues that the performance of a piece of textless music can play an invaluable role in the expansion of the way Christians imagine reality—their Christian imaginary—including in times of disruption, when unpredictable circumstances highlight the need for new and more finely nuanced insight and practice. Her essay—"'I Am Making Everything New!': Textless Music and the Expansion of the Christian Imaginary in Times of Disruption"—explores the revelatory capacity of textless music in relation to the profound and illuminating experience of divine love and presence that ensued for the author while listening to a performance of Olivier Messiaen's *Praise to the Immortality of Jesus* (a piece of textless music for violin and piano). This experience, and the meaning generated through it, offered Wakeling an enlarged perspective on reality, which she has judged to be beneficial in times of loss and change. In her essay, the musical–theological meaning-generation process is examined via a conceptual framework stemming from the work of the American semiotician Charles Peirce. Within this framework, new meaning emerges from the construction of a complex web of relations between specific musical features, extra-musical experience, and theological concepts. The imagination lies at the heart of this process.

Adrienne Dengerink Chaplin explores the work of the Chinese artist, writer, and political activist Ai Weiwei. Her essay highlights the ways that Ai's art represents an ongoing engagement with global issues, from the political oppression and corruption in his homeland China, to the migration crisis, to the weapons trade. Chaplin argues that the integration of various elements across a range of Ai's *oeuvre* creates a body of work that is not only powerful and peace-building, but also prophetic.

In her essay "Imagination and the Sacred: Contemporary Australian Fictions of Hybridity," Lyn McCredden addresses the question of how Australian writers of fiction contemplate sacredness in a highly secular nation. The essay argues that in a nation marked by significant hybridity, with its deep colonial and multicultural past, fiction's imaginative ability to summon new ways of representing sacred possibilities is transformative. From the novels of Patrick White in the mid-twentieth century, to writers such as Christos Tsiolkas, Helen Garner, and Kim Scott, imaginative, idiosyncratic, and vernacular literary language brings to birth a wide range of new ways to understand sacredness, and to explore how sacred and secular relations are problematically porous, needing to be continually constructed, in twenty-first century Australia.

The collaborative films of actor David Gulpilil (d. 2021) and director Rolf de Heer are known for their unique and compelling portrayals of Australia's past and present. The films privilege First Nations voices and perspectives and offer both an invitation and a challenge to enter the worlds of others. Katherine Rainger's essay—"'It'll Take You Way Down to the Wilderness': Theology in Conversation with the Films of Rolf de Heer and David Gulpilil"—brings two of de Heer and Gulpilil's films, *The Tracker* (2002) and *Ten Canoes* (2006), into dialogue with theologians Willie James Jennings and Denise Champion. *Ten Canoes* illuminates Jennings's theological insight of "pedagogical imperialism," the mindset prevalent in the actions of many missionaries operating in contexts of colonialism. Champion's Adnyamathanha culture, history, and songs of lament provide a theological companion for the story and songs of connection, with Country, dispossession, and survival depicted in *The Tracker*. The dialogue between film and theology reveals that in the contested space of how Australia tells its story, the films of De Heer and Gulpilil provide a poignant insight and invitation into how one might see and hear in more truthful and imaginative ways.

My essay examines the ways that Samuel Beckett's plays represent trauma, its inescapable complexities, its refusals to conform to the orthodoxies by which trauma is typically understood, and their invitation to re-examine underlying assumptions about narrative and interpretive agency. Attending to matters such as bodies, time, nature, and memory, the essay demonstrates how reading Beckett can assist those seeking to better understand and articulate the multiple entanglements that characterize trauma.

Among other things, the COVID-19 pandemic brought with it death, illness, uncertainty, and fear throughout the world. When restrictions hit across Australia, many people were prevented from travelling home, travelling to gather with family and friends, and, for many Indigenous people, returning to or visiting Country. Naomi Wolfe's family were already in Sorry Business, acute grief following the sudden death of Naomi's father. Unable to go home, unable to continue the rituals needed, and dealing with trauma and worry, a series of events happened. Family members began to break through western linear notions of time and space, and conversations occurred. Wolfe's essay recounts one person's religious, cultural, and creative way of dealing with unprecedented stress and alienation. It is a generous and gentle invitation to enter into a world that may challenge one's existing perceptions. It is also an invitation to discover one's own imaginings in uncertain times, and to return ever more hopeful in the days to come.

The cultural value of the contemporary arts is often subsumed by commercial interests and patterns of consumption. In contrast, George Gittoes is an artist and film maker whose practice is based on an ethical and spiritual response to human conflict. Rod Pattenden takes up this matter in his essay "George Gittoes: The Artist as Prophet and Mystic," arguing that a fuller understanding of arts' value is found in considering the religious roles of prophet and mystic, as evidenced in Gittoes's work. Gittoes is an artist committed to considering human futures that are conceived of using ethical and spiritual terms. Pattenden believes that understanding Gittoes's work from roles based in religion allows for an expanded and more adequate understating of the impact of his work.

Libby Byrne reflects on what it means to introduce herself as "an artist." Her essay—"Who Is an Artist, and Who Cares Anyway?"—explores questions of identity and meaning that arise for her in a complex telling that is shaped and reshaped through a series of encounters with art and people. Drawing on the experiential and material knowing that emerged in the creation and exhibition of the artefact, "Draw near with faith, and . . . ," Byrne examines what it means to be an artist—in the experience of making art, exhibiting art, and being with art and other people. She supposes that the question of whether one finds the wherewithal to think and live as an artist is really a choice about how one chooses to be with and participate in the human experience of complexity and difference.

The final essay, "'Goin' to the City': African American Folk Ritual for Communal Healing," written by Amina McIntyre, maps some of the ways that black folk religious rituals can work to heal and transform communities through attention to memory, culture, and imagination. In African American Christian culture, there is often a desire to separate or devalue folk religion due to prior demonization. But the mélange of such rituals is an integral part of African American religious history, its present practices, and its imagining of possible futures. Employing Dale Andrews's definition of African American folk religion, McIntyre's essay traces the lineage of such religion from slave narratives to Albert Raboteau to Marla Frederick, across academic and artistic disciplines. Using this knowledge, and reflecting on memory, culture, and imagination, McIntyre then examines the City of Bones ritual in August Wilson's *Gem of the Ocean*. She suggests that this ritual, a rite of passage led by Aunt Ester, offers new significance for communities experiencing trauma in the aftermath of the murders of Ahmaud Arbery, George Floyd, and Breonna Taylor, and countless more besides.

Bibliography

Adorno, Theodor W. *Aesthetic Theory*. Edited by Gretel Adorno and Rolf Tiedemann. Translated by Robert Hullot-Kentor. London: Continuum, 2002.

———. "The Artist as Deputy." In *Notes to Literature, Volume 1*, edited by Rolf Tiedemann, 98–108. New York: Columbia University Press, 1991.

———. "Art, Culture, and Society." In *Prisms*, 17–34. Cambridge: MIT Press, 1981.

———. "Marginalia to Theory and Praxis." In *Critical Models: Interventions and Catchwords*, 259–78. New York: Columbia University Press, 2005.

———. *Minima Moralia: Reflections on a Damaged Life*. Translated by E. F. N. Jephcott. London: Verso, 2005.

———. *Negative Dialectics*. Translated by E. B. Ashton. London: Routledge, 2004.

Alaran, Aishat Jumoke, et al. "Uneven Power Dynamics Must Be Levelled in COVID-19 Vaccines Access and Distribution." *Public Health in Practice* 2 (2021) e1–e3.

Arendt, Hannah. "Contemporary Issues, Undergraduate Seminar at the University of California, Berkeley, California, Spring 1955." Hannah Arendt Papers, Manuscript Division, Library of Congress, Washington, DC, USA. No. 024160.

———. *Denktagebuch, 1950–1973*. München: Piper, 2002.

———. *Eichmann in Jerusalem: A Report on the Banality of Evil*. New York: Penguin, 2006.

———. *The Human Condition*. 2nd ed. Chicago: University of Chicago Press, 1998.

Auden, W. H. "In Memory of W. B. Yeats." In *Selected Poems*, edited by Edward Mendelson, 80–83. New York: Vintage, 1979.

———. "The Poet & The City." In *The Dyer's Hand and Other Essays*, 72–89. New York: Random House, 1962.

Bazzi, Samuel, et al. "'Rugged Individualism' and Collective (In)action During the COVID-19 Pandemic." *Journal of Public Economics* 195 (2021). doi.org/10.1016/j.jpubeco.2020.104357.

Bloch, Ernst. "Etwas fehlt . . . Über die Widersprüche der utopischen Sehnsucht. Ein Rundfunkgespräch mit Theodor W. Adorno, 1964." In *Tendenz—Latenz—Utopie. Gesamtausgabe Ergänzungsband*, 350–68. Frankfurt am Main: Suhrkamp, 1978.

———. *The Principle of Hope*. Translated by Neville Plaice et al. 3 vols. Cambridge: MIT Press, 1986.

———. "Something's Missing: A Discussion between Ernst Bloch and Theodor W. Adorno on the Contradictions of Utopian Longing." In *The Utopian Function of Art and Literature: Selected Essays*, 1–17. Cambridge: MIT Press, 1988.

Bonhoeffer, Dietrich. *Ethics*. Translated by Reinhard Krauss et al. Minneapolis: Fortress, 2005.

———. "Die Kirche vor der Judenfrage." In *Dietrich Bonhoeffer Werke. Band 12, Berlin: 1932–1933*, 349–58. Gütersloh: Chr. Kaiser, 1997.

Bump, Jesse B., et al. "Political Economy of COVID-19: Extractive, Regressive, Competitive." *BMJ* 372.73 (2021). doi.org/10.1136/bmj.n73.

Camus, Albert. *Resistance, Rebellion, and Death*. Translated by Justin O'Brien. New York: Knopf, 1961.

Case, Anne, and Angus Deaton. *Deaths of Despair and the Future of Capitalism*. Princeton: Princeton University Press, 2020.

Cave, Nick. "What Are Your Plans for the Corona Pandemic? What Do You Intend to Do to Fill the Time? A Solo Performance from Home on the Piano?" https://www.theredhandfiles.com/corona-fill-the-time/.

———. "This World Is Shit. Is Shitty Art Worth Making?" https://www.theredhandfiles.com/this-world-is/.

Coolidge, Frederick L., and Thomas Wynn. "An Introduction to Cognitive Archaeology." *Current Directions in Psychological Science* 25.6 (2016) 386–92.

Cousineau, Phil, ed. *A Seat at the Table: Huston Smith in Conversation with Native Americans on Religious Freedom.* Berkeley: University of California Press, 2006.

Crawford, Anwen. "Coronavirus: Cancelling Culture." *The Monthly* (blog), March 19, 2020. https://www.themonthly.com.au/blog/anwen-crawford/2020/19/2020/1584580982/coronavirus-cancelling-culture.

De Boever, Arne. *Against Aesthetic Exceptionalism.* Minneapolis: University of Minnesota Press, 2019.

———. "Art and Exceptionalism: A Critique." *boundary 2: An International Journal of Literature and Culture* 45.4 (2018) 161–81.

De Gruchy, John W. *Led into Mystery: Faith Seeking Answers in Life and Death.* London: SCM, 2013.

Didi-Huberman, Georges. *Confronting Images: Questioning the Ends of a Certain History of Art.* Translated by John Goodman. University Park: Pennsylvania State University Press, 2005.

Evans, Michele K. "COVID's Color Line—Infectious Disease, Inequity, and Racial Justice." *The New England Journal of Medicine* 383.5 (2020) 408–10.

Fidler, David P. "Vaccine Nationalism's Politics." *Science* 369.6505 (2020) 749.

Forsyth, P. T. *The Work of Christ.* London: Hodder & Stoughton, 1910.

Frye, Northrop. *Words with Power: Being a Second Study of "The Bible and Literature."* Edited by Michael Dolzani. Toronto: University of Toronto Press, 2008.

Gould, Glenn. "Interlude: Glenn Gould Interviews Glenn Gould about Glenn Gould." In *The Glenn Gould Reader*, edited by Tim Page, 313–28. New York: Knopf, 1989.

Grady, Constance. "Why Art Matters at the End of the World." *Vox*, September 25, 2020. https://www.vox.com/culture/2020/9/25/21454442/idiot-elif-batuman-art-politics-state.

Graham, Carol. *Happiness for All? Unequal Hopes and Lives in Pursuit of the American Dream.* Princeton: Princeton University Press, 2020.

Green, Garrett. *Theology, Hermeneutics, and Imagination: The Crisis of Interpretation at the End of Modernity.* Cambridge: Cambridge University Press, 2000.

Guite, Malcolm. *Faith, Hope, and Poetry: Theology and the Poetic Imagination.* Farnham: Ashgate, 2010.

Hart, Trevor A. *Between the Image and the Word: Theological Engagements with Imagination, Literature, and Language.* Farnham: Ashgate, 2013.

Havel, Václav. *Disturbing the Peace: A Conversation with Karel Hvížďala.* Translated by Paul Wilson. New York: Knopf, 1990.

Hodgson, Derek. "Costly Signalling, the Arts, Archaeology and Human Behaviour." *World Archaeology* 49.4 (2017) 446–65.

Hogue, David A. *Remembering the Future: Story, Ritual, and the Human Brain.* Cleveland: Pilgrim, 2003.

Horkheimer, Max. "Traditional and Critical Theory." In *Critical Theory: Selected Essays*, 188–243. New York: Continuum, 2002.

Kant, Immanuel. *Critique of Pure Reason.* Edited and translated by Paul Guyer and Allen W. Wood. Cambridge: Cambridge University Press, 1998.

Krugman, Paul. "The Cult of Selfishness Is Killing America." *The New York Times*, July 28, 2020.

LaDuke, Winona, and Huston Smith. "Ecology and Spirituality: Following the Path of Natural Law: A Conversation with Winona LaDuke (Anishinaabeg)." In *A Seat at the Table: Huston Smith in Conversation with Native Americans on Religious*

Freedom, edited by Phil Cousineau, 39–57. Berkeley: University of California Press, 2006.

Le Guin, Ursula K. "Introduction to *The Left Hand of Darkness*." In *The Language of the Night: Essays on Fantasy and Science Fiction*, 150–54. New York: HarperPerennial, 1993.

Lomazzi, M., et al. "Equitable Access to COVID-19 Vaccination: A Distant Dream?" *European Journal of Public Health* 30.6 (2020) 1039–40.

Macchia, Alejandro, et al. "COVID-19 among the Inhabitants of the Slums in the City of Buenos Aires: A Population-Based Study." *BMJ Open* 11.1 (2021) e044592.

MacKinnon, Donald M. "Atonement and Tragedy." In *Borderlands of Theology, and Other Essays*, edited by George W. Roberts and Donovan E. Smucker, 97–104. Philadelphia: Lippincott, 1968.

Masters, Nina B., et al. "Vaccination Timeliness and Delay in Low- and Middle-Income Countries: A Systematic Review of the Literature, 2007–2017." *Human Vaccines & Immunotherapeutics* 15.12 (2019) 2790–805.

Millán-Guerrero, et al. "Poverty and Survival from COVID-19 in Mexico." *Journal of Public Health* (2020). doi.org/10.1093/pubmed/fdaa228.

Millett, Gregorio A., et al. "Assessing Differential Impacts of COVID-19 on Black Communities." *Annals of Epidemiology* 47 (2020) 37–44.

Mithen, Steven. "The Evolution of Imagination: An Archaeological Perspective." *SubStance Use & Misuse* 30.1/2 (2001) 28–54.

———. *The Prehistory of the Mind: A Search for the Origins of Art, Religion, and Science*. London: Phoenix, 1998.

———. *The Singing Neanderthals: The Origin of Music, Language, Mind, and Body*. London: Weidenfeld & Nicolson, 2005.

———. "Seven Steps in the Evolution of the Human Imagination." In *Imaginative Minds*, edited by Ilona Roth, 3–29. Oxford: Oxford University Press, 2007.

Murdoch, Iris. "Salvation by Words." In *Existentialists and Mystics: Writings on Philosophy and Literature*, edited by Peter Conradi, 235–42. New York: Penguin, 1997.

Péguy, Charles. "Le Porche du mystère de la deuxième vertu." *Nouvelle Revue Française* (1916) 251–88.

Pétrement, Simone. *Simone Weil: A Life*. Translated by Raymond Rosenthal. New York: Pantheon, 1976.

Pinker, Steven. *Enlightenment Now: The Case for Reason, Science, Humanism, and Progress*. New York: Viking, 2018.

Price-Haywood, Eboni G., et al. "Hospitalization and Mortality among Black Patients and White Patients with COVID-19." *New England Journal of Medicine* 382.26 (2020) 2534–43.

Quash, Ben. "Imaginative Hope: Why Art Matters in Times of Crisis." https://vimeo.com/425194618.

Rae, Murray. "Building from the Rubble: Architecture, Memory, and Hope." In *"Tikkun Olam"—To Mend the World: A Confluence of Theology and the Arts*, edited by Jason A. Goroncy, 136–51. Eugene, OR: Pickwick, 2013.

Robson, Jon. "Against Aesthetic Exceptionalism." In *Art and Belief*, edited by Ema Sullivan-Bissett et al., 213–29. Oxford: Oxford University Press, 2017.

Rosling, Hans, et al. *Factfulness: Ten Reasons We're Wrong About The World—And Why Things Are Better Than You Think*. London: Sceptre, 2018.

Rothko, Mark. "The Romantics Were Prompted, 1947." In *Writings on Art*, edited by Miguel López-Remiro, 58–59. New Haven: Yale University Press, 2006.

Roy, Arundhati. "The Pandemic Is a Portal." *Financial Times*, April 3, 2020. https://www.ft.com/content/10d8f5e8-74eb-11ea-95fe-fcd274e920ca.

Sacks, Jonathan. *To Heal a Fractured World: The Ethics of Responsibility*. New York: Schocken, 2007.

Sebald, Winfried Georg. *On the Natural History of Destruction: With Essays on Alfred Andersch, Jean Améry, and Peter Weiss*. Translated by Anthea Bell. New York: Random House, 1999. ePub.

Seghers, Eveline. "A Tale of Two Species: The Origins of Art and the Neanderthal Challenge." *Evolutionary Studies in Imaginative Culture* 2.2 (2018) 83–102.

Steinbeck, John. *The Grapes of Wrath*. London: Pan, 1975.

Steiner, George. "A Note on Absolute Tragedy." *Literature and Theology* 4.2 (1990) 147–56.

———. *Real Presences: Is There Anything in What We Say?* Chicago: University of Chicago Press, 1991.

Summers, Patrick. *The Spirit of This Place: How Music Illuminates the Human Spirit*. Chicago: University of Chicago Press, 2018.

Swinton, Tilda, and Ben Lerner. *The Seasons in Quincy: Four Portraits of John Berger*. DVD. Directed by Bartek Dziadosz et al. London: Derek Jarman Lab, 2016.

Tsuruta, Dorothy Randall. "In Dialogue to Define Aesthetics: James Baldwin and Chinua Achebe." In *Conversations with James Baldwin*, edited by Fred L. Standley and Louis H. Pratt, 210–21. Jackson: University Press of Mississippi, 1989.

Wang, Daniel, et al. "Asian-Americans and Pacific Islanders in COVID-19: Emerging Disparities amid Discrimination." *Journal of General Internal Medicine* 35.12 (2020) 3685–88.

Warnock, Mary. *Imagination*. London: Faber and Faber, 1976.

———. *Imagination and Time*. Oxford: Blackwell, 1994.

Weil, Simone. *Gravity and Grace*. Translated by Emma Crawford and Mario von der Ruhr. London: Routledge, 2003.

Whiten, Andrew, and Thomas Suddendorf. "Great Ape Cognition and the Evolutionary Roots of Human Imagination." In *Imaginative Minds*, edited by Ilona Roth, 31–59. Oxford: Oxford University Press, 2007.

Williams, Rowan. "Poetic and Religious Imagination." *Theology* 80.675 (1977) 178–87.

Williamson, Elizabeth J., et al. "Factors Associated with COVID-19-Related Death Using OpenSAFELY." *Nature* 584.7821 (2020) 430–36.

Woolf, Virginia. *The Waves*. Harmondsworth: Penguin, 1964.

Yamada, Tadataka. "Poverty, Wealth, and Access to Pandemic Influenza Vaccines." *The New England Journal of Medicine* 361.12 (2009) 1129–31.

Yeats, W. B. "The Second Coming." In *The Collected Works of W. B. Yeats, Volume 1: The Poems*, edited by Richard J. Finneran, 189–90. 2nd ed. New York: Scribner, 1997.

Zabala, Santiago. *Why Only Art Can Save Us: Aesthetics and the Absence of Emergency*. New York: Columbia University Press, 2017. ePub.

1

The Cloud of Unknowing

Jordie Albiston

§

however this Poem has come to your
possession   whether you have bought borrowed
or been warded it   you should neither read
it nor hear it nor speak it aloud unless you have   by true will & by an whole

intent   purposed yourself as a ready
pursuer of the Poem   not only
in active reading but in absolute
point of ruminative reading   the which
is possible by *time* in this present

life of a living mind yet abiding
in this deadly body   for else it is
not for you   if you shall read hear or speak
it aloud   I charge you to take the time
to read hear & speak it aloud again

§

fleshly janglers   open praisers   blamers
of others   tellers of trifles   ronners
& tattlers of tales & all manner of
judgers   care I never that they ever
saw this Poem   for mine intent was not

to write such a thing unto them   & I
would that they not meddle therewith   neither
they nor any of these curious or
lettered or unlearned readers   who though
good people   this Poem accordeth nothing

to them   but it be to those readers who
stir after the secret spirit of all
Poetry   its *specials* & *dooms*   & they
full gracious disposed to be called by the
Poem   to be one with Poetry   or none

§

ghostly friend in Poetry   fastened to
words by a leash of longing   what weary
wretched heart is that the which is not a-
wakened with the breath of the Poem &
the voice of its calling!   read on then &

briskly!   you are fortified & made whole
by no work so much   & yet it is the
lightest work of all   travail therein till
you feeleth its pleasure   both in physic
& psyche   though the first time you may find

but a darkness   {& this is the cloud of
unknowing}   you may not full understand
save that you feeleth a *something*   both in
body & mind   & if you busily
travail   I trust you shall enter the Poem

§

the Poem is the shortest work of all that
you may imagine   never longer nor
shorter than is an atom   the which {by
definition of philosophers in
the science of astronomy} is the

least part of *time*   & it is so little
that for the littleness of it   it is
indivisible & may be nearly
incomprehensible   but this is nought
to whomsoever shall dispend some term

in the reading   stalwart but mistily
& with a sharp dart of longing   for time
is neither longer nor shorter   no more
or no fewer   than exists in one hour
here on earth   as are atoms in one *now*

§

a prelude to Poetry—   all Poets
that have ever been   or ever shall be
& all the works of those same Poets should
be hid in a haze of forgetting   &
if you come to this haze   & dwell & work

therein {as I bid}   you will see the cloud
of unknowing descend on you & all
Poetry   & so position a haze
of forgetting   that you may peruse a-
new   for of all the other scribes & their

scribblings a reader may have fullhead of
knowing   but of Poetry   itself can
no reader *think*   for why?   Poetry may
be loved but never thought   by love it may
be gotten   holden   but by thought   nay so—

2

Yolŋu Scriptures and Hermeneutics

Mäṉa / Buḻ'manydji

Maratja Dhamarraṉdji
with Jione Havea[1]

Gululu[2] marrkapmirr walal.
Ṉarraka buku-gurrupan God-Waŋarranha
bokmayŋuny ṉuruk djiwarrwu
ga dhiyak munathaw wäŋaw,
gapu rapiny ga moṉuk,
dharpa warrakan gumurrŋur wäŋaŋur buṯthunamirr
ga gaḻyunamirr ga ŋunha gapuŋur guya yindi ga nyumukuṉiny
ga limurruŋ bukmakku yolŋuw ŋunhi limurr
ga nhina dhiyal munathaŋur wäŋur.
Ṉarra buku-gurrupar ga buku-nyilŋthurr Djesuwal yäkuy.

Welcome loved ones!
I am thankful to God, the creator of heaven and earth, our home,
the freshwater and the saltwater,
the trees, the animals of the sea and of the land,

---

1. We register our appreciation to Michelle Cook for her support through the development of this reflection during the difficult days of the COVID-19 pandemic, which prevented us from sitting down and talking properly.

2. The Yolŋu term *gululu* translates as "welcome," but there is a deep, complex interweaving of meanings in the term: (i) When Maratja uses *gululu* in this prayer, he acknowledges that he has the permission of his elders to welcome people into their stories and Yolŋu ways; (ii) so the welcome that he extends is on behalf of his ancestors, his elders, his people, along with the land, the sea, the wind, and all creatures and matters in the Yolŋu world; (iii) the deep welcome in *gululu* is linked to the function of the *gukuk* in *Mäṉa / Buḻ'manydji*, the subject of this essay.

the ones that fly and the ones that crawl
the big fish and the baby fish
and all the people who live here on the earth.
I give thanks and bow in the name of Jesus.

With the arrival of Christianity, the texts that were recognized, understood, and valued as "sacred" narrowed down to what "literate" people are able to read. Sacred text or scripture (as genre and object) thus became the privilege for written—meaning European, Western, White—scripts. Put differently, what counted as sacred text or scripture was determined by missionaries (and fellow keepers and protectors of western enlightenment worldviews) who favor written texts (fixed with words) over against fluid events such as ceremonies (with stories, rituals, protocols, dances), symbols (with paints, drawings, weavings, carvings), and daily practices (such as hunting, gathering, cooking).

Prior to the arrival of Christianity to the cluster of (is)lands now known as Australia, however, many sacred texts were in oral and visual forms. The scriptures of First Nations, and the art of creating them, survived "the arrival" (read: colonization) and continue even into the modern time. And, most importantly, First Nations know how to read those texts.[3] But many Second Peoples are not willing, patient, and humble enough to be taught by First Nations on how to read their scriptures.[4]

In this essay, we reflect on: (a) a Yolŋu sacred text belonging to the Dhamarrandji clan; (b) the Dreamtime story upon which it sits; and (c) the (cooking) practice that stands on and alongside the text and the story.[5] All three—(a), (b), and (c)—are sacred texts in their own right, and in different forms—painting, story, tutoring. It is thus important to stress here that among First Nations: (a) an "Indigenous or Aboriginal artwork" is a sacred text, as are (b) the Dreaming story (or stories) that inspired it, *and* (c) the law(s), protocol(s), and practice(s) that it inspires. All three texts are sacred across, and into the current, time. In these regards, a sacred text is one "page" (or dot, stroke, mark, strand) in a network of sacred texts. Therefore, to read one sacred text requires one to read it within a network of sacred texts. Put sharply: a sacred text does not sit alone. It sits in relation, and in conversation,

---

3. Back then, "reading" was taught and practiced by humans as well as by the many creatures around them. Reading was not a privilege of humans.

4. Because of such a barrier, this reflection comes with our humble invitation to cross into the world of First Nations—in this instance, with the guidance of and teachings by Maratja.

5. Some elements of this essay appear also in Dhamarrandji and Havea, "*Mäna / Buḻ'manydji* calls for Wounded Theologies," 225–38.

with other sacred texts. In that relation and conversation, sacred texts come in many "scripts" (or forms): visual, oral, practical.

Figure 1: *Mäna / Buḻ'manydji*, date and materials unknown. Photo by Michelle Cook.

The sacred text (see Figure 1) that provides the point of entry for our reflection tells and points to a sacred story of Maratja's people—Maratja's home(is)land is on the mainland of the country now called Australia, with Elcho the Island to the North East[6]—and we present it here as an invitation for those who *possess* "Indigenous or Aboriginal arts"[7] to learn the

---

6. The big name for Maratja's home island is Gurala Binyanbi (the river). One of the significant places on Gurala Binyanbi is Garraṯa, located near Lake Evella Gapuwiyak—the main town; from there, the road leads to Garraṯa homeland. Garraṯa is the place where the Yolŋu conflict resolution practice of Makarrata developed.

7. They may *possess* the "artwork," but the clan *owns* the wisdom that draws the

Dreaming stories with which those sacred texts sit *and* be respectful of the law(s), protocol(s) and practice(s) that stand alongside those sacred texts. This reflection, at the end, invites reconsideration of what counts as scripture under the long shadow of Yothu-Yindi, and what Yolŋu hermeneutics could look like.[8]

Mäna / Buḻ'manydji

At the center of this sacred text (pictured above as Figure 1) is the underside of a shark (Yolŋu: *mäna*). But only the front half of the shark is presented (in the expected form); the bottom half of the shark is covered with cross hatchings (the stretched-M shapes which look like birds in flight, bellow the belly of the shark). The cross hatchings look like a wrapping that has been put around the bottom half of the shark. In a second reading, the cross hatchings lay upon each other as if they have been kneaded together. Wrapped (like a band-aid) and kneaded (like dough), the bottom half presents the shark as wounded. The title confirms this reading because *Mäna / Buḻ'manydji* translates as "wounded shark."

In Yolŋu scripts (read: art), cross hatchings represent the waves. At the outer edges of this text, the cross hatchings are calm—the waves roll and lie peacefully alongside each other. Around the wounded shark, however, the cross hatchings toss and turn like turbulent waves. The wounded shark thus appears to be in distress. The calm waves are separated from the tossing waves by spears, which indicate that this wounded shark was the victim of a hunt.

On the head of the wounded shark stands a bronze winged pigeon (*gukuk*). Its function in this text is not clear. It could be a companion for, or it could be calling attention (of hunters and gatherers in the sea) to, the wounded shark. Also ambiguous is the hook-shaped item on the torso of the shark, around the belly-button area, which can only make sense on the basis of the Dreaming story on which this text sits, and on the basis of the cooking practice that stands upon both of these sacred texts.

Maḏayin' (Coat of Arm)

During Waŋarr (Yolŋu: Creative power), one of the terms for what is popularly known as "Dreamtime," a hunter of the Yirritja moiety named

---

links through the network of sacred texts.

8. We try to present all of these in Yolŋu and talanoa—story, telling, conversation—ways, but we are inhibited by the medium of writing (linearly).

Murayana went hunting on the beaches of Gurala (Maratja's home[is]land, now known as Elcho Island) with his wives. His wives went out to collect oysters, and they jumped when they saw a large shark (*mäna*) near the beach. As expected, the wives were afraid (as most Yolŋu would have been in that situation).

Murayana, on the other hand, was disturbed. He became violently dangerous, a state known as *madakarritj*. He entered the water in that state. He bent his spear over his head, as warriors do when they are at full attention and when they want to undermine (and scare off) their opponent. Murayana was so overtaken by madakarritj that he broke his spear in two. In that madakarritj state, Murayana wounded the shark. The wounded shark is known as *Mäna / Buḻ'manydji*. This is represented in Maratja's coat of arm (*madayin'*; see Figure 1 above), which belongs to the Dhamarrandji Djambarrpuyŋu clan.

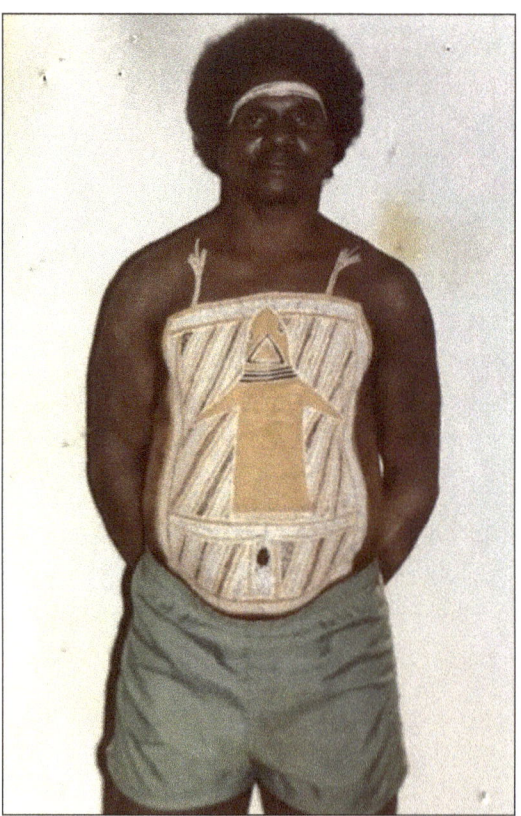

Figure 2: Maratja at his ceremony of certification in the 1970s. Photo by Kevin Inman.

The *gukuk*, the bronze winged pigeon, is a companion of *mäna* (shark). To Yolŋu people, the gukuk is also a messenger—it announces *gululu* (deep welcome).[9] It lets Yolŋu people know when (each day) the tide comes in or goes out, (the season) when sharks come to give birth, and this is connected with the blooming of the red-flowered Kurrajong (Yolŋu: Dharraṉulk / Balwurr-ya). In Yolŋu ears, the gukuk announces-and-at-once-welcomes the time when baby sharks come out, and there is plenty of fat in them—that is, they are good for eating: this is the message sung in the traditional song—*manikay yothuny djalkthuna marrtji balwurrya*. The gukuk is a bird of the air that announces events in the sea, on the island, and for the body. When the gukuk sings, it conveys *gululu* (deep welcome).

The position of the gukuk on different versions of *Mäna / Buḻ'manydji* depends on the ceremony or occasion of the text (*maḏayin'*). At Maratja's ceremony of certification in the 1970s (see Figure 2), there is no gukuk on his *maḏayin'*. But at the Dhäbi initiation ceremony of Maratja's son Justin in 1995 (see Figure 3), the gukuk stands on the head of the wounded shark (as it does in Figure 1). The difference between these two events is that Maratja's ceremony was one in which he was recognized as having authority and responsibility, whereas Justin was a young man who still needed guidance. Hence Justin was gifted with the gukuk on his *maḏayin'*.[10] Later in life, when Justin celebrates his ceremony of certification, the elders of the clan will decide where to position (or not) the gukuk on his *maḏayin'*.

Across two generations, the same sacred text (*Mäna / Buḻ'manydji*) serves different functions. The same sacred text invites different readings, in response to the ceremonies at hand. These different readings were endorsed by the elders of the clan who, by painting on these two Yolŋu bodies, gifted them with their clan's *maḏayin'*. These Yolŋu elders did for Maratja and Justin what their own elders previously did for them, and when his time comes Justin will do the same for the generations to come. Through different generations across time, the same sacred text is passed on with multiple readings—for different functions, events, ceremonies.

---

9. See n2 above.

10. This gift is known as *Raypirri'*. See Dhamarraṉdji and Havea, "Receive, Touch, Feel, and Give *Raypirri'*," 9–15.

Figure 3: Justin at his Dhäbi initiation ceremony in 1995.
Photo provided by Maratja Dhamarra<u>n</u>dji.

Cooking Tutorial

Bul'manydji was butchered at Gurala Binyanbi and segments of his body are sung today by the clan group Dhamarra<u>n</u>dji, among other Gurala clans. But the key subject in this sacred text is not only the wounded shark. In Yolŋu eyes, the two spears in Figure 1 are stingray-barbed spears called *warrŋul* (spears). This sacred text is therefore about shark *and* stingray. This relation as a consequence reveals the ambiguous item (in the first reading above) on the bellybutton of the shark as stingray barbs. The *warrŋul* and stingray barbs tell more of the story.

The Dhamarra<u>n</u>dji *ma<u>d</u>ayin'* is also a tutorial for cooking one of the favorite dishes in Maratja's home island: stingray meat with shark liver.[11] The *ma<u>d</u>ayin'* and the Dreaming story also explain how the *djukurr'* (liver

---

11. The Dreaming story of Ga<u>d</u>aka<u>d</u>a ga Wurrpa<u>n</u> (Jabiru and Emu) is also about food and sharing. See Maratja's retelling in Dhamarra<u>n</u>dji, "Ga<u>d</u>aka<u>d</u>a ga Wurrpa<u>n</u>." The English version begins at 00:11:12.

fat) and the stingray meat may be kneaded together to make them one, and tender. This kneading act is piled up in the cross hatching under the shark. Only *goŋ-manymak yolŋu* (creative Yolŋu hands) can knead that combination together. It is an art. When Yolŋu taste the dish, they will testify that it is *manymak* (very good).

The meat of the stingray is mixed with the liver fat and kneaded with water and stingray skin then rolled into large balls (like meatballs). We have in this dish Dhuwa (stingray) and Yirritja (shark)—this sacred text thus points to another sacred text, relating to moieties or skin culture, which is one of the links across the many countries of First Nation peoples in the cluster of islands now known as Australia. The Dreaming story and the totem (coat of arm, *madayin'*) help Maratja's clan remember and think. The story and the symbols are agents for verifying (through protocols, and checks and balances), and for preparing a desired dish for, the clan and their guests.

Sacred Network

We conclude this first cluster of sections with an affirmation: sacred texts *network* (verb) with one another. We began with a sacred text (*Mäna / Buḻ'manydji*) and explained it through the *madayin'* of Maratja's clan along with their Dreamtime story and a cooking tutorial. Each of those are sacred texts that come into relation, and into conversation, with each other; at that intersection, a network of sacred texts becomes meaningful, common, relevant, and practical.

Yothu-Yindi

Yothu-Yindi is the main system or network. Yindi are the owners or keepers of the law, and Yothu is the executor and caretaker for their mother's country. In Yolŋu: Yothu-Yindi translates as "mother and child."

There are checks and balances within the Yothu-Yindi network.[12] No-one is a man or woman on his or her own; no-one is a law unto himself or herself. There are checks and balances in all relationships, between moieties (or "halves"). In relationships, "I am to them, and they are to me" (similar to Ubuntu—"I am because we are"—for the people of Africa). These relationships look out to assure that everything is in order and that everything is accountable. All these relationships, which include the ancestors and creation, are conveyed in sacred texts (inappropriately known as "Aboriginal or

---

12. See Dhamarrandji and Havea, "*Mäna / Buḻ'manydji* calls for Wounded Theologies," 225–38.

Indigenous art"). And these sacred texts are passed on from generation to generation with multiple readings, for different events and functions.

In the Yothu-Yindi network, every sacred text is in relation to other sacred texts. A sacred text may be authoritative for a clan, as *Mäna / Buḻ'manydji* is to the Dhamarraṉdji clan, but in the Yothu-Yindi network, that sacred text is held *to be in relation* to other sacred texts (of other clans). A sacred text might be authoritative for a local clan, but not for all clans in the Yothu-Yindi.

Yothu-Yindi is the main overarching network or system that holds First Nations to relate to one another, and to account to, and be accountable for, one another. Under Yothu-Yindi, sacred texts are thresholds to each other.

Sacred Texts Are Porous

Gukuk lets Yolŋu people know when and for what they could go out to fish; they know how to fish in both high and low tides, but for different creatures of the sea. This message makes sense to saltwater people, and it represents what are sacred to them. But it will not make the same senses to freshwater people, who have their own cluster of sacred texts.

Mäna / Buḻ'manydji is presented and explained in this essay because Maratja is the keeper of his clan's *maḏayin'*. We cannot explain the sacred texts of other clans because we do not have their permission, but we are mindful of the network that takes place under the long shadows of Yothu-Yindi.

Whether the elders of the many clans in the cluster of (is)lands now known as Australia will at some point explain what their sacred texts convey is for those elders and their clans to decide,[13] but we stress this point here: in the Yothu-Yindi network, sacred texts are local, but they are also thresholds to each other. As we have explained above, at ceremonies and at the "kitchen" (and other places of tutoring), the sacred texts open up into each other.

What we have not explained here, because we are not the keepers of the Yothu-Yindi network, is how the sacred texts of different clans open up to each other. For us, at this point, we are thankful that Yothu-Yindi remains porous and uncolonized.[14]

---

13. If this were to happen, it would help change the attitudes toward, and commodification of, so-called Aboriginal or Indigenous arts. Those are sacred texts. They are scriptures.

14. What we propose here is contestable. Some could respond that Yothu-Yindi

Scripture Is Holey

At this end, we invite reconsideration of what counts as, and the nature of, sacred texts or scriptures and the contested assumptions concerning the nature of scriptural or biblical authority. On these matters, many elements may be kneaded on account of our foregoing reflection and the entwining spirit of Yothu-Yindi.

First, the elements of text and interpretation. What is *text* versus what is *interpretation*, a distinction that traditional biblical scholars emphasize and protect, are not separable in the Yothu-Yindi network. The three sacred texts presented above open into one another, to be *both* text *and* interpretation in relation with one another. Each of those sacred texts is holey, and we expect the same *affect* upon the sacred texts of other First Nations.

Second, the elements of private and public spaces. In the reflection above, text and interpretation *take place* in ceremonies as well as in the kitchen—both of these spaces are public as well as private. In this relation, and with respect to the Yothu-Yindi network, private and public spaces are also holey.

Third, the elements that perceive items and practices as sacred or desecrate. These too are holey, for there is sacred in the ordinary (like cooking) and desecration (like the wounding of a shark) in the sacred. The assumptions that there are divides that separate the sacred from the mundane fade under the long shadow of Yothu-Yindi.

Fourth, the elements of time. A sacred text is anchored in (but not limited to) the past, through the Dreamtime story and *madayin'*, but it is also rooted in the present, through ceremonies and tutorials. As ritual and space are holey, so is time.

Fifth, the elements of survival. The gukuk teaches us that sea and land are interconnected, and that bodies on both can listen to one another. This is not to overlook or cover-up the violence in the sacred texts read above—of sharks being wounded, butchered, and devoured—but rather to highlight the interconnection between living spaces and fellow creatures. We have read as humans; the sharks have different sacred stories to tell, and those too are under the long shadow of Yothu-Yindi.

---

too has been colonized, and some could add that many Yolŋu Christians interweave Yolŋu scripture with Christian scripture. A longer conversation is needed, but we simply note here that the controversy that we propose has to do with which sacred text serves as "the main text" and which serves as "the contextualizing text" (read: the illustration). We problematize the use of the Yolŋu scripture to illustrate Christian scripture, and not the vice versa as well. In other words, whose scripture is privileged? Whose interests are served?

Finally, in our humble opinion, the holey is holy. And both—being holey and being holy—are fitting descriptions of the scriptures under the long shadow of Yothu-Yindi. And best of all, Yothu-Yindi has room for more scriptures, and for more readings, including the ones that Christianity carries. The shadow of Yothu-Yindi is long, and welcoming. And *manymak*.

Yolŋu Hermeneutics

The art of creating First Nation's sacred texts also survived the arrival of Christianity and Western civilizations. (So did First Nation civilizations—they were wounded, but they survived.) That art (especially the wisdoms that encourage the formation *and* interweaving of multiple forms of sacred texts) would be helpful for reconsidering the practices of interpreting Christian scriptures. In this closing section, in response to the foregoing reflection, we propose three hermeneutical moves relating to: (i) First Nation cultures as Old Testament in contrast to Christian cultures as New Testament; (ii) hermeneutics being about making connections between, rather than dissecting and discriminating against, sacred texts; and (iii) hermeneutics as about making a difference to (or *affecting*) people's lives. Thus, in what follows, we revisit some of the assumptions about First Nations and invite alternative ways and attitudes—because practices are shaped by preferences and personalities—to the tasks of biblical interpretation.

At this juncture, however, we acknowledge that the phrase "Yolŋu hermeneutics" is problematic, not only because "hermeneutics" is a Western concept but also because the tasks of hermeneutics are inherent to "being Yolŋu." Reading and interpreting are components of being Yolŋu, and so hermeneutics is not a specialized field of study but rather the (scholarly) label for tasks that enable meaningful living. Put more sharply, hermeneutics was a part of First Nation cultures before the arrival of Christianity.

Testaments

The view that First Nation cultures are "Old Testament" as compared to Christian cultures being "New Testament" is shared by many in our own circles, but we have not yet engaged in careful and critical conversations on the implications of this comparison. There are two ways to conceive this comparative view, which invite careful and critical reflection:

First, the comparison may be understood in terms of time and history. First Nation cultures in the (is)lands now known as Australia have survived and accumulated over the past sixty thousand years, and they, therefore, predate Christian cultures (read: church cultures). First Nation cultures are older, and they deserve recognition and proper respect for their age and maturity. By comparison—Christian cultures are juvenile, and this comparison pays respect to First Nation cultures.

Drawing upon the first understanding, we treat First Nation sacred texts with the same respect that we extend to the Old and New Testaments of Christian scriptures.[15] In the reading above, we extended to Yolŋu sacred texts the same respect that Christian scriptures draw from us. In other words, we read Yolŋu sacred texts in the way we did above because we read Christian scriptures in the same way. In this connection, Yolŋu hermeneutics requires proper respect to First Nation sacred texts (as scriptures).

Second, the same comparative view may be understood with modern biases and discriminations. First Nation cultures are ancient (read: out of date), compared to Christian cultures which are younger and thus expected to be more suitable for modern people. This understanding is shared by modern Christians who favor the New Testament over against the Old Testament,[16] and they transfer their discrimination against the Old Testament (which borders on being antisemitic) into their perception of First Nation cultures and scriptures. They take First Nation cultures as irrelevant in the same way that they see the Old Testament—both are out of date and irrelevant.[17]

We push back at this discriminating view (of the second understanding) because we affirm the Old Testament as still talking to us in the modern world. The Old Testament talks to us and to our communities, but we do not thereby claim that it is relevant in its entirety; we treat First Nation scriptures in the same way. This affirmation does not mean that we accept both scriptures in their entirety, or uncritically. In this regard, the second understanding invites us to be critical of our scriptures: our First Nation and Christian scriptures may be out of date and parts may be irrelevant, but we cannot make this judgment in general and uncritically. In other words, the second understanding invites us to be respectful yet critical with our scriptures.

How might the two understandings above shape Yolŋu hermeneutics? With regard to the first understanding, we propose that Yolŋu hermeneutics

---

15. Here we distinguish between Christian scriptures (Old and New Testament) and Christian cultures (brought by Christian missions and churches).

16. This view is problematic because the New Testament is rooted in and hence dependent on the Old Testament. The two testaments are interconnected. It is unreasonable to favor the New Testament without also honoring the Old Testament.

17. These colleagues would also reject our proposal to read First Nation sacred texts as scriptures.

extends the same respect toward the sacred texts of other First Nations. On top of that, the key issues for us as Christian pastors is to pay proper respect to native scriptures as well as to read Christian scriptures in ways that are not supremacist. In that connection, the second understanding is a helpful check—some texts in our First Nation and Christian scriptures are hurtful and irrelevant, and Yolŋu hermeneutics thus encourages being critical and open to alternative views (e.g., for how sharks might react to the Yolŋu sacred texts—*Män̲a / Buḻ'manydji*—read above).

Connecting

Understanding sacred texts as porous and holey invites Yolŋu hermeneutics to make connections between scriptures. We did this above with *Män̲a / Buḻ'manydji* in story form, in art form, and in practical form (cooking tutorial)—three different forms of Yolŋu sacred texts (scriptures). How might this Yolŋu scripture connect with other First Nation and Christian scriptures?

First, a holey connection with other First Nations may be made in terms of *forms*. Our reflection on *Män̲a / Buḻ'manydji* problematized the privileging of written texts. Scriptures come in many forms among First Nations, and Yolŋu hermeneutics will engage with other forms, such as ritual dancing, communal singing, public and poetic speaking, and celebrating ceremonies. These are not mere cultural performances, but rather sacred texts and scriptures for First Nations. By opening up the traditional understanding of what counts as "scripture," *Män̲a / Buḻ'manydji* may be read with, for example, hunting rituals (e.g., for sharks) in neighboring First Nations. Those First Nation scriptures invite crossing into Christian scriptures, to reread texts about holy war, conquest, conversion, among others. Who are the "wounded sharks" in those sacred texts? Whose bellies are satisfied from the slaughter of those sharks?

Second, a holey connection with Christian scriptures may be made in terms of *frames*. In the Gospel stories, the final meal shared by Jesus with his companions is set in the context of the Passover (see Matt 26:17–30; Mark 14:12–26; Luke 22:7–39; cf. John 13:1—17:26). This reference connects Jesus's farewell meal to the Passover meal back in the exodus story, before the Hebrews departed from Egypt (see Exod 12), as well as forward to the Passover Seder and Eucharist–Holy Communion in modern days. Similar to *Män̲a / Buḻ'manydji*, these scripturalized meals abound in story, art, and practical forms, crossing over from the New Testament to the Old Testament, as well as from the Christian to Jewish cultures and scriptures.

Yolŋu hermeneutics gives attention to *form* and *frame*, upon which *content* unfolds. This is not to say that one is more important than the others, but rather that, in our thinking, *content* is not the only concern of Yolŋu hermeneutics.

Feed

One of Jione's claims to fame from his seminary days was twice serving as research assistant for Gustavo Gutiérrez, a Dominican priest from Peru who is among the leaders of liberation theology. In one of their conversations, Gutiérrez explained what he understands to be "good theology"—it *feeds the poor*. In honor of Gutiérrez and other companions in whose long shadows we present this reflection, we call upon sisters and brothers who contribute to the cause of Yolŋu hermeneutics to birth readings and theologies that feed the poor. We are confident that this is possible, as *Mäna / Buḻ'manydji* had done for Maratja's community.

In conclusion, and in honor of *Mäna / Buḻ'manydji* and the resulting Yolŋu cooking ritual, we add a twist to the Christian holy communion (qua ritual): the kneading of shark liver with stingray fat presses two bodies into one, and the result is a dish in which the community feeds from the sacred. In other words, a good theology is one that presses two (or more) bodies into one and enables the community to feed from the sacred. *Manymak*.

Bibliography

Dhamarrandji, Maratja. "Gadakada ga Wurrpan—Jabiru and Emu." https://ictv.com.au/video/item/6067.

Dhamarrandji, Maratja, with Jione Havea. "*Mäna / Buḻ'manydji* calls for Wounded Theologies." In *Bordered Bodies, Bothered Voices: Native and Migrant Theologies*, edited by Jione Havea, 225–38. Eugene, OR: Pickwick, 2022.

———. "Receive, Touch, Feel, and Give *Raypirri*.'" In *Indigenous Australia and the Unfinished Business of Theology: Cross-Cultural Engagement*, edited by Jione Havea, 9–15. New York: Palgrave, 2014.

3

Having Eyes to See

*An Interview with
Emmanuel Garibay*

INTERVIEW BY
ROD PATTENDEN,
APRIL 22, 2021

Emmanuel Garibay, *Selda (Prison Cell)*, 2020. Oil on canvas, 122 x 152.5 cm. Artist's collection.

Emmanuel Garibay is a leading painter from the Philippines with an international reputation for work that reflects on issues of power and injustice. His works reflect the capacity for images to wake up the imagination to the experiences of marginalization, racism, and class difference, and to therefore affect change in social, political, and religious structures.

The work *Selda*, or prison cell in English, is a work that responds to current issues facing the Philippines, and, in turn, other regions around the world in the face of the COVID-19 pandemic, increased military and political activity, and the resultant curtailment of individual freedoms. It is a large-format work made up of many smaller elements that are painted in an expressive and textured manner. The central figure of the composition is eating a golden apple, a symbol that should offer the promise to live forever, but instead has become infected with the coronavirus. To the left, a front-line health worker pales into death, sacrificed by a government that prefers to spend money on military budgets. Two authoritative figures carry a large book with the names of those who need to be sanctioned or disciplined, and then walk over a dead body. A figure in the sky is blinded by a face mask that has slipped over their eyes, a representation of delusion and false news. A woman flies a paper plane, representing the huge number of Filipino workers overseas who contribute more than ten percent of the nations' income, while a sinister yellow cat lurks in the shadows.

Below the central figure is the kalabaw, the native water buffalo which is often used as a symbol of the hard-working prosperity of the nation; but here it has died. Underneath, a friar knocks over an indigenous woman representing the ongoing impact of political and religious colonialism. To the right, a figure with a telescope, the current president, is seen spying on the helpless, while a hand comes in with a red yo-yo, an action that names "red tagging" or accusing trouble makers of having anti-government sentiments. And then, finally, tucked in near a golden door, is the historic figure of José Rizal, the great hero of the independence movement who was executed in 1896. He was a writer, artist, and scientist, and Garibay gives him a position of understated prominence in this work, affirming the role of the artist, who might see more clearly what is going on in these fractured and overwhelming times. The entire work is imbued with a golden light, full of promise and prosperity, that turns, at times, into a sulphurous yellow, toxic and decaying. The artist does not offer a possible future, but rather a contemporary view of this historical moment, full of warnings of danger that call for urgent response.

RP. This work stands in the tradition of large mural paintings that will often convey the triumph of history or the virtues of the nation. But this work is far more complex and fragmented. The viewer has to weave these disparate elements together.

EG. The fragmented nature of these works manifests the inability of most people to find a synthesized grasp of the general situation. Some aspects of what is going on tend to be intentionally highlighted, while others tend to be obscured. We have a media that is easily co-opted by those in power. You have to make an effort to dig deeper and scrutinize, to analyze, to have a more complete and bigger picture.

RP. What role do you think artists have at a time like this? Do artists help people see more clearly?

EG. Artists have an opportunity to be much more fluid and flexible, to have the greatest degree of exposure to many aspects of life. Their life situation means they are not confined to routines and patterns like a nine-to-five job. The innate qualities of an artist—such as being sensitive, observant, and analytical—enable an artist to grasp or wrestle more with seeking clarity in one's life situation and to understand the dynamics at play. This striving enables artists to have a more-complete understanding of life situations. When I paint, I listen to podcasts and lectures on theology, history, and philosophy. In other words, it enables me to have a wider basis for understanding things, not just through one perspective but through multiple perspectives.

RP. As an artist, you're not only looking, but you're also thinking about looking, and questioning your looking.

EG. In my case I prefer to paint. It's something that's been done for thousands of years. It's a direct action of you as a person. So, it is a constant affirmation of my self as a human being. Instead of exploring new technologies, it's about resisting the need to innovate. At this point, I don't see technical innovation as providing direction towards human development. I think it also helps people to slow down and to see. It also connects us to the past. What we have lost is a conscious connection to the past, and this accounts for why there is a massive loss of belief in this generation. This loss of belief makes us very vulnerable to all sorts of incursions by those in power to manipulate and control our worldview.

RP. You mean we lack an awareness of history, which means we are too buoyant, without a place of stability to make decisions about the present or the future.

EG. In the Philippines, it's the fault of the Church for having misrepresented Christianity, because it was obsessed with power and authority. It forgets Christianity is the exact opposite. So as a result, it has misrepresented belief.

RP. What would you say that faith or Christianity has to offer this moment in history?

EG. I think it is more about being truly in tune with our humanity. It is one of the problems with the theology of the church fathers in the past. It emphasized too much the divinity of Christ and very little on his humanity. The deification of Christ is really about the idea of God becoming human, so that humans can understand the mind of God. So, it is a model to be followed rather just a figure to worship. There's too much emphasis on worshipping Christ—in affect, worshipping the Church that contains this Christ. That is the main reason people have lost faith in belief.

RP. So the figure of Christ is a picturing of God. These christological images then also offer us options about what it is to be a human person.

EG. This is most emphasized in the way he lived his life, through washing the feet of his disciplines, uplifting the lowly, healing the sick, his passion for social justice. All of these are glossed over in favor of emphasizing the divinity. That is what stories are all about, and what art can do best. It can perpetuate the hope of what humanity is truly all about.

4

Why Imagination Matters

Trevor Hart

The presumption behind this volume as a whole, of course, is that it does. Imagination, that is to say. Matters. *Really* matters in our human responses to whatever reality we take ourselves finally to be faced with, and never more so than when that reality presents us with some form of crisis. I point this out at the outset because it is a presumption that, while certainly to be endorsed and celebrated, can hardly be taken for granted. Indeed, it is a presumption that appears to trouble the modern mind no end, including the minds of many for whom the scope of "reality" to be reckoned seriously with includes not just the world, but also God. A certain amount of cognitive dissonance is pretty much *de rigueur*, therefore, for hard-nosed "realists" (including *theological* realists) who, perhaps precisely to compensate for their unblinking determination to face only the facts of the matter (and whatever cool reason obliges them to build on those facts) find themselves otherwise unaccountably swayed and drawn in by acts of human *poesis* such as those we typically identify among "the arts." A little night music, a night at the opera, or a weekend in pajamas bingeing on episodes of *The Sopranos* may be just the thing as a diverting "pick you up" after some heavy lifting at the daunting coal-face of "the real world," but if concern for truth and reality are the thing, then dallying with diversions has a costly price tag attached to it, not least when the real world presents itself in ways that are indifferent, challenging, and even threatening to our well-being as a species. If, as much modern aesthetics claims, the very point of art as such is its essential lack of utility, its existence purely for its own sake, its deliberate eschewal of any practical purchase on the unwelcoming surfaces of the real world, then, no matter how cultured or accomplished, in the final analysis it surely amounts to little more than our favorite waste of time?[1] In times of crisis in particular, it seems, harboring such an admission is likely to see cognitive dissonance

---

1. For a critique of this reductionist aesthetic, see Wolterstorff, *Art in Action*.

collapse into full-blown psychic atonality, as inner voices mutter audibly about frivolity, self-indulgence, complacency, and the moral and spiritual deficit accruing to those who squander time fiddling while Rome burns. The notion of "guilty pleasures" is here translated to new, ontologically elevated heights, our participation in essentially poetic ventures having been judged *sub specie aeternitatis* and found wanting.

My focus here, though, is not to be on the arts as such, but on imagination. Of course, they are generally tarred with the same brush, the sphere of *Ars* itself being irreducibly and unashamedly imaginative. But the world of imagination is far bigger, more complex, and more pervasive than its role in enabling artists and "creatives" to enrich human lives in one way or another by doing their thing. That the arts (however broadly defined) and other outlets for "creative imagining" matter hugely—and matter precisely in times of crisis and not only in those periods of settled complacency when useless pleasures may be indulged in with impunity—is a claim I expect other essays and pieces in this book to substantiate. While I take the truth of the claim for granted, therefore, I shall not bother to say much more in its defense, other than to insist that the mattering of both (the arts and our wider human capacity to imagine) is precisely due to the organic connection between them—a deeper, generally unobserved but vital substrate in the stuff of our human responses to whatever reality we take ourselves finally to be faced with. That the arts matter, that is to say, is precisely because in their practices and products we have to do with a singular instance of our imaginative life at work in the world, and that life, far from being a frivolous distraction from the pursuit of sensible and fruitful strategies of response to the world, proves in fact to be the very thing that makes this pursuit possible at all.

So pervasive and basic is this same imaginative dynamic within our species-being and its modes of existing in the world, suggests Richard Kearney in a magisterial study of the subject, that "we wouldn't be human without it.... [B]etter to appreciate what it means to imagine" is thus, he argues, "better to understand what it is to be" as human beings.[2] No particular moral or spiritual spin should automatically be placed on such a statement. To have imagination or to be imaginative is not already to be on the side of the angels, unless we are willing even yet to identify Lucifer as well as Gabriel and Michael among their number. For, as Terry Eagleton observes, despite a venerable Romantic tradition suggesting otherwise, imagination is not an unequivocal good.[3] It is not even conveniently amoral, but finds

---

2. Kearney, *Poetics of Imagining*, 1.
3. See Eagleton, *Hope Without Optimism*, 60.

itself (like John Milton's angels) forever in the active service of either good or evil, and capable of acts of heroic magnificence on the one side only in proportion to its capacity for terrible and destructive exploits on the other. There is nothing more exquisitely imaginative than a torture chamber. Not so much despite as precisely *because* of this, though, as the engine of the very best (as well as the very worst) things of which human beings are capable in our engagements with the world, with other people, and with God, imagination matters. It always matters, because it is imagination that shapes and enables (or enfeebles) our distinctly human being in the world at every point, whether for good or for ill. In a period of crisis in particular, therefore, imagination matters because—its destructive potential notwithstanding—in it lies our only hope, humanly speaking at least. Rarely has the final clause in a sentence had more significance, no doubt; but we should not allow our reckoning with it unduly to deplete the force of what it qualifies. It is the remarkable power of human imagination *as such* to form, re-form, and transform our shared reality, as well as imagination's own final need of conscription by God in the service of God's coming kingdom, that will concern us in the remainder of this chapter.

Making It Up?

Eschewing all mention of God as one might properly expect, it is among the advocates of nihilism of one sort or another that some of the most ardent acknowledgers of imagination's power have typically been found. The conviction that human life is played out in a cosmos itself completely bereft of meaning or value and in which nothing can ever truly be known to be the case threatens to stumble early on at a considerable hurdle; namely, the fact (as we typically take it to be) that human beings live their lives for the most part as though it were otherwise. My life, and yours, that is to say, are lived as though certain things matter (and matter enough for us to invest a considerable amount of time and trouble pursuing them), certain things can be known with confidence sufficient to merit our willingness to orientate our day-to-day living around their presumed reality, and things in general ("things," let it be noted, of many different sorts) present themselves or crop up in our experience in what are for the most part regular patterns that we can identify and so, as we say, "make sense" of the various things concerned. That such patterns, meanings, values, and truths "exist" somewhere cannot be gainsaid. Any attempt to erase them from our lives completely would quickly deteriorate into well-deserved chaos and the sort of personal disintegration we tend to dub "insanity."

Facing this fact, the committed nihilist is compelled at least to add a further clause to the basic premise of his or her creed along some such lines as the following: the cosmos itself is meaningless and contains no truths, no values, no purposes *except those that we invent or "make up" for ourselves in order to make human existence bearable*. Such things exist, in other words, not objectively but precisely and only in so far as we imagine them, and this imagination matters. After all, how many of us would have the sort of constitution able to withstand the emotional drain of staring forever into the dark, chaotic abyss of "atoms and the void" (as the Greek philosopher Democritus puts it) and knowing that *this* is what "reality" amounts to, really? So, instead we supply the world with a finely imagined overlay, rich in meaning, and studded with values able to be apprehended, pursued, and defended, and, we trust, finally grasped and realized. In the face of what contemporary pop-intellectual Mark Manson refers to as the "Uncomfortable Truth" of life, that "we are inconsequential cosmic dust, bumping and milling about on a tiny blue speck,"[4] fleeting configurations of matter entirely lacking in purpose or importance and bound only for dissolution and extinction, we need something to make it worth waking up (and getting up) in the morning. "*Something* needs to matter," he writes, "because without something mattering, then there's no reason to go on living."[5] And it is on the power of human imagination quietly to construct and project meaning, value, purpose, and (significantly), narratives of hope that will sheath reality's unbearable aspect and so prevent psychic meltdown from occurring that we rely. We are, we might even say, in reality in a *perpetual* state of crisis objectively speaking, and shielded from the destructive, life-sapping, and soul-destroying invasion of our lives and communities by this crisis only by the constant vigilance and generative labors of the very same power of the human mind that elsewhere furnishes for our enrichment and enjoyment novels, poetry, music, film, paintings, drama, and all manner of other products gathered under the umbrella category of human *Ars*—the imagination, and its capacity to generate worlds and to tell stories.

A version of this same idea (which is, of course, neither new nor original, but certainly persistent) arises in the most recent publication from the erstwhile Bishop of Edinburgh, Richard Holloway—*Stories We Tell Ourselves: Making Meaning in a Meaningless Universe*. Holloway is presently, it emerges in the book, agnostic and pluralist in disposition rather than nihilist, preferring to Velcro rather than nail his colors to the mast when it comes to life's biggest questions. Strictly speaking, therefore (and despite

---

4. Manson, *Everything is F*cked*, 10.
5. Manson, *Everything is F*cked*, 10.

the subtitle of his book), his argument is predicated not on the insistence that there is in reality no meaning to be had in the cosmos, but on the more measured acknowledgment that if there *is* meaning, we cannot *know* that there is. This is an adjustment which, while it may fend off some of the existential despair intrinsic in nihilism's metaphysic (leaving just a glimmer of hope that reality may, after all, turn out to be better than nihilism itself typically suggests) leaves us in precisely the same place in practical terms: namely, with no *available* meaning, truth, or values to work with as we seek to order our lives together constructively. How, then, do we survive? Again, according to Holloway it is to imagination's capacity to fill the void that credit must be given. "Whether or not we acknowledge it," he writes, "we all live by the stories we tell ourselves to explain the mystery of our existence, the suffering that accompanies it, and the certain death that concludes it," and, we must suppose, much else besides. For "our stories . . . also supply us with rules for living the lives that we have been thrust into."[6] These being stories "we tell ourselves," of course, there are necessarily many of them and, since none of them can have any purchase on reality itself (being by definition "worlds" conjured up to compensate for reality's apparent emptiness and terrible silence), there can be no objective basis on which to adjudicate between them, let alone seek to persuade other people that our story is to be preferred to theirs. Only pragmatic criteria can be brought to bear. "If [your story] works for you, good: live by it." But rather than bothering others with noisy, misguided, and futile sales pitches, "why not cleave to it quietly and possess your soul in peace and leave others to their own stories?"[7] This is blue chip *de jure* pluralism *à la* 1970s and 1980s, and it suffers from all the logical and moral flaws of that now rather outmoded intellectual option; but, having noted its ascription to human imagination of the power to save us, weaving webs and worlds of meaning and value fit for habitation by creatures like ourselves, we must move quickly on rather than pausing here mercifully to administer the humane *coup de grâce*.

It is not necessary, fortunately, either to buy into nihilism's dismal creed or adopt one of its less muscular relativizing equivalents in order to acknowledge that, when it comes to the task of constructing a meaningful world for our indwelling, the lion's share of what is involved humanly may safely be attributed to our capacity to *imagine*. This much Manson, Holloway, and others get right. What they get wrong is their shared supposition that the need constantly to "make sense" of things, rather than inviting imaginative and intelligent responses of interpretation, requires

---

6. Holloway, *Stories We Tell Ourselves*, ix.
7. Holloway, *Stories We Tell Ourselves*, 10.

instead initiatives whereby our imagination generates the world unilaterally and then "sustains in being all that is," *making it up* as we go in a bid to fend off the howling gales of chaos and the void. Such Herculean feats of world-making would be heroic, to be sure, although bearing the burden of responsibility for maintaining them would seem likely eventually to crush even the most fertile and energetic practitioners of the art. But we need at this point to avoid making a very simple and common category error. We must not fall into the trap of reducing the scope of the imagined and highly imaginative to those variants of it whose skillful play produces what we gladly acknowledge to be "purely *imaginary*." And, in fact, for those willing to entertain any version of realism, even the fictive has its roots sunk finally in a complex reality that is given rather than being the fruit of sheer invention (were such even held to be possible). The world, as novelist and philosopher Iris Murdoch reminds us, is certainly "not given to us 'on a plate,' it is given to us as a creative task. . . . We work, . . . and 'make something of it.' We help it to be."[8] But the greatest human acts of imaginative interpretation and "sense-making" are not those claiming specious analogy with an originary, sovereign *creatio ex nihilo;* they are, rather, the myriad "sub-creative" responses to the world in which we work patiently, lovingly, and respectfully with what has been given as our starting point.

Such imaginative responses are demanded and to be found not just in the arts, of course, but, *mutatis mutandis*, in science, technology, politics, commerce, philosophy, religion, the whole gamut of human existence in the world, right down to the concrete particulars of our daily efforts to make sense of and respond well to other people with whom we have to do. Hate, novelist Graham Greene reminds us, is "just a failure of the imagination."[9] Love, on the other hand, Murdoch suggests, is born precisely out of a respectful curiosity regarding what is other than and different to ourselves, a form of successful imagining that enables both personal and impersonal others to be and become more fully themselves in their relationship with us, because of rather than despite the differences between us.[10] From the ground up, in fact, from the *micro-* to the *macro-* our apprehension of and portfolio of responses to "reality" in all its guises are enabled by our capacity to deal imaginatively with it, even (perhaps most often) when we are not aware that this is what we are doing. When, therefore, philosopher Charles Taylor writes as he does of the—often tacit but always basic—impact of cosmic and social "imaginaries" on the shape and

---

8. Murdoch, *Metaphysics as a Guide to Morals*, 215.
9. Greene, *The Power and the Glory*, 131.
10. See Murdoch, *Existentialists and Mystics*, 215–20.

substance of human living, in one sense what he has in mind is not a million miles away from Manson's and Holloway's "stories" in which meaning, value, and much else besides are to be found embedded and encountered, and without which we can have no meaningful experience of the world at all.[11] But for Taylor these "imaginaries" are anything but purely *imaginary*! They are precisely ways of making sense of the world humanly, *imaginative responses* to its self-unveiling rather than conceits dreamed up to shield us from the prospect of its terrible reality. Furthermore, arising as they do from our immersion in a world that demands to be made sense of, such imaginaries are not environments in which words like "true" and "real" can be used only when accompanied by scare-quotes declaring their playfulness and lack of either universal intent or moral seriousness. Instead, realizing that proper epistemic humility is perfectly compatible with serious conversation and even *disputation* about truth, reality, and the gains and losses of differing heuristic vantage points from which these may sought, Taylor's imaginaries (unlike Holloway's stories) are patient of meaningful adjudication even though, as imaginative responses to the world, none of them can (or has any need to) claim to be identical with "the Truth" of things, let alone the whole truth and nothing but the truth.

Making Sense of "Imagination"

We have not yet, though, offered the reader anything by way of a definition of the term "imagination," an omission the rectification of which may by now seem to be long overdue. Precise, *a priori* definitions, though, are not always appropriate to the matter in hand, and one of the overriding contributions of recent theory in various academic disciplines has been to insist that our habitual uses of the language of imagination (imaginative, imaginary, imagining, and so on) compel a picture more complex than either an essentialist approach or the hypostatizing of old-fashioned faculty psychologies (setting "*the* imagination" alongside reason, the conscience, the will, and others) are able adequately to accommodate. As one survey of the territory observes, the language "sprawls promiscuously" over a wide range of human life contexts and intellectual concerns, suggesting no single occult entity to which all uses may be taken finally to refer, but instead a range of ways of responding to the world quite different from one another in many respects, and related more by way of "family resemblance."[12] In his helpful essay on the subject, Leslie Stevenson identifies among "the most influential conceptions

---

11. See, for example, Taylor, *Modern Social Imaginaries*.
12. Stevenson, "Twelve Conceptions of Imagination," 238.

of imagination" twelve distinct claimants to the relevant underlying genetic material as follows: (i) the ability to think of something not presently perceived, but spatio-temporally real; (ii) the ability to think of whatever one acknowledges as possible in the spatio-temporal world; (iii) the liability to think of something that the subject believes to be real, but which is not; (iv) the ability to think of things that one conceives of as fictional; (v) the ability to entertain mental images; (vi) the ability to think of anything at all; (vii) the non-rational operations of the human mind, that is, those explicable in terms of causes rather than reasons; (viii) the ability to form perceptual beliefs about public objects in space and time; (ix) the ability sensuously to appreciate works of art or objects of natural beauty without classifying them under concepts or thinking of them as useful; (x) the ability to create works of art that encourage such sensuous appreciation; (xi) the ability to appreciate things that are expressive or revelatory of the meaning of human life; and (xii) the ability to create works of art that express something deep about the meaning of life.[13] We need not suppose either that this list is exhaustive in scope or that other ways of mapping the territory (or tracing the family tree) might not usefully be attempted. But Stevenson goes some way toward laying bare for us the grammar of "imagination," and the moment we begin to flesh out with concrete instances some of these abstract categories it becomes clear that our appeal to the language suggests the existence of deep underlying connections between a host of extremely varied dispositions and activities by which our daily lives are populated: expecting, planning, exploring, fearing, hoping, believing, remembering, recognizing, analyzing, empathizing, loving, conjecturing, fantasizing, pretending, and many, many others; including, of course, those specialized activities of an unashamedly "creative" and imaginative sort that we identify among the arts.

Far from being pictured as some arcane "thing" with a carefully specified and limited remit, therefore, imagination, authoritative studies suggest, is better pictured as *a way of thinking, responding, and acting* shot through the whole array of our human engagement with reality. In particular, long-established tendencies to distinguish sharply between "being imaginative" and deploying "reason" instead are found to be seriously wanting. Lending themselves as they do to the suggestion of dual agents engaged in what is at best an awkward tango and at worst a zero-sum game, accounts of this sort misrepresent the circumstance in a most unhelpful manner. C. S. Lewis, writing in his professional capacity as a philosophically trained literary critic, himself risks falling into this trap in what is in all other respects a very positive and helpful estimate of the significance

---

13. See Stevenson, "Twelve Conceptions of Imagination," 238–59.

of imagination.[14] Reason, he observes, can only do what reason does if it has something to reason *about*, and he follows the lead of the Enlightenment philosopher Immanuel Kant in ascribing to logically prior and occult activities of imagination the responsibility (and the credit) for supplying the relevant materials. What imagination supplies, Lewis clarifies, is not just a panoply of material objects (which it shapes up from data about the world supplied by our senses), but also webs of relationship or patterns within which these same objects are experienced as *meaningful*—patterns or "schemata" in terms of which alone, that is to say, we are able to *make sense* of them. Imagination, Lewis insists, might thus be described as the "organ of meaning," since what it alone is able to provide for us are those schemes of significance we must refer to if sense is to be made of anything at all. Such frameworks or *schemata* are tacit rather than available for empirical inspection (indeed, they include all sorts of things falling outside the natural range of what our senses alone can deliver to us). As well as constructing such "worlds" of meaning, therefore, imagination is also responsible for "sustaining them in being" and rendering them present as the tacit backdrop for our perpetual activities of interpretation.

Now of course, Lewis observes, "meaning is the antecedent condition both of truth and falsehood, whose antithesis is not error but nonsense."[15] The activity of imagination is thus a necessary if not sufficient condition of all our most carefully reasoned and rational engagements with the world. Apart from the force of the truth-claims they are inclined to make about the way the world actually is, therefore, those same respectable engagements share much in common with imagination's other, unashamedly fictive products, worlds of meaning ("stories" and the rest) where truth claims of that sort have little place, their uses of the indicative being understood from the outset to be bracketed entirely by the qualifications of the conditional mood. The significances of things factual and fictional alike, that is to say, issue from precisely the same source—that power of the mind which, in Paul Ricœur's felicitous phrase, "'*invents*' in both senses of the word."[16] In Lewis's preferred terms, imagination as such is only concerned to offer us an account of things that would make sense *if* certain things were the case; it has no concern with whether or not those things are *actually* the case—that is to say, with questions of "truth" as we typically intend the

---

14. See Lewis, "Bluspels and Flalansferes," 133–58.

15. Lewis, "Bluspels and Flalansferes," 157.

16. Ricœur, *The Rule of Metaphor*, 283; italics added. Ricœur's point about an eye for metaphor draws attention to the wider fact that, counter-intuitively but undeniably, in many of our most serious engagements with reality the poetic and the heuristic finally coincide rather than constituting alternatives, let alone opposites.

word. When it comes to this latter question (and thus with differentiating genuine claims about the so-called "real" world from those pertaining in the fictional worlds of the arts and those proffered by the mendacious propagation of untruths, as well as disentangling truth from error), he goes on to insist, it is *reason* that must be allowed either to offer or withhold the relevant *imprimatur*. Reason is thus "the organ of truth."[17]

Thinking Again

There is much in Lewis's account of the imaginative that is helpful, not least his acknowledgement of the breadth of the domain in which it operates and the gravity of those tasks it performs. Most readers, despite the cultural comings and goings of post-modern speculation on the subject and the cynical opportunism of those only too pleased to celebrate and exploit the suggestion that we now live in a "post-truth" world for their own political and economic gain,[18] will continue nonetheless to find it helpful to differentiate mere "meaningfulness" from "truth," as Lewis suggests that we may and must. The division of labor he proposes in this regard between imagination and reason (dependent as it is on the sort of faculty psychology alluded to above) is, though, far less obviously either helpful or sustainable for those coming to it more than eighty years after his essay on the subject was first published. It is distinctly unhelpful, in fact, in as much as it facilitates the perpetuation of the "awkward tango/zero sum game" model referred to earlier. This in its turn encourages overweening claims to be made about the power of "reason" and a corresponding baseless suspicion and relative disparagement of any circumstances where the unique contributions of imagination must be acknowledged or appealed to. If we are really concerned with the reality and truth of things, it is still sometimes suggested, then it is upon the independent adjudication of reason (held to be a conveniently safe, precisely because *imagination-free*, gauge) that we must rely. Words like "logical," "rational," and "analytical" are frequently to be found prominently displayed in such contexts in order to underline the serious intent and copper-bottomed integrity of certain sorts of intellectual exercise, compared with what are (it is implied if not explicitly stated) the altogether less reliable ("soft" rather than "hard-edged") if not downright frivolous, flaky, and even willfully mischievous epistemic offerings of that well-known weaver of untruths and illusion across the ages—"the imagination."

---

17. Lewis, "Bluspels and Flalansferes," 157.
18. See Hart, *Faith Thinking*, 219–42.

That this sort of thing can pass muster at all today as an informed account is surprising when studies undertaken in fields as diverse as psychology, philosophy, poetics, hermeneutics, ethics, and the natural and social sciences over the last fifty years or more have all increasingly come to suggest, first, that imaginative ways of engaging reality are fundamental rather than peripheral to cutting edge heuristic enterprises across the whole front of our knowing of the world, and, second, that attempts to draw a sharp line between the imaginative and the rational (between something called "imagination" and something else identifiable as "reason" to be set alongside and in tension with it) are misleading and dangerous in their entailments, so closely and necessarily intertwined are they with one another in practice. Not only is it the case, as Lewis reminds us, that "reason" is impotent without materials to work with, and must rely upon the activities of "imagination" for a ready supply of these. The reality is far more radical yet; namely, that those very activities of mind that we tend naturally to refer to as ones of "reasoning" or ratiocination are themselves activities of a highly imaginative sort. They rely, for instance, on our capacity to picture things at levels of abstraction forever unavailable to us empirically, or to follow the chains of inference or deduction permitted or prescribed by some currently favored pattern of logic or another—patterns which, again, are themselves not to be found etched on the face of things, but rather provide a backdrop necessarily summoned and sustained in the mind's eye by skilled acts of imagining. Recent ground-breaking work by authors such as Iain McGilchrist and Mark Johnson has revealed just how deep this perichoretic union between reasoning and imagining goes, insisting that the most basic conceptual and linguistic units in terms of which we are able to think or speak about anything at all are not grasped or produced by anything meaningfully described as "pure reason," but are rather wedded inexorably both to the materiality of our bodies and to the products of acts of imaginative poesis.[19] Far from enjoying any detached, "objective" perspective from which authoritative pronouncements can be made about the deliverances of imagination (or the senses), therefore, upon inspection even our most "hard-edged," "cool," and "scientific" approaches to the world turn out after all to rely upon their possession of a fairly high IQ—a high imagination quotient! That's why, earlier, I suggested that imagining, being imaginative, is itself probably best thought of as a way of thinking, responding, and acting; one, perhaps, in which the prescriptions of a given model of reasoning are more willingly departed from rather than permitted

---

19. See, for example, McGilchrist, *The Master and His Emissary*; Johnson, *The Meaning of the Body*.

to constrain operations. This permits a meaningful distinction still to be drawn between the terms "reason" and "imagination" where it is practically useful to do so; but the distinction is one drawn only within a perichoretic union in which the activity of reasoning is always also an imaginative act, and for its part imagination—even in its most "creative" projects—constantly finds itself challenged to be *reasonable*; that is, to identify, construct, and work with meaningful patterns of one sort or another.

It is frankly difficult to imagine anyone bothering to ask whether *reason* matters, either in a time of crisis or at any other time. The very formulation of the question is likely to meet with deserved incredulity, so obvious is it to all but the incurably befuddled and devotees of the most extreme postmodern *jouissance* that reason *obviously* matters, mattering to some degree and in one way or another in almost every imaginable circumstance, whatever that mattering turns out actually to amount to. To erase reason from the equation altogether is, we typically suppose, tantamount to stripping out the distinctly human dimension of things, so closely is *homo sapiens* bound up with the capacity for intelligent reflection of the sort that leads to abstractive knowledge and understanding. I have no desire whatever to understate the importance of reason, though the extent of its independent "mattering" is typically overplayed unhelpfully. *Sapientia*, though, is a more fulsome notion than what pertains under the jurisdiction of reason alone, and my argument so far has simply been to observe that within the complex manifold of our human knowing of things imagination matters every bit as much and, in one way or another, across the whole front of that knowing. To treat it as essentially frivolous in its contributions is misguided, and to suggest that where questions of truth are concerned we might either require or be able (even temporarily) to disengage the imaginative so as to permit a more authentic, more reliable approach to things is preposterous. That imagination errs and is often to be found in the service of untruth and evil cannot be doubted, and its need for redemption is great. But it is no greater than the corresponding needs in this regard of "reason," or our moral compass, or our will, or any other putative component of the composite psychic reality to which Saint Paul alludes when he reminds his readers that where our relationship with God (and thus with the reality of the world that God has created) is concerned, we are not fallen from the neck down alone, but "enemies in our minds"[20] too. Indeed, considered at its best (and without slipping into the unduly euphoric elevation of it referred to earlier), there is much to be said for the Romantic poet William Wordsworth's suggestion that, far from the two terms being set in any sort of potential deadlock,

---

20. "*Ekthrois tē dianoia*" (Col 1:21).

what we refer to as acts of imagination are in fact nothing other than "reason in its most exalted mode" or, we might better say, integral and vital to all our best thinking about anything at all.[21]

Imagining What Lies Ahead

Imagination, then, matters greatly, for it lies at the heart of all our distinctly human ways of engaging with the world, with others, and with God. From this comprehensive assessment we return now, though, to reflect on the importance of our capacity for imagination in times of crisis in particular.

We might begin simply by acknowledging what ought perhaps now to be obvious; namely, the fact that, since imagination is all about meaning and the discernment of significance, without it we should not be able to recognize a crisis in the first place even were it, as they say, to jump up and bite us on the nose. Apprehending, identifying, grasping the meaning of whatever reality confronts us with is not a passive circumstance, but rather one that demands of us skilled activities of an imaginative and constructive sort. To cite the words of Iris Murdoch again: "The world is not given to us 'on a plate,' it is given to us as a creative task.... We work,... and 'make something of it.'"[22] And what we make of it, what we take ourselves to be confronted with, will vary from one person to another contingent on a whole raft of different things, including the possession of relevant skills of recognition and interpretation, and a willingness to use these responsibly for the good of others. It is, at present, for instance, less easy than it was even five years ago to remain an avid denier of climate change, its causes in patterns of intentional human behavior, and the frightening outcomes threatening to engulf us if serious action is not taken globally and without delay. In part, this shift is due to an acceleration in the numbers of maverick "weather events" experienced and reported across the world, and crying out to be interpreted as part of a bigger picture in which environmental crisis figures large. But they *need* not be so interpreted, because that bigger picture is not itself indubitable, and it is not the only one available. As the persistence of a hard core of "climate deniers" demonstrates, it is perfectly possible not to accept the evidential weight of such events even when they stack up in this way. Evidence must be *accepted as such* before it can possess any persuasive force, and even a surfeit of freak meteorological occurrences and conditions can, viewed in the light of some alternative

---

21. This is a reality increasingly acknowledged at the frontiers of conversation between disciplines. See, for instance, McLeish, *The Poetry and Music of Science*.

22. Murdoch, *Metaphysics as a Guide to Morals*, 215.

scheme of meaning (or "imaginary"), be robbed of evidential force or have a quite different construction placed upon them. Those who have undergone a "change of mind" or heart about the reality of this or any other crisis situation, in other words, have not simply accrued a quantity of *additional* evidence to be considered; they have had a transplant of a more radical sort altogether. The imaginative backdrop in terms of which the bits and pieces of their experience were hitherto noticed, filtered, classified, selected as relevant, and made sense of has been found wanting and exchanged for another. They have, we might say, come to imagine (and so understand) their circumstance very differently and, because human meaning is mostly temporally embedded, not just their present circumstance alone, but its probable consequences in that region so reliant upon imaginative construction for its very existence—the future. If present reality can be grasped in its significance only thanks to the functioning of a rightly ordered imagination, how much more fully is this true of any reliable take on futurity, lacking, as futurity necessarily is, in the sorts of givens that confront us both in the present and in our attempts to hold on to or unearth the past?

Intentional acts of imagining are, we might usefully note at this point, always generated if not quite by actual crises then at the very least by disaffection or disappointment with what our immediate present has (or seems likely) to offer. After all, to imagine what is not actually or apparently the case takes effort, and such effort is unlikely to be deemed either necessary or worthwhile by those wholly contented with their lot. Our imaginings are, we might say, born of an insatiable itch for something more, something other, and mostly something better than we currently enjoy or must endure. They are, in other words, born of *desire*. In the case of all but the most outlandish and far-fetched of personal fantasies and the nostalgic (and generally highly selective) remembrance of things past, imagination engages itself with states of affairs in what it takes to be some possible future or other. The darker side of this, of course, is its entanglement with the generation of such emotions as fear or anxiety, whether well-founded, measured and "reasonable," or pathological and needlessly enervating, the latter variety sapping the present moment of whatever joy and peace it might otherwise hold. But it is imagination, too, which alone makes it possible for us to face the future in positive terms and, reflexively, to adjust our disposition within the present moment so as to embrace or pursue that future. There are, to be sure, different modes of such imagining. One such is optimism, a sort of cheery temperamental disposition likely to be found humming "Always look on the bright side of life" even amidst its own impending crucifixion. The optimist's imagining of the future, as Eagleton notes, possesses little rational force and no more moral virtue than "having freckles or flat feet."[23]

Of similar ilk, but on a wholly different scale of consideration, is the so-called "myth of progress," a secular, predestinarian ideology that has dominated modernity's narration of the human circumstance ever since the confident humanism of the late Renaissance and continues to stalk the corridors of power and the homes of the affluent today.[24] At the heart of this metanarrative lies a view of human history as a long, inexorable, and irreversible march through time towards a utopian goal.[25] Fired by rapid advances in science and technology, and undaunted by the thought that since, in Carl Sagan's ironic words, as a species it seems that "we have become powerful without becoming commensurately wise,"[26] the march may actually be both shorter than we once thought and in the direction of catastrophe, subscribers to the myth celebrate Progress as that axiom whereby, as time passes, things are bound to get better; better, that is to say, not just here and there or in some respectable proportion, but *as a whole*. Here, history is moving slowly but surely towards a Hollywood "happy ending" that, the abiding occurrence of bad things in the meanwhile notwithstanding, will not finally be gainsaid. There is no attempt in all this, then, to Photoshop history's horrors and terrors out of the picture; in fact, the idea of Progress itself might be seen as a way of responding to the challenge of their otherwise untamed presence by ascribing to them a meaningful place within the pattern of its narrative. Their *proper* place is in the past from which human history is still emerging, albeit at an impressive velocity, and the gradual exorcism of its traces by the powers of reason and the tools of advanced technology is already well underway, its confident completion being precisely only a matter of time. As an "imaginary" in Taylor's sense (or a "story we tell ourselves" *à la* Manson and Holloway) this has just as little rational or evidential warrant as the optimist's determination to "Always look on the bright side of life." Given its role as an ideology justifying policies and practices that have blighted generations of human lives past, present, and (it now appears certain) future, its moral standing is even less secure than that.

---

23. Eagleton, *Hope Without Optimism*, 2.
24. See Bauckham and Hart, *Hope Against Hope*, 9–19.
25. Bauckham and Hart, *Hope Against Hope*, 9.
26. Cited in Ord, *The Precipice*, 30.

Imagination and the Grammar of Hope

It remains the case, though, that human existence, being embedded in the flow of time, is vectorial rather than fixed. The present moment cannot hold our attention for long, the texture of conscious experience always involving in fact a flickering between things remembered and things anticipated, yearned for, or feared. The present, in other words, is never *pure* present at all, but is always a potentially bewildering cocktail of past, present, and possible futures; or, we might say, between the "presence" of the now and the relative absence of the "no-longer" and the "not yet." We are not, though, carried along by the tide of time like helpless passengers. While the past remains rather more present to us and more significant than we often give it credit for, we are at the last future-orientated creatures. This is intrinsically challenging, since we face and must embrace an open and unknowable future that is capable both of frightening and exciting us in equal measure; but it is always preferable to the prospect of being stuck in the limits of the moment, condemned to a perpetual revisiting of the same old, same old. Nothing is more likely, in fact, to induce in us melancholy, despair, or terminal fatigue than a Groundhog Day scenario offering the prospect of "no future," no meaningful change or development for anyone or anything, even if change should prove to bring loss rather than gain. Incarceration and stagnation in a closed, eternal present is a vision of hell worthy of Dante himself. We are creatures of desire, and we need something to look forward to, even though that may be uncertain because glimpsed only in the face of seemingly insuperable odds; otherwise, we lose heart and our soul cannot breathe as it must. George Steiner reminds us that our ability to "imagine otherwise," to reach beyond the apparent constraints of the here-and-now, relies upon our possession of language complete with a future tense. "We move forward," he writes, "in the slipstream of the statements we make about tomorrow morning,"[27] constructing "axiomatic fictions"[28] with respect to the future that will draw us forward in their wake, envisaging the possibility of a change worth waiting and striving for. We need at least to be able to glimpse a valid future from our standpoint in the (sometimes merely disappointing, sometimes unbearable) present, difficult and counter-intuitive though that might be. Indeed, as Eagleton notes, "the mere act of being able to imagine an alternative future" may itself "distance and relativise the present, loosening its grip upon us to the point where the future in question becomes more feasible."[29]

27. Steiner, *After Babel*, 160.
28. Steiner, *After Babel*, 138.
29. Eagleton, *Hope Without Optimism*, 85.

Of course, this cannot occur if what is glimpsed is only a chimera, having no foothold in the realms of genuine possibility. This, though, is a circumstance entirely likely to arise in the case of the futures imagined by cheery optimism on the one hand or unwavering faith in axiomatic Progress on the other. Furthermore, lacking as they do both in rational and moral force, neither of these impels anyone to strive responsibly to see a better future realized, each presuming, in effect, that all we must do is wait for such a future to show up. Neither in its complacency, we might reasonably say, is well-disposed to the suggestion that we ever face a genuine *crisis*. The matter stands very differently, though, with yet a third mode of imaginative reckoning with the future; namely, *hope*.[30] Like its counterparts, hope begins with the itch of desire for a better future. Unlike them, though, it never takes it for granted that the eventual satisfaction of that desire is even probable, let alone inevitable. The identification of a crisis of some sort, in other words, is intrinsic to hope, which by its very nature stares even the most intractable of realities in the face and, while recognizing their threat, is "slow to admit that all the facts are in, that all the doors have been tried, and that it is defeated."[31] After all, Eagleton notes, "only if you view your circumstance as critical do you recognise the need to transform it."[32] In hope, imagination works creatively to explore a range of possible scenarios and devises strategies by which one or more of these might be pursued and realized. It is quite distinct from mere desire as such, wedding to it the moral quality of intentionality and compelling at least the choice between action and resigned quietude. Imagination, we might note, thereby furnishes the conditions necessary for the exercise of human freedom as well as reason. More yet needs to be said, though. The decision to act in one way rather than another may well be possible and appropriate (if it seems identifiably to be the good, the right, or merely the better thing to do) quite apart from any instrumental pay-off and even when the circumstance is acknowledged at last to be hopeless. The extra distinguishing feature of *hopeful* action, though, is that it is conducted in the genuine belief that it has glimpsed a genuine possibility of rescuing, retrieving, or redeeming. Where it is not deluded,[33] hope, in the terminology of Ernst Bloch's landmark study of the subject, involves the imaginative intuition of

30. On the roles of hope, both as an imaginative disposition and more specifically within Christian faith, see Bauckham and Hart, *Hope Against Hope*.

31. Lynch, *Images of Hope*, 35.

32. Eagleton, *Hope Without Optimism*, 5.

33. The modality of hope is such that, like faith, it is fallible and can thus be mistaken, a fact which, as Eagleton observes, distinguishes it from some other imaginative dispositions towards the future. See Eagleton, *Hope Without Optimism*, 3.

a "Real-Possible"³⁴ or, further flung still, a "Not-Yet-Possible" which may yet *become* possible despite the presence of apparently insuperable obstacles, if we strive towards it or (since hope is rarely purely heroic) reach out to grasp the hand it extends to us, wedded securely as it is to the conditions and possibilities immanent within even the darkest and most threatening present reality. Without this fundamentally imaginative capacity we should simply drown, being ill-fitted to survive the challenges of existence. "Natural selection," Steiner muses, has "favoured the subjunctive."³⁵

Hoping Against Hope

It remains simply to observe that, in circumstances that are genuinely bereft of hope, the best form of imagining will be that which enables us to come to terms healthily with the imminent loss or demise that confronts us. Generating and sustaining artificial hopes ("Fido has gone to live on a farm . . .") simply fosters denial and robs us of the dignity of bearing whatever amount of reality we are able to bear even though it be unpleasant. Here, though, we face a problem of significant proportions. For, while hope may often be well grounded in the realities and possibilities immanent within nature and history, nature and history themselves (and our own fleeting involvement with them) are, the best analyses available to us confirm, finally hopeless, being bound to end at some point in death and dissolution, a scenario sufficient to call into question whatever meaning we may temporarily have traced or invested in them. Considered in themselves, that is to say, the systems of our creaturely existence afford no final grounds for hope at all, but only the facts of finitude, mortality, and transience, specters sufficient to relativize and eventually dash all hopes. And yet we persist in being hopeful. Indeed, that imaginative disposition we call "hope," William Lynch observes, "*comes close to being the very heart and centre of a human being.*"³⁶ And Christian faith, too, is irreducibly hopeful, both reflecting and fostering this facet of our humanity. What, then, are we to make of this? Is it just another cruel trick played upon us by the processes of a cosmos that is indeed finally meaningless and indifferent to our well-being? And is Christian faith either deluded and unable to give a reason for the hope that is in it or, worse, complicit in a conspiracy of artifice intended to soothe our worst fears and so avoid social tumult?

---

34. See Bloch, *The Principle of Hope*, 144–48.
35. Steiner, *After Babel*, 217.
36. Lynch, *Images of Hope*, 31.

Our answer must necessarily be brief, and is offered from the perspective of the same Christian faith which holds both that God created humans to be hopeful, and that this hopefulness finds its true counterpart and fulfilment not in any of the many "hopeful" circumstances that may arise in history, important as these undoubtedly are, but rather in a hope that transcends the finitude of history and nature as such and grants these their final meaningfulness. "Real life," said the novelist Gustave Flaubert, "is always misrepresented by those who wish to make it lead up to a conclusion. God alone may do that."[37] Christian hope, the "good news" which the church is called upon to share with the world, is an imaginary neither based on nor limited by the probabilities and possibilities latent within nature and history as such. On the contrary, its limits lie only in the boundless possibilities of the God who called nature and history themselves into being out of nothing, who made room for himself in the world by generating life in the womb of a virgin, and who, by raising his Son from death takes our imagination captive, granting us just a glimpse of a future that God has purposed for the world. We, in our turn, are called upon now to reimagine the "real world" bathed in the light of this glimpse of its true end; and not just to imagine it, but also to live as though it were already here, allowing the cognitive dissonance of discontinuity to be bodied forth in defiant acts of resistance or "guerilla theatre."[38] That the arts, those most explicit and unashamedly imaginative of all human practices, may have a vital role to play in all this seems to me to be both wholly fitting and, given the ecology of the imaginative as I have described it, inevitable.

Bibliography

Bauckham, Richard, and Trevor Hart. *Hope Against Hope: Christian Eschatology in Contemporary Context.* London: Darton, Longman, and Todd, 1999.

Bloch, Ernst. *The Principle of Hope.* Translated by Neville Plaice et al. Cambridge: MIT Press, 1986.

Eagleton, Terry. *Hope Without Optimism.* New Haven: Yale University Press, 2017.

Forsyth, P. T. *The Justification of God: Lectures for War-Time on a Christian Theodicy.* London: Duckworth & Co., 1916.

Greene, Graham. *The Power and the Glory.* Harmondsworth: Penguin, 1962.

Hart, Trevor A. *Faith Thinking: The Dynamics of Christian Theology.* 2nd ed. Eugene, OR: Cascade, 2020.

Holloway, Richard. *Stories We Tell Ourselves: Making Meaning in a Meaningless Universe.* Edinburgh: Canongate, 2020.

---

37. Cited in Forsyth, *The Justification of God*, 223.

38. See Wilder, *Theopoetic*.

Johnson, Mark. *The Meaning of the Body: Aesthetics of Human Understanding.* Chicago: University of Chicago Press, 2007.
Kearney, Richard. *Poetics of Imagining: Modern to Postmodern.* Edinburgh: Edinburgh University Press, 1998.
Lewis, C. S. "Bluspels and Flalansferes: A Semantic Nightmare." In *Rehabilitations and Other Essays*, 133–58. London: Oxford University Press, 1939.
Lynch, William F. *Images of Hope: Imagination as Healer of the Hopeless.* Dublin: Helicon, 1965.
Manson, Mark. *Everything Is F*cked: A Book about Hope.* New York: HarperCollins, 2019.
McGilchrist, Iain. *The Master and His Emissary: The Divided Brain and the Making of the Western World.* Rev. ed. New Haven: Yale University Press, 2019.
McLeish, Tom. *The Poetry and Music of Science: Comparing Creativity in Science and Art.* Oxford: Oxford University Press, 2019.
Murdoch, Iris. *Existentialists and Mystics: Writings on Philosophy and Literature.* London: Penguin, 1999.
———. *Metaphysics as a Guide to Morals.* London: Vintage, 2003.
Ord, Toby. *The Precipice: Existential Risk and the Future of Humanity.* London: Bloomsbury, 2021.
Ricœur, Paul. *The Rule of Metaphor: The Creation of Meaning in Language.* Translated by Robert Czerny et al. London: Routledge, 2004.
Steiner, George. *After Babel: Aspects of Language and Translation.* Oxford: Oxford University Press, 1975.
Stevenson, Leslie. "Twelve Conceptions of Imagination." *The British Journal of Aesthetics* 43.3 (2003) 238–59.
Taylor, Charles. *Modern Social Imaginaries.* Durham: Duke University Press, 2003.
Wilder, Amos N. *Theopoetic: Theology and the Religious Imagination.* Eugene, OR: Wipf & Stock, 2014.
Wolterstorff, Nicholas P. *Art in Action: Towards a Christian Aesthetic.* Carlisle: Solway, 1997.

5

Painting

A Contemplative Action in the Time of Pandemic

Douglas Purnell

When I retired from ministry, I had a life goal to spend fifteen years working in my studio every day. I hoped that I could produce a mature body of work. I am enjoying doing just that.

Early in the time, I wrote "My Manifesto for My Being a Painter of the Poetic."[1] It begins with the words of Audre Lord: "Poetry is the way we help give name to the nameless so it can be thought."[2]

Deep inside me, I know that I cannot paint the spirit, but only create paintings where the spirit might choose to dwell.

Over recent years, I think I have become a "contemplative" painter. My studio is a quiet place, and a place where I am not trying to create images of some "thing." Rather, it is a space in which I open myself to the possibility of making works that respond in an open way to that which I consider "mystery," and that I have no words to describe. I am lucky, in that I have a pension and do not have to sell paintings to survive. This means I can go where the process takes me.

I am reaching, in paint, for a form of expression that is beyond words. I want to paint "slower" paintings; that is, paintings which don't hit the viewer in the face, so that they recognize immediately some object or thing. I want the viewer to be engaged by the beauty of the work, and to be lured by the beauty of the work to spend time with it, that they might go to deeper places in their own "being." I don't have answers. I don't have more

---

1. Purnell, "My Manifesto for My Being a Painter of the Poetic."
2. Lorde, "Poetry is Not a Luxury," 37.

words; at this stage of my life I have paint, brushes, and an expressive form. My paintings are my voice.

Douglas Purnell, *C-V 27*, 2020. Acrylic on canvas, 122 x 91 cm. Artist's collection.

During the 2019–20 Australian summer bushfires, I didn't attempt to paint the fires. Rather, I wanted to make paintings that were evocative of the things that happened to people during the time of the fires. And, more recently, through the COVID-19 pandemic, I haven't attempted to paint "the pandemic." Instead, I am painting a series of works that might reflect my inner journey as a contemplative person, during the time of the pandemic. Hopefully, the paintings find resonance and reverberation with those who view them.

During the pandemic, I have spent each day in my studio; and, each day in my studio I add more layers to my paintings. Through the time of the pandemic, I have painted red paintings—some 183 x 122 cm, other works on paper significantly smaller, some on offcuts of canvas.

I don't know how I initially chose to paint red paintings. It was intuitional, unconscious. In the process of painting I was looking for what makes a painting "cohere," what makes it hold together; in a couple of paintings I used red to do that. Slowly that evolved into making paintings that were built up of many layers, many colors, and in each painting there were layerings of watery reds that dripped, ran, bubbled down the surface spilling over the earlier layers of paint exposed at the foot of the painting. Suddenly, they became sheets or curtains of red, breaking open to expose or hint at what was beyond the surface.

In my journal I wrote: "There is something intensely powerful in the red that I am using. I am building up multiple layers of slightly different reds. . . . Red is a color that is a symbol of blood, of energy, of passion, of love, of lust, of life, of death, of spirit, of danger, (and, more); perhaps, it is a color that is 'on the edge,' and, when it is intensified it reaches into the heart or being of the viewer and engages them deeply. I think/hope that it breaks open the heart of the viewer to deeper, richer, experiences, and awareness of 'being.' It is a color that reaches way beyond words. It is a color that engages the soul/spirit."

One of the difficulties for me as a painter is that when using acrylic paint, as I do, when the paint is wet it glistens and is vibrant in color, and then when it dries, it dries flat and dark. What seems to be singing and dancing at the end of the day seems to have fallen flat on its face the next day. What I am discovering is that it is the last 5 percent of a painting that is the hardest to paint.

Crucial to the entire process is my contemplative discipline, and my awareness that it is the process that is important, always remembering and honoring that I cannot paint the spirit, but only work to bring to life paintings in which the spirit might choose to dwell.

My dream: to fill a "chapel" space with variously-sized red paintings.

Bibliography

Lorde, Audre. "Poetry Is Not a Luxury." In *Sister Outsider: Essays & Speeches*, 36–39. Berkeley: Crossing, 1984.

Purnell, Douglas. "My Manifesto for My Being a Painter of the Poetic." http://www.dougpurnellart.com/manifesto.html.

6

The Objects of Our Loyalties and the Power of Inanimate Objects

Robin Jensen

Two of the most popular pictorial motifs found in early Christian paintings and relief sculpture are scenes depicting the three Hebrew youths from the biblical Book of Daniel. According to the story, the three handsome youths, along with their companion, Daniel, were taken by King Nebuchadnezzar as captives into the land of Babylon and installed as servants in the royal court. Once there, the palace master changed their names from Hananiah, Mishael, and Azariah, to Shadrach, Meshach, and Abednego (Dan 1:7). In art, the three are easily recognized by their garb: little peaked caps and short, belted tunics over colorful leggings. To a third- or fourth-century Roman viewer, their clothes identified them as exotic easterners. To those familiar with other Christian iconography, they are easily confused with the three magi who brought gifts to the infant Christ.

The best known of these two scenes shows the three standing in the flames of a fiery furnace, their arms raised in prayer as if appealing for divine deliverance from certain death (Fig. 1). Sometimes the composition includes a person stoking the furnace or a fourth character or creature among the flames: one with the form of a human, an angel, or a bird. According to the story, this is the one seen by the Babylonian King Nebuchadnezzar when he looked inside the furnace, someone he described as having the appearance of a god (Dan 3:25).

THE OBJECTS OF OUR LOYALTIES AND THE POWER OF INANIMATE OBJECTS   73

Figure 1: *The Three Hebrew Youths in the Fiery Furnace*, from the Catacomb of Priscilla, in Giuseppe Wilpert, Roma Sotterranea: Le Pitture della Catacombe Romane, vol. 2 (Rome: Desclée Lefebure and Co., 1903), Table 78.

The lesser-known scene depicts the incident that precipitated the youths being sentenced to death by fire: their refusal to obey the royal order to bow down to the certain cult statue (Fig. 2). In these images, one or all three of the youths make gestures to show their disavowal of a small bust mounted on a slender plinth. One of them even turns his back on the object. The king usually is depicted as wearing Roman military garb rather than the trappings of a Babylonian ruler: a short, pleated tunic under a breastplate over which a cape is draped and pinned (Fig. 2). More interestingly, the king's facial features are identical to the bust on the plinth.

Figure 2: *The Trial of the Three Hebrew Youths.* Left portion of a lid from the sarcophagus of St. Gilles, fourth century. Photo by Robin Jensen.

While the first scene matches the textual narrative fairly well, the second significantly diverges from certain details of the biblical story, which suggests that the artist was not simply illustrating the tale but rather intended to convey an additional meaning; in particular, to conflate an ancient narrative with a contemporary one.

According to the Bible, the story is set at the court of King Nebuchadnezzar II who ruled Babylon from 605–562 BCE. According to the historical tradition, around the year 587 the king's armies conquered Judah, destroyed Solomon's Temple, and took a number of Jews into Babylonia as captives. In this specific episode, Nebuchadnezzar orders the erection of an enormous golden statue and commands that everyone must fall down and worship it or be thrown into a blazing furnace. As devout followers of the God of Israel, the three refuse to obey, receive the imposed sentence of death, and are cast into the fiery furnace.

The ending, however, is a happy one. The God of Israel delivers the three alive from the flames. The king, amazed by their miraculous survival, not only rescinds his order but issues a new command that no one in his kingdom shall be permitted to utter any blasphemy against the god of Shadrach, Meshach, and Abednego (Dan 3:29).

Apart from its enormous size (sixty cubits high and six cubits wide) and its material (solid gold), the biblical text offers no information about what the statue depicts—whether it was the image of a god or of the king himself. The previous chapter of the book offers some hints, however. Here one reads that the prophet Daniel interpreted the figure in one of Nebuchadnezzar's dreams: a huge statue with a golden head, chest and arms of silver, torso and thighs of bronze, legs of iron, and feet of clay. Daniel explained that this statue symbolizes the successive destruction of the king's empire by four other empires, concluding only when the God of Heaven ultimately establishes an indestructible and eternal kingdom (Dan 2:36–45).

Nebuchadnezzar's dream statue is not at all like the colossal statue that King Nebuchadnezzar orders to be worshiped, however. That one was made of pure gold rather than of five materials (gold, silver, bronze, iron, and clay). Moreover, in the narrative, this statue does not seem to be a prophetic sign of future destruction but rather some kind of cult idol that no faithful adherent of Israel's God could venerate. Thus, the story transitions from edifying fable about the inevitable fall of human empires to a tale about one ruler's hubris and the three heroes who resist his tyrannical demands, even at the risk of their own lives.

In light of the narrative, when one turns back to consider the early Christian depictions of the story, their particular message emerges. Contrary to the biblical text, in these visual depictions the statue is neither enormous nor golden. It is also not like the one from the king's dream, made from gold, silver, bronze, lead, and clay. Instead, in these images, the youths refuse to venerate a standard, even smaller than life-sized, portrait bust of the ruler himself.

By substituting an imperial bust portrait for Nebuchadnezzar's golden colossus, and by transforming a Babylonian tyrant into a Roman emperor, the iconography infuses the biblical narrative with contemporary relevance. Specifically, it has a pointed and timely resonance for early fourth-century Christians who either had experienced state-sponsored oppression or recalled the heroism of martyrs who unjustly suffered or died for refusing to obey an imperial edict that would require them to offer sacrifices to an idol. They disobeyed the law, in effect, but a law they believed violated one set down by a higher authority.

Attributing contemporary relevance to an ancient tale is not surprising insofar as this story may originally have found its way into the biblical canon for similar reasons. While the narrative setting is the sixth-century BCE Babylonian exile of the Jews, the text is almost certainly a much later composition that most likely took final form during the persecution of the Jewish people under the Hellenistic ruler, Antiochus Epiphanes IV (c. 167–64 BCE). As a tale of survival in times of trauma and suffering, the story was composed in order to comfort and inspire the oppressed subjects of a despotic ruler. This particular king attempted to force Jews to adopt Greek practices and worship his gods, threatening them with execution if they refused. Thus, this biblical book seems to have functioned as a subversive, anti-imperial text, disguised by its writers as an unthreatening fable from a distant time and place rather than as a commentary on a current situation.

Most biblical scholars agree that texts like the Book of Daniel, in which the forces of evil are overcome by divine intervention, were written during times of national or community distress. They are not actual historical accounts but rather describe the present and predict the future through vivid narratives of trials, tribulations, and cosmic battles in which the protagonists eventually overthrow the forces of evil with the help of heavenly agents. The conclusion to the Book of Daniel, like that of the New Testament Book of Revelation, portrays the ultimate defeat and punishment of the wicked and the deliverance and final reward of the good. In the end, persecution or subjugation of the holy ones will end, and a perpetual era of peace, security, prosperity, and justice will dawn.

Millennia later, this story still resonates with oppressed communities; in particular, with African Americans who were enslaved and, even later as freed men and women, who were oppressed and abused in the era of Jim Crow discrimination. They recognized their own story in that of the Jews who were captured and transported to Babylon as involuntary servants to their captors. Like the three Hebrew youths whose names were changed by their new overlords, they too were commanded to give up their own customs and to worship their captors' gods. Thus, these biblical heroes came again to have a contemporary relevance, especially for the American Civil Rights Movement.

In one of the most influential documents from this era, Martin Luther King Jr.'s *Letter from Birmingham Jail,* King specifically refers to the three Hebrew youths as models of civil disobedience, and furthermore associates them with the early Christian martyrs. King writes:

> Of course, there is nothing new about this kind of civil disobedience. It was seen sublimely in the refusal of Shadrach, Meshach, and Abednego to obey the laws of Nebuchadnezzar because a higher moral law was involved. It was practiced, superbly by the early Christians who were willing to face hungry lions and the excruciating pain of chopping blocks before submitting to certain unjust laws of the Roman Empire.[1]

As King here argues, the heroic youths, like the Christian martyrs, refused to cooperate with unjust laws and they resisted corrupt authorities, but they also did this knowing that they would most likely

---

1. King, "Letter from Birmingham Jail," 3.

be arrested, tried, and cruelly punished for their witness. They accepted the consequences of their civil disobedience. They refused to sit at the back of the bus and insisted on sitting at whites-only lunch counters. They disobeyed segregationist laws that they regarded as immoral and unjust. Unlike the biblical three Hebrew youths, however, the Christian martyrs and Dr. King were not divinely delivered from suffering and death. Yet, their courage was more significant than their martyrdom as models for members of oppressed communities seeking to defeat ethnic, racial, or religious discrimination, subjugation, and hatred.[2]

King and many of those who participated in the Civil Rights Movement found inspiration in songs sung by the enslaved Africans on southern plantations. Studies of these songs have uncovered the coded messages and symbols alluding to escape to freedom and resistance to their oppressors. They also offered hope for divine deliverance, if not in this life then in the next. Like the origins of the story of the three Hebrew youths, the oppressors did not realize that these songs, many of them drawn from the Old Testament, were much more than edifying fables or pious Bible stories. Their songs, like *Go Down Moses*, did not just refer to the Israelites' flight from enslavement in Egypt, but also expressed hope for their own liberation. Another example, *Didn't My Lord Deliver Daniel*, expresses yearning to be delivered, like that biblical prophet, from tyrannical bondage. The song refers also to the three Hebrew youths and asks, again and again, if Daniel why not everyone? One of the most famous recordings of this spiritual was that by Paul Robeson, which was recorded on his own Othello label in the 1950s and made available more recently on the Smithsonian Folkways African American Legacy series.[3]

---

2. See a similar analysis in Augustine, "The Fiery Furnace, Civil Disobedience, and the Civil Rights Movement." Here, however, Augustine discusses a "martyrdom" or "suffering servant" theology, by which he means the often-deadly consequences of one's disobedience to unjust laws.

3. See Smithsonian Folkways, "Paul Robeson."

Figure 3: Cover of sheet music for the song *Shadrack* (*Shadrach*), written and composed by Robert MacGimsey, 1931. Ink on paper, 30.48 x 22.86 cm. National Museum of American History, Washington, DC, USA.

The story of the three Hebrew youths was not as prominent in the songs of enslaved Africans, but it turned up later, in the 1930s, in the song, *Shadrack*, composed by Robert MacGimsey. MacGimsey, a white man who grew up in a small Louisiana town, wrote his songs in the style of African American spirituals (Fig. 3). Based on this style, many assumed him to be African American himself. Ironically, one of the first recordings of *Shadrack* was made by Robert Merrill in 1946. However, it was probably most famously performed by Louis Armstrong and released on an album, *Louis and the Good Book*, in 1958. The lyrics incorporate the sound of jazz instruments, perhaps intentionally echoing the somewhat comical

THE OBJECTS OF OUR LOYALTIES AND THE POWER OF INANIMATE OBJECTS   79

repetitions in the biblical story of the sounds of horn, pipe, lyre, trigon, harp, drum, and entire musical ensemble:

> There was three children from the land of Israel
> Shadrack, Meshach, Abednego!
> They took a little trip to the land of Babylon
> Shadrack, Meshach, Abednego!
> Nebuchadnezzar was the king of Babylon
> Shadrack, Meshach, Abednego!
> He took a lot of gold, and made an idol
> Shadrack, Meshach, Abednego!
>
> And he told everybody when you hear the music of the trombone,
> And he told everybody when you hear the music of the clarinet,
> And he told everybody when you hear the music of the horn,
> You must fall down and worship the idol!
> Shadrack, Meshach, Abednego!
>
> But the children of Israel would not bow down!
> Shadrack, Meshach, Abednego!
> Couldn't fool 'em with a golden idol!
> Shadrack, Meshach, Abednego!
> I said you couldn't fool 'em with a golden idol!
> Shadrack, Meshach, Abednego!
>
> So the king put the children in the fiery furnace
> Shadrack, Meshach, Abednego!
> Heaped on coals and red-hot brimstone
> Shadrack, Meshach, Abednego!
> Eleven times hotter, hotter than it oughtta be!
> Shadrack, Meshach, Abednego!
> Burned up the soldiers that the king had put there
> Shadrack, Meshach, Abednego!
>
> But the Lord sent an angel with the snow-white wings
> Down in the middle of the furnace
> Talkin' to the children 'bout the power of the Gospel
> Shadrack, Meshach, Abednego!

Well they couldn't burn a hair on the head of
Shadrack, Meshach, Abednego!
Laughin' and talkin' while the fire jumpin' round
Shadrack, Meshach, Abednego!

Old Nebudchanezzer called "Hey there!"
When he saw the power of the Lord
And they had a regal time in the house of Babylon
Shadrack! Meshach, Abednego!
Oh, Abednego!

In recent years, active repudiation of different kinds of statues have become the centers of defiance and repudiation, and symbols of resistance. In the United States, these have included the monumental figures of Southern Civil War heroes or civic leaders discovered to have been slave holders. Their statues grace city parks and squares around the country. Protests against the existence of these offensive monuments, and efforts to remove them, have often been met with violent backlash. For example, in August 2017, the planned removal of a Confederate General's statue from a city park in Charlottesville, Virginia, prompted an organized demonstration by white nationalists who objected to its removal. This in turn sparked a counter demonstration by those who wanted the statue destroyed. While no king or emperor had demanded that citizens bow down to and worship the statue, the ensuring controversy was often characterized as a culture war in which certain disrespectful members of the public were desecrating a kind of sacred history, pitted against those who wanted to preserve and even reinstate brutal, unjust, and racist social structures.

Contrary to common assumptions, most of the statues at the center of the controversy were, in fact, erected not at the end of the US Civil War to honor fallen heroes, but rather during the times when Jim Crow laws enforcing the racial segregation of black and white citizens were promulgated in the US, at the end of the nineteenth century and beginning of the twentieth century, or when Civil Rights tensions were especially fraught in the late 1950s to the mid 1960s. Based on this timing, one may reasonably view these monuments as having intentionally been erected to reinforce messages of white superiority and the validity of regarding African Americans as second-class and disenfranchised citizens. Because of these racist associations, the statues became galvanizing symbols. In other parts of the world, groups of citizens have risen up to demand the removal of figures of Cecil Rhodes or Captain Cook.

Defenders of such monuments have argued that, like them or not, they serve a useful, even educational, purpose; that eradicating them is tantamount to denying or trying to expunge the historical record. They often suggest that the statues might be supplemented with didactic labels to provide helpful context and to educate viewers about both their positive and negative significance. Others, either from an interest in historical artifacts or perhaps regarding them as aesthetically valuable, have proposed moving them to museums. Protesters have responded that the problem is not that people have forgotten (or might forget) the past, but rather that these objects serve to galvanize those who cherish their memories and would like to return to the past and restore the old regimes. For their part, museum curators are usually unwilling to accept the offered statues as works of art worthy of display or long-term storage.[4]

Events like these demonstrate the power of inanimate objects, whether they function as symbols, either of other people's gods, venerated ancestral customs, or despised reminders of past injustices. The protests in Charlottesville prompted a domino-like movement. Groups of citizens around the country were galvanized to destroy or at least desecrate similar monuments, sometimes spray painting them with the message "Black Lives Matter."

A half century after King's death, societies still grapple with the reality of systemic racism, cultural subjugation, and political exclusion. In the past few years, the world has witnessed a marked resurgence of nationalist pride and the equation of patriotism with bowing down to secular gods, whether they be statues, flags, or political leaders.

African Americans and members of various groups who are regarded as non-conformists are still killed, incarcerated, and persecuted, often simply for refusing to obey individuals who regard themselves as empowered to abuse anyone they deem uncooperative. In protest to such attitudes and their consequences, modern Shadrachs, Meshachs, and Abednegos might choose to take a knee during the playing of the secular National Anthem before a football game as a demonstration of their higher loyalty and refusal to identify nationalism with true religion. They refuse to bow down and worship the new golden idol. This choice, this non-compliance, of course has consequences: they are thrown into a modern form of a fiery furnace.

---

4. See, for example, Woolf, "What to do with America's Confederate Statues and Monuments."

Bibliography

Augustine, Jonathan C. "The Fiery Furnace, Civil Disobedience, and the Civil Rights Movement: A Biblical Exegesis on Daniel 3 and Letter from Birmingham Jail." *Richmond Public Interest Law Review* 21.3 (2018) 243–62.

King, Martin Luther, Jr. "Letter from Birmingham Jail." https://www.csuchico.edu/iege/_assets/documents/susi-letter-from-birmingham-jail.pdf.

Smithsonian Folkways. "Paul Robeson—'Didn't My Lord Deliver Daniel?' [Official Audio]." *YouTube*, March 26, 2009. https://www.youtube.com/watch?v=bcHT6XVFtRo.

Wilpert, Giuseppe. *Roma Sotterranea: Le Pitture della Catacombe Romane*. Rome: Desclée Lefebure and Co., 1903.

Woolf, Christopher. "What to Do with America's Confederate Statues and Monuments." https://www.pri.org/stories/2017-08-17/what-do-america-s-confederate-statues-and-monuments.

7

The Shadow of the Cross[1]

Robert Cording

Once, in the silence of a church in Taos,
I saw the so-called mystery painting—

Christ stands in the pinkish light
of early morning beside the Sea of Galilee

just before filling the disciples' nets with fish
in places they'd sworn there were no fish.

What makes the painting a mystery is not
the full-bellied nets of abundant, unexpected life

to come but the other scene that appears
exactly where this first one is

when the lights are turned off inside
the special recess that holds the painting.

In the penetrating dark, Christ
carries the weight of the cross where once

the sea glimmered in the morning light.
There is no accounting for why this is so—

---

1. This poem was inspired by Henri Ault's *The Shadow of the Cross*, 1896. Oil on canvas, size unknown. San Francisco de Asis, Rancho de Taos, USA.

experts agree it is not a trick of light or paint.
Some see more in the darkness than others—

Christ's plodding movement, or the gloom
of clouds shuttering the light. Neither painting

is very good, but standing before it,
I could see how, together, they made visible

how everything is more than one thing—
the haul of fish which are always there,

the daily fear we live with, of something,
inevitably, we will be asked to bear.

8

"If I Say..."

Poetry "after God" in Times of Eco-social and Ecclesial Trauma

ANNE ELVEY

"I AM MAKING A list 'post-god,'" says the speaker in M. T. C. Cronin's *God Is Waiting in the World's Yard*.[1] Titled "Somewhat More than God," the poem in which this line appears concludes: "What did you think you were going to do after God. Ambushed like fear by prayer?"[2] In my subtitle, I have situated this essay in a contemporary field of intersecting and concurrent traumas: the eco-social traumas of colonial invasion, violence, especially against women and minors, climate change, biodiversity loss, pollution, poverty, pandemic and militarism, and the ecclesial trauma around institutional responses to child sexual abuse.

The intersecting eco-social challenges that have traumatic effects for Earth and its many creatures, including humans, call forth a metanoia. This has been called an "ecological conversion" that for me requires that I do not presuppose what it might mean to speak of God, but rather, as a priority, that I turn toward Earth in a mode of attentiveness to its lively unfolding, contemporary ecological stresses, and otherness.[3] This metanoia requires in some senses a "not speaking of God," and I am aware of the irony of speaking of God in this essay.[4] For me, refraining from speaking of God does not suggest that eco-social trauma presses me to a "post-God" position. Rather, I am prompted to put aside the question of God

---

1. Cronin, "Somewhat More than God," 136.
2. Cronin, "Somewhat More than God," 136.
3. On turning toward Earth, see Rose, "Rupture and the Ethics of Care in Colonized Space," 190–215, 261–63. On ecological conversion, see Edwards, *Ecology at the Heart of Faith*, 2–4.
4. See Elvey, "Ashes and Dust," 33–42.

for a contemplative orientation toward Earth. This orientation does not take Earth as divine, nor does it imply pantheism or panentheism, but sits with or within an apophatic spirituality in which God, if there is any, will arrive in God's own time.[5] It is a disposition characterized, but not circumscribed, by openness to the possibility of God.

The concurrent human-focused trauma of the institutionalized failure to address child sexual abuse in the Roman Catholic church, and I can only speak of my experience in that Christian tradition, however, places my study "after God." This is not the place to detail my involvement as one of a small group of lay whistle-blowers and as a secondary witness in the 1990s, except to say that my reading of Volume 16, Number 2, of the Royal Commission's report into Institutional Responses to Child Sexual Abuse[6] established for me that my experience with Melbourne Archdiocesan authorities was anything but unique. Rather, the failures to act adequately and promptly were both systemic and not innocent. In the aftermath of such a report, I would have expected sustained public repentance from church authorities and their lay supporters. Instead, since 2017, I have observed, and on occasion encountered in conversation, defense and apologetic from both liberal and conservative Catholic clergy. This failure of response redoubles the initial failures. Questions remain about the way not only the structures of the church but also its theologies made the criminal cover up possible. These questions are beyond the scope of this essay. The area that is potent for me in relation to poetry is the old lure of, and subsequent loss of faith in, sacrament as related to the divine, and the persistence of sacrament as a mode of relation that is material and materially transformative.

From an ecological perspective, especially one informed by the new materialism, the honoring of matter that is central to sacramental traditions is a gift.[7] In the aftermath of the Royal Commission it is gift as remainder "after God," that is, after even the most subtle theologizing of God (in a Roman Catholic tradition). As I write, I hear committed Christian readers objecting, with all the objections that come down through the decades in the word "lapsed" which have somehow sounded like "didn't try hard enough," "wasn't open enough," "had a swag of wrong images of God," but which ignore that "lapsed" might just be an ethical stance.[8] I want to claim

---

5. See Elvey, "Leaf Litter," 65.

6. Royal Commission into Institutional Responses to Child Sexual Abuse, *Final Report*.

7. For a foundational new materialist perspective, see Bennett, *Vibrant Matter*.

8. See, for example, Dux, *Lapsed*. In this memoir retracing her Roman Catholic heritage in the light of the Royal Commission, Monica Dux argues for "lapsed" Catholics to take action by refraining from identifying as cultural Catholics, for example, in

this space, which is not unique to me, "after God," as a space within which poetry in Australia is speaking. The poetry I deal with is from contemporary settler writers. It is not in my purview to write of First Nations' poetry that is resurgent and has excellent First Nations' reviewers and scholars.[9]

If this essay has an argument, it is this:

> If I say there is no god
> I do not mean there is no
>
> god. There is no
>   There is
>
> the bound energy
> of the melaleuca, light
>
> tossed back from the underside
> of a leaf, peeled bark
>
> of the body where
> translation
>
> is the impossible –
> insistent, necessary.[10]

I intend to engage with poetry in this moment "after God" without a great deal of theorization, but letting the poetry lead the inquiry. The central part of the essay will focus on Cronin's *God is Waiting in the World's Yard*. Two concepts guide me: the material sacred and creative witness. To introduce, the material sacred, I begin with breath.

Poetry and Breath: The Material Sacred

> Pared back to the clarity
> of line   flowing into

---

the census. Her view is that Roman Catholic church authorities can use census data, which is effectively inaccurate if it counts "lapsed" Catholics, to exert influence on governments unduly.

9. For example, Wiradjuri academic and poet, Jeanine Leane, writes long form reviews of contemporary First Nations' poetry. Among her many fine reviews are Leane, "Staring Back," and, "On the Power to Be Still."

10. Elvey, "If I Say," 65.

line   maybe

every poem is
about breathing
about re-inscribing

the certainty
    for now   at least
of rise

    and fall
an anchor
    in wild waters   and calm

the almost unbearable simplicity of

in
    and
out

the cool air I invite into the habitation of my body
its invisible conduits

the welcome tide of bright blood and spark
of neuron

that searches me out
washing me in the salty pathways of life

the warmed breath that flows from me and
back into the world

    I am its creature
a body   swimming in channels of air

the steady and the variable beating of
words   and white spaces

    pulsing   an interplay of
                  note
    and rest

    ornament and pause   while always
    the deep thrum of silence

        its potential to disrupt   to splinter

    the sheen of surface[11]

In her poem, "Poetry and Breathing," Rose Lucas uses the spaces on the page and a steady rhythm to evoke the embodied relation between poetry and breath. Breath becomes visible on the page. The reader's breath is the medium of the poem.[12]

Breath is an important part of language, of the space between words, inhabiting different sounds and cadences, making the music of poetry (its speech and song) possible.[13] Often translated as "spirit," the biblical Greek word *pnuema* also means "blowing," "breathing," "breath," "(life-)spirit," and sometimes also "wind."[14] The Hebrew word *ruach* has a similar range of meaning. As Theodore Hiebert explains, *ruach* signifies a concept that connects air, wind, breath, and the sacred.[15] For Hiebert, *ruach* is "the air of both atmospheric winds and animal respiration."[16] As in Lucas's poem, these biblical concepts of *ruach* and *pnuema* signal the lively interconnectedness of breathing creatures with air, atmosphere, wind, and climate. For Lucas, the lulling rhythms of breath, especially through poetic (and meditative) attention, shift toward a silence that is not only calming but potentially disruptive, moving poet and reader into a splintered world, beyond "the sheen of surface."

Lucas writes of "the almost unbearable simplicity of // in // and // out." By describing the everyday quality of the body's inhalation and exhalation of air as "almost unbearable," the poet touches on what I call the material

---

    11. Lucas, "Poetry and Breathing," 28–29.

    12. See Pinsky, *The Sounds of Poetry*, 8. The following two paragraphs are adapted from Elvey, *Reading with Earth*, Chapter 3.

    13. See, for example, David Abram's comments on the breathing spaces between the consonants of unpointed Hebrew, in Abram, *The Spell of the Sensuous*, 99.

    14. See Bauer, *A Greek–English Lexicon*, 674–75.

    15. See Hiebert, "Air, the First Sacred Thing," 9–19.

    16. Hiebert, "Air, the First Sacred Thing," 13.

sacred. The frisson of a material transcendence inhabits the most basic bodily acts of living. Just as breathing enacts the necessary relationship between the body and the air, through the senses bodies are sites of co-relation of matter with matter, of shared material-corporeal agencies, of experiencing the self-in-relation materially.[17] Imaging the sacred as a quality of matter, and its organized forms including human bodies, I suggest that matter has a quality of transcendence, a material transcendence.[18] This has echoes in Lyn McCredden's analysis of the sacred in Australian poetry, when she writes: "the contemporary sacred seeks to recognize and reconstruct what [Luce] Irigaray has often referred to as the incarnate, 'sensible transcendent' . . . , a refusal to separate the corporeal and the spiritual, but a languaged, creative proposing of the one with the other."[19] The concept of the material sacred picks up this inseparability of the material, the corporeal, and the spiritual, not as a "nice" "new-age-y" coincidence, but rather with the frisson of the numinous that Lucas gestures toward in her references to splintering and "the almost unbearable," and in the breathy space created by her poem's contemplative rhythms. The material sacred has the quality of the *mysterium tremendum et fascinans* that, as Vine Deloria writes, "upsets our intellectual beliefs with a devastating display of energy, and remains with the individual as a fascinating, attractive presence and reminder that there are dimensions to life we cannot possibly imagine."[20] This is the energy of sacrament and sacramentality, the correspondence of matter and the sacred, conveyed through the correlation between breath and poesis, matter and its alterities.

Poetry and Situation: The Wound and the Sacred

Situational materialities, such as those outlined in the first paragraphs of this essay under the tropes of eco-social and ecclesial trauma, are inseparable from the material sacred, and inhabit the sacramentality of the everyday, often as wound. Poetry is well-placed to attend to the material situation of the wound:

> The incision – mine anyway –
> begins below the back of the neck

---

17. See Logan, *Air*; Serres, *The Five Senses*.
18. See Elvey, "Material Elements," 54–56.
19. McCredden, "Contemporary Poetry and the Sacred," 154. See also Irigaray, *An Ethics of Sexual Difference*, 148.
20. Deloria, "The Sacred and the Modern World," 1446.

and ends just above the coccyx.
Surgical stitches quietly dissolve,

leave a thick scar – a blurred, insistent line.
As each layer of skin dies, it whispers to the next

the form and story of the wound.
This is how I continue, intact.

Yet now, as I strain to lift this
too-heavy object, the long suture ruptures

in my head – the scar tearing open.
You might think this visceral confession

only an image of mine. But you are becoming
this unstitching, this sudden opening.[21]

    Andy Jackson's poem, "Opening," begins with a seeming description of the aftermath of a surgery and its memory; then the body and the poem together become "the form and story of the wound." The rupture is not, or not only, in the body but also in the psyche of the speaker, though this is not the crux of the poem. That comes in the last three lines, with the second person address, apparently an address to the reader but also to the poet-speaker as witness: "You might think . . ." The poem turns from the confessional to confront the reader with their positioning as wound itself, as a space of "unstitching" and "opening." "Opening" is the first poem of Jackson's new collection *Human Looking*, of which the back cover note explains: "The poems in *Human Looking* speak with the voices of the disabled and the disfigured, in ways which are confronting but also illuminating and tender."[22] Where confessional poetry can fail to convey the sacred weight of the wound, for example, in those cases when the speech becomes mired in its speaker's raw suffering, in Jackson's "Opening" confession shifts toward the reader-witness called into the space of the wound as both invitation and conviction.

---

21. Jackson, "Opening," 3.
22. Jackson, *Human Looking*, back cover note.

Poetry and/after God

What I have tried to capture in the short phrase "after God" is a particular wound in the idea and experience of the divine, as inherited and mediated through western Christian theologies and practices, especially sacramental traditions that both offer and withhold so much. This "after God" holds questions that are not new, but that come with current nuances. On one hand, the human power to extinguish life, culture, and biological diversity on massive scales, through genocide, nuclear weaponry, extinction of species, and anthropogenic climate change, prompts questions concerning just what a divine creator might permit creatures to enact in relation to the creation of which they are part. On another hand, the suppressed suffering of children prompts questions concerning of what kind is creation and the partiality or otherwise of the divine creator.[23] This may seem well-traversed territory for theologians, but poets offer ways of addressing these questions of God with an immediacy of corporeal, breathy engagement that does not seek direct answers but, at its best, opens to collective life-giving possibilities in the face of finitude, tragedy, and the horrors of human power misused.[24] Both surprisingly and unsurprisingly, in an ostensibly secular society, biblical and more broadly religious, including Jewish and Christian, themes become part of poets' vocabularies, often given their own pitch, as is the case in Cronin's *God Is Waiting in the World's Yard*.

Hard to categorize, *God Is Waiting in the World's Yard* is a series of prose poems exploring the possibility and impossibility of someone or something called "God" from the vantage of a domestic, sometimes idyllic, and sometimes troubling, backyard—the "world's yard." The left-facing pages carry (prose) poems that are left justified and have individual titles. The right-facing pages carry prose poems that are fully justified and are each titled "The World's Yard." Every one of these poems on the recto pages of the book begins: "Right at the back of the world's yard I am sitting." Since the book's title affirms "God is Waiting in the World's Yard," a reader may wonder if the "I" refers to God, the poet, or both. When with a play on "dog" as "god" reversed the poet writes, "God comes back with the stick I threw about five years ago," it seems likely that the "I" and "God" are distinct.[25]

---

23. See, for example, Ivan's "Rebellion" in Dostoyevsky, *The Brothers Karamazov*, Book V, Chapter 4.

24. My appeal to collective life-giving possibilities echoes Eric Santner's emphasis on "new possibilities for collective life," in his exploration of "neighbor love" through the lens of political theology. See Santner, *On Creaturely Life*, 58, 133.

25. Cronin, "The World's Yard," 89.

This kind of playful imagery recurs in the collection, but whimsy is juxtaposed with the horror, for example, of extinction.[26] In his review, Luke Beesley describes Cronin's book as gothic.[27] Death is a theme throughout the book—deaths are questions put to the idea of God; death resonates in the book's affirmation and disaffirmation of the "death of God." The God of Cronin's collection is almost invariably male. While the imagery ranges widely and sometimes wildly; while the recognition of "God" as a human construct stands with the possibility of God as more than any human construction; while affirmations of and withdrawals from this "God" accompany something like the possibility of God, the book scrutinizes divine indifference, the (failed) promise of divine protection, as well as traditions of divine sexual assault. These last remind me of the problematic imaginary created by William Butler Yeats's "Leda and the Swan" or John Donne's invitation to God in his sonnet, "Batter my heart . . . "[28] One way of reading *God is Waiting in the World's Yard* could be as an exorcism of this patriarchal God, which does not quite succeed. The remarkable persistence of the patriarchal, imperial divine "after God" infects the book itself, but this is part of the point of Cronin's shifting reverie in the collection. "After God" the book produces not only the God who was supposed, but refuses, to be dead to contemporary thinking, even to belief, or the kind of god or gods who might emerge in response to current need, but also the poet-speaker as themself waiting on God. While the title suggests that it is God who is waiting, by the final poem—the only one to span left and right-hand pages—it is the poet-speaker who is waiting. The book ends in a moment, somewhat of an anti-climax after all the God talk, with the poet saying: "Occasionally we find something to do with ourselves in which waiting plays no part."[29]

The anti-climactic quality of the book echoes for me in the close of Jacques Derrida's *The Gift of Death*. Having evoked the lure and the violence of the divine (e.g., in the akedah tradition of the sacrifice of Isaac), the fear and trembling associated with a particular God, Derrida refuses to leave the reader with an image of awakening to alterity through a kind

---

26. See Cronin, "Plus God," 52.

27. See Beesley, "Luke Beesley Reviews Three New Poetry Collections."

28. Yeats, "Leda and the Swan," 221; Donne, "Holy Sonnets 14," 222; cf. Cronin, "Under God," 178. While Cronin does not refer to Yeats or Donne explicitly, many of the verso poems in *God is Waiting in the World's Yard* include quotations from or rewordings of other writers, and the endnotes refer to authors including Wallace Stevens, Fernando Pessoa, Edmond Jabès, Michael Taussig, Voltaire, Hafiz, Dana Gioia, Rosemarie Waldrop, and Friedrich Nietzsche.

29. Cronin, "God Is Waiting," 193.

of faithfulness to a question "that takes us further than the response."[30] He shifts to end (in the English translation) on the word "make-believe," but perhaps with the possibility that "make" relates not only to belief as fantasy but also to belief as being compelled.[31]

In her poem, "The Antidote to the Antidote," Cronin seems to ask what makes faith possible in a post-faith world.[32] Sarah Kirkland Snider's "Credo," in her *Mass for the Endangered*, comes to mind. The text of the Mass comes from poet Nathaniel Bellows and is interlaced with a traditional Latin Mass; the libretto "embodies a prayer for endangered animals and the imperiled environments in which they live."[33] In the "Credo," belief shifts from the divine creator toward creation, both that which is and that which might soon be endangered by human action. This "Credo" celebrates the material sacred as subject of faith, faith in "stone," "moss," "tooth," "the voiceless," "the stalwart," "the silenced," and their advocates.[34] This kind of faith echoes in the call-response captured in Cronin's one-line poem ""Address"" that comes like its title, in double quotation marks: "What you call God, I call out to you."[35] Later, Cronin writes: "Seated there are the humans. They are being counselled on the limits."[36] And closing the same poem, with a bracketed aside: "(Someone should grieve. Everything is worth that.)"[37] Read beside Snider's *Mass for the Endangered*, and with the echo of extinction in earlier poems, some of these limits and griefs are ecological.

Poignantly, Cronin, in "The World's Yard," evokes the muted terror and complexities of the apocalyptic eschatological imaginary accompanying the eco-social traumas of this moment which many now call the Anthropocene:[38]

> Right at the back of the world's yard I am sitting. Guts of the resurrection spilled at my feet. Having tempted flesh from flesh in an ongoing Armageddon, time passes and does not pass. Overhead, a small face, fearful against the plane's window,

---

30. Derrida, *The Gift of Death*, 115.
31. Derrida, *The Gift of Death*, 115.
32. See Cronin, "The Antidote to the Antidote," 66.
33. Snider, *Mass for the Endangered*. Album booklet, 2.
34. Snider, *Mass for the Endangered*. Album booklet, 3.
35. Cronin, "Address," 56.
36. Cronin, "The World's Yard," 117.
37. Cronin, "The World's Yard," 117.
38. On a contemporary apocalyptic eschatological imaginary and its complexities, see Keller, *Facing Apocalypse*. On the Anthropocene epoch, see, for example, Zalasiewicz et al., "The Anthropocene," 1033–40.

sees forever the small boats on their untending sea. A light green moth lands in the centre of a prayer. I dare, as an atheist, to mention God and from a wound in my side, sand pours.[39]

An "ongoing Armageddon" features in a popular cultural imaginary; for example, in climate impact movies such as *The Day after Tomorrow* or where the planetary threat from human action shifts to an extra-terrestrial agent, such as an alien species (e.g., *Independence Day*) or asteroid (e.g., *Armageddon*). One of the linking factors is not only an endangered planet but also a male savior, similarly in a pandemic film such as *Outbreak*. In Cronin's poem, "Armageddon" is not a matter of months or years broken by the advent of an all-too-human male savior, but rather occurs post-resurrection, with "guts of the resurrection spilled" at the speaker's feet. This "Armageddon" is ongoing. Where in biblical theology *he basileia tou Theou* (the divine rule or reign) is reckoned as occurring *already but not yet*, Cronin's "Armageddon" shares this relation to time that "passes and does not pass." The poem shifts to "a small face, fearful against the plane's window," and I am reminded of flying in the years post the fall of the twin towers in New York on September 11, 2001, when air travel lost its child-like appeal. The sea the traveler looks out on is described as "untending." My spell checker wants to change this to "unending," a cliché, or "unbending," which would be interesting. To describe the sea as "untending" from the perspective of the "small boats" is to summon both its power and its indifference to human interests.

Next, touchingly, the poem introduces a moth landing "in the centre of a prayer." The poet-speaker of this particular poem then identifies "as an atheist," and invokes two related gospel episodes (John 19:31–37 and 20:24–29). In the first, at the Roman execution of Jesus by crucifixion, seeing he has died, "one of the soldiers pierced his side with a spear, and at once blood and water came out" (John 19:34). In the second, Thomas, described as "one of the twelve" (the Johannine Jesus's inner circle of male disciples), is absent when the risen Jesus appears. Hearing of the appearance from the other disciples, Thomas says: "Unless I see the mark of the nails in his hands, and put my finger in the mark of the nails and my hand in his side, I will not believe" (John 20:25). This disciple comes down to us as the proverbial "doubting Thomas." In John's Gospel, Jesus appears again post-resurrection, this time with Thomas present, and says to him: "Reach out your hand and put it in my side. Do not doubt but believe" (John 20:27). In Cronin's poem, it is the poet-speaker's side that is wounded, from which neither blood nor water pours but rather sand, as if the body is in drought. But I think the sand

---

39. Cronin, "The World's Yard," 45.

refers neither to an absence of nor a desire for faith. There is no simple one-to-one correspondence between the biblical stories and the poem; rather, the allusion to the wounded body (of Jesus) in the context of a question of belief invites poet and reader to reach perhaps into the side of the questioner. At the site of the question concerning what comes "after God" in this moment of eco-social trauma, of "ongoing Armageddon," the speaker embodies a kind of drought, when lives are endangered and male saviors, even if they may be useful at times, will not suffice.

The poem also suggests that as an image "ongoing Armageddon" is not an endpoint. As Catherine Keller argues, the apocalyptic imaginary that lies behind end-time narratives of climate change, for example, can be part of the problem, and needs to be met with counter-apocalyptic theopoetics and politics, to resist the pull of destructive eschatologies.[40] This kind of resistance to destructive imaginaries, as they inhabit social, cultural, political, and theological worlds and their constructions, is part of the poetic impulse in Cronin's *God Is Waiting in the World's Yard*.

In contemporary ecological thought, alternatives exist to the designation of Anthropocene for this epoch. Glenn Albrecht, for example, prefers the term Symbiocence, emphasizing mutuality and cooperation, co-being and co-relation; in his approach, hope exists in a deliberate lived affirmation of our ecological enmeshments and entanglements.[41] In trinitarian theologies, God is already more than singular, is already in relation. Beside Cronin's "world's yard," this relationality is unsettled by human constructions of God, by God-talk, and by the impossibility of faith that is not also fantasy. So "God's Companion":

> God never comes alone. To be even more precise, is always
> brought by someone else. Or at least this is the story you
> get from those who talk a lot about being God's friend.
> But God's friend, God's true companion, doesn't take God
> anywhere. God's companion has an imaginary friend that
> he can't convince anyone of.[42]

Nonetheless, the emphasis on companionship unsettles any suggestion that faith is *only* fantasy.

At one point early in *God Is Waiting in the World's Yard*, the poet says: "I probably believe in God."[43] This slant affirmation comes in a recto poem featuring attention, lightness, and humor, what might be considered

---

40. See Keller, *Apocalypse Now and Then*; Keller, *Facing Apocalypse*.
41. See Albrecht, "Exiting the Anthropocene and Entering the Symbiocene."
42. Cronin, "God's Companion," 90.
43. Cronin, "The World's Yard," 5.

a contemplative "being in the moment." But for Cronin's backyard sitter, the *here* and the *now* that constitute this moment are also in question.[44] They, too, are the impossible.

Meditation, contemplation, and the accompanying experience of the numinous remain potent when Cronin writes of "The Experience of God": "Swooning and / falling into the open arms of God, who with the void in his / hands, makes you what's left."[45] If the moment "after God," which nonetheless retains the possibility of God, is a moment when the creature pauses on the edge of an abyss, the poet suggests that the divine also holds that empty space. Moreover, that divine embrace of the loss—the manifold deaths, of God, of others, of extinction (what Deborah Bird Rose describes as a "double death")—has a remainder, "you," the addressee, the poet-reader as witness.[46]

The void remains. In the world's yard, windows open onto emptiness.[47] But then the poet says: "On the soft green grass birds burst into flight. They think they are entering the ocean but it is my heart. My heart which keeps letting go . . ."[48] A short poem, "Strange," reads: "The jug of water I left on your step has been found by all / the world. How strange, then, that the water from God is in / no-one's cup."[49] There is a dance of engagement with a more-than-human world, a spiritual hungering, and the possibility of openheartedness to what might be. In "My Flaws," Cronin writes: "I am what God understands. Huddled under his heart without humiliation."[50] The final phrase, "without humiliation," reminds me of the Lukan Mary singing of humiliation, possibly due to sexual assault, divinely seen and undone in the Magnificat (Luke 1:48, 52), against a backdrop of Roman imperial power and the realities of poverty, hunger, and oppression.[51] This is not to say Cronin intends this intertextual association.

As I noted earlier, *God Is Waiting in the World's Yard* resists categorization. The shifts in imagery and tone, the approach and retreat from belief, the allusion to Christian (e.g., the resurrection) and Jewish (e.g., the western wall) themes, the quotations and paraphrases from writers such

---

44. See Cronin, "The World's Yard," 77; Cronin, "God Is a Survival Instinct," 96; Cronin, "The World's Yard," 97; Cronin, "No Resurrection," 112.

45. Cronin, "The Experience of God," 100.

46. Rose, "Double Death."

47. Cronin, "The World's Yard," 113.

48. Cronin, "The World's Yard," 113.

49. Cronin, "Strange," 108.

50. Cronin, "My Flaws," 104.

51. See Reid, "Women Prophets," 54–55; Elvey, *Reading the Magnificat in Australia*, 53.

as Hafiz, make it difficult to situate the poet in relation to any particular religious tradition.[52] This appears intentional. References, further, to what I have called contemporary eco-social trauma are seldom overt and they do not form a catalogue, but arrive, for example, in mentions of extinction and other violence. The interlaced sequences of "God" poems (each with their own title) and "world" poems (each titled "The World's Yard") create a searching conversation that does not presume faith or divinity, but observes aspects of belief, constructions of God, and the possibility of an alterity existing beyond human comprehension, which may or may not require the name "God." Party to and creator of this conversation is the poet-speaker, seated "right at the back of the world's yard," practicing a critical, generous, and tender attention that is whimsical, sharp, and poignant, making space for the reader as compassionate witness.

Poetry as Truth-telling and Healing

To be compassionate witness, as reader or poet, is to risk the kind of writing represented by Andy Jackson in his collection *Human Looking*, from which the poem "Opening," cited above, comes. Two recent collections by Claire Gaskin bear this quality of empathetic testimony and daring: *Eurydice Speaks* and *Ismene's Survivable Resistance*.[53] *Eurydice Speaks* is a series of 57 linked fourteen-line poems (modern sonnets), related by recurring lines or near-lines as one poem gives way to the next. The poems weave a devastating play of family, pain, trauma, and unease. Appearing as the last line of sonnet 48 and as the first line of sonnet 49, I read: "it's hard to believe a pain so historical could ease."[54] The latter sonnet speaks of "a language barrier between the binaries," of "possession," of "eyewitness," and of being "locked into" "martyrdom" as a kind of "rage" that is the speaker's "motivation."[55] Where "martyrdom" appears in sonnet 49, the near identical line in sonnet 48 has "marriage" in place of "martyrdom," and "mother" in place of "my motivation."[56] The place of the maternal in the speaker's journey with and through trauma is a feature of the word play in the series, and the classical Greek character of Eurydice becomes a vehicle for female testimony as she is given voice in the book.

52. See Cronin, "Endnotes," 197–200.
53. Gaskin, *Eurydice Speaks*; Gaskin, *Ismene's Survivable Resistance*.
54. Gaskin, "48," 48; Gaskin, "49," 49.
55. Gaskin, "49," 49.
56. Gaskin, "48," 48.

Another Greek character, Antigone's less-celebrated sister Ismene, plays a parallel role in *Ismene's Survivable Resistance*. Where Antigone does not survive her resistance, Ismene, Gaskin suggests, enacts a kind of resistance that can be survived. The extent to which survival and compliance coincide is a questioning echoing in the collection.[57] Dominique Hecq writes of *Ismene's Survivable Resistance*: "Though Gaskin draws on Sophocles' plot and constellation of characters, this is not a tragedy. The tragedy has already occurred. As in *Eurydice Speaks*, Gaskin assumes the voice of the voiceless in a contemporary setting. Here Ismene is a poet grappling with her traumatic past. The reader of her poems is in the position of witness."[58] The poet-speaker testifies to trauma and its afterlives.

While there are warnings of ecclesial trauma in *Eurydice Speaks*,[59] in *Ismene's Survivable Resistance*, the Royal Commission receives explicit notice in the poem "Ismene after the Royal Commission":

> the truth is I went back
> to the ruins of the house
> I paid with my being to live in
>
> the gate like an opening and closing in the heart
>
> my dead mother still living in the one room not burnt out
>
> the floor forever giving
>
> someone swallowed a mouthful of her dressmaking pins
>
> you have a persecution complex she would say
>
> now *they* stand accused
> I watched it burn
>
> my history wearing a meaning mask
>
> don't cause conflict she would say

---

57. See esp. Gaskin, "Ismene in a Twelve Step Programme," 23.

58. Hecq, "Sheltered."

59. For example, "the broken rosary," Gaskin, "14," 14; and the eucharistic echoes in "my body was broken," Gaskin, "7," 7.

I couldn't save my mother

my heart is not banging in the walls
it is the wall of words I push through
realising it's a bead curtain

you are over sensitive

I go to say something and . . .
there is a vacuum
there is an empty space at the table for me

I couldn't save my sister

forgetting is a stone

the only place she looks alive is in my dreams

the pretending was so profound it became forecasting

all that is left of the window is the brown crucifix of a wooden frame

the floor tilting towards the viewer

emptied of arrival

there are three wooden chairs summoning resurrection.[60]

    Hecq comments that in this collection "body and mind and language are inseparable."[61] In "Ismene after the Royal Commission," the ruined house, and the mother and sister the poet-speaker fails to save, are inseparable from the afterlives of Christianity. The fractures in family understanding—"you are over sensitive"; "don't cause conflict she would say"—echo in the burnt-out house. Given the poem's title, the house that fails to be a family "home" crosses with churches and the burnings that seem to follow,

---

60. Gaskin, "Ismene after the Royal Commission," 39–40.
61. Hecq, "Sheltered."

decades later, the abuses that occurred there.[62] The speaker keeps making a costly return to the place of trauma: "I paid with my being"; the rhythms of the language and repetitions of imagery and words indicate that this return is not once for all but recurrent. The poem hints, too, at something more than repetition; a gate is both a closing and an opening that is incorporated into the flow of blood through the valves of the heart.

In the emptiness of the loss, which encompasses a loss of the hope that home and church are safe spaces for relationship and spiritual growth, a window remains. It is cruciform. Perhaps echoing Andrei Rublev's icon, but with empty chairs where the ancient figures sit, the poem concludes with "three wooden chairs summoning resurrection." This is not a statement that the Christian story fixes anything. Rather, it is something like a prayer, that in pushing through a "wall of words," which might be the writing of the poem as witness, the poet opens and is open to the possibility that abuse is not the last word. Poetry is a making in this instance of the possibility of living *with* and *beyond* trauma; it is a summoning of this possibility.

Another shorter poem, just five lines, "mother of mercy," pivots on the word "sheltered."[63] Hecq writes: "To be sheltered is opposed to the claustrophobic interior space of a self collapsed onto self, held back . . . by a patriarchal system that gagged her until she feels she has 'the authority' to speak up, 'let go and allow love being.'"[64] Writing and reading as empathetic witness is a kind of shelter, if not healing; but it is not a comfortable one. It suggests the possibility of the poem as enacting a kind of hospice.

Conclusion

In a time of eco-social and ecclesial traumas that unsettle old notions of divinity, poets like Jackson, Cronin, and Gaskin are finding creative ways of "staying with the trouble."[65] Here poesis does not substitute for theology but courageously inhabits a place of tension between the material sacred and the failures of institutions, including religious ones. Through corporeal enmeshments of breath and language, poetry becomes a kind of sacrament or sacramental, with the capacity to embody and prompt empathetic witness.

Early in this essay, I quoted a poem by my friend and colleague Rose Lucas, and situated poetry as a materialization of the breath with the capacity to evoke the frisson of the material sacred. In closing, and taking up

62. For example, Mills et al., "Fire at St. James Church in Brighton."
63. Gaskin, "mother of mercy," 45.
64. Hecq, "Sheltered."
65. This term comes from Haraway, *Staying with the Trouble*.

the capacity of poetry to enact a kind of hospice, I cite another friend and colleague, Anne Carson, and a poem she wrote in memory of her friend Christina McCallum:

> Nestled in the space
> between one note
>
> > and the next. At the end
> > of the phrase, the stave.
>
> Before the next instrument
> throws its voice into the
>
> > auditorium. At the end
> > of the piece, before the
>
> applause, coloured by the relief
> and grief of finitude. Briefly,
>
> > at the end of the poetic
> > line, longer at the end
>
> of the sentence, the stanza.
> Hidden in plain view
>
> > in the page's white space.
> > After the engine's throat
>
> closes, the chainsaw's
> racket fades. After the last
>
> > bird farewells the day.
> > After a breath, a life ... .[66]

This poem appears as the epilogue to Carson's collection *Two Green Parrots*. In modest language and with a gentle rhythm the poet performs a eulogy not simply for Christina McCallum, to whom it is dedicated, but for all that passes in a life, in a day: the music, the language, the destruction, the

---

66. Carson, "( )," 81.

lives of otherkind, their voices. Carson moves gently from the finitude of the living, as grief and relief, to the finitude of a poem—the possibility that at the close, the language, the en-mattered breath, makes way for the attentive embodied life. As Jackson, Cronin, and Gaskin remind me, this conscientious attention to the living and the dead is costly, disturbing, and tender.

Bibliography

Abram, David. *The Spell of the Sensuous: Perception and Language in a More-Than-Human World.* New York: Vintage, 1997.

Albrecht, Glenn A. "Exiting the Anthropocene and Entering the Symbiocene." https://glennaalbrecht.wordpress.com/2015/12/17/exiting-the-anthropocene-and-entering-the-symbiocene/.

Armageddon. DVD. Directed by Michael Bay. Burbank/Santa Monica/Hollywood: Touchstone Pictures/Jerry Bruckheimer Films/Valhalla Motion Pictures, 1998.

Bauer, Walter. *A Greek–English Lexicon of the New Testament and Other Early Christian Literature.* Translated and augmented by William F. Arndt et al. 2nd ed. Chicago: University of Chicago Press, 1979.

Beesley, Luke. "Luke Beesley Reviews Three New Poetry Collections by MTC Cronin, Jordie Albiston, and Michael Farrell." *Australian Book Review* 422 (2020). https://www.australianbookreview.com.au/abr-online/archive/2020/june-july-2020-no-422/810-june-july-2020-no-422/6518-luke-beesley-reviews-in-god-is-waiting-in-the-world-s-yard-by-mtc-cronin-element-by-jordie-albiston-and-family-trees-by-michael-farrell.

Bennett, Jane. *Vibrant Matter: A Political Ecology of Things.* Durham: Duke University Press, 2010.

Carson, Anne M. "( )." In *Two Green Parrots*, 81. Port Adelaide: Ginninderra, 2019.

Cronin, M. T. C. "Address." In *God Is Waiting in the World's Yard*, 56. Waratah: Puncher and Wattmann, 2019.

———. "The Antidote to the Antidote." In *God Is Waiting in the World's Yard*, 66. Waratah: Puncher and Wattmann, 2019.

———. "Endnotes." In *God Is Waiting in the World's Yard*, 197–200. Waratah: Puncher and Wattmann, 2019.

———. "The Experience of God." In *God Is Waiting in the World's Yard*, 100. Waratah: Puncher and Wattmann, 2019.

———. "God Is a Survival Instinct." In *God Is Waiting in the World's Yard*, 96. Waratah: Puncher and Wattmann, 2019.

———. "God Is Waiting." In *God Is Waiting in the World's Yard*, 192–93. Waratah: Puncher and Wattmann, 2019.

———. *God Is Waiting in the World's Yard.* Waratah: Puncher and Wattmann, 2019.

———. "God's Companion." In *God Is Waiting in the World's Yard*, 90. Waratah: Puncher and Wattmann, 2019.

———. "My Flaws." In *God Is Waiting in the World's Yard*, 104. Waratah: Puncher and Wattmann, 2019.

———. "No Resurrection." In *God Is Waiting in the World's Yard*, 112. Waratah: Puncher and Wattmann, 2019.

———. "Plus God." In *God Is Waiting in the World's Yard*, 52. Waratah: Puncher and Wattmann, 2019.
———. "Somewhat More than God." In *God Is Waiting in the World's Yard*, 136. Waratah: Puncher and Wattmann, 2019.
———. "Strange." In *God Is Waiting in the World's Yard*, 108. Waratah: Puncher and Wattmann, 2019.
———. "Under God." In *God Is Waiting in the World's Yard*, 178. Waratah: Puncher and Wattmann, 2019.
———. "The World's Yard." In *God Is Waiting in the World's Yard*, 5, 45, 77, 89, 97, 113, 117. Waratah: Puncher and Wattmann, 2019.
Deloria, Vine, Jr. "The Sacred and the Modern World." In *Encyclopedia of Religion and Nature, Volume 2*, edited by Bron R. Taylor and Jeffrey Kaplan, 1446–48. London: Thoemmes Continuum, 2005.
Derrida, Jacques. *The Gift of Death*. Translated by David Wills. Chicago: University of Chicago Press, 1995.
Donne, John. "Holy Sonnets 14." In *The Norton Anthology of Poetry*, edited by Alexander W. Alison et al., 222. 3rd ed. New York: Norton, 1983.
Dostoyevsky, Fyodor. *The Brothers Karamazov: A Novel in Four Parts and an Epilogue*. Translated by Constance Garnett. New York: Macmillan, 1922.
Dux, Monica. *Lapsed*. Sydney: HarperCollins, 2021.
Edwards, Denis. *Ecology at the Heart of Faith: The Change of Heart That Leads to a New Way of Living on Earth*. Maryknoll: Orbis, 2006.
Elvey, Anne. "Ashes and Dust: On (Not) Speaking about God Ecologically." *Concilium* 3 (2009) 33–42.
———. "If I Say." In *On Arrivals of Breath*, 65. Montrose: Poetica Christi, 2019.
———. "Leaf Litter: Thinking the Divine from the Perspective of Earth." In *What's God Got to Do with It? Essays from a One-Day Conference Exploring the Challenges Facing Feminism, Theology, and the Conceptions of Women and the Divine in the New Millennium, August 2nd 1999, Sydney University*, edited by Kathleen McPhillips, 59–68. Hawkesbury: New Humanities Transdisciplinary Research Group, University of Western Sydney, 2000.
———. "Material Elements: The Matter of Women, the Matter of Earth, the Matter of God." In *Post-Christian Feminisms: A Critical Approach*, edited by Lisa Isherwood and Kathleen McPhillips, 53–69. Aldershot: Ashgate, 2008.
———. *Reading the Magnificat in Australia: Unsettling Engagements*. Sheffield: Sheffield Phoenix, 2020.
———. *Reading with Earth: Contributions of the New Materialism to an Ecological Feminist Hermeneutics*. London: T. & T. Clark, 2022.
Gaskin, Claire. "7." In *Eurydice Speaks*, 7. St. Lucia: Hunter, 2020.
———. "14." In *Eurydice Speaks*, 14. St. Lucia: Hunter, 2020.
———. "48." In *Eurydice Speaks*, 48. St. Lucia: Hunter, 2020.
———. "49." In *Eurydice Speaks*, 49. St. Lucia: Hunter, 2020.
———. *Eurydice Speaks*. St. Lucia: Hunter, 2020.
———. "Ismene after the Royal Commission." In *Ismene's Survivable Resistance*, 39–40. Waratah: Puncher and Wattmann, 2021.
———. "Ismene in a Twelve Step Programme." In *Ismene's Survivable Resistance*, 22–24. Waratah: Puncher and Wattmann, 2021.
———. *Ismene's Survivable Resistance*. Waratah: Puncher and Wattmann, 2021.

———. "mother of mercy." In *Ismene's Survivable Resistance*, 45. Waratah: Puncher and Wattmann, 2021.
Haraway, Donna J. *Staying with the Trouble: Making Kin in the Chthulucene*. Durham: Duke University Press, 2016.
Hecq, Dominique. "Sheltered: Dominique Hecq Reviews Claire Gaskin's *Ismene's Survivable Resistance*." *Rochford Street Review* (2021). https://rochfordstreetreview.com/2021/08/31/sheltered-dominique-hecq-reviews-claire-gaskins-ismenes-survivable-resistance/.
Hiebert, Theodore. "Air, the First Sacred Thing: The Conception of *ruach* in the Hebrew Scriptures." In *Exploring Ecological Hermeneutics*, edited by Norman C. Habel and Peter L. Trudinger, 9–19. Atlanta: Society of Biblical Literature, 2008.
Independence Day. DVD. Directed by Roland Emmerich. Los Angeles: Centropolis Entertainment, 1996.
Irigaray, Luce. *An Ethics of Sexual Difference*. Translated by Carolyn Burke and Gillian C. Gill. Ithaca: Cornell University Press, 1993.
Jackson, Andy. *Human Looking*. Artarmon: Giramondo, 2021.
———. "Opening." In *Human Looking*, 3. Artarmon: Giramondo, 2021.
Keller, Catherine. *Apocalypse Now and Then: A Feminist Guide to the End of the World*. Boston: Beacon, 1996.
———. *Facing Apocalypse: Climate, Democracy, and Other Last Chances*. Maryknoll: Orbis, 2021.
Leane, Jeanine. "On the Power to Be Still: Jeanine Leane on Ellen Van Neerven." *Sydney Review of Books* (2020). https://sydneyreviewofbooks.com/review/van-neerven-throat/.
———. "Staring Back: Jeanine Leane on Evelyn Araluen." *Sydney Review of Books* (2021). https://sydneyreviewofbooks.com/review/araluen-drop-bear/.
Logan, William Bryant. *Air: The Restless Shaper of the World*. New York: Norton, 2012.
Lucas, Rose. "Poetry and Breathing." In *This Shuttered Eye*, 28–29. Seddon: Liquid Amber, 2021.
McCredden, Lyn. "Contemporary Poetry and the Sacred: Vincent Buckley, Les Murray, and Samuel Wagan Watson." *Australian Literary Studies* 23.2 (2007) 153–67.
Mills, Tammy, et al. "Fire at St. James Church in Brighton a Relief, Says Actor Rachel Griffiths." *The Age*, March 30, 2015. https://www.theage.com.au/national/victoria/fire-at-st-james-church-in-brighton-a-relief-says-actor-rachel-griffiths-20150330-1mawmo.html.
Outbreak. DVD. Directed by Wolfgang Petersen. Burbank: Warner Brothers, 1995.
Pinsky, Robert. *The Sounds of Poetry: A Brief Guide*. New York: Farrar, Straus, and Giroux, 1998.
Reid, Barbara E. "Women Prophets of God's Alternative Reign." In *Luke-Acts and Empire: Essays in Honor of Robert L. Brawley*, edited by David M. Rhoads et al., 44–59. Eugene, OR: Pickwick, 2011.
Rose, Deborah Bird. "Double Death." https://www.multispecies-salon.org/double-death/.
———. "Rupture and the Ethics of Care in Colonized Space." In *Prehistory to Politics: John Mulvaney, the Humanities and the Public Intellectual*, edited by Tim Bonyhady and Tom Griffiths, 190–215, 261–63. Carlton South: Melbourne University Press, 1996.

Royal Commission into Institutional Responses to Child Sexual Abuse. *Final Report: Religious Institutions. Volume 16, Book 2*. Barton: Commonwealth of Australia, 2017. https://www.childabuseroyalcommission.gov.au/sites/default/files/final_report_-_volume_16_religious_institutions_book_2.pdf.

Santner, Eric L. *On Creaturely Life: Rilke, Benjamin, Sebald*. Chicago: University of Chicago Press, 2006.

Serres, Michel. *The Five Senses: A Philosophy of Mingled Bodies (I)*. Translated by Margaret Sankey and Peter Cowley. London: Continuum, 2008.

Snider, Sarah Kirkland. *Mass for the Endangered*. Conducted by Gabriel Crouch with Gallicantus. Words by Nathaniel Bellows. New Amsterdam Records 075597920055, 2020, compact disc.

The Day After Tomorrow. DVD. Directed by Roland Emmerich. Los Angeles: Centropolis Entertainment, Lions Gate Films, and Mark Gordon Company, 2004.

Yeats, William Butler. "Leda and the Swan." In *The Collected Poems*, edited by Augustine Martin, 221. London: Vintage, 1992.

Zalasiewicz, Jan, et al. "The Anthropocene." In *The Geologic Time Scale 2012*, edited by Felix M. Gradstein et al, 1033–40. Boston: Elsevier, 2012.

9

Timpani

Julie Perrin

The chamber orchestra concert is in a country basketball stadium.[1] The crowd is swelling, lending their warmth to hard-edged surfaces. We've arrived early to the plastic chairs in the front row with a close-up view of the percussion section. A slight young woman is on timpani—three large bowl-like kettle drums. Erica Rasmussen stands graceful and attentive over the gleaming copper drums. Her stillness and concentration are mesmerizing; already you feel the place has expanded past its usual steely functionality. She arms herself with beaters—a pair in each hand to play across the skins of the three drums.

Erica leans over the timpani, watching and listening, ready to strike. As soon as she has struck the beater, she lifts and holds it away from the drum skin while the sound resonates. Simultaneously she spreads her fingertips so the pads touch the drum skin and quell the sound.

I am moved by the grace of her action. I love the shift between a big round resonant sound and the immediate stilling. It was not just a stopping; the movement is stilled; a cleaner sound is given by the halt to the resonating drum. It allows a decisive and contained presence amidst the surrounding sounds of the orchestra.

As a child I had an uneasy relationship with the movement to calm. The quelling of my exuberance felt like a heavy-handed requirement of the worried-adult-world. I learned to both obey and resent the need to quieten; there was only so much amping-up the household could bear. The flinch of undiagnosed PTSD lived in our house, haunting my father after his wartime service.

It has taken me a long time to welcome the dance between a big presence and contained stillness. Quiet, for a long time, was a kind of thwarting. I did not have agency in my own capacity for quietening—it

---

1. A version of this story appears in Perrin, *A Prayer, a Plea, a Bird*, 51–52.

was imposed rather than sought. In my late teens I held onto my reclaimed exuberance with a ferocity that saw me dancing on other people's furniture and grabbing hold of microphones.

In my late twenties I taught drama to a group of tertiary students. In the process of brainstorming ideas, a mature-aged student took a breath to speak but allowed space for someone else who had simultaneously begun. When that person had finished, I asked the woman who had drawn a breath if she wanted to speak. "No," she said, "it's alright. Sometimes I just get *too excited*." It immediately struck me that I didn't know you could get too excited. I'd worked so hard at shaking off the need to gag excitement that I hadn't seen the gift in restraint.

Recently I confessed to my shiatsu practitioner that I was confused about the Yin and the Yang energies. "Which do I need?" I asked. "Ah!," she said, "it's not one energy over the other, we need both—the activity of the Yang and the rest of the Yin. They are constantly turning towards the other, turning into each other, as day folds into night, as night opens into morning."

In the beauty in Erica's timpani, I felt a similar sense of flow. She was in charge of both the fullness and the quelling. I wept watching her. The poetry of the conversation between sound and stillness.

The timpanist's work had spoken to my own writing practice. Erica's composed posture reminded me to pay attention to my own stance, not in order to press a point of view, but to ready myself to use my tools deftly. In early drafts I usually write by hand, using a fountain pen. Sometimes I slow the whole process down by writing with my non-dominant hand. This slowing can also be experienced on the breath, so the rhythm of words and sentences does not outrun the capacity to speak or to read them.

There is a holy wisdom in this. The narratives need to leave space for things to settle, for the reader to make their own connections. My goal is not for the final flourish that neatly wraps up the conclusion and sets a seal on it. I want to invite readers to bear witness to the astonishments and sorrows we walk amidst.

This sense of the Divine as present in our most ordinary interactions allows delight and laughter to sit in loving proximity to lament and stillness. As I read the Gospels, I find there a permission to be with both faith and doubt, to go between knowing the presence and absence of God. For how will we navigate life's relinquishments if we have not also taken hold of curiosity and dwelt with wonder and praise?

Bibliography

Perrin, Julie. *A Prayer, a Plea, a Bird*. Richmond: MediaCom Education, 2020.

10

Hope at the End of History

Scott Kirkland

Prelude: On Becoming Pākehā

In the first panel of Colin McCahon's *Parihaka Triptych* (1972), he writes: "An ornament for the Pākehā." McCahon himself, a white New Zealander, Pākehā, adopts the form of the triptych, which has its roots as an altar painting in early Christian art, often centering the cross in the middle panel. This became a common medieval, western European form. McCahon adopts the form, and places in the center a tau, or St. Anthony cross, with the words at its base—"a monument to Te Whiti."

Te Whiti, as we will see in the second half of this essay, was a Māori prophet or messianic figure who led, along with Tohu, a non-violent resistance to European land confiscation at Parihaka, in Taranaki, Aotearoa. McCahon we know was taken by these figures, and was acutely aware of the ongoing effects of colonization and dispossession, having grown up in an impoverished part of Auckland. The European seizure of Māori lands was not simply the theft of the material wealth of the Māori peoples of Aotearoa, however; it was an act of violence to a people who understood themselves less as possessors of the land, and more as belonging to the land. Dispossession, in that sense, is apocalyptic, world ending.

McCahon's painting, beginning with the first panel proclaiming an "ornament for the Pākehā," unsettles. The ornament here is ambiguous. Is Te Whiti's inhabiting the shape of the cross to become decorative of the altars of the colonizing, white New Zealander? However, the use of the language Pākehā demands our attention. Pākehā is a Māori term for white New Zealander, and as such, when the white New Zealander is asked to identify themselves with this language, there emerges, as it were, a recognition of one's relation to the other as colonizer. One cannot simply fade into the faux universality, invisibility, and transparency of whiteness; one is seen as Pākeha. So it is that the image demands a form of unsettling recognition.

Colin McCahon, *Parihaka Triptych*, 1972. Acrylic on canvas, 175.4 x 437.0 cm. Gift of the artist, 1973. Held by the Govett-Brewster Art Gallery, New Plymouth, Aotearoa New Zealand, for the people of Parihaka. He tākoha nā te ringatoi, 1973. E tautiaki ana te whare whakairi toi o Govett-Brewster mā te iwi o Parihaka.

As we move into the center panel, we see that this "monument for Te Whiti" takes the shape both of a cross and of the mountain, Taranaki, the spiritual center of Taranaki. Tohu is quoted, "I stand for peace," and we are presented with Te Whiti's monument, transfigured not as the crucifix of western European art brought to "save" the Māori, but as the very instrument of this apocalyptic dispossession. "To the people throughout the world," "and for the people of Parihaka," McCahon writes in stark white, as if below the earth, against the deep blacks of the bottom of the panel. The universality of whiteness is interrupted by the solidarity to be found in Te Whiti's life, a solidarity to be found in dispossession and loss in the face of the Pākehā.

It is our present that McCahon is pointing to, not our past. As long as the force of dispossession remains, justice cannot flow. "War shall cease and no longer divide the world," McCahon writes, echoing Te Whiti, to the right of the cross, in hope and apocalyptic expectation. The division between Pākehā and Māori remains, and it remains as long as the Pākehā refuse to recognize themselves as such, as colonizer, as dispossessor, not in the past, but in the present. In this sense, what follows in this essay is an attempt to think similarly to McCahon, to attend to Te Whiti and Tohu, to Parihaka, and so to understand the violence that founds the project called "New Zealand."

Doomsaying

Doing political theology at the moment can seem to require becoming a prophet of doom. Until recently, Donald Trump, a reality TV star and career con man, was "leading" the "free" world; England has decided to drag the United Kingdom out of the European Union in order to get the imperial band back together; the Middle East has been in flames for at least half a century; peoples have been and are being displaced by the millions globally in the wake of the destructive forces of globalization and borderless, endless wars; we are now witnessing the effects of catastrophic levels of global emissions, choking ourselves to death; and we are now in the middle of a global pandemic exposing the brutality of all that is and claims to be legitimate.

Australia, where I currently live, is seeing some of the first effects of this apocalypse, and serves politically as an almost too neat illustration of these global ills. A country that continues to rip coal from the ground for its own economic benefit, barricading its borders to those seeking shelter from conflicts it has helped fuel and placing them in the legal zone of indistinction that is detention, participating wholeheartedly in the project of neoliberal globalization at the expense of the local and global poor, all of which is bound up in the ongoing histories and logics of white-supremacist violence and exclusion.

My political consciousness really began in 2000–01, and has since been caught between promised hopes and an almost immediate mourning of lost futures—from watching climate activist Al Gore's lost presidential bid in 2000, to watching disorientedly as much of the West marched unthinking to war in Afghanistan ("Operation Enduring Freedom") and Iraq ("Coalition of the Willing" [or "of the Shilling," as Tariq Ali called it]—beginning with operation "shock and awe") from 2001–04, to the hope gathered and immediately lost in the wake of Barack Obama's election in 2008 and the ensuing global financial crisis (2007–09), to the rage of the sovereign debt crisis and the crushing of progressive economic solutions by rigid austerity in the Europe of 2010, which acted as a prelude to the absolute dismay of 2016—Brexit, Trump—and onto the Australian present in which politicians who casually joke about our island neighbors' homes being swallowed by the unrelenting rise of the ocean now carve a path through the Great Barrier Reef for more multinational miners to get their ships to port.

Perhaps less a prophet of doom than a realist.

And yet it can be rather dull to rehearse the all too familiar and numbingly depressing news items. We are largely a culture for whom apocalypse is entertainment, after all. A perverse addiction to despair, a kind of disaster fetishism—all too easy to embrace—should not form the ground of our political–theological imaginations. In fact, what I want to suggest is that it is perhaps precisely our waiting for a sovereign to save us that is the root of our inability to perform hope in the present. After all, people who claim to follow a messiah who was tortured, mocked, and crucified should hardly expect those same powers of crucifixion to provide hope for another world. Mourning, turning to melancholia, awaits us on that road. I want to suggest that hope is precisely in the opposite—in the refusal of sovereignty, in the unsovereign weakness of self-resignation and resistance. This resignation finds its home in practices of attention, of what Simone Weil calls "decreation," the unmaking of the will to mastery, a turn toward the problem in order to remain with it.[1]

The End of the End of History

From August 13, 1961 until November 9, 1989, a wall snaked its way through Berlin. The wall was quite literal, but in its mere twenty-seven miles it symbolized something of meta-historical importance: the ideological, political, and social division between the communist East and the capitalist West. As the wall was torn down, the American political theorist Francis Fukuyama opined that we were witnessing the "end of history." We were not seeing, as some predicted, a synthesis between capitalism and socialism, but, in Fukuyama's words, "an unabashed victory of economic and political liberalism." He wrote:

> What we may be witnessing is not just the end of the Cold War, or the passing of a particular period of postwar history, but the end of history as such: that is, the end point of mankind's ideological evolution and universalization of Western liberal democracy as the final form of human government. This is not to say that there will no longer be events to fill the pages of *Foreign Affairs*'s yearly summaries of international relations, for the victory of liberalism has occurred primarily in the realm of ideas or consciousness and is as yet incomplete in the real or material world. But there are powerful reasons for believing that it is the ideal that will govern the material world *in the long run*.[2]

What Fukuyama thought was happening as the wall was enthusiastically torn down by Berliners of all ideological persuasions was the final chapter in ideological history. That here was the visible, material symbol of

---

1. See Weil, *Gravity and Grace*, 55–60.
2. Fukuyama, "The End of History?" 4.

the victory of the forces of western liberalism over the last great rival to its ideological hegemony in Soviet Communism.

This idea of Fukuyama's was adapted from the Russian–French émigré philosopher, later architect of the European Economic Community, and (we now know) Soviet spy, Alexandre Kojève. In his lectures on the great German philosopher Hegel's *Phenomenology of Spirit*, first published in French in 1947, Kojève proclaimed that we were entering into the "post-historical" condition.[3] Karl Marx had prophesied something similar when articulating the historical dialectic that would lead inexorably to the dictatorship of the proletariat. But Marx's vision was, according to Fukuyama, upside-down. Fukuyama is a representative of a school of interpretation of Hegel in which history is seen as a series of developmental ideas. Ideas breed material change, and so serve as something of the canaries in the coalmines of history.[4] For Marx, however, things were the other way around. Material change led to change in the ideal or ideological superstructure.[5] This is why we speak of a historical materialist dialectic.

As the long-90s progressed it looked for a short while—if, and I stress *if*, you fixed your eyes in certain directions—that Fukuyama might be proven right. The neoliberal revolution marched on, reaching something of a climax in the formation of the World Trade Organization (WTO) in 1995. The formation of the WTO, Clinton's New Democrats, Blair's New Labour, and Germany's Chancellor Gerhard Schroeder all promised a world of free trade, borders porous to the movement of capital. Capitalism freed itself from the constraints of national democracies in the establishment of international institutions and cosmopolitan trans-national treaties guaranteeing the flow of goods and capital independently of democratic controls. The North American Free Trade Agreement (NAFTA), the General Agreement on Tariffs and Trade (GATT) which became the WTO, the Eurasian Economic Union, the International Monetary Fund, and the Comprehensive and Progressive Agreement for Trans-Pacific Partnership (what was initially the Trans-Pacific Partnership Agreement), are all illustrative of the development of the ideological triumph of liberal capitalism. These international institutions and treaties often function beyond the level of state sovereignty, and so beyond democratic control, disciplining the shape of the global

---

3. Kojève, *Introduction to the Reading of Hegel*, 161.

4. The problem with history, however, is that the grand old men who are in charge of it rarely read the best thinkers.

5. While this language is formalized in work by later Marxists, it is present in the structure of Marx's inversion of Hegelian dialectics, where ideological conditions flow from material relations, not vice versa. For a discussion, see Williams, "Base and Superstructure in Marxist Cultural Theory," 3–16.

economic and political environment. It might seem, then, that Fukuyama was right. The great ideological battles of history are over, we are simply ironing out the details down here on the ground.

The political theorist Wendy Brown has noted that this world that Fukuyama was so optimistic about, on closer examination produces something of a paradox. In a world in which capital and goods flow across borders with unprecedented ease, lubricated by the legal instruments of world trade, increasingly we find ourselves in a world in which walls are being resurrected to stem the flow of those peoples displaced precisely by these globalizing forces.[6] Think, for instance, of the relationship between the United States and Mexico. NAFTA has established a free-trade zone between the US and Mexico such that American manufacturing can exploit the labor conditions of the Mexican market and move the goods produced back over the border without incurring tariffs to compensate for the loss of American labor. Trump—who, ironically, was going bankrupt after a misadventure with the Atlantic City Taj Mahal at the end of history—rode into power in 2016 on the slogan, "Build that wall!"—a wall we were told would be paid for by the Mexican Government. The apparent paradox is that while we in the west want the flow of goods, we do not want the exchange with real human persons this might entail. Money will not hold together social bonds. The various nationalist insurgencies we are now seeing globally—be it in the US, the UK, Hungary, or Brazil—might not so much be a revolt against globalization but rather something of a doubling down on its logic of exclusion.

Brown reminds us that these walls are notoriously ineffectual. Walls do not stop human trafficking, the movement of illicit drugs, or the movements of peoples. "Moreover, the contemporary walls often dramatically intensify criminal smuggling industries, gang control of borderlands and their proximate communities, and conflicts or tensions between neighboring nations, thus constituting new threats and erosions of nation state sovereignty."[7] But, they do serve as political theatre, as the material signification of the reassertion of sovereignty, of nativism, of xenophobia. The spectacle of borders hardened by walls involves "deliberate manipulations of space and time, cause and effect."[8] The wall so often serves as the cause of that which it ostensibly protects us from.

Fukuyama, watching the Berlin Wall come down in 1989, thought that we were simply going to see the liberal project ironed out over the next few decades. What we are seeing now instead is the return of those forces he

---

6. Brown, *Walled States*.
7. Brown, *Walled States*, 8–9.
8. Brown, *Walled States*, 9.

thought were vanquished. Not only that, it perhaps turns out that the ideological conditions of the end of history, the globalization of liberal capitalism, are precisely those that are productive of a new end of history. Our ecosystems stand on the brink—if they have not already been pushed over—of collapse, and we in the west are experiencing the period of greatest political instability since the fascisms of the 1930s. It is hard not to bind these two factors together, and in Australia to bind them to our history of capitalism, mineral extraction, and colonial destruction of carefully managed indigenous country. Any hope we might have had in history "progressing" are beginning to look naïve at best, violent at worst. We appear to be caught in something more like a vicious return of the same. The question remains for us, then, in the absence of hope in progress, to where do we turn?

In what follows, I would like to provide a few brief reflections on time and hope. I want to provide a reading to my, and my home country's shame, of an event with which I am having to familiarize myself after my education in the public schooling systems of New Zealand. The impulse running through this reading is that hope is not to be found on the outside, at the end of history, or by striving for an outside. Rather, hope might appear as something more like a practice of attention, something like prayer, something like the refusal to be told that this is the end, the refusal of the mastery over the world the end—absolute sovereignty—provides us with.

Parihaka and the Logic of Refusal

The Announcement of Freedom from Pākehā Authority

In Aotearoa New Zealand, there was a treaty signed in 1840. This treaty, however, was not signed by all Māori chiefs.[9] There was no single Māori nation, and so no single *iwi* could represent everyone. Te Tiriti o Waitangi was not signed by the chiefs in the Taranaki region of the west coast of the North Island, some three million acres. After 1840, there was a rapid increase in the Pākehā population. Land was being surveyed, stolen or purchased, parceled up, and sold to settlers. War broke out in Taranaki over land around Waitara—and 3,500 troops were brought in from Australia in support—a war that provided so-called justification for the confiscation of lands under the Native Lands Act, 1862.

Te Whiti-O-Rongomai III and Tohu Kākahi refused to simply cede land to the European settlers. Wars were slowly destroying the Māori population, and the Europeans began to outnumber Māori significantly. Te Whiti drew

---

9. See Binney, *Encircled Lands*, 17–66; Anderson et al., *Tangata Whenua*, 171–235.

on Māori and Christian traditions "in looking for a way to end the slaughter without surrendering the land. Instead of a bush fortress he proposed an open village where his people could defend themselves by powers strange and untried."[10] Those strange and untried powers were the powers of passive resistance, the refusal of violence and activity that resisted by highlighting injustice and illegality. Te Whiti stated that "what iron has broken, iron will rebuild." That is to say, "iron scissors cut calico, the iron needle rejoins it. The fabric of life torn by iron, the mission teaching, would be stitched together by iron, the new beliefs at Parihaka."[11] So it is that the village of Parihaka was established, nestled beneath Te Maunga Taranaki.

Parihaka served as a refuge for those who had been scattered by conflict, but it was also a place that refused to acknowledge the sovereignty of the crown over Taranaki lands. Ngati Ruanui, Taranaki, and Atiawa, the three tribes in the geographical area, had not signed the treaty. They refused to be sublimated to the crown. Reading the Māori translation of the Treaty, in any case, we see that Māori did not surrender *rangatiratanga* (sovereignty, chieftainship) over their lands. This refusal to be sublimated, however, was accompanied always with an invitation to speak to the Pākehā.

Scott writes: "Te Whiti announced a programme that had four stages: the day of *takahanga*, his 1869 announcement of freedom from Pākehā authority; the *akarama*, the Aceldama, the transaction of Judas Iscariot; *tuupaapaku*, the day of death; and *aranga*, the day of reckoning or resurrection when the results of struggle would rise to the surface and be harvested."[12] So it is that Te Whiti models the logic for passive resistance upon a rich weaving together of Māori culture and a complex reception of the biblical narratives themselves. The announcement of freedom from the authority of the crown was complete; now it was time for the transaction.

The Field of Blood

Robert Parris, Civil Commissioner in New Plymouth, wrote a series of reports on the state of Taranaki in 1874, in the wake of the wars, and perhaps

---

10. Scott, *Ask That Mountain*, 28. For an overview of the New Zealand Wars from 1845–72, see O'Malley, *The New Zealand Wars*.

11. Scott, *Ask That Mountain*, 28. Scott immediately cites Te Whiti's use of the tribes of Israel to describe the coming together at Parihaka. Mark Brett has argued that the Kingitanga movement, drawing similarly on Hebrew Bible motifs, looks to ways of thinking covenant in order to establish something other than the absolute sovereignty of the likes of Bodin and Hobbes, embodied in colonial doctrines of discovery. See Brett, *Locations of God*, 132–49.

12. Scott, *Ask That Mountain*, 36.

in the middle of them. Parris believed, as Danny Keenan notes, that the answer to the Māori's troubles was "acquiescence to the Crown's bidding, which was most desirable for their 'advancement.'" It frustrated Parris that Māori did not simply acquiesce in this way, and he identifies the "'baneful influence of the Parihaka Councils' where monthly meetings were 'kept up with as much devotion and adoration of Te Whiti as ever.'"[13] Te Whiti became the target of Parris's attempts at seduction.

In order to acquire the land, an open-ended budget was provided by the Land Purchase Officer, Donald McLean. This resulted in the use of tactics such as attempts to entrap Māori in debt, and the use of bribes and alcohol in order to dispossess Māori. Te Whiti, however, refused such lures from Parris time and time again. Scott writes that "Lamenting the aloofness of 'this singular man,' Parris said of Te Whiti in 1872 that 'the absence of all desire for money, or anything we have to offer him, renders it difficult, if not hopeless to obtain any active aid from him.'"[14]

"Te Whiti dramatised this aspect of his policy with the phrase: *E kore e piri te uku ki te rino, ka whitia e te ra*, clay will not cling to iron when the sun shines. Iron was the Pākehā, clay the Māori, and the bond between land-seller and land-buyer was moisture or money. When the money was gone, common ties would evaporate."[15] (Thus the vision of *rangatiratanga* was lost through the ephemeral allure of capital). This was not simply Te Whiti rejecting money as useless; it was also an allusion to his larger political–theological vision, that of relations between Māori and Pākehā grounded on peaceful respect for one another rather than on sovereign domination. Money would not bind the two people together; it would vanish and the covenantal bond along with it.

The Crown found itself under pressure in 1878, with many Pākehā finding themselves economically doing it tough in parts of Aotearoa. Te Whiti wanted an agreement (perhaps, covenant) that would secure Māori rights to the land while allowing Europeans to remain present, and agreed to attend a meeting in Waitara (North Taranaki). However, a lavish feast full of bribery, with attempts to lure the chiefs and the Māori king "travestied everything that Te Whiti had hoped for." Instead of a conversation, an opportunity to speak to one another, they were faced with the lure of Judas's fifty pieces of silver, again. Deception and entrapment in debt was the only method the Pākehā would deploy, and failing that, violence. As Scott notes, during this meeting one of the chiefs, Rewi Maniopoto, was lured, and as a result failed

---

13. Keenan, *Te Whiti O Rongomai*, xxv.
14. Scott, *Ask That Mountain*, 48.
15. Scott, *Ask That Mountain*, 48.

to achieve anything for his people. Te Whiti commented: "having emptied the main stores of New Plymouth, Rewi would not return.... In this way the second stage of Te Whiti's prediction, the Aceldama, the field of blood, the plot of ground bought with Judas' silver, was fulfilled."[16]

The Day of Death

In 1879, the community at Parihaka, under the leadership of Te Whiti and Tohu, began employing tactics of passive resistance to illegal surveying (a prelude to theft and "purchase") of their land. On May 26, Māori ploughmen began ploughing fields in Oakura, just a few kilometers from New Plymouth, the major settlement in Taranaki. The same thing took place in other locations around Taranaki. Ploughmen worked "from daylight to dark on Pākehā occupied land ... they were unarmed, good tempered—and firm. Te Whiti was not ploughing the land, he is only ploughing the belly of the government, the intruders blandly explained to irate onlookers."[17]

This gesture was intended as a response to the theft of land in North Taranaki, which represented a broken promise by the then governor who promised peace (a complaint which the Waitangi Tribunal has now vindicated). This provoked the Pākehā greatly, with threats of violence being issued in newspapers, and frustrated farmers banding together in groups of vigilantes. Tohu, responding to a question over what to do with the ploughmen should they be shot, said: "Gather up the earth on which the blood is spilt and bring it to Parihaka."[18]

Dick Scott recounts oral histories of a speech of Te Whiti's at the monthly meeting:

> Go, put your hands to the plough. Look not back. If any come with guns and swords, be not afraid. If they smite you, smite not in return. If they rend you, be not discouraged. Another will take up the good work. If evil thoughts fill the minds of the settlers and they flee from their farms to the town, as in the war of old, enter not you into their houses, touch not their goods nor their cattle. My eye is over all. I will detect the thief, and the punishment shall be like that which fell upon Ananias.[19]

---

16. Scott, *Ask That Mountain*, 51.
17. Scott, *Ask That Mountain*, 55.
18. Scott, *Ask That Mountain*, 56.
19. Scott, *Ask That Mountain*, 57.

Again: "If any man molests me I will talk with my weapon—the tongue. I will not resist the soldiers if they come. I would gladly let them crucify me."[20]

Te Whiti drew a broad coalition together in solidarity. Former soldiers, folk who had offered violent resistance in the past, peoples scattered by Europeans, those enticed by his message, and some prosperous Māori. In response, the Taranaki jails started to fill as ploughmen were arrested. Te Whiti then stated at the next meeting:

> The governments of the earth have built up a structure that exists only by the power of money. The head of the land—the Queen—is honoured in proportion to the pomps and vanities of her immediate attendants. Her governors all hold out their hands for their wages, without which their patriotism would shrivel up. The legislators, the magistrates, the police etc., make laws and put them into force at so much per day. From the highest to the lowest, money is the motive force. . . . I have built up my power by the force of will—no worldly considerations affect my followers. They are disinterested, they are superior to the power of money. . . . Their hearts are being purified in anticipation of the great day that is at hand. I have a uniform and distinct path that I travel continuously—peace and goodwill to men is the password. The wayfarers are clothed in love and charity; the end of the journey to those who enter is joy everlasting.[21]

One might remember the earlier saying in which iron will not cling to clay after the moisture leaves. Money cannot form a lasting social bond, for it passes and leaves us isolated from one another. Te Whiti wanted to ground solidarity elsewhere—in a commitment to peace. There is a very real sense here that money is a motive force of apocalyptic destruction of sociality. The crown, confiscating lands and liquidating them in order to generate money both for itself and for settlers, destroys any potential solidarity, any peace. As long as money remained the motivating force, that which is would be consumed.

Many of the ploughmen who were arrested were then held without trail and shipped to the South Island, a long way from Taranaki. This required the use of extraordinary powers, generating something of a state of exception. Keenan states: "Parliamentarians who supported the measure agreed . . . that it was 'indispensable for the peace and safety of the colony that the ordinary course of law be suspended and the trial of such natives

---

20. Scott, *Ask That Mountain*, 57.
21. Scott, *Ask That Mountain*, 59.

should take place under special legislation'. . . . [After some resistance and debate] Māori would not be tried in court, as was their right, but instead would be detained with trial dates to be set at the discretion of the governor. When the Act was passed, 170 Taranaki Māori were in prison in Wellington and twenty-five in Dunedin."[22] Many of these men would be held illegally for over two years.

The Government continued to incur into the land through the building of roads. This met with the passive resistance tactic of building fences to block the roads, with Māori offering no resistance when arrested. It seemed that the Crown would not relent, and continued to incur into Māori lands, only meeting passive resistance each time. Te Whiti's teaching, however, was being distorted through the local newspapers and through other reporting. Mistranslations provided occasion for scare tactics, and passive resistance was cast as aggression and transgression of law. The West Coast Settlement Reserves Act was also passed in September 1881, which allowed the Government to confiscate and sell lands retained by Māori. This Act would allow dispossession through surveys that would determine the alienability of the land. This essentially robbed Māori of the management, custodianship, or *rangatiratanga*, of the reserves, handing them to the governor.

As forces gathered outside Parihaka on November 4, 1881, the night before invasion—*tuupaapaku*—the day of death—Te Whiti and Tohu are recalled as having said:

> The canoe [*waka*] by which we are to be saved is forbearance. It has been prepared by Tohu during months and years, and is now launched, and will bear us safely through all tempests. It will save us all. . . . What matter to us what happens; we have our ark, as Noah of old. I now say come into the ark. . . . Let us wait for the end; there is nothing else for us. Let us rest quietly upon the land. . . . If any man thinks of his gun or his horse, and goes to fetch it, he will die by it. . . . [P]lace your trust in forbearance and peace . . . let the booted feet come when they like, the land shall remain firm for ever."[23]

Tohu said: "We look for peace and we find war. Be steadfast, keep to peaceful works, be not dismayed: have no fear. Let your dwelling be good in this place oh my tribe, until works such as this are frustrated."[24]

---

22. Keenan, *Te Whiti O Rongomai*, 132.

23. Scott, *Ask That Mountain*, 106. Modified according to the account in *Appendix to the Journals of the House of Representatives of New Zealand*, 9–10.

24. Scott, *Ask That Mountain*, 117.

As the Crown's forces marched into Parihaka, one constabulary officer, Colonel Messenger, recalls: "There was a line of children across the entrance to the big village, a kind of singing class directed by an old man with a stick. The children sat there unmoving, droning away, and even when a mounted officer galloped up and pulled his horse up so short that the dirt from its forefeet spattered the children they still went on chanting, perfectly oblivious, apparently, to the pakeha [sic], and the old man calmly continued his monotonous drone."[25]

Again Messenger: "I was the first to enter the Maori [sic] town with my company. I found my only obstacle was the youthful feminine element. There were skipping-parties of girls on the road."[26]

The leader of the force, Captain Bryce, ventured into the village on a white horse—suitably apocalyptic, and Napoleonic—and they met no resistance, making their incursion somewhat Quixotic. The soldiers were shocked as they imagined somehow they would be met with an attack, but all they were met with was peace. Bryce was offered the chance to speak with Te Whiti, should he descend from his horse. Bryce's refusal to speak as equals led to the arrest of Te Whiti and Tohu, who were led away wearing *korowai* cloaks. As he left, Te Whiti stated: "This day's work is not my doing. It comes from the heart of the pakeha [sic]. . . . On my fall the pakeha [sic] builds his work: but be you steadfast in all that is peaceful."[27]

The constabulary then began arresting and removing those who had found refuge and hope in Parihaka, returning them forcefully to where they came from. They arrested all the men, and left only women and the elderly *kaumatua*. A pass system was established to allow people in and out, and the buildings on site were destroyed. Women were raped, and children born of rape. The forces remained on Parihaka. The day of death, *tuupaapaku*, had arrived.

Resurrection

History had for too long been written to vindicate the Crown's horrendous actions. However, in 1996 the Waitangi Tribunal produced *The Taranaki Report: Kappa Tuatahi*. On Parihaka, it stated that Māori children "were schooled to believe that those of their forebears whose images they should have carved with pride were simply rebels, savages, or fanatics," and further, that "New Zealanders were not to know that forced removals, pass

25. Scott, *Ask That Mountain*, 118.
26. Scott, *Ask That Mountain*, 118.
27. Scott, *Ask That Mountain*, 118.

laws, and other suspensions of civil liberties, so often criticised of governments elsewhere, had been applied here. We were not to know, when paying tribute to Gandhi and King, that their policies and practices had first been enunciated by Maori [sic]."[28] Further, the report begins that this problem remains with us even in the recognition of the history: "If war is the absence of peace, the war has never ended in Taranaki, because that essential prerequisite for peace among peoples, that each should be able to live with dignity on their own lands, is still absent and the protest over land rights continues to be made."[29]

In 2017, the Crown offered an acknowledgement of the crimes of Parihaka, and signed a reconciliation agreement. However, this history does not leave us. It remains the problem with which we must abide. It is not my place at this time to interpret Te Whiti's use of Christianity; nor is it my place to identify with the struggle of Parihaka. First of all, I must be unsettled by it. As we face the apocalypse in the present, the end of history, perhaps we can be unsettled. I grew up in the shadow of the same mountain under which this violence was perpetrated. I cannot undo this history, but I can remain with it as a window into another world we keep shutting the door upon as we continue to insist that capital, money, will form another world.

Coda

It is the absence of freedom that gives rise to the collective struggle for freedom. It is the absence of optimism that gives rise to the performance of hope. We have been disarmed of optimism in the present—there is at one and the same time no space for fantasy, and nothing but fantasy, in the present. There is little occasion for this. Optimism is nothing more than a wish. Hope can only be performed. Hope comes as we struggle together, as we embrace the absence of optimism. Hope is a pilgrimage. It is not the pilgrimage of the attempt to escape the world, but rather a pilgrimage into the world, into the problem, a commitment to remain with the problem even—especially even—in the face of contradiction and failure.

We might think the end of history otherwise. The end of history took place two thousand years ago, when God was slain upon the cross and rose again from the dead. The history of domination by force, the history of colonization, the history of white supremacy, met its supreme conflict in the refusal of Christ, the absolute, God himself, to resist these forces. Hope is not located in violent resistance; it is located in identification with

---

28. *The Taranaki Report*, 206–07.
29. *The Taranaki Report*, 2.

this self-abnegation, in the movement of refusal to repay violence with violence. This is not a hope that in the end "history" will turn out okay for all concerned; it is deeper than that. It is a hope grounded in God's own being, made manifest to us as that which refuses to dominate; and precisely in that refusal, it is sovereign, unsovereign even. (It is certainly totally unlike "sovereignty" as we know it, so totally other as to refuse it.) This practice of passive resistance to the ravages of history is precisely that which ended history. Only in participating in that end, we await resurrection. The same life that refuses is the life that is supposed to enliven and empower communities of resistance, of contradictory hope.

I want to end by adding one layer to the history I lingered over above. I want to remember that in 2019, a heavily armed twenty-eight-year-old white Australian man walked into a mosque in Christchurch and opened fire. He was greeted by a seventy-one-year-old Muslim man, Haji-Daoud Nabi, who said: "Hello, brother. Welcome."

Bibliography

Anderson, Atholl, et al. *Tangata Whenua: A History*. Wellington: Williams, 2015.

Appendix to the Journals of the House of Representatives of New Zealand, in the Forty-sixth and Forty-seventh Years of the Reign of Her Majesty Queen Victoria, Being the Second Session of the Eighth Parliament of New Zealand. Volume 1. A. Legislative and Political. B. Finance. C. Crown Lands. Wellington: Order of the House of Representatives, 1883.

Binney, Judith. *Encircled Lands: Te Urewera, 1820–1921*. Wellington: Williams, 2009.

Brett, Mark G. *Locations of God: Political Theology in the Hebrew Bible*. New York: Oxford University Press, 2019.

Brown, Wendy. *Walled States, Waning Sovereignty*. 2nd ed. New York: Zone, 2017.

Fukuyama, Francis. "The End of History?" *The National Interest* 16 (1989) 3–18.

Keenan, Danny. *Te Whiti O Rongomai and the Resistance of Parihaka*. Wellington: HUIA, 2015.

Kojève, Alexandre. *Introduction to the Reading of Hegel: Lectures on the "Phenomenology of Spirit."* Assembled by Raymond Queneau. Edited by Allan Bloom. Translated by James H. Nichols Jr. Ithaca: Cornell University Press, 1980.

O'Malley, Vincent. *The New Zealand Wars, Ngā Pakanga o Aotearoa*. Wellington: Williams, 2019.

Scott, Dick. *Ask That Mountain: The Story of Parihaka*. Rosedale: Raupo, 2008.

The Taranaki Report: Kaupapa Tuatahi: A Waitangi Tribunal Report, 1996. Wellington: Legislation Direct, 1996.

Weil, Simone. *Gravity and Grace*. Translated by Emma Crawford and Mario von der Ruhr. London: Routledge, 2003.

Williams, Raymond. "Base and Superstructure in Marxist Cultural Theory." *New Left Review* 1.82 (1973) 3–16.

11

Home

Petra White

London, July 2020
1
The door opens—
the equilibrium of my organs as if in a jar!
And down five flights.
A shoal of dead leaves rushes past—the brittle,
weightless summer.
Then Tower Bridge, I pat it like a pet.
Little boats on the surging river
shudder in fresh wind,
my feet on the bridge.
O the world—its passages!
Odysseus could have circled
his living room ten years—
telling Penelope the same story
each morning, until the story grew faint
as the threads she wove and unwove,
and they stood, mythless,
bare feet on the pale carpet,
home at last with the worn-out dog,
the still-shining ship moored in the carport,
the merely looked-at sea crashing, howling,
back forth, back forth,
as if trying to prove the years.

Penelope knew about staying home,
one task that burnt through the days,
the singing days, loud busy birds and dew
disappearing in the sun that came
from the sea to blind her
without tidings. She pulled like levers
absence, then presence,
absence and presence,
which one? She had to keep guessing,
a figment of light,
perched at the heart of a thousand stories.
In the evening she stands on the cool grass,
and looks as I look at the setting sun.
I tell my daughter it is travelling home—
word that is a steadying, a loss,
dark water pushes a boat out to sea, the journey
begins, irreversible as a birth.
Once departed, return is an idea,
as Odysseus knew, sailing through entire lives towards
the little orange light in Penelope's window.

My English grandmother, never at home
in Adelaide, sprawled there with her dogs by the fire,
like a woman who has landed
on the earth in a city.
Her river for walking by, her garden that contained
eternity, so I imagined, alphabet bird seed
scattering infinity of language, moon
visiting us alone through the branches
of a tree that grew in the middle of the delicate web
of all things I thought to be home—
cupped in her hand like the earth
cupped that vanished tree.

2

In the otherwise empty Trafalgar Square, the homeless men
for whom the city is neither inside nor outside,
stale home on cobblestones, a wandering sense,

stand up, sit down, roam back and forth, sidle into
the blue July sky.
Twenty years ago, on the Nullarbor Plain
I walked, or knelt,
enveloped in the hygiene of space.
My fragile brain set like a flower in the desert,
thoughts flew, none could be caught,
believing only in a fizzing distance
in which my gaze could dissolve,
naked in desert air, shitting in soft holes,
desperately becoming,
this wild source.

It would take an Odysseus to return, the sea beneath him
fluid time slamming onto land, his legs
wobbling and rippling,
as things were made solid, his depths
settled, disguise came easily, lit his eyes, this home
small, busy with itself,
it could not know him, he could walk
streets of silent olive trees thick with childhood
as stranger, no longer knew this island, this woman
that yet he loved,
came and did the deed that only he could do,
and sat among his people, his son, and in his chair
sank a little heavier into the earth.

12

Every Life Can Sing

Trish Watts

As one who was blessed with a singing father and a vivacious, faith-filled mother, I was voiced into life by the rousing four-part harmony of hymnody. My local rural church choir instilled in me a dream that spirited singing was a way of life and a medicine for all. I believe passionately that "Every life can sing!" It was in the days when singing around a piano was "normal." My siblings and I would invent harmonies, perform for our farming neighbors, and participate in all the musicals, school choirs, and concerts we could. Rehearsing our songs by serenading the sheep, horses, and cows was a daily habit. For me this was bliss! A freedom that I now, never take for granted.

For three years, between 2015–17, I lived and worked in Cambodia, for a not-for-profit startup group called *Cambodia Sings*. You can imagine my shock when I experienced the "noise pollution" and discordant chaos of Phnom Penh. The only experience I had of Cambodia was as a seven-year-old, witnessing my brother boarding a country train, "conscripted" to the army to fight in Vietnam. I remember my father switching TV channels whenever violent images of Vietnam or Cambodia were shown. It was confusing to see images which had no explanation, only the "silent witness" of what was so terrifying.

These images flashed through my mind when I was invited to work with Cambodian children and families, to start choirs, in the hope of rekindling the love of singing in schools, on streets, and in villages. Was the idea insane? Yes! Did my heart feel called? Yes! Did I believe in the medicine of community singing! Yes! Even though the yesses felt strong, no one could have prepared me for the total auditory collision my ears would experience. The loss of any resemblance to harmony, rhythm, melody, and song was a harsh reality on the ground. Gone were the peaceful harmonies of choral singing, the grounded rhythm of structured music, and the melodious comfort of birdsong. In its place was dirt, choking dust, loud fractured sounds of construction diggers, with workers hanging off scaffolding singing off-key, loudly, to distorted radios! I had arrived in an urban reconstruction zone.

Cambodia was once known as the "Jewel of Asia." Her color, inventiveness, wealth and community life, rose from a rich cultural life of the performing arts. Music, song, dance, and visual art were at the heart of Khmer life and present at every ceremony and community gathering. Its musical heritage was unique, covering both artistic stylization and earthy folklore. During 1975–79, the country was gripped by civil war as the Khmer Rouge took control. During these years, over two million people lost their lives, through slaughter and starvation. The country and its people lived in absolute terror under the leadership of Marxist dictator Pol Pot who attempted to create a "master race" through social engineering. The regime stole the heart and soul of the people, crushing their spirit and trust in each other.

Families were torn apart, labor camps and enforced marriages replaced the sacred ritual practices of treasured family life. Children were separated from their parents and ritually brainwashed with songs of a hateful, cruel regime, turning them against their own kin. It was nothing short of horrific. The land still weeps; it still bleeds for the generations lost, caught in a time warp of survival and living with the ghosts of those who suffered. The sacred dreaming and the rituals that held the medicine for community life were severely fractured, almost severed. How can you safely talk, let alone sing, when all is swallowed down? How do a people express grief and heal intergenerational wounds? These questions have plagued me the past four years.

Ninety percent of the artists, musicians, teachers, doctors, and other professionals were killed during these years. Now forty years later, it is hard to find a grandparent wandering the streets. People with silver hair are either sitting on crooked benches in the markets, chopping heads off fish, begging on the stony streets, or are hidden behind closed doors watching television soaps, numbed down by medication, placating secret wounds too horrendous to murmur. Into this broken environment I stepped and met a warm-blooded people, hungering for understanding, for change, and for teachers who could walk with them and believe in their worth and goodness.

As a professional singer and Voice Movement Therapy practitioner, I know deep in my bones that the lived experience of communal singing is our birthright! Our ancestors passed down songs and stories because of their love for us; passing on goodness to build resilience and identity, to affirm our belonging to our tribe, to enrich our lives with culture, and to instruct us in living and sharing peacefully together. When we are denied access to the health and faith of our elders and ancestors, then our spirits and souls ache for what is missing. Songs carry the collective memory of the generations. When they are prohibited or forgotten, the stories of our lives weaken and we can become lost, ungrounded, grief stricken, and spiritually ill.

Working side by side with Elain Younn, a Khmer business woman of vision, we gathered children to sing on a Sunday. Through an interpreter, I asked the parents if they would like their children to sing in a regular singing group? After much discussion between themselves the answer came back—"Why?" I was shocked, and thought I'd catch the next flight home to Australia! What they were really saying was: "Will singing help with their employment as they grow up? Will it bring in money for the family? Will it make their lives easier?" I knew I needed to provide an answer that would satisfy this question, so I said: "It's a great way to learn English." A strong "Yes" came back; "We want our children learning English, it will give them a chance of a better life."

Youth School EYC (Empowering Youth Cambodia) in partnership with Cambodia Sings, Phnom Penh. Photo supplied by Trish Watts.

Figuring out how to offer singing in a country that has lost its songlines was challenging, especially as I didn't speak Khmer. I found that I desperately needed to sing myself, to move the flood of emotion that was being triggered within. I needed songs to hold my own psyche safe, songs connected to my own credo and values. It was, therefore, sheer relief to find the Music Arts School in Phnom Penh, and to offer singing workshops in world music, a cappella, and fragments of Khmer folk songs. I knew from my Methodist roots of singing with my choir-conducting dad that consistent singing with heart could seed oak trees and move mountains of doubt. He was with me!

An adult community choir began consisting of Khmer, Filipinos, and ex-pats from France, Spain, the United Kingdom, the United States of America, New Zealand, and Australia. We sang every Sunday afternoon through monsoons, mosquitos, dripping humidity, and hair-raising stories, and with copious liters of coconut water. This humble circle of about a dozen singers became a refuge, a sanctuary, a space of sanity where we could connect heart to heart and soul to soul, and "water" a dream for singing freely. Together, we could experience the wellspring of goodness within humanity and remember what was common between us. Together, we could sing up unity in a country that carries the ghosts of generational trauma, where to give voice could cost you your life.

When we sing, we come home to ourselves. We remember who we are—that we each matter and that we're stronger together. Voicing is primal to our ability to survive and thrive. It is the vehicle we use to announce our arrival, to protect, guard, instruct, and communicate our intentions to each other. Our bones dance to the tone of happiness, and our adrenals jump at the sound of a cry for help. It's an inbuilt wiring that connects us all.

Young adults under the age of thirty are exploding in numbers in Cambodia, making up 80 percent of the population. Moto's (motorbikes) roar up and down the streets carrying young families, sometimes up to five on a bike. A young spirit fills the air. It's exciting, exposing, and contains an element of genuine danger. The energy is ripe for new life.

What if Khmer youth could reclaim their birthright to have a voice, to have their song, to sing again? What if community singing could open a doorway of trust and joy? What if songs could ignite imagination and the capacity to dream again?

A father pulled up on his motorbike with a big smile on his face. He told me he heard a delightful song being sung. He turned around and realized it was his four-year-old son singing with abandon "Arappy Ya," a popular folk song sung in Khmer, to the other riders in the street.

Cambodia Sings created opportunities for over one thousand children to sing weekly with beautiful singing leaders in Phnom Penh. In slums, on the streets, in factories, and in villages, the voice of youth is rising again, bringing hope and healing to a re-emerging, resilient country, one humble note, at a time.

13

"I Am Making Everything New!"

Textless Music and the Expansion of the Christian Imaginary in Times of Disruption

JENNIFER WAKELING

Introduction

THE PERFORMANCE OF A piece of textless music can play an invaluable role in expanding the way Christians imagine reality—their Christian imaginary[1]—including in times of disruption, when unpredictable circumstances highlight the need for such expansion.

The term, Christian imaginary, is similar in connotation to the notion of Christian worldview, but it reflects an embodied (Christian) understanding of reality—one seated in the imagination—which avoids risk of reduction to a set of static propositions. The Christian imaginary is formed within communities not merely through Christian teaching but also through immersion in Christian worship and practice. One learns what it is like to be Christian not only in terms of the conscious, cognitive, explicit, and propositional dimensions of Christian faith, but also through its nonconscious, pre-cognitive, implicit, practical, and affective dimensions. By unifying and synthesizing Christian experience and knowledge, the Christian imaginary enables and limits Christian attempts to live with logical and pragmatic conviction, coherence, and continuity. Openness to the expansion of the Christian imaginary through new experiences is therefore vital. Disruptive events, such as those pertaining to current crises—including the COVID-19 pandemic, climate change, and escalations

---

1. The term "Christian imaginary," and its connotations here, are based on James K. A. Smith's discussion of Christian social imaginaries in *Desiring the Kingdom*, 68–69. Smith's use of the term stems from Charles Taylor's notion of social imaginaries in Taylor, "Modern Social Imaginaries," 106.

of various ethnic, religious, and political tensions and conflicts—may (or ought) not fit neatly within preconceived assumptions concerning God's presence and action in the world. Deeper and more finely nuanced Christian insight and practice may be needed.

This essay explores the capacity of textless music—as situated within the embodied realm of feeling qualities—to fuel the imagination and thereby expand the Christian imaginary in relation to challenges posed by current times. In particular, Olivier Messiaen's *Praise to the Immortality of Jesus*, a piece of textless music for violin and piano (the final movement of Messiaen's *Quartet for the End of Time*), can be shown to offer great potential for timely Christian insight. I present a musical–theological reflection on the piece whereby feeling responses, creative speculation, and prior knowledge conjoin for theological implications to be derived. I then explore a conceptual framework for understanding this process of musical–theological meaning-generation. The imagination is central to this process.

A Musical–Theological Reflection

I have always been moved profoundly by *Praise to the Immortality of Jesus*. Recently, while listening to a particular recording of this piece,[2] I was overcome by a sense of something I understood to be a tangible encounter with the divine. I felt disarmed by divine love. Divine presence was felt with intense tangibility as if suffusing the depths of all humanity in intimate loving union and communion, evoking something like the ecstatic heartbeat of God blissfully loving Christ and the world, as Christ's life is offered sacrificially and completely to the Father and as the world is drawn into this loving dialogue, responding to Christ with desire, praise, and exaltation. Serenity, tenderness, triumph, and longing formed a unified whole. At the end of the piece, the sounds disappeared into an extended silence. I cannot decide whether the silence was charged with presence so illuminative that it exceeded what can be conveyed through sonically perceived frequencies, or whether the ceasing of sound confronted me with absence, abandonment, and loss.

In times of disruption, we can find ourselves in strange new places which make no sense. Such crises can result in experiences of loss and disempowerment. Many people suffer great devastation, and many others are forced to surrender attachments to plans, ambitions, and projects. Familiar life patterns and habits previously adopted for understanding reality can seem to lose their relevance, or prove inadequate or problematic.

---

2. Gruenberg and Béroff, performance of "Louange À L'Immortalité De Jésus."

Praise to the Immortality of Jesus could be understood as presenting us with that enlarged, exhilarating vision of reality in which all of life, humanity, and creation is caught up through Christ in the temporally unfolding eternal dynamic of divine–human union and communion. Yet, the Christ event reveals that *kenosis* (self-emptying) lies at the heart of such a vision.[3] Christ emptied himself completely (to the point of death) to attain fully to such union and communion. Thus, we are called to allow ourselves, in solidarity with Christ, to be emptied and to become participants in this union and communion with increasing fullness. Self-emptying is tied up inextricably with (fuller) divine–human union and communion.

Perhaps the disruptive events of our times could be seen to make explicit what is always true—in hardship or happiness: the centrality of *kenosis* in the Christian vocation. Everyday life, especially grief, pain, and loss, or the thwarting of plans, ambitions, and projects, can lead us to new levels of participation in Christ's self-emptying.[4]

Messiaen's piece could be heard as imbuing *kenosis* with enlightening overtones. A quality of stasis—suspension in time and space—is elicited throughout the entire piece. Stasis can suggest the dimension of our existence and experience underlying all that we plan, achieve, and believe, whereby we are fundamentally and purely receivers of life given by and in divine love. "Naked I came from my mother's womb, and naked I will depart."[5] This original (logically, not temporally, speaking) nakedness of pure receptivity is already participation in divine love, regardless of circumstances.

Stasis coexists in the piece with intense expression of desire, a sense of progression towards a goal, and ecstatically triumphant attainment of that goal. This is perhaps the dimension of our participation in divine love that involves our impassioned yearning for it, our efforts to manifest it in our lives, and our most tangible, enrapturing experiences of it. However, what is yearned for seems to slip quietly away in the silence (following the piece), as if beyond our grasp. For all the impassioned yearning, what has been glimpsed or attained seems elusive. Such elusiveness can become manifest in everyday life through disappointing and extremely painful circumstances. Perhaps it is by allowing this elusiveness to be made present to us that we can begin to hear the almost imperceptibly quiet call of divine love to be—to return to the original nakedness of pure receptivity.

Embracing this nakedness is emptying before it is liberating. It is loss and death. It involves severance from previously comforting but subtly

---

3. Phil 2:1–11.
4. See Bourgeault, *The Heart of Centering Prayer*, 180.
5. Job 1:21.

stifling attachments, including even Christian insights, affections, and acts of goodness that have become (perhaps perplexingly and painfully) like old wineskins, unable to contain the perpetually new wine of divine love. As Messiaen's piece can show, relinquishing ourselves to divine love in this way becomes indissoluble from the praise of Christ. If we let ourselves be carried to this place of relinquishment-as-praise/praise-as-relinquishment, including perhaps through disrupting events, we may find ourselves open to participating in the gradual unfolding of divine love through Christ in new and unexpected ways. Not only may this musically-embodied vision console and uplift those who are marginalized and suffering, it can call us to be agents of Christ's renewal and restoration of the world. Perhaps we can become more open to hear the groaning of creation and to seek its regeneration. We may see more clearly, through Christ's loving universal embrace of all humanity, our oneness with those we categorize as "other" and those who suffer, seeking new ways to elicit reconciliation and healing.

The Musical–Theological Meaning-Generation Process

As shown in this reflection, that which was originally a qualitative, pre-conceptual, musical experience became for me a poignant medium of divine encounter and theological reflection facilitating potential expansion of the Christian imaginary. However, the experience could have yielded a wide range of meanings (theological or otherwise), or none at all. How is it that I found myself in that place, with that experience, with that piece of textless music? How can such an experience be accounted for in an analytically rigorous way?

I propose that through a blend of speculation, creativity, reason, and prior knowledge, a complex, intricate web of relations was constructed between specific musical properties and structures, feeling qualities, extra-musical entities (material and mental), real-life experiences, and theological notions. In what follows, I investigate aspects of this construction process, and the role of the imagination within it, in relation to the semiotic theory of Charles Peirce (1839–1914), an American philosopher, scientist, and logician. Peircean semiotics—the study of how things function as signs—offers a highly developed account of the logical (as prescinded from, e.g., the neurophysiological and psychological) dimensions of the interpreter's interaction with the sign (in this case, textless music).

Indeterminate Musical Meaning to Determined Theological Meaning

Textless music such as *Praise to the Immortality of Jesus* (heard apart from its title and composer's intentions) is indeterminate theologically. Logically precedent to any forthcoming theological implications, the flow of sounds presents the listener with pure qualitative possibility. This possibility emerges at a fundamental level from the specific musical properties and structures.

According to Peircean semiotics, pure qualitative possibility (for Peirce, a rhematic sign) is intrinsic to all meaning-generation. It constitutes what Peirce refers to as *Firstness*: "the mode of being of that which is such as it is, positively and without reference to anything else."[6] Firstness can be likened to blurred vision or inarticulate sound. It is like an infant's vague experiences of the world prior to categorizing them. It is a comma-looking thing, a sore throat, or the sound of a musical piece logically prior to (respectively) identification, diagnosis, or description.

Because we are meaning-making creatures, qualitative possibility (Firstness) tends to become attached to entities (e.g., physical objects, feelings, ideas, images) so that indeterminacy is relinquished for something temporal and particular, whereby we are impacted in some way. This is *Secondness*: "the mode of being of that which is such as it is, with respect to a second but regardless of any third."[7] Secondness resembles focused vision or articulate sound. It is like the infant growing up to categorize experiences and name objects. It is identifying a comma-looking thing as a comma requiring one to pause in a sentence, diagnosing a cold on account of a sore throat, or describing a musical piece as melancholy or in terms of a particular narrative scheme (e.g., equilibrium–disequilibrium–new equilibrium) or theological notion. In such cases, one entity functioning as the sign (e.g., the music's feeling quality) is brought into relation with a second entity (e.g., melancholy), that to which the sign refers.

Relations between entities are not automatic or necessary. They are not purely dyadic. They are mediated by general understandings and habits: the convention of relating comma-looking things to pausing in a sentence; common knowledge linking sore throats to colds; and generally understood notions such as melancholy, narrative, and aspects of Christian theology. This phenomenon of mediation (semiosis) is *Thirdness*: "the mode of being of that which is such as it is, in bringing a second and third

---

6. Peirce, *Collected Papers*, 8:328.
7. Peirce, *Collected Papers*, 8:328.

into relation to each other."[8] There is no meaning apart from mediation. Meaning-generation is genuinely triadic.

In musical–theological meaning-generation, transition from the musically-elicited indeterminacy of pure qualitative possibility (Firstness) to determined theological meaning (Secondness) requires the listener to bring musically embodied feeling qualities into relation with extra-musical entities (material or mental), including those of a theological nature, via pre-conceived epistemological structures—theological and otherwise (Thirdness). It is through the imagination—the capacity whereby humans structure and interpret experience—that entities from different domains (e.g., music and theology) can be brought into relation. Concepts are exchanged between domains and sensory images are accessed, combined, and transformed with various degrees of inventiveness for meaning to be generated.[9] Such inventiveness is vital for the formation and expansion of the Christian imaginary.

This musical-to-theological transition is not clear, simple, linear, prescribed, or necessary. As mentioned above, a perplexingly complex multi-dimensional web of relations—rhizomatous in structure—is constructed through the imagination. It would require an impossibly long time and an enormous amount of insight, knowledge, and detail (including knowledge not yet attained or attainable) to examine every part of this process (much of which is nonconscious). However, some salient elements will be defined here.

Processes of the Imagination

According to Peircean semiotics, there are three kinds of relations between entities (signs and that to which signs refer): resemblance, contiguity, and convention. (Peircean terminology for these are, respectively: iconicity, indexicality, and symbolicity). These relations are recognized or established via three reasoning stages: abduction, deduction, and induction.

Resemblance and Abduction

Resemblance involves bringing two entities into relation based on perceived likeness, such as when a portrait suggests a subject (correctly or incorrectly) through its perceived likeness with the subject, or a rumbling sound indicates thunder (correctly or incorrectly) by sounding like thunder. The perception of resemblance stems from our capacity to seek

---

8. Peirce, *Collected Papers*, 8:328.
9. See Roth, "Imagination," 443–47.

comparisons between entities (based on our experience of them)[10] which may be, but are not necessarily, connected. Sonic structures have no (necessary) connection to the world of feelings, narrative, and theology. However, a piece of music can be heard as melancholy, as depicting a narrative scheme of equilibrium–disequilibrium–new equilibrium, or in terms of some theological notion because the flow of sounds has an affect which feels like melancholy, is perceived to be structured like a narrative based on an equilibrium–disequilibrium–new equilibrium scheme, or seems to bear likeness in some way with a theological notion.

Relations of resemblance do not constitute fact, but they can participate in the perception of facts, such as when a rumbling sound resembles the sound of thunder in an actual instance of thunder. Significantly, resemblance can reveal otherwise undisclosed insight, such as when the realm of rationalistic certainty falls short. For example, within the theological sphere, we are faced inevitably with a "virtual frontier"[11] beyond which we can only ascertain imaginatively and creatively how things are, or may be. Analogy (and metaphor)—the perception of similarities (in conjunction with dissimilarities) between aspects of temporal–material experience and transcendent reality—is vital to theological knowledge and understanding.

Peirce refers to the kind of creative, imaginative speculation required for perceiving resemblance as abduction: a guess, a flash of insight. Abduction directs "us as if we were in possession of facts that are entirely beyond the reach of our senses."[12] Abduction is fallible, but, according to Peirce, it is a necessary stage in the reasoning process whereby new knowledge can be acquired.[13] It is like the generation of a hypothesis. It enables leaps over closed circuits of deduction and forges gaps through impenetrable mountains of induction.

Meaning-generation through textless music (and art in general) relies heavily on abduction and resemblance and can thus enable new perspectives and deeper insights in relation to over-familiar theological themes. Textless music can offer potentially vital analogical links where other logical chains fail, such as when connecting the effect of musical sounds to the feeling of a heartbeat, and, in turn, to the notion of God's love for the world. However, abduction and resemblance cannot be relied upon entirely. Deduction and relations of contiguity must be involved also.

10. See Johnson, *The Meaning of the Body*, 31.
11. Hughes, *Worship as Meaning*, 151.
12. Peirce, *Collected Papers*, 5:173.
13. See Peirce, *Collected Papers*, 2:96; 5:181.

Contiguity and Deduction

Perception of contiguity involves grouping entities based on cause–effect links, temporal–spatial proximation, and/or temporal sequencing.[14] For example: because the sun emits light, daylight will tend to be associated with the sun. Because knives and forks are used together, the thought of a knife could reasonably invoke the thought of a fork. Because a main meal follows an entrée, an entrée would tend to bring to mind the idea of a main meal.

Relations based on contiguity are the most reliable, factually speaking. Perceiving such relations involves deduction: a logical progression from a premise to a conclusion, such as concluding from the presence of daylight that the sun has risen. Deduction is a vital stage in the reasoning process for testing the feasibility of abductions. For example, one hypothesizes that rumbling in the distance indicates thunder. However, the rumbling also sounds like, and could therefore potentially indicate, an airplane, truck, or some fierce, giant, mythical animal. One therefore needs to apply deduction to arrive at a reasonable conclusion, such as deciding the rumbling sound indicates thunder because it coincides with lightning (contiguity is perceived). Thus, deduction guards against fanciful abductions which may prove incongruent with reality.

While musical meaning-generation is heavily oriented towards abduction and resemblance, it can be deemed somewhat reasonable through the involvement of deduction and contiguity in terms of biological and physical cause–effect processes.[15] For example, physical gestures and vocal tones which express melancholy produce a particular kinetic shape (cause–effect). It makes sense then that a musical gesture (phrase) or tone producing such a kinetic shape (cause–effect) could be likened to melancholy (resemblance). Titles, commentaries, specified programs, and performance contexts can be brought into relation with textless music by deduction on account of temporal proximity. If a textless piece is performed during a Christmas Eve service directly following the reading of Luke 2:1–20, for example, the meaning of the piece could be deduced by listeners as pertaining to the birth of Jesus.

While deduction alone is insufficient for theologizing, deduction and contiguity play a vital part in establishing theo-logic chains (albeit dependent upon assumed theological premises). For example, a logic chain can be established between the words and actions of Jesus at the Last Supper and identifying Christians gathered for worship as the body of Christ. Logic

---

14. See Massecar, "Peirce's Interesting Associations," 196–97.

15. See, for example, biological explanations for musical–somatic mapping in the work of Cox, "The Mimetic Hypothesis and Embodied Musical Meaning," 195–212.

chains are vital to musical–theological meaning-generation. For example, in relation to the Messiaen case, I was already aware that self-emptying (death) is made contiguous with new life (resurrection) in the Christ event, and this self-emptying/new life pattern is made contiguous with followers of Christ through a range of scripture passages.[16]

Convention and Induction

Entities can be also brought into relation by virtue of convention, such as when a red traffic light means stop, the word 'cat' signifies a particular kind of animal, and a funeral service indicates someone has died. Conventional relations are largely (though not necessarily entirely) arbitrary. They can change and evolve over time, and vary across different socio-cultural contexts.

Conventional relations are perceived through induction: generalizing from a representative sample of data. For example, if, in one's experience, 'cat' has been connected to a particular kind of animal in many previous instances, it is very likely 'cat' will be suitable for that same kind of animal in a new singular instance. Induction is more reliable than is abduction, but less reliable than is deduction. For an English speaker visiting Germany, previous cat-naming experiences cannot be relied upon to connect such an animal correctly to the word *Katze*.

There are a range of musical conventions that enable music to make sense (inductively) in particular ways. For example, within the Western tonal system, single tones within a melody tend to be heard in terms of various degrees of stability and instability. Typically, a melody is a play of stability and instability, and often begins and ends with stability. Listeners are affected by the music according to their familiarity with such play, and the expectations that arise from it. Listeners unfamiliar with, for example, the use of microtones (such as in South Asian and Middle Eastern music) or Messiaen's own unique tonal language, may require multiple hearings and/or guidance to ascertain meaning from such music. Listeners' responses are affected also by their familiarity with common music–context pairings within their socio-cultural context (e.g., in ritual music, movie soundtracks, advertising).

When theologizing, Christians rely on a particular range of conventional ways of imagining reality (centered on the Christ event) which are adopted through practical and theoretical indoctrination of shared, agreed-upon results of prior Christian theologizing (within particular socio-cultural contexts). This involves induction. As demonstrated in the cat example

16. E.g., Matt 16:25.

above, induction ought not be confused with deduction. It is possible, as the history of Christianity shows, for some Christian theoretical and practical conventions to fade out, evolve, and/or become more finely nuanced when incongruences and new complexities are discovered. In other words, the Christian imaginary can undergo expansion.

Apart from the use of textless music, for example, in marketing when a jingle becomes associated with a specific product, textless music does not relate typically to extra-musical notions in one-to-one correspondence by convention. However, in musical–theological meaning-generation, Christian conventions can be brought into relation with textless music through contiguity. In the Messiaen example, linking the feeling of a heartbeat specifically with God's love for the world requires prior Christian knowledge and belief. Such knowledge and belief can be brought into play by markers (textual or contextual) accompanying (temporally proximate with) the musical performance.

It will probably be apparent that all three kinds of relation work in conjunction with various degrees of prominence within a singular case of musical–theological meaning-generation. Myriad relations are established within a complex dynamic musical–theological space which can be stretched over time; as in my case, through ongoing reflection on my original experience of the Messiaen piece. As mentioned previously, this space emerges through interfacing the musical domain—the field of meaning-generation possibilities offered by *Praise to the Immortality of Jesus*—with the theological domain. A particular theological field of meaning-generation possibilities is elicited, in this case, by the piece's title, the composer's commentary, and ascension theology (more specifically, the constraints of my awareness of, and knowledge and beliefs regarding, these entities).

The Theological Domain

The title of Messiaen's piece refers to the notions of praise and of Jesus's immortality. Messiaen elaborates: It is a eulogy "addressed . . . to the second aspect of Jesus—the man Jesus—to the Word made flesh, resurrected immortally to grant us life. It is all love. Its slow ascent towards the extreme high register is the ascent of [humanity] towards . . . God, of the Child of God towards [their] Father, of the deified Being towards Paradise."[17]

This information points to ascension theology which provides further ideas to bring into relation with the piece's feeling qualities. As the "climax

---

17. Pople, *Messiaen*, 81, translating Messiaen, "Preface," ii.

of redemption,"[18] the ascension to heaven of Jesus's risen body is a crucial part of the entire Christ event. Having been raised from the dead, Christ ascends into heaven to fill everything—the whole universe—in every way[19] as "Center and Upholder of the universe."[20] His final victory over evil forces becomes assured and he attains "the glory of Divine Sonship": "intimate union and communion" with the Father.[21]

Furthermore, as the "first fruits" of humankind, Christ paves the way through the ascension for the modification of the condition of humankind. "Human nature in its totality, the embodied human person, is now glorified with Christ,"[22] as if drawn up to God by Christ. The boundaries of human finitude have been pierced and the possibility has been established for humankind to enter a new level of divine–human communion to be temporally and progressively grown into through Christ's advocacy and the empowering work of the Holy Spirit.[23]

Thus, the ascension constitutes not so much Jesus's departure from the world as it does the perdurance of his presence and rule in a "new mode."[24] Humanity is assured of, and immersed within, the finality and reality of Christ's reign and presence in the world, the hope that it generates, and the joy and praise that it elicits.

Interfacing the Musical Domain with the Theological Domain

It is now clearer, I hope, why particular theological notions were understood by me as embodied in the Messiaen piece. However, the piece needed to elicit, through its specific musical properties and structures, a particular musical field of meaning-generation possibilities which could be brought reasonably into relation with these (and not other) theological notions. Four main feeling qualities were elicited (as indicated earlier): stasis, progression, desire, and ecstasy.

Stasis (suspension in time and space) was generated through factors such as an unnaturally slow tempo; an imperceptible meter; a rhythmically static piano part; the piano's slow harmonic rhythm; a tonal scheme (the octatonic scale) lacking pitch hierarchy (minimizing the impetus of tension

---

18. Kapic and Lugt, "The Ascension of Jesus," 24.
19. See Pss 47; 93; Eph 1:23; 4:10.
20. Toon, "Historical Perspectives," 295.
21. Milligan, *The Ascension*, 39–40, cited in Toon, "Historical Perspectives," 294.
22. Murray, "Ascension of Jesus Christ," 772.
23. See O'Loughlin, *The Eucharist*, 29–30. See Heb 9:24–28; 10:19–23.
24. Catholic Church, "The Ascension of the Lord," 845.

and resolution); and the slow-moving, almost continuous, and mostly conjunct violin melody which rises and falls without coming to rest. The kinetic character of the flow of sound emerging from such factors was brought into relation with the theological notion of divine–human communion in its eternal dimension. The flow of sound was experienced as a disposition of calm, spellbound receptivity. One is fully enveloped by, and sustained in the eternal present through, loving divine presence.

Seemingly paradoxically, a feeling quality of progression was also attained due to the gradual ascent throughout the piece from the violin's low register to its extremely high register. In each of the piece's two sections there is a climactic arrival point in the violin's high register. Additionally, Messiaen incorporates a second tonal scheme (E major) which does involve the impetus of tension and resolution, albeit in a gentle manner. The kinetic character of such musical ascent and arrival—mapped onto the notion of progressing towards a goal—was brought into relation with Christ's and the world's ascent towards, and attainment of, union with the divine. Furthermore, the general understanding of divine life as unfolding progressively in the world was brought into play. Hope for the unfolding of divine life was elicited along with encouragement to participate in the activation of such hope. Hope is sustained by the belief that what is unfolding is already attained, just as stasis and progression cohered musically, evoking a sense of goal-orientation yet circularity.

Desire was felt qualitatively via the expressive intensity of the violin part: its long, sustained, penetrating tones; expressive dissonances, leaps, and appoggiatura-like notes; and use of vibrato and glissando. Desire was also realized through the gradual increase in volume and the stretto-like effect (whereby note values are shortened) as the violin's melody approaches its two climactic points. The closer the arrival point, the more intense the attraction or compulsion towards it. The feeling of intense desire, evoked through the physiological responses prompted by these musical features, was brought into relation with the notion of desire for God—for being drawn to increasingly intimate levels of divine–human communion. The visceral nature of such desire can be likened to the lover in Song of Songs opening the latch for the beloved only to find he had departed.[25] There is a range of mystic writings, biblical stories, and psalms whereby desire for God can be expressed in exhilarating and/or agonizing ways which fuel wholehearted and sacrificial devotion and action along the way—perhaps involving relinquishment of other objects of desire in emphatic praise to

---

25. Song 5:4–6.

God. Painful circumstances in life could be seen as related to the (as yet) unfulfilled dimension of ultimate desire for God.

Finally, an ecstatic feeling quality was embodied most poignantly through the piece's ending. The ultimate climactic point is powerfully triumphant on account of the violin's note sequence and the overall intensity of volume reinforced by the piano chords which are like church bells in their clanging, repetitious effect, or perhaps a pounding heartbeat. However, stunningly and unexpectedly, the violin's pitch continues to soar beyond the climactic point, diminishing gradually in intensity (as does the piano). The violin melody leaps to the final, extremely high note (supported by the piano's extremely high register). It is as though the summit of finitude has been reached and can be succeeded only by what seems to be an entirely different realm of reality. This final note is sustained unnaturally in length while continuing to diminish in volume until fading into the most affecting, extended silence.

Such extreme musical features were heard as otherworldly and were brought into relation with the notion of paradisiacal divine–human communion—the dimension of divine–human communion that can be glimpsed but ultimately transcends earthly life. Recalling the image of the disciples looking into the skies after Jesus ascended into heaven[26] can imbue the (post-musical) silence with ecstatic bliss and/or bewilderment—perhaps a uniquely nuanced blend of hollowness, abandonment, confusion, awe, empowerment, and ecstatic joy.[27] One is disarmed before—one returns to the nakedness of pure receptivity to—the mystery of loving, divine presence-in-absence. One is perhaps opened to new visions and manifestations of God's presence and action in the world, as was the case for the disciples.

For the overall experience and theological implications to emerge as presented, the broadly-defined relations specified above, and myriad others, were recognized and established (consciously and nonconsciously) through interfacing a specific musical field of meaning-generation possibilities with particular theological and experiential fields of meaning-generation possibilities. As discussed earlier, the experiential field incorporates current crises. Firstness (musically-elicited qualitative possibilities) gave way to Secondness (theological implications) via Thirdness (the process of bringing a wide range of entities into relation). Webs of relations could be spun indefinitely (with increasing Thirdness) to attain further theological refinement and nuance, and different webs could be spun for different listeners, leading to different meanings. However, the meaning at any stage stems

---

26. Acts 1:9–11.

27. Luke 24:52–53.

from the specific musical properties and structures of the piece and of the listeners' prior knowledge and experience, including that pertaining to Christian faith and that which is recalled (mentally) and suggested (contextually) within the listening and reflection process. The meaning is constrained by these factors. This means firmly established dimensions of the Christian imaginary can play a crucial role. At the same time, the meaning can constitute an expansion of previous knowledge, experience, and belief due to the imagination's capacity to bring entities together in new, previously unconceived of, combinations. Thus, the Christian imaginary can be expanded. *Praise to the Immortality of Jesus* is particularly rich in potential for enabling such combinations.

It is perhaps helpful to note that I have not mentioned explicitly the work of the Spirit. However, I suggest that it is only by looking through a dichotomous lens that (artificially) severs spirituality from humanity that a reader would fail to see the work of the Spirit implied continuously throughout this essay. Could we not say that the Spirit's work (historic and immediate) can be evident potentially in every abduction, deduction, and induction, no matter how (seemingly) mundane (rather than a factor we recruit to fill otherwise inexplicable gaps)?

Conclusion

Musical-theological meaning-generation has been explicated here as a creative and logical process centered in the imagination that brings into relation a wide range of entities—musical, extra-musical, and theological—to form a complex, rhizomatous network. It is not possible to investigate such complexity more fully here. However, wondrously, what is fundamentally a series of sonic events can give rise to experiences which generate deeper insight to expand the Christian imaginary. Such expansion can be important for negotiating disruptive events in a way that extends the love of Christ to all humanity, and indeed to all creation. Significantly, it has been shown that creative, imaginative engagement with textless music can be involved in theological meaning-generation intrinsically, not as some fanciful, esoteric, optional pursuit. It can play an invaluable role in the unfolding and proliferation of the great divine purpose fulfilled in Christ—"I am making everything new!"[28]

---

28. Rev 21:5.

Bibliography

Bourgeault, Cynthia. *The Heart of Centering Prayer: Nondual Christianity in Theory and Practice*. Boulder: Shambhala, 2016.

Catholic Church. "The Ascension of the Lord (Year C)." In *St. Paul's Sunday Missal: Sunday Masses for the Three-year Cycle*, 845–50. Strathfield: St. Pauls, 2012.

Cox, Arnie. "The Mimetic Hypothesis and Embodied Musical Meaning." *Musicae Scientiae* 5 (2001) 195–212.

Gruenberg, Erich, and Michel Béroff. Performance of "Louange À L'Immortalité De Jésus," by Olivier Messiaen, *MESSIAEN: Quatuor pour la fin du Temps, Le Merle noir*. Recorded at Abbey Road Studios, London, October 14–16, 1968. EMI Records, 1969, compact disc.

Hughes, Graham. *Worship as Meaning: A Liturgical Theology for Late Modernity*. Cambridge: Cambridge University Press, 2003.

Johnson, Mark. *The Meaning of the Body: Aesthetics of Human Understanding*. Chicago: University of Chicago Press, 2007.

Kapic, Kelly, and Wesley Lugt. "The Ascension of Jesus and the Descent of the Holy Spirit in Patristic Perspective: A Theological Reading." *Evangelical Quarterly* 79 (2007) 23–33.

Massecar, Aaron. "Peirce's Interesting Associations." *Transactions of the Charles S. Peirce Society: A Quarterly Journal in American Philosophy* 48 (2012) 191–208.

Messiaen, Olivier. "Preface." In *Quatuor pour la fin du Temps pour clarinette en si bèmol, violon, violoncelle et piano*, i–iv. Paris: Durand, 1942.

Milligan, William. *The Ascension and Heavenly Priesthood of Our Lord*. London: Macmillan & Co., 1892.

Murray, J. C. "Ascension of Jesus Christ." In *New Catholic Encyclopedia*, edited by Berard L. Marthaler, 1:768–72. 2nd ed. Detroit: Gale, 2003.

O'Loughlin, Frank. *The Eucharist: Doing What Jesus Did*. Strathfield: St. Pauls, 1997.

Peirce, Charles. *Collected Papers of Charles Sanders Peirce*. Vols. 1–6, edited by Charles Hartshorne and Paul Weiss. Vols. 7–8, edited by A. W. Burks. Cambridge: Belknap, 1958–66.

Pople, Anthony. *Messiaen: Quatuor pour la fin du Temps*. Cambridge: Cambridge University Press, 1998.

Roth, Ilona. "Imagination." In *The Oxford Companion to the Mind*, edited by Richard L. Gregory, 443–47. 2nd ed. Oxford: Oxford University Press, 2004.

Smith, James K. A. *Desiring the Kingdom: Worship, Worldview, and Cultural Formation*. Grand Rapids: Baker Academic, 2009.

Taylor, Charles. "Modern Social Imaginaries." *Public Culture* 14 (2002) 91–124.

Toon, Peter. "Historical Perspectives on the Doctrine of Christ's Ascension, Part 2: The Meaning of the Ascension for Christ." *Bibliotheca Sacra* 140 (1983) 291–301.

14

Journal de l'Année de la Peste

KEVIN HART

How quickly Paris shrinks to just a room
That holds its silence like a reservoir.
The Gardens closed again, I fiddle round,

Listing in French each part of that old bike
I see chained up, time sleeping in today,
And watch men heaping high their cars' back seats

And women pushing trolleys, stuffed with food,
Toward Montmartre where some trains still run.
I'm put on hold for half an afternoon

Trying to fly away and, when it's three,
I'm hearing myself say *le frein* aloud.
No métro after midnight, sighs the news,

Maybe no taxis after Macron talks.
I let *la bicyclette* return to rust
And feel my stomach tighten once again.

Perhaps one day the world will end like this,
Advertisements still coming on iphones
For special deals on shoes and candy bars,

Small shops all boarded up, police with masks
And retro guns outside sieged pharmacies,
Rumor like rain that cowers half the town,

And no one picking up in offices,
Bright boulevards half-dead and looking lost
Like disused sets from *Breathless* left around,

Soft locks upon each afternoon that bite
As evening comes, and fast, thin dreams in sleep,
And empty buses trundling down dark roads.

15

Setting the Record *Straight*

The Prophetic Art of Ai Weiwei

ADRIENNE DENGERINK CHAPLIN

> I hope I can change at least the spirit of the times with art. I think we'd have a better society if imagination, fantasy or passion—the qualities realised through art—were more valued.[1]

Earthquake

WHEN, ON MAY 12, 2008, Chinese artist Ai Weiwei (b. 1957) first heard about the devastating, magnitude-eight earthquake that shook the mountainous Sichuan province in southwestern China, he felt too overwhelmed to speak.[2] He stopped his prolific daily blogging and all other social media activity and fell into a long silence. As he recalls: "It was devastating: more than 80,000 lives disappeared. Many of the dead were young people at school and university. I'd been writing a daily blog—about modern Chinese society, the government, and art—but I stopped suddenly. People asked me why but, faced with such a tragedy, I was silenced. I couldn't find the right vocabulary."[3]

Soon after, he drove to the affected region to find out more so that he might write something of relevance. It was while there, however, that he discovered a shocking truth: in contrast to most other multi-story buildings that had stayed upright, hundreds of school buildings with thousands of classrooms had inexplicably collapsed, crushing the children within them.

---

1. Ai, in Marlow, "Ai Weiwei in Conversation," 26.

2. "Weiwei" is Ai Weiwei's first name and "Ai" his family name. Hereon he will be referred to by his family name—"Ai."

3. Ai, "The Artwork That Made Me the Most Dangerous Person in China," lines 5–9. See also Ai, "Ai Weiwei on the Project That Awoke His Political Voice."

As became gradually clear, not only were many schools built on seismic fault lines but most of them were built in violation of essential building regulations, their shoddy construction a direct result of corrupt practices by developers and colluding politicians.

Middle School, Sichuan earthquake, 2009. Photo by Xieyouding.

When Ai eventually found the words to speak, he did not waste them. He used his presence on the internet to voice his critique of the Chinese authorities and to start his own inquiries. He also made several significant works of art that engaged directly with the earthquake and its aftermath. The works can be considered an important turning point in Ai's life as an activist and artist. This essay will examine some of the works made in the period between 2008 and 2012, showing how they influenced his new way of engaging with our age's crises, not only in China but also internationally and globally.

Exile

Ai is no stranger to crises. From an early age, he and his family were victims of the whims of China's communist regime. His father, the renowned poet Ai Qing (1910–96), had initially been close to Mao Zedong and his circles, but fell out of favor after having expressed some criticism of the Party's policies. In the year that Ai was born, Mao unleashed his Anti-Rightist campaign that was meant to purge all intellectuals and artists whose works were not considered to conform to Party ideology. Ai Qing and his young family—alongside hundreds of thousands of other intellectuals—were exiled from Beijing to Shihezi in the Northwest of China to undergo "reform through labor."[4] Ten years later, Mao's growing zeal for radical reforms led him to launch the Great Proletarian Cultural Revolution, encouraging his followers to "'smash the four olds'—old ideas, old culture, old customs, old habits."[5] Intellectuals bore the brunt of hostile treatments, which involved public denunciation meetings and humiliating punishments. When Ai was ten years old, Ai's father was forced to move even further north, this time to a large agricultural production unit in a region known as "Little Siberia." There they lived for five years in a disused dugout left by early pioneers—a square hole in the ground covered by branches for a roof. His father's new job was to clean the communal latrines.[6] It was not until after Mao's death and the end of China's ten-year Great Proletarian Cultural Revolution in 1976 that his father was rehabilitated, and his family allowed to return to their home in Beijing.[7]

At age nineteen, Ai began his first formal education and enrolled at the Beijing Film Academy to study animation. His studies coincided with the post-Cultural Revolution emergence of a new generation of Chinese avant-garde artists who embraced the Western idea of art as self-expression as an antidote to the state-approved socialist realism that had prevailed until then. Ai became one of the founding members of "Stars," one of the many contemporary art collectives that sprung up across China.

New York

As one of the first of his generation, Ai went abroad to study and pursue other opportunities.[8] After studying English in Philadelphia and San Francisco, he briefly enrolled at the Parsons School of Design in New York City. Unable to afford the fees—and underwhelmed by the courses—he left after six months and survived as an undocumented citizen doing odd

---

4. Ai, *1000 Years of Joys and Sorrows*, 114.

5. Ai, *1000 Years of Joys and Sorrows*, 94.

6. For more on Ai's time in "Little Siberia," see Ai, *1000 Years of Joys and Sorrows*, 93–99.

7. For a comprehensive account of Ai Qing's life, see Ai, *1000 Years of Joys and Sorrows*, 3–153.

8. For more on his New York period, see Ai, *1000 Years of Joys and Sorrows*, 165–95.

jobs, including drawing street portraits, while observing and exploring New York's urban life and art scene. He was particularly taken by the conceptualism of Marcel Duchamp and Andy Warhol, and, in 1988, put on his own solo show—*Old Shoes, Safe Sex*—that included several conceptual pieces of "found art." Ai's acute skills of observation found their way into photography. During his time in New York, he took over ten thousand photographs documenting the city's life, several of which were bought and published by American newspapers.[9]

While he was in New York, the surge of new experimental art in China came to an abrupt halt in 1989, when the Government launched a brutal attack on pro-democracy demonstrators in Tiananmen Square, resulting in over ten thousand deaths and many more arrests and detentions. After that, Chinese contemporary art changed from embracing modern ideals of authenticity, freedom, and self-expression, to a "postmodern sensibility of cynicism, satire, pastiche and kitsch."[10] Ai describes the two categories of contemporary art thus: "The first presented gloomy, violent themes in dark, oppressive shades, while the second was quite the opposite: colorful and ribald, so-called political pop-paintings, featuring pink, bald-headed men and seductive, preening women, with an overlay of Cultural Revolution imagery. Though they differed in their degree of self-mockery, decadence, absurdity, and cynicism, both idioms captured elements of our nonsensical, contrived reality."[11] Although met with suspicion and hostility by the authorities, this new wave of contemporary Chinese artists drew considerable attention from the international art market.

Beijing

In 1993, when his father's health deteriorated, Ai returned to Beijing where he lived with his parents in their traditional courtyard house, the kind that was rapidly disappearing under the building boom of Deng Xiaoping's capitalist reforms.[12] During that time, Ai spent most of his time writing art-critical essays. Drawing on his experience in New York, he sought to bring the modern art he had encountered in America into conversation with developments in contemporary Chinese art.[13] Together

9. A selection of 227 photographs is published in Ai, *Ai Weiwei: New York Photographs*.
10. Zhang and Frazier, "Playing the Chinese Card," 4.
11. Ai, *1000 Years of Joys and Sorrows*, 201.
12. See Tancock, "Born Radical," 34–35.
13. See Ai, *The Black Cover Book*; Ai, *The White Cover Book*; Ai, *The Gray Cover Book*. Also, Tung, "Black, White, and Grey," 55–64.

with his stepbrother Ai Dan, he also scoured the local antique markets for vases, furniture, and other items from the Ming (1368–1644) and Qing (1644–1911) dynasties, which were being salvaged from old buildings that were bulldozed to clear space for new construction. Ai's 1995 photographs, *Dropping a Han Dynasty Urn*, originally started as a means to try out the continuous capture function on his camera, can be interpreted as a reference to this rampant destruction of traditional Chinese culture. In 1997, he made his first art works using parts of antique furniture—*Table with Two Legs on the Wall*—a surreal configuration that fused American conceptualism with traditional Chinese craft.

In 1999, he designed and built his own studio house at Caochangdi, a village on the outskirts of Beijing. Its minimalism and use of commonplace materials drew the attention of national and foreign architects, and launched Ai's career as a successful architect with his own company, FAKE Design, founded in 2003.[14] Ai's house and studio became a magnet for many other artists, and the village soon turned into a thriving art district, with a plethora of studios and galleries.

Internet

In 2005, because of his fast-growing profile and influence, Ai was invited by China's largest internet platform, Sina, to start a blog commenting on Chinese art, design, lifestyle, and society more generally. Although at that time unfamiliar with the internet and unable to type, he quickly recognized the unprecedented opportunity this provided him to express and share his views with large numbers of people.[15] As yet unhindered by any government restrictions, he believed the internet could herald a new dawn of democracy and social reform. As he wrote in his memoir: "On the internet, social coercion is nullified and the individual acquires a kind of weightlessness, no longer subordinate to the power structure."[16]

For the next five years, he devoted most of his days—and many nights—to writing blogs, which were read and shared by an average of ten thousand people a day.[17] Energized by this exposure, he became increasingly outspoken and political, thereby inevitably drawing the Chinese

---

14. For more about the building of his studio, see Ai, *1000 Years of Joys and Sorrows*, 214–20.

15. For more about Ai's use of the internet, see Ai, *1000 Years of Joys and Sorrows*, 227–32.

16. Ai, *1000 Years of Joys and Sorrows*, 228.

17. See Ai and Samman, "The Internet Is My Life."

Government's attention, resulting in the blog's eventual closure in May 2009. The main reason for the closure—and the final straw for the Government—was Ai's use of his blog after the earthquake in 2008. In order to understand exactly what happened, it is important to pick up the story some days after that event.

Citizens' Investigation

In the days following the earthquake, calls for more information from the bereaved families were met with silence by the authorities. A large convoy of state-appointed soldiers took control of the clearing-up operation and local people were kept at a distance. Many parents were prevented from retrieving their children's belongings—backpacks, notebooks, pens, etc. that lay scattered among the rubble—and some children were even denied a proper burial. Even the children's names were being withheld. In Ai's words: "The Chinese government censored and controlled all of the information about the earthquake, so people didn't know the details of what really happened. I wanted to know how many students had lost their lives. Schools built by the state are supposed to be very secure—they should not collapse. I made hundreds of phone calls to the education department, the police and civil departments, to ask questions about the student casualties, but of course nobody would talk to me."[18]

In response to the cover-up by the authorities, Ai started his own online Citizens' Investigation, using his blog to call on volunteers to help him compile a list of names of the children that had perished, together with information about their date of birth, gender, school class, and so on.[19] He felt that this was the least he could do for the bereaved families. Over the course of the next year, a team of over one hundred volunteers knocked on the doors of the villagers to gain details about the lost children, with Ai posting all information on his daily blog. After a year, they had collected 5,196 names. Ai also recorded and filmed all his conversations, and produced the powerful investigative documentary *Little Girl's Cheeks* (2008). The film is one of China's first works of socially engaged art conceived as art that "directly affects people's feelings and living conditions, their freedom and how they look at the world."[20]

---

18. Ai, "The Artwork That Made Me the Most Dangerous Person in China," lines 10–16.

19. For more on the Citizens' Investigation, see Ai, *1000 Years of Joys and Sorrows*, 246–56.

20. Ai, cited in Bracker, *Ai Weiwei*, 13.

Throughout the year, the team faced many challenges. Many investigators were arrested and detained, their findings confiscated and deleted, turning their efforts into a Sisyphean struggle. Eventually, on May 28, 2009, the Government shut down Ai's blog completely.[21] As he describes the day in his memoir:

> I got a call from a Communist Party official at the Writers Association who exhorted me to keep quiet during the days to come—the period leading up to the twentieth anniversary of the massacre in Beijing on June 4, 1989. I told him I could give no such assurance. No sooner had the call ended than I discovered I had disappeared from Chinese cyberspace. I was unable to log in to my blog; the three thousand posts I had written and the ten thousand photographs I had uploaded over the course of three years and seven months were gone; and even an online search for 'Ai Weiwei' drew a blank—my name was now taboo.... I felt as though my body was being torn apart."[22]

Ai subsequently moved to Twitter—by 2012, he had sent sixty thousand tweets—and, from 2011 onwards, to Instagram. Soon after that the Chinese Government started to censure and ban all independent social media platforms, and Ai could no longer post anything online. With the introduction of ever-more firewalls and filters, all searches involving his name were being blocked.[23]

Two months after the closure of his blog, Ai and ten other investigators were in Chengdu, the capital of Sichuan, for the trial of a local activist. During the night before the trial, their hotel rooms were invaded by a group of police officers who forcefully kept them locked in their rooms until after the trial was finished.[24] In the process, Ai was so badly beaten that he developed a life-threatening brain haemorrhage that required urgent emergency surgery.[25]

Remembering

The surgery took place in September in Munich where Ai was preparing his exhibition—"So Sorry"—in the *Haus der Kunst*. He had used the

---

21. For a collection of some of Ai's blogs, see Ai, *Ai Weiwei's Blog.*
22. Ai, *1000 Years of Joys and Sorrows*, 264.
23. See Hornby, "Chinese Artist Ai Weiwei Makes Internet His Medium."
24. See Branigan, "Chinese Police Detain 11."
25. For more on the attack on him in Chengdu, see Ai, *1000 Years of Joys and Sorrows*, 268–74.

opportunity of the exhibition to create a large memorial for the children, called *Remembering* (2009), consisting of nine thousand brightly-colored school backpacks spelling the Chinese sentence "she had been living happily for seven years [in this world]," a phrase taken from a letter to Ai from the girl's mother saying that all she wanted was the world to remember that.[26] It had been the haunting image of the children's unattended backpacks in the midst of the debris that had prompted Ai to use this particular item as a symbol for the children's innocent pre-earthquake lives. The work was installed on the museum's façade, a poignant reminder of the fact that the *Haus der Kunst* had originally been built in 1937 for Hitler, as a home for the socialist realist Nazi art that was to counter the "degenerate" modern abstract and surrealist art of the time.[27]

Remembering was both a culmination and a turning point in Ai's life as an artist. As he describes it: "Given all our social and political investigations, [*Remembering*] was about how, in Chinese society, with censorship and control, individuals can still take action to defend their very, very fragile rights. It was also the culmination of all my years on the internet. I've been blogging since 2005, so when that show happened in Munich in 2009, it was like all my efforts were coming to a head."[28] Put differently, it was the tragedy of Sichuan that brought Ai's art and politics together in a deeper and more existential way—"the artwork that made me the most dangerous person in China"—than ever before and signaled a new artistic period: "I have made many other works relating to the Sichuan earthquake, but this one had a profound impact on how I deal with social and political issues. It's about a real-life tragedy, the human condition, civil rights—an embodiment of my passion and imagination. If I hadn't engaged with that tragedy, I would not be the artist I am today. I cannot imagine I'd still be making art if I wasn't reflecting my political views."[29]

---

26. Ai, "The Artwork That Made Me the Most Dangerous Person in China," lines 36–37.

27. For more about the exhibition "So Sorry," see Ai, *1000 Years of Joys and Sorrows*, 274–75. For a documentary on the tensions between Ai and the Government named after the 2009 exhibition in Munich, see Ai, "So Sorry."

28. Ai, "The Artwork That Made Me the Most Dangerous Person in China," lines 40–45.

29. Ai, "The Artwork That Made Me the Most Dangerous Person in China," lines 64–69.

Sunflower Seeds

In the light of Ai's own comments on *Remembering*, another installation made by him around the same time, *Sunflower Seeds* (2008–10), could be seen as a transitional work. Conceived in the period before the earthquake, *Sunflower Seeds* consists of a ten-centimeter-deep layer of millions of small, hand-crafted, porcelain "sunflower seeds." It was first shown in the cavernous Turbine Hall of the Tate Modern in London, where the "seeds" were spread out on the entire floor—a vast expanse of greyness blending seamlessly with the industrial steel architecture of the hall itself.[30]

The floor installation can be seen to represent Chinese society: on the one hand a uniform mass of indistinguishable citizens; yet, on the other, a plurality of individuals, each with their own unique features. When it first opened in October 2010, the "seeds" could be walked on—suggesting the people of China as downtrodden—but after ceramic dust that was released created health concerns, the work could only be viewed from the sides, or from above. This did not seem to diminish, and in some ways did enrich, its ultimate impact. As part of the installation there was a video feed enabling visitors to ask Ai questions after he had returned to his studio in Beijing. The questions and responses were recorded and subsequently put on the internet.[31]

The "seeds" themselves were "made in China," but not the China associated with cheap, mass-produced goods. This was the China of traditional crafts and specialized workshops. The "seeds" were made by local people in the province of the Chinese city of Jingdezhen, where porcelain had been made for Chinese emperors for thousands of years.

For Ai, the "seeds" also represented something else: sunflower seeds were a common street snack in China and were shared as a little indulgence among friends and families. As he recalls: "In China, when we grew up, we had nothing. . . . But for even the poorest people, the treat or the treasure we'd have would be the sunflower seeds in everybody's pockets."[32] For him, they symbolized the simple acts of friendship and moments of joy in the midst of lives of hardship. Finally, the "seeds" also refer to the sunflowers on propaganda posters, with their faces turned to Mao and his red sun halo as the source of all life bringing light.[33]

---

30. See Tate, "Tate Modern Exhibition: The Unilever Series."
31. See Tate, "Ai Weiwei, a One-to-One."
32. Ai, in Ai et al., "Quotes from a Conversation with Ai Weiwei," lines 1–2.
33. For more on the installation *Sunflower Seeds*, see Ai, *1000 Years of Joys and Sorrows*, 276–77, 283–86.

Ai Weiwei, *Sunflower Seeds*, 2008–10. Handcrafted porcelain. Tate Modern, London, England. Photo taken May 17, 2011.

While *Remembering* was a direct response to a specific human rights incident, *Sunflower Seeds* is a more oblique and general comment on Chinese culture and society. Yet, *Remembering* and *Sunflower Seeds* were only the beginning. When, about a year after the earthquake, Ai found out that local people were putting up the mangled rebar for sale as scrap metal, he decided to buy the lot. Although not even sure then what to do with it, he wanted to avoid this "evidence" being melted down and forgotten. Once the rods had been transported to his studio, he gathered a team of blacksmiths and instructed them to straighten them out, one by one, until they were restored to their pre-earthquake state.

Detention

By that time, all Ai's activities were under constant surveillance, with the first security cameras installed outside his studio house shortly after the start of his Citizens' Investigation in July 2008. Looking for reasons to silence him, the Government arrested Ai on April 3, 2011, at Beijing International Airport for alleged tax evasion and other "economic crimes" against the state. Significantly, he had been due to board a plane to Taiwan to attend the first large survey exhibition of his work in a Chinese-speaking country. Instead, he was hooded and taken to a secret facility where he was detained in a small windowless cell, watched over constantly by two guards. Back home, his studio was raided and his hard drives and computers confiscated. His wife, Lu Qing, his studio staff, and several lawyers were arrested and detained, and were not told anything about Ai's whereabouts. Interestingly, Ai's business account books were left untouched, raising doubts about the police's stated reason for his arrest.[34]

It was only because of a large international campaign that Ai, after eighty-one days, was released.[35] At the same time, he was forbidden to go online or to speak to the media about his detention. He had to ask permission to go out, and was not allowed to leave Beijing or, for that matter, China, as the police were holding on to his passport. As a result, he missed several openings of exhibitions of his abroad.

It was during his detention that he started to reflect on the hardships suffered by his late father, and regretted that he had not taken more opportunities to ask him about his experiences of state oppression. This sparked the idea to write down his father's and his own life story for his son, Ai Lao, so that he, when he was older, would have the opportunity to learn about his family's history.

Straight

In his memoir, Ai recalls that one of the first things he heard upon his return to his studio after his release in July 2011 was the clanging of metal by his assistants, who had continued their labor to straighten the rods despite the uncertainty about Ai's future.[36] When, after two years of hard work, all two hundred tons of twisted rods were finally straightened, Ai used the materials

---

34. See Ai, *1000 Years of Joys and Sorrows*, 305.

35. For more about his arrest and detention, see Ai, *1000 Years of Joys and Sorrows*, 294–327.

36. See Ai, *1000 Years of Joys and Sorrows*, 333.

to create both an amazingly simple *and* a most multi-layered work of art called *Straight* (2008–12). He had the rods arranged in piles of varying lengths and heights within the overall shape of a large rectangle. The result was an exquisite, minimalist floor sculpture with a gently undulating surface, both peaceful and ominous in its allusion to the seismic swelling and surging of the earth below. Viewed from the side, it can be seen to resemble the curves of a Richter scale graph. The individual rods could be said to represent the individuals that had perished on that fatal day.

Like much of Ai's work, *Straight* draws on the modern art he encountered in New York. It echoes, for example, some of the minimalism of sculptures by Carl Andre (*Equivalent VIII*, 1966) or Donald Judd (*Untitled*, 1969). Unlike these, however, Ai's work is not merely purely formalist but brims with multi-layered metaphoric meaning. Its monumental size alone creates a physical, "sublime" experience of feeling overwhelmed.

Ai Weiwei, *Straight*, 2008–12. Steel. Royal Academy of Arts, London, England. Photo taken September 15, 2015. Photo by Malcolm Park editorial.

Straight also hints at the conceptualism and "readymades" of Marcel Duchamp (*Fountain*, 1917) and Andy Warhol (*Brillo Soap Pads*, 1969); but, again, his use of the "found" rods is not merely to raise inhouse philosophical questions about definitions of art and non-art, but rather to pose questions about the concrete materials themselves—their origins, context, and ways of use. They are a reminder of the fact that these strong rods did not provide the children the protection they were meant to give had the schools been built to proper standards.

Ai has a strong interest in materials and processes of production. He celebrates traditional skills and craft because of its understanding of a material's potential and, as his sculptures made out of antique furniture show, often pushes its boundaries. Ai himself is a highly-skilled draughtsman, having learned drawing from his father's artists' friends while in exile.[37] Both *Straight* and *Sunflower Seeds* took years to make, and involved numerous skilled laborers and crafts people. In the case of *Sunflower Seeds*, each ceramic "seed" required over twenty different stages to produce. From the original cutting and firing to the final sanding and painting, it had taken 1,600 skilled artisans two-and-a-half years to manufacture and paint the "seeds."[38] The straightening of the steel rods, too, had taken over two years, each rod requiring thirty hammer strokes.

Straight was first shown at the survey exhibition, "Ai Weiwei: According to What," at the Hirshhorn Museum in Washington, DC (2012–13), followed by the Venice Biennale (2013), and the Art Gallery of Ontario in Toronto (2013). In 2015, it was the large centerpiece of a comprehensive retrospective at the Royal Academy in London (2015). Because Ai was still not allowed to leave China, he had co-curated the exhibition remotely from his studio in Beijing, advising staff on site by means of screen images as "through a mirror."[39] Just under two months before the opening, his passport was returned as unexpectedly and inexplicably as was its confiscation. The President of the Royal Academy heard the news while writing his Foreword for the exhibition's catalogue.[40]

An integral part of *Straight* is the long list of names of the children that Ai had been able to collect. When the installation was shown in Toronto, three hundred volunteers read out the names during a four-hour performance—*Say Their Names, Remember*. The recording was incorporated into the installation allowing visitors to hear the names while reading them.[41]

---

37. See Ai and Obrist, *Ai Weiwei Speaks*. For an interview about the background and making of *Straight*, see Royal Academy of Arts, "Ai Weiwei in Conversation with Tim Marlow."

38. See Tate, "Ai Weiwei—Sunflower Seeds."

39. Ponsford, "Ai Weiwei."

40. See LeBrun, "President's Foreword," 6.

41. See Art Gallery of Ontario, "Say Their Names, Remember—I"; Art Gallery of Ontario, "Say Their Names, Remember—II"; Toronto Star. "Say Their Names."

Ambivalence

Prior to 2000, the Chinese Government had been largely antagonistic towards contemporary art. But after witnessing its growing success on the international art market, contemporary art came to be seen as a useful asset to raise the country's profile and promote its "soft power." This also applied to the Government's dealings with Ai. Keen to be seen to be liberal in their attitude towards subversive art, the Government had even condoned Ai's controversial exhibition "Fuck Off" being shown at a private gallery alongside the Third Shanghai Biennale in 2000, albeit that the exhibition was only open to international visitors.[42]

In 2002, following his growing fame as an architect, Ai was invited by the Swiss architectural firm Herzog & de Meuron to serve as "the Chinese art consultant" on the team tasked by the Chinese Government to design the Beijing National Stadium that was to hold the Olympic Games in the summer of 2008. The resulting "Bird's Nest" design was to fuse modern Western architecture with traditional Chinese ceramics design.[43]

In January 2008, just five months before the earthquake, Ai had been awarded the lifetime achievement award at the Chinese Contemporary Art Lifetime Achievement Award, and, in March of that same year, had been invited by a local government official to build a large new studio in a rural area on the outskirts of Shanghai with a view to developing a similar art district as Ai had created in Beijing. Even so, as soon as it was finished two years later, state officials ordered its demolition on the grounds that it lacked the required planning permissions.[44]

Such events show the difficulties Ai and other artists face in negotiating the fine line between being able to work as independent, creative artists and being used by the state for its self-serving propaganda. Looking back, Ai regrets having got involved with the stadium: "The Beijing Olympics have oppressed the life of the general public with the latest technologies and a security apparatus of 700,000 guards.... It was merely a stage for a political party to advertise its glory to the world.... I became disenchanted because I realised I was used by the government to spread their patriotic education. Since the Olympics, I haven't looked at (the stadium)."[45]

---

42. Zhang and Frazier, "Playing the Chinese Card," 10.

43. For more on his work on the "Bird's Nest," see Ai, *1000 Years of Joys and Sorrows*, 221–26, 232, 249–50.

44. For more on the building of his new studio and its subsequent demolition, see Ai, *1000 Years of Joys and Sorrows*, 287–90. See also Locke, "Chronology," 79.

45. Ai, cited in Artlyst, "Ai Weiwei," lines 14–17. See also Ai, *1000 Years of Joys and Sorrows*, 249–50.

It was, however, the earthquake and the Government's response that left an indelible impression on him: "Sometimes when I make an artwork . . . it requires my life. This is quite a responsibility. It can be unpredictable and dangerous. If you cut into a tree and look at its rings, you can see certain years have left more of a mark in the wood. That's what the Sichuan earthquake did to me."[46]

Art and Activism

Ai is not only ambivalent about the Chinese art world, but also about that of the West with its circuit of art critics, curators, and collectors. He deplores its elitism, exclusivism, and commercialism, and is equally wary of being annexed by it. Despite being ranked the number one influential contemporary artist in the world by *The Art Review* "Power 100" in 2011, he carries his international fame and success lightly: "Art should be recognized, yes, but not in the form of expensive collectibles to be deposited in MoMA [New York's Museum of Modern Art] storage to molder—that's simply a waste. My vision of contemporary art took a very different form. To me, art is in a dynamic relationship with reality, with our way of life and attitude to life, and it should not be placed in a separate compartment. I have no interest in art that tries to keep itself distinct from reality."[47] For Ai, there is no real division between art and activism: art is a "form of social intervention, promoting the values of justice and equality."[48]

Straight functions both as an autonomous work of art for aesthetic contemplation in a gallery *and* as a public memorial, defying common modernist assumptions that these two roles cannot be combined. Public memorials play important roles in processing painful memories, both individually and collectively. For Ai, a nation that cannot face its past has no future. As he puts it: "To remove the memory of the past is to rob what is left of an individual, because our past is all we have. Without it, there is no such thing as a civilised society or nation. Any attempt to destroy, remove or distort memory is the act of an illegitimate power."[49]

Sadly, the very people for whom this memorial is primarily meant—the parents and families of the children—are not able to see the work, at least not in China where all Ai's works are banned. Even so, *Straight* can still play

---

46. Ai, "The Artwork That Made Me the Most Dangerous Person in China," lines 75–78.
47. Ai, *1000 Years of Joys and Sorrows*, 234.
48. Ai, *1000 Years of Joys and Sorrows*, 350.
49. Ai, "The West is Complicit," lines 54–57.

an important prophetic role by drawing attention to injustice and the plight of others, and by calling those responsible to account. As he points out, "the freedom that Westerners so enjoy loses its meaning if the West does not fight for freedom elsewhere."[50] Ai considers the West's avoidance of issues of freedom of speech and citizen's rights in its business dealings with China as "one of the most glaring moral failures of our time ... [and] tantamount to a neocolonialist exploitation of developing nations."[51]

Ai himself now lives in the West as a kind of political refugee. After his release from detention in 2009, he was put under increasing surveillance with the police having built a small two-story building right next to his compound with a window directly facing his front gate. All his comings and goings were meticulously recorded and he was followed by plain clothes police officers wherever he went.[52] The final straw was his discovery that they also took photographs of his two-year-old son Ai Lao in his stroller. At that point he felt that it was no longer safe for his family to stay in Beijing. As he wrote in his memoir: "What father would not recoil at the thought that he cannot protect his own child? I could practically feel a lurking assailant breathing down my neck."[53] In August 2014, his partner Wang Fen and their son left Beijing for Berlin, followed by Ai a year later as soon as he had been handed back his passport in July 2015. In 2019, they moved to Cambridge for Ai Lao's education, but Ai also has a base in Portugal where he spends much of the year.

Freedom

Ai is as critical of the West's individualism and capitalist consumerism as he is of China's totalitarianism and egalitarian socialism. Reflecting on his time in New York, he comments: "I came from a society where everything's restricted. Everything. Suddenly, you come to a place where even if you were found dead in your apartment, nobody would care. . . . You can call it freedom, but you also can call it something else. It is an entirely different society."[54]

He is similarly shocked by the refugee crisis and the scenes he saw on Lesbos, the Greek island where many refugees landed in fragile boats: "This is Europe, and I never expected that this could happen. Not even in

50. Ai, *1000 Years of Joys and Sorrows*, 350.
51. Ai, *1000 Years of Joys and Sorrows*, 291.
52. See Ai, *1000 Years of Joys and Sorrows*, 333.
53. Ai, *1000 Years of Joys and Sorrows*, 343–44.
54. Ai, *Conversations*, 117.

my imagination could I expect to see people, on one side, desperately trying to save their own lives or their children's lives and, on the other side, nobody paying attention. . . . It seemed as if they didn't exist, as if they were ghosts, and of course ghosts don't exist."[55] Or, as he wrote in the Afterword to his memoir: "[Seeing these boats] broke apart all preconceived notions and confronted me with a world of suffering and desperation. Seeing [these boats] stirred me so deeply, it had the force of a sacred revelation."[56] Viewed in that light, it is telling that most of his post-Sichuan works are no longer focused on events in China but rather on crises globally—climate change (*Roots*, 2016), global migration (*Human Flow*, 2017), the arms race (*History of Bombs*, 2020), and others. For Ai, all these issues are deeply intertwined.

Freedom, for Ai, is not merely about saying and doing what you like, but also about speaking out on and standing up for human dignity and human rights. It was this understanding of freedom that sustained him when he was in detention and was told that he would be there for more than ten years: "At the time being an artist or not being an artist didn't seem very important. But what did make me satisfied was that I had spoken my mind clearly before I got into this situation. I had no regrets about having to stay there a long time for that reason."[57]

Religion

Ai is not religious, at least not in a traditional sense: "I definitely believe in some kind of God, but I still don't know what kind."[58] But his convictions and beliefs in justice and integrity resonate deeply with Christians and those of other faiths. For Ai, self-sacrifice is at the heart of all religion: "In any kind of religion, to save one life or to help one life is the highest ritual. Nothing can be higher than that."[59]

One of Ai's most powerful post-detention works has a religious title—*S.A.C.R.E.D.*—and was first displayed in the religious setting of the Church of Saint Antonin in Venice. The installation consists of six large iron diorama boxes, each with a small opening—similar to those found on a prison cell door—through which viewers can peer inside. Each box contains a tableau of the cell in which he was detained in 2009; each represents a different moment in what was his daily routine. Located in the church, the work evokes

55. Ai, *Conversations*, 99.
56. Ai, *1000 Years of Joys and Sorrows*, 365.
57. Marlow, "Ai Weiwei in Conversation," 23.
58. Ai, *Conversations*, 62.
59. Ai, *Humanity*, 7.

the stations of the cross, suggesting connections between Ai's ordeal and the martyrdom of the saints, even Christ. Ai himself would most definitely resist such interpretations. Instead, as John Tancock observes: "His riposte to detention is to turn the gaze of the world upon the actions of his oppressors. Through *S.A.C.R.E.D.* the watchers are becoming the watched."[60]

The fact that the detention cell in *S.A.C.R.E.D.* was reduced to half its size enabled people to feel that the experience was "more like a play than a reality."[61] Ai is a master in exposing the absurdity of the state's Kafkaesque measures and behavior, through playfulness and humor. Upon his release from detention—and as an act of defiance—Ai decorated all surveillance cameras outside his studio with a Chinese lantern and put out a daily bunch of fresh flowers into his bicycle basket parked near his front door.[62] He has made replica surveillance cameras and handcuffs out of jade and marble—precious materials traditionally associated with power and opulence—and put them on display to be admired as objects for aesthetic contemplation. Exactly a year after his arrest and detention, he installed his own "surveillance" webcams in his house (including one over his bed and one over his computer) with a livestream on the internet, letting the secret police know that he does not have any secrets, and showing his supporters that he is still alive and safe at home.[63] Arguably one of the best interventionist art projects of all time, it was banned and removed by police after only three days. He also made a music video—*Dumbass* (2013)—featuring him and two actor guards in his cell going through the daily rituals accompanied by Chinese heavy metal music.[64] Still suffering from nightmares, he finds this way of processing his traumatic experience a "kind of self-therapy."[65] Ai understands how art can "objectify"—in visual forms, sounds, and gestures—otherwise ineffable feelings so that they can be made available to the conscious mind. He also understands that socially engaged art does not have to sacrifice imagination or be message driven. Were that the case, it would lose its unique capacity to foster free and independent thinking. Art, understood as the imaginative exploration of our affective, lived experience, does not offer didactic assertions or prescriptive messages. Instead, it seeks

60. Rosbottom, "Architecture Can Also Be Silent," 50.
61. Marlow, "Ai Weiwei in Conversation," 21.
62. See Ai, *1000 Years of Joys and Sorrows*, 342.
63. See Branigan, "Ai Weiwei Installs Studio Webcams." See also Ai, *1000 Years of Joys and Sorrows*, 342.
64. See Shanghaiist, "Ai Weiwei."
65. Ai, cited in Branigan, "Dumbass," line 5.

to develop new aesthetic languages that can represent and capture as well as mold and shape the feelings and moods of a time.

Ai's hope for his own art is that it can, in some way, "change the spirit of the times."[66] But he has no illusions that it will indeed do so. He is acutely aware of the momentous challenges, as well as of his own frailty and weakness in the face of them. Ten days before his sudden arrest at Beijing Airport, he was asked whether he was scared of anything or worried about being detained. He replied: "As a person . . . I'm quite weak. . . . You have to constantly ask yourself if physically, mentally you are strong enough for that. I have to always, everyday ask myself, 'How long could I last, if I'm in extreme conditions such as jail?'"[67] The interviewer later referred to the comment as "eerily prophetic."[68]

The art produced by Ai can certainly be called "prophetic"; not in the sense of foretelling or intuiting future events—Ai always stresses the contingent and unexpected character of life—but rather in the sense of speaking truth to power. Ai never refrains from confronting corrupt authorities and calling out the injustices on their watch. This connects him with the prophets of the Hebrew Bible for whom prophecy often involves both foretelling and *forthtelling*. Like Ai, they often used imaginative forms of social intervention to convey their message. In one instance, Jeremiah is called to buy, wear, and bury a new waist sash and then to dig it up again, to find it ruined for further wear, in order to show how God would "ruin the pride of Judah and the pride of Jerusalem" (Jer 13:1–10). In another instance, he is told to buy a pot on the market and to smash it in front of the leaders of Israel to show how God would smash the people of Israel and Jerusalem "just as this potter's jar is smashed and cannot be repaired" (Jer 19:11). Unlike Ai, ancient Israel's prophets were aware that they were called by God directly to remind the Israelites of their divine covenant. But Ai's dropping of a precious urn can be seen to be no less "prophetic" in its exposure of the Chinese authorities' routine destruction of traditional temples and ancient antiques to make space for their hubristic program of modernization.

Ai's truth-telling, forensic, memorial art, stands in the kind of prophetic tradition that warns against social and cultural complacency.[69] Art, so Ai says, should be "a nail in the eye, a spike in the flesh, gravel in the shoe: the reason why art cannot be ignored is that it destabilizes what seems settled

---

66. Marlow, "Ai Weiwei in Conversation," 26.
67. Lodish, "China," lines 5–7.
68. Lodish, "China," line 2.
69. For a comparable movement, see Forensic Architecture, "Investigations."

and secure."[70] In that context, his self-professed weakness becomes a source of power: "I feel powerless all the time, but I regain my energy by making a very small difference that won't cost me much. I think many people give up because they don't know how to change just a little bit to reach a better position."[71] Or, as he put it in his memoir: "If in a pitch-dark room I find a single candle . . . I will light that candle. I have no choice."[72] May that serve as an inspiration for all those who seek to make art in a time of crisis.

Bibliography

Ai, Weiwei. *1000 Years of Joys and Sorrows: A Memoir*. Translated by Allan H. Barr. London: Bodley Head, 2021.

———. *Ai Weiwei: New York Photographs, 1983–1993*. Beijing: Three Shadows, 2010.

———. "Ai Weiwei on the Project That Awoke His Political Voice—The Start Podcast." *The Guardian*, February 15, 2018. https://www.theguardian.com/artanddesign/audio/2018/feb/15/ai-weiwei-on-project-political-voice-sichuan-earthquake-the-start-podcast.

———. *Ai Weiwei's Blog: Writings, Interviews, and Digital Rants, 2006–2009*. Edited by Lee Ambrozy. Cambridge: MIT Press, 2011.

———. "The Artwork That Made Me the Most Dangerous Person in China." *The Guardian*, February 15, 2018. https://www.theguardian.com/artanddesign/2018/feb/15/ai-weiwei-remembering-sichuan-earthquake.

———. *The Black Cover Book*. Hong Kong: Tai Tei, 1994.

———. *The Grey Cover Book*. Hong Kong: Tai Tei, 1997.

———. *Humanity*. Edited by Larry Wash. Princeton: Princeton University Press, 2018.

———. "So Sorry." *YouTube*, December 15, 2012. https://www.youtube.com/watch?v=MrL8WlHplqo.

———. "The West Is Complicit in the 30-year Cover-Up of Tiananmen." *The Guardian*, June 4, 2019. https://www.theguardian.com/commentisfree/2019/jun/04/china-tiananmen-square-beijing.

———. *The White Cover Book*. Hong Kong: Tai Tei, 1995.

Ai, Weiwei, and Brook Larmer. "Ai Weiwei." *Harvard Business Review*, April 2012. https://hbr.org/2012/04/ai-weiwei.

Ai, Weiwei, and Hans Ulrich Obrist. *Ai Weiwei Speaks: With Hans Ulrich Obrist*. London: Penguin, 2016.

Ai, Weiwei, and Nadim Samman. "'The Internet Is My Life and Twitter Is My Nation': Ai Weiwei Is Online." *Sleek*, March 9, 2015. https://www.sleek-mag.com/article/ai-weiwei-is-online-rare-earth.

Ai, Weiwei, et al. *Conversations*. New York: Columbia University Press, 2021.

Ai, Weiwei, et al. "Quotes from a Conversation with Ai Weiwei on 31 May 2010 and 1 June 2010, Beijing." https://www.tate.org.uk/whats-on/tate-modern/exhibition/unilever-series/unilever-series-ai-weiwei-sunflower-seeds/unilever-0.

70. Ai, *1000 Years of Joys and Sorrows*, 201.
71. Ai, in Ai and Larmer. "Ai Weiwei," lines 44–47.
72. Ai, *1000 Years of Joys and Sorrows*, 280.

Art Gallery of Ontario. "AGO LiveStream | Say Their Names, Remember—I." *YouTube*, July 27, 2016. https://www.youtube.com/watch?v=578VpKVTT7Q.

———. "AGO LiveStream | Say Their Names, Remember—II." *YouTube*, June 27, 2016. https://www.youtube.com/watch?v=D159XmvNAc8.

Artlyst. "Ai Weiwei: I Wish I Never Designed Birds Nest." https://www.artlyst.com/news/ai-weiwei-i-wish-i-never-designed-birds-nest.

Bracker, Alison. *Ai Weiwei: An Introduction to the Exhibition for Teachers and Students.* London: Royal Academy of Arts, 2015.

Branigan, Tania. "Ai Weiwei Installs Studio Webcams for Supporters and Security Services." *The Guardian*, April 3, 2012. https://www.theguardian.com/artanddesign/2012/apr/03/ai-weiwei-webcams-supporters-security-services.

———. "Chinese Police Detain 11 Who Planned to Attend Activist's Trial." *The Guardian*, August 12, 2009. https://www.theguardian.com/world/2009/aug/12/china-detentions-activist-trial-earthquake.

———. "Dumbass: Ai Weiwei Releases Heavy Metal Music Video." *The Guardian*, May 22, 2013. https://www.theguardian.com/artanddesign/2013/may/22/dumbass-ai-weiwei-music-video.

Forensic Architecture. "Investigations." https://forensic-architecture.org.

Hornby, Lucy. "Chinese Artist Ai Weiwei Makes Internet His Medium." *Reuters*, March 5, 2010. https://www.reuters.com/article/us-china-artist-aiweiwei/chinese-artist-ai-weiwei-makes-internet-his-medium-idINTRE62423620100305.

LeBrun, Christopher. "President's Foreword." In *Ai Weiwei*, edited by Tim Marlow and John Tancock, 6. London: Royal Academy of Arts, 2015.

Locke, Arian. "Chronology." In *Ai Weiwei*, edited by Tim Marlow and John Tancock, 66–97. London: Royal Academy of Arts, 2015.

Lodish, Emily. "China: Ai Weiwei's Prophetic Interview." *The World*, April 7, 2011. https://www.pri.org/stories/2011-04-07/china-ai-weiweis-prophetic-interview.

Marlow, Tim. "Ai Weiwei in Conversation." In *Ai Weiwei*, edited by Tim Marlow and John Tancock, 16–29. London: Royal Academy of Arts, 2015.

Ponsford, Matthew. "Ai Weiwei: Trapped in China, I Saw My Creations 'Through a Mirror.'" *CNN*, September 21, 2015. https://edition.cnn.com/style/article/ai-weiwei-royal-academy-passport/index.html.

Rosbottom, Daniel. "Architecture Can Also Be Silent." In *Ai Weiwei*, edited by Tim Marlow and John Tancock, 46–65. London: Royal Academy of Arts, 2015.

Royal Academy of Arts, "Ai Weiwei in Conversation with Tim Marlow: Part 2." https://vimeo.com/135463659.

Shanghaiist. "Ai Weiwei—Dumbass (Heavy Metal Music Video)." *YouTube*, May 21, 2013. https://www.youtube.com/watch?v=lyQZ-oLshOQ.

Tancock, John. "Born Radical." In *Ai Weiwei*, edited by Tim Marlow and John Tancock, 30–45. London: Royal Academy of Arts, 2015.

Tate. "Ai Weiwei, a One-to-One." https://www.tate.org.uk/art/artists/ai-weiwei-8208/ai-weiwei-one-one.

———. "Ai Weiwei—Sunflower Seeds | Artist Interview | Tate." *YouTube*, October 14, 2010. https://www.youtube.com/watch?v=PueYywpkJW8.

———. "Tate Modern Exhibition: The Unilever Series: Ai Weiwei: Sunflower Seeds, 12 October 2010–2 May 2011." https://www.tate.org.uk/whats-on/tate-modern/exhibition/unilever-series/unilever-series-ai-weiwei-sunflower-seeds.

———. "The Unilever Series: Ai Weiwei: Sunflower Seeds: Interpretation Text." https://www.tate.org.uk/whats-on/tate-modern/exhibition/unilever-series/unilever-series-ai-weiwei-sunflower-seeds/unilever.

Toronto Star. "Say Their Names." *YouTube*, August 19, 2013. https://www.youtube.com/watch?v=oeY9foHSJic.

Tung, Stephanie H. "Black, White, and Grey: Ai Weiwei in Beijing, 1993–1997." *Yishu* 16.6 (2017) 55–64.

Zhang, Lin, and Taj Frazier. "'Playing the Chinese Card': Globalization and the Aesthetic Strategies of Chinese Contemporary Artists." *International Journal of Cultural Studies* 20.6 (2015) 1–18.

16

What Do I Paint Now?

Alfonse Borysewicz

SOMETIME IN THE EARLY or mid-1990s a peculiar moment occurred (which now looking back seems prophetic) when my Jesuit mentor and friend for thirty years, Michael Paul Gallagher, SJ,[1] was visiting me in New York City. We met for lunch and caught up on various subjects. Before we said goodbye, Michael Paul had a strange request: he wanted to visit Trump Tower to ascertain, believe it or not, if he could pray there! We then walked over to Fifth Avenue and rode those now infamous escalators. He was silent as we went up and then right back down. I never asked him directly if his prayer attempt was what—successful? I was just bewildered by this whole episode. Who does that and why? Michael Paul died in 2015 and I still live here in the city, having endured the Trump years and now the COVID-19 pandemic; it has all taken its toll. Looking back, and filtering it as a man known for his "spiritual/religious" paintings, now in my sixties, the world has seemed to take on a darker hue. What do I paint now, and why?

Unlike previous epochs of painting where emphasis on spiritual emotion was beckoned from elaborate movement, vivid color wheels, and optical illusions, my painting engages the spiritual by being muddled, scratched, and scarred. These distortions, however, at least to me, reflect the quality of the sublime. This is obvious in two recent paintings, the first whose narrative bespeaks this theme of struggling to see (or to recognize) within and outside oneself. The first painting is my attempt to depict the resurrected Lord in the Gospel story about the road to Emmaus (Luke 24:13–35). Christ is a stranger, blurred, and struggling to emerge, to be seen again, among his disciples. In the story, of course, the disciples cannot recognize who they are walking with. They are riding the escalator blind, so to speak, like I was with my friend. Who does he think he is? Here in this place? Not only can our

---

1. Gallagher served as a professor at the Pontifical Gregorian University in Rome, and was the author of *Faith Maps*.

vision be blurred, but also our faith can be lacking, being with the Lord or with a friend. My painted image of the Lord, very textured, peeling almost, in pink, brown, and white, depicts one who yearns to be brought into focus, unbound, recognized, and, most importantly, to be in relationship with us. With persistent eyes, the self is opened to receive him—an *anagnorisis*, to know again—and, by extension, others in the breaking of the bread.

Alfonse Borysewicz, *Road to Emmaus*, 2017–20. Oil and wax on linen, 45.72 x 35.56 cm. Artist's collection.

The second painting, *NEOWISE COMET*, is about seeing externally, outside oneself; in this case, once in six thousand years something far away—the NEOWISE comet! I was fleeing New York City to Michigan for a week vacation of sorts while the comet was flying outside our solar system. My family beckoned me late at night to come out and look up at the night sky. It took a while to refocus my eyesight. I finally recognized its white tail between all the fingers pointing to it. Suddenly, I could feel my Icarus wings wanting to chance another flight towards the sun. Do I dare?

Both paintings speak of vision (or lack thereof) and of the effort it takes to really see—whether within or outside ourselves, whether it be someone on the path we meet or in another solar system. The plague of willing obfuscation in our current times is prevalent everywhere; not wanting to explore our inner selves or what lays beyond our walls. We have a call to ride that escalator, if you will, in the most impossible circumstances and uncomfortable places . . . to discover the more genuine creation God has bestowed on and within us.

Bibliography

Gallagher, Michael Paul. *Faith Maps: Ten Religious Explorers from Newman to Joseph Ratzinger*. London: Darton, Longman, and Todd, 2010.

Alfonse Borysewicz, *NEOWISE COMET*, 2017–20. Oil and wax on linen, 45.72 x 35.56 cm. Artist's collection.

17

Imagination and the Sacred

Contemporary Australian Fictions of Hybridity

Lyn McCredden

> Sometimes it seems to me that, in the end, the only thing people have got going for them is imagination. At times of great darkness, everything around us becomes symbolic, poetic, archetypal. Perhaps this is what dreaming, and art, are for.[1]

To be a writer of fiction in Australia, a profoundly hybrid nation—inhabited for sixty thousand years or more, violently colonized, and ambivalently offering a home to diasporic peoples—is a steep challenge. Who is your audience? Are you seeking to address all of your fellow citizens? A small group? One gender or many? Indigenous and/or non-Indigenous? The old cultures of former homelands? The future? Or just yourself? Over the past seventy years, authors have addressed themselves to this particularly plural set of parameters: writing to, or for, or beyond a nation which many have described as deeply secular and materialistic; a nation rapidly divorcing itself from the older religious traditions generated in Europe, and, equally, becoming aware of the ancient religions of Buddhism, Hinduism, Islam, and many others—which have been emerging as strong presences. Amongst all of this, and perhaps the most urgent questions—of Indigenous/non-Indigenous relations in Australia—what imaginative understandings of sacredness emerge in the late twentieth and early twenty-first centuries in such a place as this?

---

1. Garner, *Everywhere I Look*, 152.

Australian Secularity?

The Pew Research Center's 2014 report on national belief profiles states that "Many people in the Asian/Pacific and Latin American regions . . . link faith and morality. For example, Indonesians, Pakistanis, Filipinos, and Malaysians almost unanimously think that belief in God is central to having good values. People in El Salvador, Brazil, Bolivia, and Venezuela overwhelmingly agree. However, most Australians take the opposite position—that it is *not* necessary to be a believer to be a moral person."[2]

Further, in the Pew statistics, Australia came in at an extremely low 23 percent of the population (the fourth lowest globally) who thought that it was "necessary to believe in God to be moral."[3] Of course, the many factors of age, education levels, and ethnicity would complicate these statistics, but it is clear that the majority of Australians hold secular beliefs, especially in this instance, in relation to acting justly. From the middle of the twentieth century, and supporting this picture of secularity, the iconic words of historian Russell Ward, in his *The Australian Legend*, are often cited: the typical Australian is a "hard case . . . sceptical about the value of religion and of intellectual pursuits generally."[4]

However, within, and perhaps in response to, the many claims about entrenched Australian secularism, this essay will argue that in Australian imaginative writing post-1950 an amazing flow of subterranean sacred concerns and narratives is evident. This essay defines "the sacred" not merely as religion, or as denomination, and not just as institution, but rather as a sense of reality that embraces the places and times where meaning is encountered and made, both by individuals and communities. The sacred might be experienced in abstract terms, involving ideas, traditions, doctrines; but it is also earthy, material, involved in the here and now. In relation to "the sacred," "the imaginary" and "imagination" are often invoked by writers and literary scholars. All these categories are related to the visionary, artistic, sometimes subconscious worlds drawn on by writers and other artists. However, everyday definitions of "imaginary" and "imagination" might give us pause. The Merriam-Webster dictionary defines the "imaginary" as "existing only in imagination: lacking factual reality."[5] It is fascinating that the imaginary and its relative, "imagination," can be so easily reduced or dismissed by some, just as the sacred often is, and in similar ways: as illusory, the opposite of the hard-nosed, "sceptical," secular real.

2. Pew Research Center, "Worldwide," lines 20–30.
3. Pew Research Center, "Worldwide," line 8.
4. Ward, *The Australian Legend*, 2.
5. *Merriam-Webster*, s.v. "Imaginary," line 5.

Australian Fiction and the Sacred

This essay sets such oversimplifying polarities aside. It will ask what some of Australia's pre-eminent writers—exemplified here by Patrick White, Helen Garner, Nick Cave, Christos Tsiolkas, and Kim Scott—reveal about imagination and the sacred, across the past seventy years. While in 1958 *The Australian Legend* emphasized the "hard case" of Australian skepticism, musician and lyricist Nick Cave, in 2020, moves in a different direction. Cave has recently written out of the depths of personal loss and grief, of times when "things—both animate and inanimate—take on an added intensity and meaning . . . this feeling . . . of alertness to the inner-spirit of things—this humming—comes from a hard-earned understanding of the impermanence of things . . . our own impermanence. This lesson ultimately animates and illuminates our lives."[6]

This is a dual understanding, of the hard-earned, and of illumination, yoked together and experienced by those seeking to find and create a sacred purpose in imaginative writings, and in their lives. In his description of White, and of the impermanence and torturous ministrations of humanity upon itself, so evident in World War II, fellow writer David Malouf recalls White's returning to Australia in 1948. Malouf powerfully creates the world White had been living in "the over-refined and divided Europe of the 1930s, which he had watched slide towards the barbarous destruction of Barcelona in 1938, to be followed by London, Hamburg, Dresden, and the organised murder of the Nazi concentration camps."[7]

Indeed, an overwhelming, sometimes tragic sense of impermanence, and an understanding of human cruelty, informs White's work from very early in his career. Patrick White and Nick Cave might be separated by fifty years, one a reclusive Nobel Laureate and the other a popular singer and lyricist. However, Cave, responding frankly and with emotional rawness to questions from his audience on his blog *The Red Hand Files*, is not such a strange bedfellow when considering White and his twelve extraordinary, mid-century novels.

From White's middle period, across fifteen years in the 1950s to the 1960s, novels of immense imaginative and sacred struggle emerge: *The Tree of Man* (1955), *Voss* (1957), *Riders in the Chariot* (1961), *The Solid Mandala* (1966), and *The Vivisector* (1970). In these novels, White's central characters are characteristically outsiders, excluded and sometimes barely visible to their fellows. They are simpletons, like Mary Hare or Arthur Brown; obsessives like Voss; sometimes they are silent figures, unable to use words, like Stan Parker or Ruth Godbold; and there are the speckled "monsters"

---

6. Cave, "Issue #106," lines 26–28, 32–36.
7. Malouf, "Patrick White Reappraised."

such as Hurtle Duffield, or Theodora Goodman. But each of them is given some aspects of the visionary by White, able to reach beyond the vicious suburban landscapes that White creates; but equally, able to seek meaning within material and earthy realities. Each of these characters, in Cave's words, demonstrates, or grows towards, an "alertness to the inner-spirit . . . a hard-earned understanding of the impermanence of things."

Patrick White's *Voss* (1957)

In 1957, White published his fifth novel, *Voss*, which won the inaugural Miles Franklin Literary Award. White had arrived back in Australia in 1948, after the Second World War, which he spent as an intelligence officer, and six years living in the Middle East with his partner Manoly Lascaris. He had already begun to imagine something of the political and historical contexts from which *Voss*, with its austere German hero, emerged. Out of the barbarities of the war, the whirlpool of modernist experimentation in art, a gay, cosmopolitan man returned to Australia.

The first cover design for *Voss* was provided by Sidney Nolan, White's then friend, one of a number of painter friends—Roy de Maistre, Francis Bacon, Brett Whitely, and others—who White admired, and would, he said, have liked to have emulated.

Sidney Nolan, *Book jacket design for Patrick White's novel* Voss, *1957*, 1957. Ink, wash, wax crayon, pen, and ink on card, 8.9 x 13.9 cm. Mitchell Library, State Library of New South Wales and courtesy of The Trustees of the Sidney Nolan Trust, ML 743, Sydney, Australia.

This first cover suggests many of the core ideas of the novel: the lone, hubristic, somewhat awkward figure of Voss; the desolate, thinly populated Australian landscape "waiting" to be explored and fenced; the myopic man with his large spectacles, and at the same time the visionary, seeing what others could not see. As to whether Voss, modelled on the heroic, doomed figure of Ludwig Leichardt, and to a lesser extent that of Edward Eyre, can in any productive way be seen as a transcendent figure, needs further thought.

Arriving in 1840s colonial Sydney and preparing to enter with his expedition into the "unmapped" parts of Australia, Voss has unexpectedly encountered another human being who exhibits the capacity to understand and question him, intellectually, psychologically and emotionally: Laura Trevelyan, the niece of Voss's benefactor. Voss, troubled by his first meeting with Laura, is described in this way as he returns to his solitary rooms:

> At once the German, beneath his tree, was racked by the fresh mortification to which he had submitted himself. But it was a discipline for the great trials and achievements in store for him in this country of which he had become possessed by implicit right. Unseeing people walked the sandy earth, eating bread, or sat at meat in their houses of frail stone foundations, while the lean man, beneath his twisted tree, became familiar with each blade of withered grass at which he stared, even the joints in the body of the ant.[8]

It is not easy to put frames around the complex character of Voss: a man subjecting himself to mortification and self-abnegation, but also an ego seeking great achievements, above the calling of "unseeing people." In a famous interview, White described himself as "a lapsed Anglican egotist agnostic pantheist occultist existentialist would-be though failed Christian Australian."[9] We might describe Voss in some of these terms (perhaps not Anglican), but it is arguable that if he is depicted as an imperialist, then he is equally a searcher after meaning; if an egotist, then he is also deeply attentive to "each blade of withered grass," "the joints in the body of the ant."[10] Voss is someone who takes on the infinite, but who has an understanding of the "frail stone foundations" of humanity, living as "the lean man, beneath his twisted tree."[11] It is possible to hear humor in White's intensification of this image, the man beneath his tree, the lean man beneath his twisted tree. There is in the novel an undermining of the megalomania of heroism, its claims to knowing and possessing unequivocally, but there is also great admiration for the vision and purpose of the explorer.

8. White, *Voss*, 27.
9. Cited in Wetherell, "Uncheery Soul," 253.
10. White, *Voss*, 27.
11. White, *Voss*, 27.

White is arguably employing the figure of Voss to think through his own christology, his responses to God enfleshed, the fully human, earthy, bodily Son of God. Voss has been read as a transcendent, Christ-like figure, but also as a megalomaniac, an imperialist, fearful of women, an arrogant lone-traveler. He is certainly one of the most porous imaginative figures in literature, drawing a range of ambivalent responses from readers. But this is hardly surprising, as White himself, possibly the most poetic of Australian authors, long exhibited those centrally modernist, post-war traits of the imagination: uncertainty, ambivalence, unfinishedness. Multiplicity of meaning, and no single, monolithic meaning, characterizes such imaginative work.

British author Nicholas Shakespeare cites historian Manning Clark's story of a near-encounter with the great novelist, as Clark "passed [White] once in Sydney, walking down George Street, and was taken aback by White's expression. 'It is the face of a man who wants something he is never going to get . . . something possibly no human being can give him.' But what? Clark ruminated: 'a hunger for forgiveness in a man who places himself through his pride and pessimism, beyond the reach of forgiveness.'"[12]

As in White's aesthetics and psychology, so arguably in his theology. One critic describes White's journey with Christianity in this way: "he continued the cycle of attraction and repulsion with Anglican Christianity for many decades, before finally making 'a retreat into his private faith.'"[13] Critic George Watt summed up one thrust of the critical framing of White, in the following list of journal titles: "Prophets with Honour"; "Yearning for Sainthood"; "Confessions of St. Patrick"; "Glabrous Shaman or Centennial Park's Very Own Saint . . . ?" Watt, in 1994, argued of these titles: "the very terms of which are out of kilter with most definitions of literary modernism. According to popular perception in Academe, Western literature apparently ceased to bother about God, faith, or transcendence after 1900. This is not true of White."[14]

It is not hard to hear the skepticism oozing from such editorial witticisms. But White is, arguably, a step ahead of his editors. Rather than a pious circling around the figure of Voss, as a static symbol of meaning, the novel works through modernist approaches, with multiple, oscillating movements, rather than any straightforward plotline or set of meanings. For readers trying to read the novel, as much as for the figure of Voss himself, White places tensions: between attraction and repulsion of the earthly,

---

12. Shakespeare, "Patrick White," lines 105–8.

13. Michael Giffin citing White. Cited in Wetherell, "Uncheery Soul," 253. See also Giffin, *Patrick White and God*.

14. Watt, "Patrick White," 273.

libidinal flesh and its inevitable melting into nothing; between egotism and the annihilation of martyrdom; between myopia and vision. We are in the same christological territory here as in the 1988 Martin Scorsese film *The Last Temptation of Christ*. The figure of Voss, as with Scorsese's Christ, is an incarnational conundrum, even to himself. This reading of the novel's imaginative and theological restlessness, and its context in White's own beliefs and uncertainties, leads us to ask the central question of this volume, *Imagination in an Age of Crisis*: what role does the imagination play for artists and thinkers caught in the jaws of belief and un-belief?

Again, Nicholas Shakespeare gives fascinating insight into the ways imagination and creativity often operate, emerging out of chaos, seeking desperately for meaning, perhaps particularly in the post-WWII era:

> [White] claims to have conceived *Voss* during the London Blitz, in a bedsitter in Ebury Street, close to where he was born, as German bombs rained down. But *Voss*'s lineaments can be discerned further back, in a poem about a 'mad Messiah' that White wrote at Cheltenham, where his mother had sent him at thirteen for an English education, and in which he tried to make sense of "the emotional chaos of which I was in possession." In that poem, a man with "wild eyes and flowing beard" cries out: "I am the Resurrection and the Life." At school in Cheltenham (which he remembered as "a prison") and afterwards at King's College, Cambridge, White looked just like Voss—thin, angular, with those blue eyes—and behaved in the same prickly and perverse way. "He didn't like himself very much, and had times of loathing himself," said his cousin Betty Withycombe. "His mouth was always set very hard. He had a strain of stubbornness in him."[15]

In terms of the broader historical context, sociologists may argue that the 1950s was socially a time of polarities, politically and aesthetically: peace at last, but with acute memories and experiences of war; economic boom, but many hungry souls stripped of vocation and a place to belong; reunited families, but with scars and traumas persisting. Enter the imagination of White, humorist and curmudgeon, European and Australian, with a powerful vision of earthed, visceral, human life, but equally with a desire for the transcendent. The imagination in White's oeuvre produces both salvific and doomed possibilities—comforting, transforming, renewing, but also productive of a hellish vision. In Laura Trevelyan's often quoted words, from *Voss*, when the man of vision or obsession disappears into the

---

15. Shakespeare, "Patrick White," lines 95–104.

land: "true knowledge only comes of death by torture in the country of the mind."[16] Knowledge and death exist, side by side, in *Voss*, this simultaneity leaving us with an understanding of the imagination as a crucible of uncertainty, ambivalence, unfinishedness.

Patrick White's *The Solid Mandala* (1966)

The Solid Mandala, published a decade after *Voss*, moves the scene from colonial Sydney and the "outback," to the poisonous and farcical fictional suburb of Sarsaparilla in the 1950s, a place where on Sunday people go home from church "to sharpen knives for the week."[17] White depicts twin brothers Waldo and Arthur Brown, two manifestations of *suburbanum hominem* in what is a dreary, parochial Australia. Waldo embodies the petty hatreds and denials, the arrogance, and the suffocation of joy and eroticism, that White observed in his home country. Arthur, the supposed simpleton, is one of White's suburban saints. He finds, makes, and shares meaning and sacred purpose in his small, circumscribed life. Arthur navigates life as a victim of his brother's disgust for his doltish ways and club foot; but he is never simply a victim. He sees and feels the suffering of those around him, struggling to create his idiosyncratic system for making and sharing new meaning. The marbles Arthur, boy-like, carries in his pockets become symbols of the eponymous mandala, which in turn becomes a symbol of totality. Arthur does not necessarily *know* the meaning or significance of the mandala, but he *does something*, transforming the material objects into tools or symbols with which to alleviate the pain he sees in his neighbors' lives. Accompanying his neighbor Mrs. Poulter on a picnic into the bush, Arthur spontaneously begins to dance: "Till in the centre of the mandala he danced the passion of all their lives, the blood running out of the backs of his hands, water out of the hole in his ribs. His mouth was a silent hole, because no sound was needed to explain."[18]

As critic Anthony Uhlmann persuasively argues in his essay "The Symbol in Patrick White":

> It seems that the mad, foolish, the failed, themselves do not attempt an understanding. Rather than fixating on the meaning of totality, Arthur Brown sets out to create or find the mandala. That is, rather than attempting an understanding, he creates a sense of the meaningful beyond the obvious. Arthur Brown

---

16. White, *Voss*, 451.
17. White, *The Solid Mandala*, 49.
18. White, *The Solid Mandala*, 267.

creates the mandala, not the understanding of the mandala ... it may be that it is not that there is no meaning but, rather, that there is no communicable understanding, that there is an apprehension which does not necessarily involve or allow comprehension and is, therefore, not easily shared.[19]

As Arthur dances the mandala, silently, wordlessly, for his neighbor in her pain, he bears for White the marks of a moving, clown-like Christ, the bleeding hands, the pierced ribs, the compassion. No certitudes or dogmas emerge from his lips—"a silent hole"—no explanations are shared. He is a child, a figure on the edge of absurdity. But he is not seen as such by his audience. Critic Rob Tomlinson writes attentively of this culminating scene:

> Just before Arthur's gifting of the gold mandala marble to Mrs. Poulter ... Arthur dances a mandala. ... It is barely two pages in length, yet consists of a wordless, hypnotic, semi-epileptic trance of a dance that Arthur spontaneously performs in front of Mrs. Poulter. Like some shamanic ritual, the elderly twin shuffles from corner to corner of an imaginary Mandaic square in the space formed by a curved bank of blackberry bushes. It is an intensely devotional performance, with the four corners being associated in Arthur's mind with Mrs. Poulter, the trio of himself and Dulcie and Leonard, his brother Waldo, and himself alone. Arthur performs it in silence and observes that Mrs. Poulter is "obviously moved" by this. At the end, his energy is spent and he falls down and in a stupor. It is clearly intended as a unifying episode, a kind of crescendo delivered with White's prose elevating Arthur onto a transcendental plane.[20]

It is worthwhile thinking about how such a passage seeks to affect readers. Some will see it as White's imagination warped by "transcendental" desires and might either embrace or reject such "meaning." But what *is* the scene's meaning? Arthur's meaning? Arthur is in a trance, but no solid or religious meaning emerges. Or does it? Arthur has made his sacred vision and his meaning, and has shared it with Dulcie and Mrs. Poulter, and himself.

However, as Uhlmann has further argued, the two central figures, Waldo and Arthur, representing denial and affirmation, are complex foils for each other, just as opposites define their other: "Affirmation affirms meaning, but when it collapses it is not that there is now no meaning; rather, it is no longer possible to say exactly what its meaning is. Meaning itself then does not collapse; it merely returns us to uncertainty. Yet

---

19. Uhlmann, "The Symbol in Patrick White," 72.
20. Tomlinson, "The Solid Mandala," lines 243–53.

paradoxically, with the new failure of denial, while meaning is now uncertain, it is now certain that there is meaning."[21]

At the end of the novel, Arthur fears and mourns the death of his brother, even as he sees him clearly, in all his denial and anger. But Arthur on his own does not represent or embody affirmation and meaning. Sometimes meaning is in the silence, the uncertainty, the proper humbling of mortality. For Arthur, seeking to give the gift of the mandala, its totality, its empathic meaning, to his neighbors and to himself, there must be spentness, stupor, the marks of crucifixion. Just as for Nick Cave, in the midst of grief, "this feeling . . . of alertness to the inner-spirit of things—this humming—comes from a hard-earned understanding of the impermanence of things . . . our own impermanence."[22] Arthur's totality involves fragmentation and loss, a hovering close to absurdity. In this novel, and equally in White's *The Riders in the Chariot* (1961), it is in the speckled, the hybrid, the excluded, that the grains of sacredness can be found.

Fictions of Sacredness: Patrick White and Christos Tsiolkas

Patrick White's imagination often engages with the absurd, its language and narrative innovations extremely challenging for many (most?) readers then and now. Not only is it the hybrid who move closest to the sacred, but further, White also sees such capacities in characters that embody an "excremental vision . . . which sees poetry and wonder and God in the viscosity and excrement of life."[23] This description applies to many of White's works, and also to another, younger novelist, Christos Tsiolkas, who was twenty-five, and just beginning his career as a writer when White died in 1990. Tsiolkas expresses how deeply he was indebted to White in a critical volume, *Patrick White: Writers on Writers* (2018). In novels such as *Loaded* (1995), *Dead Europe* (2005), *The Slap* (2008), *Barracuda* (2013), and *Damascus* (2019), Tsiolkas takes his readers on a gyroscopic journey through hellish, fantastic landscapes, as well as more realistic, suburban settings arguably no less horrifying and passive-aggressive than is White's Sarsaparilla. What operations does the imagination of this novelist perform? And what affiliations can we see between these two novelists?

In *Patrick White*, Tsiolkas describes what he sees as the core of White's sacred vision:

21. Uhlmann, "The Symbol in Patrick White," 75.
22. Cave, "Issue #106," lines 32–35.
23. Giffin, *Arthur's Dream*, 13–14.

a defiant celebration of the wanderer, the exile and the pilgrim; and also, a spiritual dimension to his writing, a language of transcendence that finds the sacred in the material world and in the accidental moments when strangers bestow kindness on one another. White's notion of the sacred is never sentimental; nor is his championing of the exile. A suspicion of madness and self-delusion taints . . . the gargantuan folly of explorer Johann Ulrich Voss. . . . But madness, folly, and naivety do not diminish any of [his] characters. Their vividness is a transcendence that we as readers comprehend and are shaken by. This is the foundation of my love for Patrick White.[24]

It is this nomad spirit that Tsiolkas identifies as (ironically) White's imaginative and spiritual home, against which all the ugliness, pettiness, racism, classism, and unimaginative stasis of Australian suburbia are judged. This notion of the nomad, the excluded or self-excluded one, recurs, differently, in Tsiolkas's suburban worlds—multicultural-, working-, and middle-class suburbs based on his Melbourne experiences. In *Loaded*, *Barracuda*, and *The Slap* these suburbs are peeled back in all their raw material crassness and tribal competitiveness. *Barracuda* is visceral in its exposing of the classist, sexist, and racist foundations of Australian middle-class life. As young Danny begins his career at the private school which has awarded him a swimming scholarship, we read:

> The gold leaf of the lion's crown and the crucifix and the burning flame. Cunts College. It's my first day at Cunts College, thought Danny. His mother pushed him out of the car and he was trying to hide in the folds of the jacket which seemed heavy on his shoulders and the thick fabric of the trousers was chafing the skin between his thighs and behind his knees. He thought he must stink of chlorine, and that he must be walking like a retard, he was walking slowly up the drive that seemed too long and too wide, too grand for a school, all that bluestone and gravel, all those statues and granite steps, the buildings reeking of the centuries, not looking like a school, no portables, no concrete sheeting, looking more like a cathedral, a cathedral where the Pope would live. Danny walked up one two three four five six seven steps, following the stream of boys through an arch and into an entrance hall as big as a house, taller than a house, lined with stained-glass windows that towered above him, smooth

---

24. Tsiolkas, *Patrick White*, 25.

cream walls from which portraits of old men stared down at him, all moustaches and bald pates.[25]

Tsiolkas introduces us, through the eyes of Danny the working-class Greek boy, to a world of self-congratulatory privilege as prickly and discomfiting as is his new uniform. The conjoining of material privilege with the trappings of the institutional sacred and religious—the crucifix, the school's appearance of a cathedral where the pope would live, the stained-glass windows—introduces us to a hierarchical world where Danny is about to be tortured.

Similar in some ways to Helen Garner's short story collection, *Cosmo Cosmolino* (1992), Tsiolkas's social satire links arms with an idiosyncratic, individual journey of physical, psychological, and spiritual transformation. For both Garner and Tsiolkas, it is a deeply secular world, but one in which sacred struggle becomes evident. As we have seen in White's works, there is an exploration of sacred struggle inseparable from the secular world, infused with uncertainty and ambivalence in the central characters. Tsiolkas's fiction fuses the rejection of social inequalities and injustice with a positive vision of alternative, sacred possibilities, imagined and idealistic. The visceral, spotty, hybrid, and unruly Danny is a nomad in the world of high privilege. He is taken deep into the bowels of loss and degradation, but he is also the hero.

However, it is in Tsiolkas's monumental and more linguistically experimental, risk-taking novels, *Dead Europe* and *Damascus*, that the nomad spirit fully emerges. As does the visceral. *Damascus* opens with the brutal stoning of a sinful woman condemned to death for blasphemy. Watching on is the self-righteous figure of Saul. The opening section is entitled "Saul 1: 35 Anno Domini," and we know we are setting out on a torturous journey—across time, and in the life of Saul, who is to become Paul. After watching the stoning, Saul is caught in conversation with the young Arab gravedigger:

> "She denied the Lord," Saul answers in Syrian, "the Lord of her people. She abandoned her family. She had to be punished for her blasphemy."
>
> At this, the old man snorts. "She was just a chick of a girl—what does she know of blasphemy?"
>
> He wipes his nose and rubs his hand across his straggle of chest hairs. His next words are a sneer: "Did you hunt her down? Was she one of yours?"
>
> As if Saul were a filthy mercenary, a slave trader, a collector of tax for the dirty Romans.

25. Tsiolkas, *Barracuda*, 15–16.

A thousand curses are on his lips. Shut your foul mouth, you Arab piece of shit. Child of a whore. But no sound comes forth. His head is heavy, the light is banished and the curses are snatched from his lips. The din is a madness in his head, and he has to cover his mouth to keep the words from escaping: If you are without sin, then cast your stone. Brazen, unholy words; the devil's words. He knew those words were for him, that she was judging him. As if he were the one who stood condemned.

"Are you ill, uncle?" The naked boy is before him, his hand raised, seemingly about to touch Saul.

He jerks away from the filthy deathworker. "Do your foul work," he spits at him. "You've been paid."

Saul turns from them, abandons the judgement ground, and climbs up the hill, thistles scratching across his calves. He can hear the vile old Stranger laughing; he hears the thud as the girl's corpse is thrown onto the cart.

Someone calls out after him; the torrent of violence in his head is such he can't discern if it is the apprentice or the old man.

"Do we bury her or do we burn the cunt?"

To earth or to fire, the girl is lost to the Lord. He does not reply.

*

Death's breath is on his skin; he can smell it. The blood and meat and sin and poison of the girl. He wants to be careful not to touch anyone, lest he stain them with his pollution, but the market-sellers have set up their tables and the streets are full of people and slaves, beggars and labourers, scavenging dogs and bleating goats. Saul keeps close to the walls, ducks into narrow passages to avoid contact. In this way, slowly, he weaves through the back streets and manages to avoid the crowds. He breathes deeply with relief. He has reached the wide marble steps leading to the Temple. The mansion of the Lord reaches up to the heavens, the smooth face of the rock glistens from the touch of the sun. He smells incense and burning wood; wisps of smoke curl around him. He unties his sandals, delivers his prayer, and enters the bathing pool.

He washes death off himself.

Finally, rocking back and forth on his knees, he begs the Lord, the One, the only One, to cleanse him and forgive him.

I am not a filthy child killer.[26]

---

26. Tsiolkas, *Damascus*, 9–11.

Tsiolkas's prose here is earthy and sensual, with its logics of smell and sound, touch and taste. It is a sensuality continually butting up against unresolved feelings and thoughts in the seemingly untouchable central character. Saul's understanding of sacred duties and principles is given ironic juxtapositioning with his violent, unholy thoughts. The words he would express to separate himself from the deathworkers and the stoned girl are almost physically stopped up in his mouth, as he negotiates the proximity of earth and death to his own holy self-image.

But Tsiolkas's nomadic imagination is already at work, fracturing the strict borders between Arab and Jew, sinner and righteous leader, rational and sensual humanity. Saul is compelled to tell the Arab deathworker "shut your foul mouth," but it is Saul who cannot or does not speak—it is his mouth that is shut. He has condemned the sinning girl to death, but it is *he* who washes death off himself, asking for cleansing and forgiveness.

Helen Garner's Secular Meditations

For White and Tsiolkas, sacredness is most often defined by its absence, even its opposite. Satire is White's way of doing that, through his repudiation of vicious hypocrisies and lack of imagination in the characters he creates. For Tsiolkas, it is pushing the libidinal and taboo to extremes, in order to "get at" what is (still, possibly) productive of meaning and justice. Sacredness, or just a glimpse, a possibility of meaning or purpose or joy or insight, is similarly defined by its absence in Helen Garner's description of Janet, her central character in *Cosmo Cosmolino*: "She scorned many things. All she believed in was the physical, the practical, the stoical. Bite the bullet, she said. Plug on, one foot in front of the other and keep going. She had no children. Her family was scattered. She was too proud to take advice or sympathy: to a woman like Janet, nothing is more enfeebling than pity: and so she fell out with all her friends."[27]

There is a tension here, if not a contradiction, between the dogged, dull plugging on of the character, and the way the energy of Garner's prose pulses—those short, crisp sentences, reflecting a sinewy if repressed vigor, in the author, and also unrealized by Janet at first. Such vigor seems to undermine, or at least set up a gap in which the reader might want to question the nature of, Janet's repression. So much scorning and stoicism, everything practical and resolved, plugging on, supposedly. In the wonderfully named "Sweetpea Mansions," surely, the reader might be prompted to look out for the old serendipities of late '60s urban bohemianism: shared

---

27. Garner, *Cosmo Cosmolino*, 52.

houses (possibly not including the hell-holes in Garner's *Monkey Grip*), warm echoes of connection, shared meanings, even renewed understandings of the sacred in community? Instead, Garner at first writes purposively and overtly of failed dreams, of Janet's bleak nostalgia, of the characters' thoughtlessness and lack of community, and of ways to repress such emotions and needs, so that Sweetpea Mansions becomes an almost gothic scene of the *anti-sacred*, a series of secular dead-ends: Janet's abortive communal dinner where no-one turns up; Maxine's ironized baby-longings, her petty thefts, and her own not-quite-immaculate conception and angelic escape; and Ray and Alby's fecklessness. The leftovers of 1960's idealisms.

And yet, the tiny pin-pricks of remembered, shared meaning, remembered joy, keep Janet, if not afloat, then recalling possibilities *against her own will*:

> sometimes, now, in the empty house, she heard her own footsteps hurry past on the other side of a wall, her own voice, more girlish, laughing in a closed room. Unwelcome memories of happiness rustled behind her or pounced from doorways. She remembered being the youngest person present, being a student with a job; how it was to tie on an apron and slap together sandwiches in a shop, taking orders, chiacking with the customers; to have sore feet from standing up all day to serve; and later, the surprised pride of being on a payroll and a promotions list, of belonging to a union and knowing where she fitted into her society.[28]

In a fascinating essay on Garner, critic and writer Teagan Bennett Daylight writes in praise of this section of *Cosmo Cosmolino*: "The sheer careering speed of this passage, our original third person meeting with the protagonist Janet, is phenomenal. This book is full of trams, chattering, and chiming their ways down avenues; and the book itself is like a tram. It chatters and chimes and rocks but never leaves the tracks; it speeds absolutely surely through its landscape."[29] I agree with this description of Garner's writerly deftness, the energy and verve of the prose. But again, we might ask about something else that hovers, or bubbles, beneath the prose, and in the other two stories of *Cosmo Cosmolino*, "Recording Angel" and "The Vigil": a less tram-like—slower, unspoken—yearning for what has been lost, a mixture of past connections, friendship, youth, purpose, family, but also for some hope of futurity. Hopelessness hovers, but is papered over with busyness, stoicism, scorn, and reliance on coincidence.

---

28. Garner, *Cosmo Cosmolino*, 53.
29. Daylight, "Consider This," lines 133–38.

For some readers, a desire to move *with* the *energy* of the writing, and with the strength of the unspoken longings of the characters for meaning and direction, causes the stories to twist and turn around possible redemptions, unseen possibilities, hints of longed-for epiphanies just out of reach. For other readers, the sourness of Janet is overwhelming.

Garner's stories certainly don't allow *thematically* for a rest between bouts of bleakness. In the leaky, haunted rooms of Sweetpea Mansions there doesn't seem much point in looking for any sense of sacredness, or even just skerricks of past joy. Some reviews of *Cosmo Cosmolino* touched on Garner's own personal, emotional battles at the time, in order to explain the dolor of the stories. Some even raised Garner's newly-expressed interest in *the numinous* as an explanation for the power of something in the stories, something greater than the characters' wills and experiences, the remembered joy of which seems to haunt them.

In a published letter to Bennett Daylight, Garner wrote:

> When [*Cosmo Cosmolino*] came out I was stupid enough to agree to an interview with that hard-nosed leftie rationalist Craig McGregor and even stupider to blurt out my strange experience with the shadowy presence. After I'd spoken to him, I panicked and called him, naively asked him to cut that part. He says oh don't worry I hardly even mentioned it. The piece comes out and my mysterious visitor is the backbone of the story. People who hadn't read the book ran round saying Garner's got religion etc. One neighbour said with a sort of patronising laugh "what you needed was a big hug." . . . None of this matters to me now. But it taught me that in Australia you can't write about experiences of "the numinous" without opening yourself to sneering and cynical laughter. Back then, anyway.[30]

Daylight's response to Garner here needs to be appreciated:

> It seems a terrible shame to me that critics, in their rush to disavow something so tasteless, so unfashionable as belief, missed something so rich and deep in Garner's work. By becoming helpless before God she also became helpless before metaphor. We are the richer for it. We don't condemn Toni Morrison or Marilynne Robinson or even Herman Melville for their use of biblical metaphor. We try to be respectful of other beliefs, of Islam, of Hinduism, of Aboriginal spirituality. Is there room for us to treat Christianity with similar respect? Could we perhaps

---

30. Garner, cited in Daylight, "Consider This," lines 380–92.

banish the sneering and cynical laughter for long enough to
read this book as it deserves to be read?[31]

The critic admires the "sheer careering speed" of Garner's prose, as
it moves "absolutely surely through its landscape"; and at the same time
to demur at "critics, in their rush to disavow something so tasteless, so
unfashionable as belief, missed something so rich and deep in Garner's
work." What can we make of these different registers of speed (energy,
deftness, power) and depth (that "something" possibly numinous or sacred)? Do the final scenes of *Cosmo Cosmolino* resolve anything, produce
anything like a sacred context? Another way of thinking about these *contemporary sacred/secular epiphanies*, if that is what they are, is the idea
of theorist Sharon Kim, that: "As the dark spots left on the retina by a
light, epiphany reveals the state of *not* having seen, and intuits that there
is something that yet cannot be seen."[32] A little negative theology at work
here. This comes very close to Uhlmann's observation, quoted above in
regard to White, that "while meaning is now uncertain, it is now certain
that there is meaning."[33]

Sacredness, Abjection, and Hybridity: Kim Scott

One crucial question underlies this essay: how do the contemporary imaginations of fiction writers in Australia negotiate the hybridity of the world
they observe, experience, and represent? One way of responding to this
question is to argue that for many of these writers, borders between sacred and secular are imbricated. What could it mean to be self-righteous
and "pure" in a world suffering from multiple forms of violence; to know
unequivocally; to separate flesh and spirit imperially; to be full of unques-
tioned certitude? And what does it mean to possess and wield privilege and
ownership in an impoverished world? Such questions are being powerfully
and purposefully asked in the works we have been examining, perhaps
nowhere more urgently than in the new relations being forged between
Indigenous and non-Indigenous Australians.

Noongar novelist and cultural warrior Kim Scott has written,
as well as been a leader in language renewal, across three decades. In
works such as *True Country* (1993), *Benang: From the Heart* (1999), *That
Deadman Dance* (2010), and *Taboo* (2017), Scott's vision is shaped by a

---

31. Daylight, "Consider This," lines 393–402.
32. Kim, *Literary Epiphany in the Novel*, 10.
33. Uhlmann, "The Symbol in Patrick White," 75.

growing awareness that, rather than any exclusionary or monolithic notion of identity, there is a need to fully acknowledge the multiple, hybrid elements of the world—Indigenous and non-Indigenous, multicultural, sacred and secular, Arab and Jew, simple and intellectual—and to ask how such hybridity might be incorporated into respect for the past, but also hope for the future. This is not a vision of a level playing field, or of simplistic homogenization. In the work of Patrick White, Helen Garner, Christos Tsiolkas, and Kim Scott, we are urged to confront the realities of difference, and the pain of what exclusion means for speckled, "impure," supposedly unlovely characters. Such confrontation challenges readers to move towards awareness of sacred processes and meanings.

In *That Deadman Dance*, Scott introduces us to the figure of Bobby Wabalanginy, a fresh-faced, curious Noongar boy living in the first decades of the nineteenth century in what is now South East Western Australia. Bobby grows up just as his people are brought face to face with the whalers, grog merchants, and land grabbers of white invasion. He learns—for survival, amidst the injustices, *and* with an infectious joyfulness—to sing the whalers' songs, to interpolate his own tongue into their lyrics, to perform, in hybrid forms and costumes, "that deadman dance," and in multiple ways to attest to the mighty traumas of colonial invasion, as well as to his people's energy and resilience.

In the closing scenes of a twisting narrative, Bobby, now an old man, is pictured singing and performing for a few coins from tourists. He can be read here as an abject figure of confusion, a clown who has lost the purity of his identity. But at its core, *That Deadman Dance* also presents us with something beyond abjection, in a complex and hybrid vision of reality and invention working together:

> Bobby sang, and it happened just as in this song: the boats left the shore and home receded, but the singer was on the boat not on the shore like in the old songs. . . . Singing, Bobby thought of the marks he made when he was on the lookout: his pen and paper, his chalk on the slate, his *roze a wail*. . . . The business of a white man thinking he was too good for a Noongar was not in Bobby's song, but instead the men on board ship, black and white and Chinaman, too, if we want to keep saying people are this or that, and Yankees and convicts and Froggies and soldiers. . . . They all joined voices with Bobby as the melody grabbed them, held them, hauled them along behind. For some it was recognising the words—their whaling language in the midst of all the blackfella talk, and they called out, putting their voice beside the singer, trusting him and themselves to get to the end.

> ... One of those blackfella songs, they said, but with some of our words in it. They caught familiar words and snatches of melody, but something in the sound and the rolling momentum of liquid syllables moved them, put them at sea again and full of spirit.[34]

Here, Scott depicts Bobby as a hero, a leader who has survived through matching his wit and energy and imagination against any difference: learning the invaders' language, bringing his own language into the presence of hegemonic English, counting himself as equal. The voice of the character and the narrator seem to meld momentarily in this passage, as the hybrid frontier characters are described: "the men on board ship, black and white and Chinaman, too, if we want to keep saying people are this or that, and Yankees and convicts and Froggies and soldiers." While Scott does not shy away from describing frontier barbarities, he also records that Indigenous and non-Indigenous "all joined voices with Bobby as the melody grabbed them, held them, hauled them along behind." It is in the music, the dance, the languages, the common working relations, that the frontier, at least in this moment of Scott's representation, is being forged. Scott enacts the hope that the power of the imagination, in the *forging of culture*, together, is how the future will be made.

A purely political view might critique this vision as too forgiving, too idealistic, a contemporary gloss. After all, can imaginative work really be stood up against the losses and horrors which Indigenous peoples across this nation endured, and are still enduring? At its barest, this seems like so much idealism. But at its richest, and with the guidance of those who have been subjected to such losses, a sacred context can be, and is being, imagined and created. If we read the important 2017 Indigenous document, *Uluru Statement from the Heart*, we can glimpse what Scott is saying. The *Statement* ends not with an exclusionary set of principles, but rather with a vision of relationship and an invitation. In the *Statement*, Indigenous peoples express communally their desire for their children:

> They will walk in two worlds and their culture will be a gift to their country. . . . Makarrata is the culmination of our agenda: *the coming together after a struggle*. It captures our aspirations for a fair and truthful relationship with the people of Australia and a better future for their children based on justice and self-determination. We seek a Makarrata Commission to supervise a process of agreement-making between governments and First Nations and truth-telling about our history. In 1967 we were counted, in 2017 we seek to be heard. We leave base camp and

---

34. Scott, *That Deadman Dance*, 317–18.

start our trek across this vast country. We invite you to walk with us in a movement of the Australian people for a better future.[35]

The necessary and joyful hybridity of *makarrata*—walking in two worlds, coming together after a struggle, relationship with the people of Australia, agreement making, being heard, a movement of the Australian people for a better future—these are the *relational* dialogic terms so generously offered by Indigenous peoples to all Australians, in an imaginative coming together for "our trek across this vast country."

For White in the mid-twentieth century, the vision of a future Australia was still distant, questioning. He nevertheless imagined and gave voice to many speckled, hybrid, faulty, and earthed saints existing in this place, seeking meaning. Garner too draws our heart to uncertain, faulty characters characterized by self-questioning and a nomadic struggle for lost joy and purpose. Tsiolkas and Scott, beginning from contemporary Greek Australian and Indigenous contexts, respectively, construct divided Australias; but equally they envisage Australia as a hybrid nation imaginatively wrestling to make sacred meaning, not as dogma or monolithic power or hierarchy—not even as policies of homogeneity pre-eminently—but as multiple, imaginative, and continuously reimagining possibilities. "Perhaps this is what dreaming, and art, are for," Helen Garner reminds us.[36]

Bibliography

Cave, Nick. "Issue #106." https://www.theredhandfiles.com/how-to-understand-experience-of-loss/.

Daylight, Tegan Bennett. "Consider This: Helen Garner's *Cosmo Cosmolino*." *Sydney Review of Books*, May 2016. https://sydneyreviewofbooks.com/essay/consider-helen-garner-cosmo-cosmolino/.

Garner, Helen. *Cosmo Cosmolino*. Ringwood: McPhee Gribble, 1992.

———. *Everywhere I Look*. Melbourne: Text, 2016.

Giffin, Michael. *Arthur's Dream: The Religious Imagination in the Fiction of Patrick White*. Paddington: Spaniel, 1996.

———. *Patrick White and God*. Newcastle upon Tyne: Cambridge Scholars, 2017.

Kim, Sharon. *Literary Epiphany in the Novel, 1850–1950: Constellations of the Soul*. New York: Palgrave Macmillan, 2012.

Malouf, David. "Patrick White Reappraised." *The Age*, January 27, 2007. https://www.theage.com.au/entertainment/books/patrick-white-reappraised-20070127-ge42xi.html.

Merriam-Webster, "Imaginary." https://www.merriam-webster.com/dictionary/imaginary.

35. "The Uluru Statement from the Heart."
36. Garner, *Everywhere I Look*, 152.

Pew Research Center. "Worldwide, Many See Belief in God as Essential to Morality." *Pew Research Center*, March 13, 2014. https://www.pewresearch.org/global/2014/03/13/worldwide-many-see-belief-in-god-as-essential-to-morality/.

Scott, Kim. *That Deadman Dance*. Sydney: Picador, 2010.

Shakespeare, Nicholas. "Patrick White." https://www.nicholasshakespeare.com/writing/patrick-white/

Tomlinson, Rob. "The Solid Mandala." https://www.rob-tomlinson.com/a-good-read/solid-mandala.

Tsiolkas, Christos. *Barracuda*. Crows Nest: Allen & Unwin, 2013.

———. *Damascus*. Crows Nest: Allen & Unwin, 2019.

———. *Patrick White: Writers on Writers*. Carlton: Black, 2018.

Uhlmann, Anthony. "The Symbol in Patrick White." In *Remembering Patrick White: Contemporary Critical Essays*, edited by Elizabeth McMahon and Brigitta Olubas, 65–75. Amsterdam: Rodopi, 2010.

"The Uluru Statement from the Heart." https://ulurustatemdev.wpengine.com/wp-content/uploads/2022/01/UluruStatementfromtheHeartPLAINTEXT.pdf.

Ward, Russell. *The Australian Legend*. Melbourne: Oxford University Press, 1958.

Watt, George. "Patrick White: Novelist as Prophet." *Literature and Theology* 10.3 (1996) 273–79.

Wetherell, Rodney. "Uncheery Soul." *Meanjin* 64.1–2 (2005) 243–54.

White, Patrick. *The Solid Mandala*. London: Eyre & Spottiswoode, 1966.

———. *Voss*. London: Eyre & Spottiswoode, 1957.

18

Process Sequence

Paul Mitchell

Process Theology a)
I'm planning to write a poem tomorrow
it'll seem a lot like life.　　　Not quite mine

or yours
or anyone like ours

just a life spent lying
under a tree on college grounds

staring through branches at the sun
because class was skipped, a soul was saved

and what else was there to do but listen
to Brian Eno on headphones and cassette

'til sunset, marriage, childbirth and rapture?

Well, let's not get ahead of ourselves:

there was the fact the college grounds
overlooked a cemetery

and the college motto was

Aedificamus in Aeternum.

We could, instead, get behind ourselves
recognise that when a Rubik's cube's
solved it should simply be

tossed in the air, so why not

a soul that's saved?

There's little more to say
than this: tomorrow's
life could be an improvement upon

today's poem. But today's does have something:

a line or two into
the best future I planned.

Process Theology b)
I am writing today a poem I planned to write
yesterday. It looks and sounds exactly
like my life: a cold, windowless office

at the back of a weatherboard shed.
A power saw cutting through the morning's
peace, the ticking of a novelty clock

my latest son bought for Father's Day
a pigeon, choking and chortling
traffic from six lanes that office walls

try to turn to ocean waves
and thick glass on the door pane

working against every plane
Tullamarine takes in a day.

Computer stares at me
with a day's work inside
while I pen this onto a foolscap

pad on a fool's errand to write
a poem that might outlast my life.

It looks exactly like this.

Process ~~***Theology c)***~~
Today's poem has no good news
so go read your horoscope . . .

Nope? Max Dupain's bloke's lying
on the beach in sepia in a brochure

sticking out of a rack in the café
oblivious to the poem I based

on the image in two-thousand
that was published in *The Australian*.

Looking at me, Max's photo?
Inspiring me, Max's photo?

I recall it wasn't that photo
I based my poem on. It was

another Dupain. My inner critic
can't even get his artwork

in order. What hope the poet
sorting out the process?

19

"It'll Take You Way Down to the Wilderness"

*Theology in Conversation with the Films
of Rolf de Heer and David Gulpilil*

KATHERINE RAINGER

Introduction

FILMS TELL OUR STORIES. They reveal to us the human condition with its universal longings lived out in particular contexts. Theology also aims to tell our stories, making room for both the universal and the particular. This essay is based on the premise that filmmakers have much to offer in the quest to foster theological imagination that is orientated towards justice, hope, and truth.

Films from North America, Europe, and increasingly from other parts of the globe have been the subject of theological reflection. With a few notable exceptions, Australian films, and, in particular, films on Indigenous themes or that involve Indigenous collaboration, have been largely overlooked by those interested in film and theology.[1] This essay aims to address this omission by focusing on the collaborative work of two Australian filmmakers: director Rolf de Heer and actor David Gulpilil. In particular, *The Tracker* (2002) and *Ten Canoes* (2006) provide rich conversation partners for theological reflection that is attentive to both the strength of First Nation cultures and the impacts and legacies of colonialism.

"Settlement" and Survival

The arrival of the British, in 1788, in the lands now known as Australia led to widespread dispossession and crisis for First Nations people. In 1988,

---

1. The work of Australian director Peter Weir is one such exception. See Leonard, *The Mystical Gaze of the Cinema*.

Australia celebrated the bicentenary of British "settlement." Common usage of the word "settlement" hides both the resistance to British invasion by First Nations people and also the violence that First Nations people endured as their lands were stolen. Furthermore, settlement implies that the land was not already cultivated and cared for by First Nations people, something that Bruce Pascoe's work convincingly refutes.[2]

Ramingining artists and Djon Mundine, conceptual creator and artist, Bandjalung people, *The Aboriginal Memorial*, 1987–88. Natural earth pigments and binder on eucalyptus wood, 327 (H) cm (height irregular). National Gallery of Australia, Canberra, Australia. Purchased with the assistance of funds from National Gallery admission charges and commissioned in 1987, 1987.2240.1-200.

Along with historians such as Pascoe, artists have also used various mediums and platforms to resist the narrative that Australia was settled peacefully. For example, *The Aboriginal Memorial*, commissioned in 1987 and completed in 1988, is a striking three-dimensional artwork that is permanently installed in the forecourt of the National Gallery of Australia. The work contains two hundred memorial poles (hollow log coffins used for storing the bones of the deceased). The poles symbolize two hundred years of dispossession since the First Fleet landed on the lands of the

2. See Pascoe, *Dark Emu*.

Gadigal clan of the Eora Nation (now Sydney) in 1788. Forty-three male and female Yolŋu artists who live in Ramingining and the surrounding communities in the Northern Territory made the memorial poles using their specific ancestral designs.[3]

The poles are situated according to the location of the artists' Country[4] along the Glyde River and its tributaries. The path through the Memorial imitates the course of the river that flows through the Arafura Swamp to the sea. A viewing platform on the first floor of the Gallery provides an aerial perspective of the work that shows the curve of the river. Visitors to the Gallery are encouraged to walk the path through the memorial to experience Yolŋu culture and connection with place.

The work is also a political statement that expresses the grief and injustice of murder and dispossession. Djon Mundine, a Bundjalung man, was the Conceptual Producer of *The Aboriginal Memorial*. He was an art advisor at Ramingining in the 1980s. Mundine explains that the Memorial commemorates the lives of Aboriginal and Torres Strait Islander people who were killed in the process of colonization: "Since 1788 at least several hundred thousand Aboriginal people were murdered in the colonisation of this continent. They weren't necessarily warriors. They were just your average Aboriginal families, men, women, children, older people—living in peace with the land. For these people, these unsung people, this Aboriginal Memorial was created."[5]

The Aboriginal Memorial relates to the films of David Gulpilil and Rolf de Heer in a number of ways. De Heer and Gulpilil's most ambitious film, *Ten Canoes*, was filmed in the Arafura Swamp. The opening scene contains an aerial shot that meanders along the Glyde River, drawing the viewer into

---

3. The names and clan designations of the forty-three artists are recorded on three plaques on walls adjacent to the artwork: Djardie Ashley, Joe Patrick Birriwanga, David Blanasi, Roy Burrnyila, Mick Daypurryun, Tony Dhanyula, Paddy Dhathangu, John Dhurrikayu, Jimmy Djelminy, Tony Djikululu, Dorothy Djukulul, Tom Djumburpur, Robyn Djunginy, Charlie Djurritjini, Elizabeth Djuttara, Billy Black Durrgumba, Gela Nga-Mirraitja Fordham, Tony Gabalga, Daisy Ganyila, Philip Gudthaykudthay, Neville Gulaygulay, Don Gundinga, George Jangawanga, David Malangi Daymirringu, Jimmy Mamalunhawuy, Terry Mangapal, Agnes Marrawurr, Andrew Marrgululu, Clara Matjandatjpi (Wubukwubuk), John Mawurndjul AM, Dick Smith Mewirri, George Milpurrurru, Peter Minygululu, Jack Mirritji, Jimmy Moduk, Neville Nanytjawuy, Victor Pamkal, Roy Riwa, Frances Rrikili, William Watirri, Jimmy Wululu, Wurraki, and Yambal Durrurrnga.

4. In this essay, Country is capitalized when it refers to the specific place that is culturally and spiritually connected with a First Nations people such as the Yolŋu or Adnyamathanha people.

5. Mundine, "The Aboriginal Memorial."

the place where the story will occur, introducing them to the river and to those who call it home.

Like *The Aboriginal Memorial*, *The Tracker* remembers Aboriginal people, including unarmed family groups, who were killed in the Frontier Wars. Although not the focus of this essay, *Charlie's Country* (2013), also made by de Heer and Gulpilil, asks viewers to consider the implications that connection to Country and the legacy of colonial violence continues to have in remote communities today.

Rolf de Heer and David Gulpilil on the set of *The Tracker*. Photo by Matthew Nettheim.

Ten Canoes, *Charlie's Country*, and *The Aboriginal Memorial* are testament to the survival of Yolŋu culture and language. The sensory medium of film and the immersive artwork are an invitation to experience place through an Aboriginal lens where people, land, and water are interconnected and in relationship with one another. In these works, land and water are markers of identity, something that the British colonizers largely ignored as they entered into places that were soaked with spiritual and cultural meaning and saw only empty space—*terra nullius*, land belonging to no one.

How we relate to place, and to each other, is a theological concern for both Willie James Jennings and Denise Champion. Bringing the work of these two theological voices into conversation with the films of de Heer and Gulpilil is the aim of this essay. When viewed and read together, compelling insights relating to Christianity's role in colonialism emerge, along with new ways of imagining relationality between peoples, and between people and the rest of creation.

Throughout this dialogue the work of the filmmakers and the theologians retain their own integrity. The purpose is not to appropriate the films for the purpose of theological reflection. Rather, the films are brought into conversation as an equal and autonomous partner. From this encounter, deeper understanding has the opportunity to develop.

A brief overview of de Heer and Gulpilil's body of work is provided followed by a discussion of three specific insights from the conversation between theology and Gulpilil and de Heer's films: (i) overcoming pedagogical imperialism; (ii) encountering creation as animated and interconnected; and (iii) lament for stolen Country.

Although I lived for three years on Gurindji Country in the remote community of Kalkaringi in the Northern Territory, a context similar to Ramingining where *Ten Canoes* and *Charlie's Country* were filmed, my own life experience is very different to that of the Yolŋu filmmakers. I am a middle-class, non-Indigenous woman whose ancestors came to Australia as English convicts at the end of the eighteenth century and as German migrants in the mid-nineteenth century. I benefit from the dispossession of First Nations people through wealth that was accumulated on land where the traditional owners were never compensated. Today I work and live on Ngunnawal land. I am a Christian and an ordained leader in the Anglican Church of Australia. These characteristics are part of the standpoint that I bring to this essay.

Setting the Scene

David Gulpilil Ridjimiraril Dalaithngu AM, known professionally as David Gulpilil, was one of Australia's most prominent actors, known for his charismatic on-screen presence. Gulpilil passed away in 2021. He was a Yolŋu man from Arnhem Land in Australia's Northern Territory. His language group on his mother's side was Ganalbingu, and on his father's was Mandhalpingu. Gulpilil's acting and dancing career started at age sixteen when director Nicolas Roag cast Gulpilil in *Walkabout* (1971). This cinematic debut catapulted Gulpilil onto the world stage and required him to navigate two very different cultures.

Gulpilil viewed himself as a cultural ambassador for Yolŋu people and as a conduit for greater understanding between First Nations people and other Australians. He was also an advocate for justice for his people, a theme that comes through strongly in films such as *The Tracker*, *Charlie's Country*, and *Another Country* (2014).[6] Megan Davis describes Gulpilil as "easily the greatest actor this country has ever had," adding that "his oeuvre speaks to the unresolved grievance this country bears."[7]

Rolf de Heer is a non-Indigenous Australian with Dutch heritage who spent his childhood in Indonesia. Jane Freebury, in her comprehensive account of de Heer's oeuvre, argues that de Heer's films have a distinct place in public discourse due to his boldness in terms of style, form, and content.[8] While de Heer's willingness to deal with diverse themes and issues make it difficult to synthesize his work, Freebury discerns the inclusion of marginalized characters as a constant theme. Viewers are invited into unique and compelling visions of "outsiders" whose voices are not usually heard. Freebury distinguishes de Heer's style from the social-realist and art-house flavor that characterizes much of Australian cinema. De Heer focuses instead on elements such as character psychology, dramatic interpersonal tension, and the subtle use of humor.

De Heer first met Gulpilil when he cast him in the lead role in the film *The Tracker*, a film which unflinchingly reveals Australia's violent colonial past through the intricacies of the relationships between three police officers and their Aboriginal tracker. The professional connection between the director and actor became a personal friendship when Gulpilil invited de Heer to his Country in Ramingining, Arnhem Land. Gulpilil requested that the two of them work on another film project set in his Country. This invitation was the genesis of *Ten Canoes*, a film that is set in pre-contact times and interweaves two distinct stories of ancestors in a tale of romance, revenge, and lore. *Ten Canoes* is the first Australian film to be made entirely in First Nations languages. The collaboration extended to incorporate the community at Ramingining, including Peter Djigirr who co-directed the film.

6. On Gulpilil's work, see Johnson, *Gulpilil*; Rielly, *Gulpilil*.
7. Davis, in Adelaide Festival, "David Gulpilil Retrospective."
8. See Freebury, *Dancing to His Song*.

Seven years after *Ten Canoes*, Gulpilil and de Heer's third feature film, *Charlie's Country*, was released. This film was co-written by Gulpilil and de Heer, and co-produced by Peter Djigirr. Along with *Charlie's Country*, the "country suite" includes *Still Our Country* (2014) and *Another Country* (2014), two documentaries filmed in Ramingining, written with Gulpilil, directed by Molly Reynolds, and produced by de Heer and Djigirr. In 2021, the documentary film *My Name is Gulpilil*, a collaborative piece made by Gulpilil, de Heer, Reynolds, and Djigirr, premiered at the Adelaide Film Festival.

Overcoming Pedagogical Imperialism

De Heer and Gulpilil's body of work contains many avenues for theological reflection. The work of Willie James Jennings provides useful insights to focus the conversation. Jennings is Associate Professor of Systematic Theology and Africana Studies at Yale Divinity School, in the United States, and an ordained Baptist pastor. In his book, *The Christian Imagination: Theology and the Origins of Race* (2010), Jennings provides a comprehensive account of the connection between Christianity and colonialism, and the detrimental impact that this connection has on Christian theology today.

In a later essay titled "Disfigurations of Christian Identity: Performing Identity as Theological Method," Jennings argues that three identities were predominant in the colonial project—the merchant, the soldier, and the missionary. These three identities were at work as Europeans entered the lands of others with a sense of divine sanction to use the natural resources seemingly on offer and exerted control of the local people by forcing them into webs of economic exchange such as slavery and servitude, alongside conversion to Christianity. His description of the "way of the missionary" includes a critique of the forms of relationality that the missionaries imported. While generalizations are at play in Jennings's assessment, his overall summation provides a poignant framework for analyzing the relationship between missionaries and Indigenous peoples. For example, Jennings argues that "pedagogical imperialism" was the *modus operandi* as missionaries entered the space of Indigenous peoples imagining it to be shaped by fundamental deficiencies in the social, intellectual, and cultural spheres. While Indigenous peoples were capable of receiving salvation, which implied a shared humanity, what was on offer was "a Christianity and Christian theology encased in evaluative mode" that resulted in an irreversible asymmetrical mode of relating where Indigenous Christian life was "never in the position of teacher."[9]

---

9. Jennings, "Disfigurations of Christian Identity," 80.

Subverting Pedagogical Imperialism in *Ten Canoes*

Ten Canoes is a film made for two distinct audiences—the community at Ramingining who wanted to use their culture and language to make a film for their children; and non-Yolŋu viewers who are invited into this Yolŋu film.[10] The posture of the film towards the non-Yolŋu audience is one of invitation. However, the Storyteller (a voiceover by Gulpilil) is the knowledgeable guide and "owner" of the story. The following quotations are from the opening and closing scenes:

> *Scene 1 Storyteller*: It's not your story . . . it's my story . . . a story like you never seen before. But you want a proper story, eh? Then I must tell you some things . . . of my people, and my land. . . . Then you can see this story, and know it.

> *Scene 153 Storyteller*: But now you've seen my story. It's a good story. (The breeze blows through the reeds, the sound of magpie geese echoes across the swamp). Not like your story, but a good story all the same.

Screenshot from *Ten Canoes*. Photo by James Geurts.

---

10. See Palace Films, "Ten Canoes."

Viewers are invited by the Storyteller into the story, to "know it." This invitation subverts the "pedagogical imperialism" of the way of the missionary. The way of the missionary is reimagined so that the knowledge bearer retains ownership of their story while also offering hospitality to the audience.

Film analysts Kim Clothier and Debra Duduk observe that the non-Yolŋu viewer is invited and guided into every aspect of the film by the Storyteller and the subtitled dialogue.[11] The exception to this is the scene depicting Ridjimiraril's death dance. The Storyteller continues to instruct the viewer regarding what is happening. There are, however, people who will always know more than the non-Yolŋu viewer, people who do not need to be told how to respond to what has taken place:

> *Storyteller*: And the people know . . . (Small groups of people begin to emerge from different part of the bush, all coming in the same direction.)
>
> *Storyteller*: See? They know. They come out from the bush, from everywhere. They are coming for Ridjimirail.

The singing and wailing during Ridjimiraril's death dance do not contain subtitles. This has the effect of positioning non-Yolŋu Matha[12] speakers as outsiders whose audio-visual participation in this ceremony is limited. The cinematic experience of coming close to the ceremony but with limited comprehension can overcome the "obsessive evaluative gestures born of the missionary."[13]

Furthermore, the Storyteller's insider knowledge schools the viewer in waiting for knowledge to be revealed and accepting the discomfort of limited comprehension. The film's unresolved ending also contributes to this sensation. The "happily ever after," a conventional ending in Western stories, is disrupted:

> *Storyteller*: And they all lived happily ever after . . . (laughs). No, I don't know what happened after that. Maybe that Dayindi found a wife. Maybe he didn't. It was like that for my people.

---

11. See Clothier and Dudek, "Opening the Body," 82–92. The inclusion of English subtitles and English spoken by the Storyteller in the theatrical release version (as opposed to the version that contained no subtitles or spoken English used for screenings with Yolŋu viewers) is a mark of language survival and a gesture of hospitality to the non-Yolŋu viewer who does not know the Yolŋu languages in the film and who requires translation and subtitles.

12. Yolŋu Matha is a collection of languages that Yolŋu people speak.

13. Jennings, "Disfigurations of Christian Identity," 82.

The ending mirrors the disruption to the conventional Western beginning in Scene 1:

> *Storyteller*: Once upon a time, in a land far, far away . . . (laughs). No, not like that. I am only joking. But I am going to tell you a story.

This playful approach to Western storytelling conventions is contained within a framing device for the entire film, which privileges the Storyteller and his knowledge. The non-Yolŋu viewers are reminded of their place as outsiders who are invited into the narrative world of the Storyteller.

The pedagogical imperialism of the missionary can be further transformed in the world in front of the film. Djungadjunga Yunupingu and Dhanggal Yunupingu discuss their experience of being Yolŋu and being Christian:

> We see spirituality as having shaped Aboriginal people in the way that something is put together as an arrangement of parts and built as a framework. Our faith grows stronger when we have ceremonies, song and dance, when our people are close to us every day of our life, mainly in ceremonies, and there is a feeling of unity and wholeness. What European missionaries taught us did not respect Yolŋu ways of life; we were as one tree cut in half. Wholeness came only when we could express our spirituality in a Yolŋu way.[14]

Listening to Yolŋu people onscreen and offscreen broadens and redefines the way of the missionary to one of reciprocity and the assertion of, rather than the reduction of, Indigenous agency.[15]

Jennings argues that Indigenous Christians have inherited a diminished form of Christian imagination in the way of the missionary where to be Christian required alignment with European culture. In response, Jennings proposes that Indigenous Christians can embody Christian practices through "native religious and cultural performance enacted in Christian form."[16] *Ten Canoes* is not an example of Yolŋu and Christian performance. Rather, it is an audio-visual performance of Yolŋu culture, humor, and spirituality that subverts and challenges the pedagogical imperialism found in the way of the missionary.

---

14. Yunupingu and Yunupingu, "Mungulk Dhalatj," 94.

15. For further discussion of what "listening" to *Ten Canoes* might involve, see McCredden, "*Ten Canoes*," 45–56; Henderson, "Stranger Danger," 54–70.

16. Jennings, "Disfigurations of Christian Identity," 82.

Belonging to Country

> I got tears falling down, I been crying seeing that movie, it's such a good movie. . . . It will hold them in the heart, the people who will see it, it'll take you way down to the wilderness.[17]

Jennings challenges the deficit discourse nurtured by Christian theology that disproportionately placed the burden of alignment and adaptation onto First Nation peoples. In addition, Indigenous peoples were required to align themselves with a faith "that slowly drained the earth, animals, landscape, and places of their signifying power and turned it all into underdeveloped private property and underutilized foodstuffs."[18]

According to Jennings, one of the characteristics of the colonial, Christian mindset was the way that identity was transferred from place, land, animals, kinship, and language, and located solely in the body. Jennings argues that skin color became the dominant way of describing identity as other forms of identity were intentionally severed through separation of Indigenous peoples from land, family, and language. The films of Gulpilil and de Heer subvert a colonial understanding of identity by showing the deep connection with Country that Indigenous peoples have.

In the documentary *Still Our Country*, Gulpilil states: "I live in the land and land lives in me. We live together."[19] In *Ten Canoes*, this is communicated on screen by the Storyteller who shares with the audience his creation story attached to particular sounds and images shown in the opening scene of the film as something that the audience needs to know if they are going to understand the film: "A story like you've never seen before. I must tell you something of my people and my land. This land began in the beginning. Yurlunggur, that great water goanna, he travelled here. Yurlunggur made all this land—he made the water and he made the swamp that stretches long and gives us life. I come from this waterhole."[20]

Gulpilil's creation story and the particularities of the land formations and waterways are evocatively portrayed on screen. The curve of Yurlunggur's body travels through space and forms the land and water of the Arafura Swamp. Land, water, and the Storyteller are intimately connected in a "sacred cosmology of kinship."[21] The curve of the swamp that the camera tracks in the opening scene is followed by the Storyteller's voice-over. The movement

17. Gulpilil, in "*Ten Canoes*," Press Kit, 12.
18. Jennings, "Disfigurations of Christian Identity," 82.
19. Gulpilil, in Reynolds, *Still Our Country*.
20. De Heer, *Ten Canoes*.
21. Victorin-Vangerud, "From Metaphors and Models to Maps," 80.

of the great water goanna travelling and creating the land and water is connected with the aerial view of the swamp that opened the film.

A colonial vision of people and place has led to some fundamental shortcomings in Western Christian doctrines of creation, with private property and utility driving the discourse. Rather than a static resource waiting to be extracted, *Ten Canoes* asks viewers to see creation as interconnected, animated, life-giving, relational, and embedded with story. Viewers are invited to "overhear" creation through the wisdom and experience of Yolngu people and in doing so to enter their Country as guests. This way of entering Country is a fundamental reversal to the colonial attitude. It is a starting point for a renewed dialogue that will wait for knowledge to be revealed, and ask questions rather than impose answers.

Lament for Stolen Country

> The past is always present. The past is always with us. We are all defined by our past.[22]

Connection and identity are retained by Gulpilil's character in *The Tracker* as he uses his knowledge of the land to subvert the mission of his officer companions.[23] The officers are constantly out of place, while the tracker is able to discern signs in the land and waterways even though he is not on his Country. The film ends with the tracker returning to his Country while the youngest of the colonial officers is left in the ambiguous position of needing to find his way home.

Aunty Reverend Dr. Denise Champion is an Adnyamathanha woman of the Ararru (north wind) moiety and an ordained minister of the Uniting Church in Australia. As she explains, "Adnyamathanha" is made up of two syllables and means "rock (adnya) group (mathanha)." Her identity is located in her land and her family. Aunty Denise's Adnyamathanha name, Warrikanha, indicates that she is the second born and female in her family.[24]

Aunty Denise's Country, Adnyamathanha Country (the Flinders Ranges), is where *The Tracker* was filmed. Like the discussion of *Ten Canoes* above in relation to Jennings, I am proposing that *The Tracker* provides an audio-visual companion to Champion's theology. In particular, it reflects Champion's account of the animated and connected nature of land,

---

22. Foley, "Duplicity and Deceit," 3.
23. See Screen Australia, "The Tracker."
24. See Champion and Budden, "First Peoples," 33–45.

animals, sky, water, and people, and her lament for the disconnection that has occurred due to stolen Country and culture.

Screenshot of David Gulpilil in *The Tracker*. Photo by Matthew Nettheim.

"Knowing" Country and "caring for" Country remain important for Adnyamathanha people. However, due to the colonial disruption that has taken place, Champion describes her people as exiles and refugees in their land. This tension between relating to the land and the colonial atrocities that have taken place are also powerfully communicated in *The Tracker*.

In her book, *Yarta Wandatha*, which means "the land is speaking," Champion expresses her Adnyamathanha culture and language alongside her identity as an Adnyamathanha Christian pastor. Champion's storytelling, which brings together her Adnyamathanha culture and Christian faith, demonstrates that her Christian belief is not limited to European ways of knowing. She speaks honestly about her Christian, Adnyamathanha, and

Australian identities. She records some of the struggle for identity she experienced in mission contexts, such as when Elders decided to stop Adnyamathanha ceremonies because the knowledge of how to do them properly was disappearing due to colonization.

Champion describes relatedness with land and place in familial terms. The quotations below demonstrate Champion's theological method where she weaves together her relationship with her land and the biblical account of land as the source of life and divine connection, in Genesis 2.

> We are not separated from the land our mother. We always talk about the land as our mother, which fits very closely with the story of Genesis of the Lord God forming humankind from clay. . . . I always say Australia is like one gigantic storybook. There's a story in every part of the land and sky and sea. When we, as Adnyamathanha, gather and tell our stories we always say *yarta wandatha*—"the land is speaking." We also say *yarta wandatha ikandadnha*. The people are speaking as if the land is speaking. So the land is speaking to us and through us in these stories. There's a oneness there.[25]

The "gigantic storybook" that Champion refers to includes the Adnyamathanha Dreaming stories. These stories explain how to live in right relationship with the Creator, the creation, and with other humans.[26] Dreaming stories incorporate hills, rocks, waterholes, plants, and animals, explaining how each one came to be. The particularities of land formations are evidence of the Creator Spirit and ancestral creation beings who traversed the landscape during the Dreaming.

For Adnyamathanha people, a spiritual dimension is present in the land, which is why land autonomy and the preservation of sacred sites (places where particular activity from ancestral beings in the Dreaming can be discerned) are essential.

Champion also recognizes Adnyamathanha peoples' "long memory" of the Creator God in their stories and their land.[27] She includes Christ as hidden in the Adnyamathanha stories and therefore hidden in the land. For example, the story of *Yurnda Akananadha: The Creation of the First Day*, explains the daily movement of the sun. Christ, like the sun, is dependable and provides the light needed to see and to grow. Champion reads John 1 and Psalm 119 alongside *Yurnda Akananadha* to explore the meanings of light and dark, and the guidance that God provides.

25. Champion, *Yarta Wandatha*, 19, 29.
26. See Prentis, "What Can the Birds of the Land Tell Us?" 21.
27. See Champion, *Yarta Wandatha*, 29.

Screenshot of Grant Page, Damon Gameau, Gary Sweet, and David Gulpilil in *The Tracker*. Photo by Matthew Nettheim.

There is no explicit reference to Adnyamathanha stories in *The Tracker*; however, through the setting, and techniques such as wide shots, the viewer gets a sense of the character of the land and its importance in the film. The landscape that seems barren and oppressive to the police party is a source of nurture and sustenance for the tracker. It is almost as if the land is on the tracker's side.

The tracker can find food easily and uses plants medicinally. He hears and sees things to which the others in the police party remain oblivious. The power dynamics that are so central to the plot of the film ultimately come down to who can survive in the environment. The police party are aware that despite their guns and supplies, which are ultimately futile and finite, it is the tracker who is key to their survival.

Songs of Lament

The soundtrack of *The Tracker* is an essential and evocative element of the film. The haunting songs, written by de Heer, function as part of the script. These songs become the inner voice of the tracker, positioning him as central to the story. *The Tracker* is a lament in the sense that it involves truth-telling, naming injustice, and speaking about the unspeakable.

The songs convey a sense of lament in a particular way. The soundtrack includes world-renowned singer and songwriter Archie Roach singing in English and in his father's language, Bundjalung. These songs of lament are also a sign of the continuity and survival of people, language, and culture. For example, in the song "My People" we hear:

> In this land long ago
> We lived our own way
> Now we're no longer free
> We are dispossessed.
> People of mine.[28]

The connection between land and people has been broken, and this is a cause for lament. This sense of lament for the broken relationship between land and people is also seen in Champion's work. She has written an Adnyamathanha lament paraphrasing the first chapter of the biblical book of Lamentations. Lamentations uses vivid language and imagery to depict Jerusalem's destruction and exile into Babylon. Champion's Adnyamathanha lament grounds the cry of dispossession in her country:

> Strangers have come and taken the land of our
> Fathers and Mothers,
> away from Adnyamathanha children.
> But where can we go?
> We have nowhere to go!
> Now strangers in our own land.
> The Adnyamathanha suffer much,
> made to work hard for the new owners.
> She lives among the nations but has no rest.
> Ngaingka! Who will hear us crying?[29]

Champion's Adnyamathanha lament and the songs from *The Tracker* speak of dispossession. They are laments arising from the land we now call Australia. Echoing the cries of Jerusalem in Lamentations 1:12, Champion asks her readers: "Who will hear us crying?"[30] The viewer of *The Tracker* becomes a witness to the colonial atrocities that took place. "Hope Always,"

---

28. De Heer, "My People."
29. Champion, *Yarta Wandatha*, 23–24.
30. Champion, *Yarta Wandatha*, 24.

the final song in *The Tracker*, reminds the viewer that the effects of history linger in the present:

> Hope's all we have until we find our way,
> for all around to respect what we say,
> Chain our hands, take our lands, we stay.
> It's where our future goes
> searching for those who will carry the burden with us.
> Always we hope.[31]

Both *The Tracker* and Champion's writing and ministry include a commitment to truth-telling and an invitation to non-Indigenous peoples to "carry the burden," as the song suggests. For Champion, hope lies in a sense of return after exile and in the person of Christ. Christ is not only a "safe place of refuge," but is also "a sacred place" whose presence is experienced in the stories of the land and in the biblical witness; for example, in Mary's song in Luke 1 where justice and freedom are proclaimed.[32]

Conclusion: "It'll Take You Way Down to the Wilderness"

David Gulpilil describes the experience of viewing *Ten Canoes* as being taken "way down to the wilderness."[33] The wilderness, in biblical imagery, conjures up notions of revelation, identity, and purpose in the midst of struggle, testing, and temptation. The wilderness experience is a crucial aspect in ancient Israel's story, and in the story of Jesus.

If films can tell our story, what might the experience of wilderness in *Ten Canoes* have to teach us? In the contested space of a nation telling its own story, de Heer and Gulpilil make a specific contribution that highlights both the hospitable relationship that First Nations people experience with their land and the disruption that has taken place.

De Heer and Gulpilil invite their audience to see, hear, and imagine creation through the lens and guidance of Yolŋu storytellers and filmmakers on Yolŋu Country. For non-Indigenous viewers, such as myself, the wilderness of *Ten Canoes* is both revealing and disorientating. Where the colonial Christian lens saw empty land, the film reveals land, plants, and animals that are animated by story and kinship. A patient guide is needed to translate this, and yet there will always be knowledge that is untranslatable.

31. De Heer, "Hope Always."
32. See Champion, *Yarta Wandatha*, 25.
33. Gulpilil, in "*Ten Canoes*," Press Kit, 12.

For Gulpilil, the experience of wilderness is connected with emotions that cannot be divorced from the experience of watching *Ten Canoes*. He has "got tears falling down" as he watches the film. For the people who will see it, the film "will hold them in the heart."[34] Watching *Ten Canoes* is not designed to be an exercise in the accumulation of facts about First Peoples. Rather, through its storytelling, like *The Aboriginal Memorial*, it is an invitation to be immersed in a sensory experience where the past and the present cannot be separated.

The past and the present are also connected in *The Tracker*. Along with Champion's theological insights, the invitation in this film is to truth-telling, lament, and resistance. These are essential elements for any honest constructions of Australia's story, and are part of the contribution that de Heer and Gulpilil make to a more truthful account of the impacts of colonization and where we find ourselves today.

As the credits role in *The Tracker*, haunting lyrics fill the screen—"chain our hands, take our lands, we stay." The films of David Gulpilil and Rolf de Heer are part of what it means to "stay," to be visible, and to have agency over the ways that history is told and land is understood. To be taken "way down to the wilderness" is not comfortable, but it is necessary for the learning that is required to take place. Entering, remaining, and coming through the wilderness with a clearer vision is the gift and challenge of Gulpilil and de Heer's body of work.

Bibliography

Adelaide Festival. "David Gulpilil Retrospective." https://www.adelaidefestival.com.au/events/gulpilil-retrospective-series/.

Champion, Denise. *Yarta Wandatha*. Salisbury: Uniting Aboriginal and Islander Christian Congress, 2014.

Champion, Denise, and Chris Budden. "First Peoples, Ancient Spirit, and the Uniting Church Preamble: Opportunity and Challenge." In *Postcolonial Voices from Downunder: Indigenous Matters, Confronting Readings*, edited by Jione Havea, 33–45. Eugene, OR: Pickwick, 2017.

Clothier, Kim, and Debra Dudek. "Opening the Body: Reading *Ten Canoes* with Critical Intimacy." *Kunapipi* 31.2 (2009) 82–92.

De Heer, Rolf. "Hope Always." In *The Tracker: Soundtrack*, performed by Archie Roach. Melbourne: Mushroom Records, 2002, compact disc.

———. "My People." In *The Tracker: Soundtrack*, performed by Archie Roach. Melbourne: Mushroom Records, 2002, compact disc.

———. *Ten Canoes*. DVD. Directed by Rolf de Heer and Peter Djigirr. Produced by Rolf de Heer and Julie Ryan. Chippendale: Palace Films, 2006.

---

34. Gulpilil, in *"Ten Canoes,"* Press Kit, 12.

Foley, Gary. "Duplicity and Deceit: Rudd's Apology to the Stolen Generations." *Melbourne Historical Journal* 36 (2008) 1–6.

Freebury, Jane. *Dancing to His Song: The Singular Cinema of Rolf de Heer*. Strawberry Hills: Currency, 2015.

Henderson, Ian. "Stranger Danger: Approaching Home and *Ten Canoes*." *South Atlantic Quarterly* 108.1 (2009) 54–70.

Jennings, Willie James. *The Christian Imagination: Theology and Origins of Race*. New Haven: Yale University Press, 2010.

———. "Disfigurations of Christian Identity: Performing Identity as Theological Method." In *Lived Theology: New Perspectives on Method, Style, and Pedagogy*, edited by Charles Marsh et al., 67–85. New York: Oxford University Press, 2017.

Johnson, Darlene. *Gulpilil: One Red Blood*. DVD. Directed by Darlene Johnson. Produced by Tom Zubrycki. Jotz Productions/Ronin Films, 2002.

Leonard, Richard. *The Mystical Gaze of the Cinema: The Films of Peter Weir*. Melbourne: Melbourne University Press, 2009.

McCredden, Lyn. "*Ten Canoes*: Engaging Difference." *Studies in Australasian Cinema* 6.1 (2012) 45–56.

Mundine, Djon. "The Aboriginal Memorial: Introduction." https://nga.gov.au/aboriginalmemorial/home.cfm.

Palace Films. "Ten Canoes." https://www.palacefilms.com.au/ten-canoes.

Pascoe, Bruce. *Dark Emu*. Adelaide: Griffin, 2014.

Prentis, Brooke. "What Can the Birds of the Land Tell Us?" In *Grounded in the Body, in Time and Place, in Scripture: Papers by Australian Women Scholars in the Evangelical Tradition*, edited by Jill Firth and Denise Cooper-Clarke, 19–30. Eugene, OR: Wipf & Stock, 2021.

Reynolds, Molly. *Still Our Country*. DVD. Directed by Molly Reynolds. Produced by Peter Djigirr et al. Vertigo Productions/National Film and Sound Archive/Bula'Bula Arts Aboriginal Corporation, 2014.

Rielly, Derek. *Gulpilil*. Sydney: Pan Macmillan Australia, 2019.

Screen Australia. "The Tracker." https://www.screenaustralia.gov.au/the-screen-guide/t/the-tracker-2002/16248/.

"Ten Canoes." https://www.yumpu.com/en/document/read/20796705/in-english-cannes-international-film-festival.

Victorin-Vangerud, Nancy M. "From Metaphors and Models to Maps: Thinking Theology with an Archipelagic Imagination." In *Theology That Matters: Ecology, Economy, and God*, edited by Kathleen Ray Darby, 75–90. Minneapolis: Augsburg Fortress, 2006.

Yunupingu, Djungadjunga, and Dhaggal Yunupingu. "Mungulk Dhalatj: A Calm Wisdom." In *Aboriginal Spirituality: Past, Present, Future*, edited by Anne Pattel-Gray, 94–98. Blackburn: HarperCollinsReligious, 1996.

20

Grass Cloak

Penny Dunstan

> There are consequences of the old ways with which I feel easiest: walking as enabling sight and thought, rather than encouraging retreat and escape; paths as offering not only means of traversing space, but also of ways of feeling, being and knowing.[1]

To dwell in Australia is to dwell with deep time. I feel time thick and sticky as I walk, my feet meeting earth along the paths that have always been walked upon. Although Australia is often thought of as a young country, always there are traces of the old ways. The old civilization that came before colonization still exists in memory and in fact. The grindstone resting at my front gate. A scared tree next to a river bank. A stone all-purpose knife sitting on top of a dam bank in a four-times reworked mine site. And indigenous crops. Grasses. Tall. Holding their grain and waiting for harvest. I rub the awns of Weeping grass (*Microlaena stipoides*) between my hands to liberate the grain in the same way as one does for wheat (*Triticum aestivum*, *Triticum durum*). The raw grain is nutty to taste, but I have never collected enough to bake into a loaf in the fire coals as the old people did before. If I were to walk without the knowledge that I am on Wonnarua Country, I would puzzle over the remnants of the old ways. But since I know, the very air sings with old time and old ways of understanding.

I walk my way into the grass-world with my dog. The earth pushes up to greet me bearing gifts of grass seeds and bindiis (*Soliva sessilis*). The grass seeds make their way through my boot eyelet holes to bury themselves in the flesh of my ankle. The bindiis spike into the paws of the dog. We stop. One paw, three seeds.

---

1. Macfarlane, *The Old Ways*, 24.

Penny Dunstan, *Grass Cloak*, 2020. Local harvest Microlaena stipoides, embroidery cotton, steel, and forest redgum (*Eucalyptus tereticornis*), 160 x 120 x 25 cm. Artist's collection.

It is a windy wet afternoon. A woman with dark skin and dark hair strides through the Kangaroo Grass (*Themeda triandra*)-clad road embankment and slows to walk beside me. She is made of dark swirling fog and her shoulder-length hair bounces as she walks. Warm, light rain wafts around us. My dog walks determinedly in front, leash stretched to the maximum.

Time has collapsed. Old and new are meeting. She turns her head to speak to me. *Why do you walk this funny way?*

My head is full of lockdown art. Zoom painting groups. Pre-COVID painting lessons. And a deadline for an exhibition at Curve Gallery in Newcastle. I have nothing finished. It's starting to really bother me that I have too many choices. What is my new mentor talking about? How do I answer? My mentor reads my mind: *This is not the path you know*, she says as she leaves me, crossing the road to stride her way through the trees towards the Williams River.

The dog and I turn to walk home. What path? An old path? I know that my house is built on an old meeting ground. There is a spring near the top of the hill and I have found two grindstones. It was and is a sheltered place to meet under the lee of an east-facing hill where the westerlies cannot reach. There must be lots of paths that lead to the meeting place. Making my way back by the treed small rural blocks I puzzle about her words. And then as I round the corner into my driveway, I understand her advice. *Choose the path you know*. On the side of the long driveway, a crop of *Microlaena stipoides* waves to me. *Choose the path you know*. I am an agronomist, interested in soils and plants. And an indigenous grain crop is waving to me.

The grass swooshes in the breeze, its full grain seed heads curling over to knee height. My driveway grass, home to quail, lizards, and mice, cloaks the ground with food and forage. I have done nothing but not mow it. Underground vast networks of grass roots, with their mycorrhizal fungi extensions, feed worms, bacteria, and other small lifeforms in turn feeding the soil and trees. Mantle of green, grass of plenty: the old ways speak of perennial Indigenous agriculture. Old time flows into present day. I know what to make now.

Bibliography

Macfarlane, Robert. *The Old Ways: A Journey on Foot*. London: Penguin, 2013.

21

"My Past Has Thrown Me Out"

Reading Samuel Beckett's Plays in an Age of Trauma

Jason Goroncy

As a direct response to the earthquake and tsunami that hit Japan on March 11, 2011, and that caused such catastrophic loss and disaster, the Japan Society for the Promotion of Science undertook to begin a project on trauma in the work of the Irish novelist, playwright, poet, and theatre director Samuel Beckett (1906–89). It follows a similar project on Beckett and pain,[1] and companions attention to Beckett in work by theatre director and playwright Yuta Hagiwara, most notably his award-winning *Waiting for Godot in Fukushima* (2011), a play set near Futatsunuma Park, some 20 km from the Fukushima Daiichi Nuclear Power Plant. *Waiting for Godot in Fukushima* was performed on August 6, the anniversary of the United States of America's 1945 terrorist attack on Hiroshima. In Hagiwara's play, bodies exposed to radiation wait for one who "won't come this evening."[2]

---

1. Tanaka et al., *Samuel Beckett and Pain*. There is, in fact, considerable interest in Beckett's work in Japan. See, for example, Okamuro, "Make Sense Who May," 21–40; Gontarski, "An Interview with Director Makoto Sato," 186–94; Kyong, "A Portrait of the Writer in Beckett's *Ohio Impromptu*," 147–64; Kataoka, "Structure of Images," 19–37; Yoshiko, "The Effect of Translated Plays," 113–22.

2. Hagiwara was inspired by the artist collective Chim↑Pom, who were really the first artists to respond to the Fukushima disaster, and particularly by their massive "guerrilla style installation," *Level 7 feat. "Myth of Tomorrow."* See Chim↑Pom, "Level 7 feat. 'Myth of Tomorrow.'" The same year, 2011, The New National Theatre of Japan, in Tokyo, put on *Waiting for Godot*, directed by Mori Shintaro. In 2019, the same play ran again, this time at the Kanagawa Arts Theatre in Yokohama, directed by Junnosuke Tada. Around the same time, Hagiwara turned again to Beckett, this time to *Happy Days*, with performances at Keio University, Tokyo, in 2018, and at the CAVE, Yokohama, in 2019. Hagiwara returned to performing *Happy Days* in 2021 against the backdrop of the COVID-19 pandemic. He writes: "The body of Winnie that can't move at all

For Hagiwara, "doing theatre by taking a risk of radioactive exposure was the only way for the artist to acquire the status of *tojisha*, the affected, in the time of crisis."[3]

Scene from *Waiting for Godot in Fukushima,* directed by Yuta Hagiwara. Featuring Honami Shimizu, Shintaro Yokote, and Ichiro Matsubara. Near Futatsunuma Park, Fukushima, 2011. Photo by Takashi Fujii.

For Mariko Hori Tanaka, Yoshiki Tajiri, and Michiko Tsushima, "What Beckett writes," they said, "made us think of the way we could overcome our own trauma."[4] But why Beckett? What is it about his work that might prove to be of interest to those who seek to understand, to live with, and to "overcome" trauma in its many guises?[5] The answer, they suggest,

---

is a good metaphor for the pandemic period. But 'why' can't we move somewhere? My artistic theme is focused on 'Public'. In the period of pandemic, people have the image that someone from outside brings a virus, which means we can't make it public. Yes, for Winnie, outside is the existence of God. . . . [S]he prays a lot. The more she prays, the more she can't move." Yuta Hagiwara, email to author, June 12, 2021. For a survey of the performative responses to the tragedy at Fukushima, see Uchino, "After the Quake."

3. Uchino, "After the Quake," 6.

4. Tanaka et al., "Acknowledgements," xi.

5. The collection of essays published in the *Journal of Beckett Studies* 17.1–2 (2008) provides much evidence of Beckett's interest in neuroscience and clinical psychology. See also, for example, Jones, *Samuel Beckett and Testimony*; Jones, "Strange Pain," 135–50.

lies in the way that Beckett's work manages to traverse the spaces between understanding trauma as unrepresentable (or anti-representational) and examining trauma through its social and cultural contexts, spaces that represent something of an impasse in trauma theory and its accompanying debates.[6] What follows here is an examination of the ways that Beckett's plays represent trauma, its inescapable complexities, its refusals to conform to the (Freudian and other) orthodoxies by which trauma is typically understood, and their invitation to re-examine underlying assumptions about narrative and interpretive agency. Attending to matters such as bodies, time, nature, and memory, this essay demonstrates how reading Beckett can assist those seeking to better understand and articulate the multiple entanglements that characterize trauma.

Haunted Bodies, Surviving Bodies

There is, for a start, the fact that the bodies of Beckett's characters are always haunted and compromised—Hamm, Clov, Nagg, and Nell in *Endgame*, the bedridden and pebble-sucking Molloy in *Molloy*, Malone's physical limitations, Mouth's "practically speechless"[7] testimony of her survival, her "prayer unanswered,"[8] in *Not I*, for example. In this way, Beckett's characters bear witness to the ways that "trauma is not locatable in the simple violent or original event in an individual's past, but rather in the way that its very unassimilated nature—the way it was precisely *not known* in the first instance—returns to haunt the survivor later on."[9] The haunting is located, carried, in the body.[10] There is Estragon's feet, Vladimir's prostate issues, and Pozzo's blindness in

    6. See Tanaka et al., "Introduction," 4–5; Tanaka, "The Global Trauma of the Nuclear Age," 173–93.

    7. Beckett, "Not I," 219. *Not I* is a good example of what Cathy Caruth would describe as "the narrative of belated experience." Caruth, *Unclaimed Experience*, 7. Mouth appears as a kind of open wound that, in Caruth's description of trauma, "addresses us in the attempt to tell us of a reality or truth that is not otherwise available" (Caruth, *Unclaimed Experience*, 4), but does so in ways that "the reality of the event becomes unclear, and seems permanently obscured by incomplete descriptions and vague inferences." Tranter, *Beckett's Late Stage*, 114.

    8. Beckett, "Not I," 222. For an extended discussion about *Not I* and trauma, see Tranter, *Beckett's Late Stage*, 113–28.

    9. Caruth, *Unclaimed Experience*, 4. See also Tonning, "*Not I* and the Trauma of Birth," 21–34. More recently, Christopher Langlois has argued that "Beckett's orientation of thinking in literature is enthralled to an *eternal return of terror*." Langlois, *Samuel Beckett and the Terror of Literature*, 10.

    10. On Beckett's bodies, see Rabillard, "The Body in Beckett," 99–118; Gontarski, "The Body in the Body of Beckett's Theatre," 169–77; Jones, "*Insignificant Residues*," 71–93; Rada, "Boring Holes," 22–39; Sigg, "Bodily Object Voices in *Embers*," 116–31; Tsushima, "The Skin of Words," 94–115.

Waiting for Godot. There is blind and poor old Billy in *Rough for Theatre I* who "scrapes his fiddle," and his wheelchair-bound amputee neighbor who sits there "in my lair, in my chair, in the dark, twenty-three hours out of the twenty-four."[11] There is, in *Ohio Impromptu*,[12] that indelible conversation of "buried" thoughts—of movement from speech to silence to speech to silence to lonely speech to solitary silence, that knock, the haunted *Selah* defying nostalgia and wounded by memory—between "Listener" and "Reader" (the character and their own ghost, or alter ego, or divided self).[13] What a description of hell is there—"Buried in who knows what profounds of mind. Of mindlessness. Whither no light can reach. No sound."[14] It is literature written during, and in the aftermath of, the Second World War, from a Europe still horrified by the First World War.[15] It is literature scarred by these facts. It is literature that resists being defined by that fact. It is literature that makes visible trauma's somatic memory. It is literature that witnesses to the ways that violence renders the entire world unsafe. One might recall here Jean Améry's observations about the tortured, observations that have also been employed to describe, for example, victims of rape:

> Whoever has succumbed to torture can no longer feel at home in the world. The shame of destruction cannot be erased. Trust in the world, which already collapsed in part at the first blow, but in the end, under torture, fully, will not be regained. That one's fellow man was experienced as the antiman remains in the tortured person as accumulated horror. It blocks the view into a world in which the principle of hope rules.[16]

And yet, so much of Beckett's work is marked by a kind of imperturbable survivalism. Such is undeniably present in his four major plays, where couples Vladimir and Estragon in *Waiting for Godot*, Hamm and Clov, and Nagg and Nell in *Endgame*, the two Krapps, thirty years apart, in *Krapp's Last Tape*, and Winnie and Willie in *Happy Days*, shelter in place for time both undetermined and unresolved. They "go on" under a kind of

---

11. Beckett, "Rough for Theatre I," 67, 69.
12. Beckett, "Ohio Impromptu," 283–88.
13. A pattern seen also in *Krapp's Last Tape*, *Footfalls*, *That Time*, and *Waiting for Godot*. See Laing, *The Divided Self*. For an extended discussion about *Footfalls* and trauma, see Tranter, *Beckett's Late Stage*, 145–61.
14. Beckett, "Ohio Impromptu," 288.
15. On which, see Knowlson, *Damned to Fame*, chap. 14; Moody, "The *Non-Lieu* of Hunger," 261–74.
16. Améry, *At the Mind's Limits*, 40; cf. Waxman, "Rape and Sexual Abuse in Hiding," 132.

sequestration, even when they "can't go on like this."[17] They seem to be waiting out something; perhaps life itself. "The end is in the beginning and yet you go on."[18] "It's the way of doing it that counts, the way of doing it, if you want to go on living."[19]

Scene from *Krapp's Last Tape*, directed by Dominic Hill. Featuring Gerard Murphy as Krapp. Citizens Theatre, Glasgow, 2012. Photo by Tommy Ga-Ken Wan.

Elusive Selves, Empty Words

Another way to answer such questions—about why Beckett, and what is it about his work that addresses those who seek to understand and to live with trauma—is to draw attention to the ways that trauma eludes concrete identification: "Nothing is more real than nothing."[20] Unlike most plays where the narratives and scenes are made coherent to the audience by way of connection with cultural and historical signs by which the audience can revisit and reappraise things, Beckett's plays make other demands on the audience. As Rhys Tranter has observed:

17. Beckett, *Waiting for Godot*, 60.
18. Beckett, "Endgame," 69.
19. Beckett, *Waiting for Godot*, 38.
20. Beckett, *Malone Dies*, 16.

> In place of realistic representations that can immerse us in the past, we have unreliable voices emanating from unclear sources. Instead of illumination, the curtain opens on darkness and obscurity. The protagonists of these shady texts are unreliable, both in their appearance and in what they relate to us: some are mere fragments, a disembodied mouth or an isolated head; others are perhaps without a body altogether. Their narratives are partial and unclear, circling around distressing events and traumatic blackouts. But the repetition of these narratives, the acting out of neurotic symptoms, does not bring closure on Beckett's stage. Instead of returning us to a moment in the past, repetition, like rehearsal, only projects us toward a later unforeseeable future. These gestures of repetition, whether they are spoken or acted out, do not bring the past within grasp of the present, but break down our grip on what we think the present to be.[21]

This is to recall Sigmund Freud's belief that to identify the trauma would be to "dispose of" it, for the act of identification is an act of mastery. Among the realities that makes—and what *keeps*—trauma trauma is that one "no longer [has] any possibility of preventing the mental apparatus from being flooded with large amounts of stimulus, and another problem arises instead—the problem of mastering the amounts of stimulus which have broken in and of binding them, in the psychical sense, so that they can then be disposed of."[22] Trauma's deepest work, therefore, happens off stage, as it were. What one is given to see are the ghosts, the residues, the indicia of trauma, the denial or deferral of meaning carried in hyperaroused bodies ever alert to and expecting danger, intruded bodies marked with the indelible imprints of trauma's moment of genesis, and constricted bodies habituated by numb responses of surrender.[23]

Insofar as this is true, trauma not only eludes concrete identification; it also punctuates it. This is certainly true in Beckett's plays wherein language, presence, and subjectivity are deconstructed and, above all, fragmented. The intrusive and irrepressible "imperative to tell"[24] is met by inadequacy, by "empty words,"[25] by failing words,[26] by perpetually repeating "the old

21. Tranter, *Beckett's Late Stage*, 161.
22. Freud, *Beyond the Pleasure Principle*, 23–24.
23. See Herman, *Trauma and Recovery*, 35.
24. Laub, "An Event without a Witness," 78. Cf. Beckett, *Waiting for Godot*, 41: "VLADIMIR: To have lived is not enough for [the dead voices]. ESTRAGON: They have to talk about it."
25. Beckett, *Happy Days*, 38.
26. So Beckett, *Happy Days*, 24: "Words fail, there are times when even they fail."

questions, the old answers,"²⁷ by "the impossibility of telling,"²⁸ or by silence. One exchange between Vladimir and Estragon in *Waiting for Godot* provides but one example:

> [*Long silence.*]
>
> VLADIMIR: Say something!
>
> ESTRAGON: I'm trying. [*Long silence*]."
>
> VLADIMIR: (*in anguish*). Say anything at all!
>
> ESTRAGON: What do we do now?
>
> VLADIMIR: Wait for Godot.
>
> ESTRAGON: Ah!
>
> *Silence.*
>
> VLADIMIR: This is awful!
>
> ESTRAGON: Sing something.
>
> VLADIMIR: No no! (*He reflects.*) We could start all over again perhaps.²⁹

What Time Is It?

Beckett's three short plays—*What Where*, *That Time*,³⁰ and *Ohio Impromptu*—provide three further examples of this. In the worlds Beckett creates,

---

27. Beckett, "Endgame," 38. Cf. Butler, *Bodies That Matter*, 2.

28. Laub, "An Event without a Witness," 79.

29. Beckett, *Waiting for Godot*, 40–41. This is an example of what Laura Brown and Robert Jay Lifton refer to as "psychic numbing," or what Caruth calls "amnesiac reenactment." See Brown, "Not outside the Range," 100, 104; Caruth, "An Interview with Robert Jay Lifton," 136; Caruth, "II. Recapturing the Past," 153. Writing of Shoah survivors, Dori Laub observes: "None find peace in silence, even when it is their choice to remain silent. Moreover, survivors who do not tell their story become victims of a distorted memory, that is, of a forcibly imposed 'external evil,' which causes an endless struggle with and over a delusion. The 'not telling' of the story serves as a perpetuation of its tyranny. The events become more and more distorted in their silent retention and pervasively invade and contaminate the survivor's daily life. The longer the story remains untold, the more distorted it becomes in the survivor's conception of it, so much so that the survivor doubts the reality of the actual events." Laub, "An Event without a Witness," 79.

30. For an extended discussion about *That Time* and trauma, see Tranter, "Without Solution of Continuity," 115–28; Tranter, *Beckett's Late Stage*, 129–44.

people exist in a perpetual state of flux, wherein earlier versions of the self tend to be elusive and foreign and readily discardable. So Krapp: "Just been listening to that stupid bastard I took myself for thirty years ago, hard to believe I was ever as bad as that. Thank God that's all done with anyway."[31] And yet, the histories of traumatized bodies remain inescapable: "Shall we hold hands in the old way?" says Vi to Ru and Flo, in *Come and Go*.[32] Or as Beckett would write elsewhere: "Yesterday is not a milestone that has been passed, but a daystone on the beaten track of the years, and irremediably part of us, within us, heavy and dangerous. We are not merely more weary because of yesterday, we are other, no longer what we were before the calamity of yesterday."[33]

Scene from *Come and Go*, directed by Marc Atkinson Borrull and Nicholas Johnson. Set by Colm McNally. Costumes by Liadain Kaminska Ní Bhraonáin. Featuring Siobhán Cullen, Ellen Flynn, and Ellen Patterson. Samuel Beckett Theatre, Dublin, 2012. Photo by Colm McNally.

Such work is, like trauma, marked by a disorientating absence of time, of self, and, very often, of place.[34] Like trauma, it remains "elusive, troubling the borderlines between what exists and what does not."[35] So Tranter:

31. Beckett, "Krapp's Last Tape," 24.
32. Beckett, "Come and Go," 195.
33. Beckett, *Proust*, 3.
34. See Moorjani, *The Aesthetics of Loss and Lessness*, 175; Kennedy, "Introduction," 1; Boxall, *Since Beckett*, 3.
35. Tranter, *Beckett's Late Stage*, 19.

> The status of trauma in Beckett's writing appears to resist concrete or meaningful understandings. Its appearances are, by definition, peripheral and fragmentary. . . . Beckett's work appears to designate a space for the representation of trauma or traumatic experience, but it is a space that is constantly shifting in tone and perspective: from pathos to tragedy to humour, categories of action and being, past and present, are continually called into question.[36]

In this sense, Beckett's work may be representative also, as Anna-Verena Nosthoff has argued, of a kind of "inverse theology" that first and foremost questions itself, "a historico–dialectical reflection on and an unconditional confrontation with a renewed theodicy" laden, however inconspicuously, with modes of "inverted messianic promise" while culminating in "a form of reasoning that transcends the existing without hypostatizing any specific form of transcendence."[37]

To be sure, Beckett's work represents trauma in idiosyncratic ways, ways that stand as a warning against those moderns who would employ trauma as a "hermeneutical tool . . . and literary trope"[38] for reading any text, something that has become especially popular—and often deeply troubling—in relation to the reading of modern and postmodern texts, as well as ancient texts such as the Bible. It is something of an irony, as Jonathan Boulter has noted, that the same postmodernism that "celebrates the shattering and loss of traditional metaphysical and ontological categories such as truth, ethics, and the subject" should read texts through the lenses provided by trauma therapists concerned to reintegrate these concepts "precisely as they work toward discovering, narrating, working-through (to borrow Freud's term) the originary loss."[39] *Not I* is one complicated example of this, of speech trying, impossibly so, to "fill in gaps in memory," to create a life narrative, and thereby both decontaminate the present and "overcome resistances due to repression."[40] Mouth has "something she had to— . . . tell,"[41] however unreliable or lacking in concreteness, however irreducible or "unresponsive to rational investigation, temporal logic, or the meaning of

---

36. Tranter, *Beckett's Late Stage*, 19, 22–23. See also McMullan, "The Eye of Judgement," 82–96.
37. Nosthoff, "Beckett, Adorno, and the Hope," 37–38.
38. Boulter, "Does Mourning Require a Subject?" 332.
39. Boulter, "Does Mourning Require a Subject?" 332–33.
40. Freud, "Remembering, Repeating, and Working-Through," 148.
41. Beckett, "Not I," 221.

linguistic terms"[42] her account might prove to be. As Tranter rightly avers: "Working through in *Not I* is not simply an attempt to reconcile oneself with the past, but to rehearse a traumatic experience of disorientation and temporal suspension."[43] In this way it is not too unlike Christian communities celebrating the Eucharist.[44] And again:

> *Not I* operates like a discourse on trauma that forbids all meaningful and coherent gestures, a discourse that does not find a comfortable end in truth and closure but instead rehearses trauma's uncanny themes of loss, absence and disorientation. In *Not I*, memory itself is an acting-out procedure that defines the human subject while simultaneously disowning it. All memory is, to some extent, traumatic: the impossible integration of the human and language, of the corporeal body and the articulation that allows it to exist.[45]

For Boulter, what makes thinking about trauma through Beckett's work both interesting and radical is the way that it "manages to avoid this ghostly metaphysical haunting, this nostalgia for an originary subject and scene of loss. It avoids this haunting precisely because the Beckettian narrator is unable to present itself as a stable, unified (or potentially unified) subject"—a subject, that is, "without history or memory, without, that is, those preconditions for trauma and mourning. . . . Certainly the narrator has undergone (or claims to have undergone) some radical alteration. This change places him 'now' (whenever that is) in a state of being beyond categories of life and death. He is alive, yet dead; alive in death. The narrator is postlife, postdeath, postgrave."[46] Writing about *Endgame* (although the same might be observed about any number of Beckett's plays), Theodor Adorno notes:

> History is excluded, because it itself has dehydrated the power of consciousness to think history, the power of remembrance. Drama falls silent and becomes gesture, frozen amid the dialogues. Only the result of history appears—as decline. What

---

42. Tranter, *Beckett's Late Stage*, 117. This idea of working-through is far from straightforward in *Not I* because the idea relies on a kind of stability and correspondence between the past and the present that is not present in Beckett's play. See Tranter, *Beckett's Late Stage*, 119–21.

43. Tranter, *Beckett's Late Stage*, 122; see also 162.

44. See Goroncy, "The Catholicity of Time," 22–44; Goroncy, "Live Bread for the Starved Folk," 75.

45. Tranter, *Beckett's Late Stage*, 127–28.

46. Boulter, "Does Mourning Require a Subject?" 333, 338.

preens itself in the existentialists as the once-and-for-all of being has withered to the sharp point of history which breaks off.[47]

And yet, it is precisely Beckett's skill in being able to witness to history's *results* that means that history remains included in some ways. His works are not in fact ahistorical in character at all, even as they illustrate just how impossible fully understanding or making meaning from history itself remains. In this way, Beckett's texts are about *both* the transhistorical and the historical dimensions of trauma.[48] It is this that reveals so clearly his acute grasp of the *zeitgeist*, and that makes his work so significant for thinking about trauma, and for doing theology. For both, history is an unreliable necessity.

Throughout much of his work, Beckett appears to be uninterested in identifying the original trauma; at other times it is made quite explicit. "Birth," says the speaker in "A Piece of Monologue," "was the death of him,"[49] a statement that reflects something of Beckett's own appreciation of Otto Rank's *Das Trauma der Geburt*, an appreciation seen especially in his early works such as his poems collected in *Echo's Bones and Other Precipitates*.[50] It was an appreciation that he certainly did not share with Freud. There is, however, enough of Freud in Beckett to observe here his recognition of the idea that birth induces in us all a primal anxiety. But what matters throughout his work is the attention given to documenting, to bearing witness to, the ever-contemporary effects of that event. Beckett's is not the witness of faith that overcomes the night to see again the morning. It is, rather, the witness of an Ishmael condemned by Abraham to live out his days in the wilderness; or, as in Herman Melville's version, on the sea, citing Job—"And I only am escaped alone to tell thee."[51] Life is what happens between funerals. Beckett recognizes, brilliantly in fact, that what makes trauma trauma is that it is always, in Freudian terms, a "contemporary event."[52] This is the work of mourning, of mourning loss. To see—indeed, to see "the whole thing"—is, according to Becket, to come face to face with the unassailable fact that "the dark I have always struggled to keep under is in reality my most . . . unshatterable association until my dissolution."[53]

47. Adorno, "Trying to Understand *Endgame*," 125.
48. See Garrison, "Faintly Struggling Things," 105; Gibson, *Samuel Beckett*, 21–22.
49. Beckett, "A Piece of Monologue," 265.
50. See Rank, *Das Trauma der Geburt*; Beckett, *Echo's Bones and Other Precipitates*; Freud, *Inhibitions, Symptoms, and Anxiety*, 6; cf. Carville, "Smiling Tigers," 155–72.
51. Melville, *Moby Dick*, 509. The citation comes from Job 1:15, 16, 17, 19.
52. Freud, "Heredity and the Aetiology of the Neuroses," 154.
53. Beckett, "Krapp's Last Tape," 21.

But what happens to trauma when that mourning has no identifiable subject? Engaging with Beckett's *Texts for Nothing*, Boulter suggests that what we are confronted with therein is a kind of "aporetic mourning and trauma because we have a narrating subject without subjectivity."[54] He continues:

> We have a subject who cannot maintain with any certainty that the experiences he describes are in fact his own; we have a narrating subject who cannot discern if his voice is his own; we have a subject who cannot tell if he has a body; and most crucially, we have a subject who has no sense of personal history, no memory. We have, in short, a subject whose ontology denies the viability of mourning and trauma, yet who seems to display the symptomology of mourning and trauma.[55]

In other texts, Beckett explores the mystery of time and the reliability—and the downright cruelty—of memory, which he understands as "some miracle of analogy," as an "*accident*," and as "a clinical laboratory stocked with poison and remedy, stimulant and sedative."[56] Through the device of repetitive cyclic pattern and unavoidable linear progression, through the repercussions of history toward some inconsolable end[57]—or "not now"[58]—*Endgame*, for example, depicts time—its present, future, and past—as simultaneously meaningless[59] and entirely meaningful: "What time is it? / The same as usual."[60] "Yesterday! What does that mean? Yesterday!"[61] And, riffing on T. S. Eliot's *Four Quartets*: "The end is in the beginning and yet you go on."[62]

54. Boulter, "Does Mourning Require a Subject?" 337.
55. Boulter, "Does Mourning Require a Subject?" 337.
56. Beckett, *Proust*, 22, 54.
57. See Beckett, "Endgame," 36.
58. See Moorjani, *The Aesthetics of Loss and Lessness*, 179.
59. Adorno, for example, avers that "Understanding [*Endgame*] can mean nothing other than understanding its incomprehensibility, or concretely reconstructing its meaning structure—that it has none." Adorno, "Trying to Understand *Endgame*," 120. Nosthoff helpfully argues that "Adorno's reflections on Beckett are best understood as meditations on theology in the age of its impossibility." Nosthoff, "Beckett, Adorno, and the Hope," 36. She suggests that rather than following Adorno's reading of Beckett as an example of the end of metaphysics *per se*, we should read Beckett's work as an example of "a deconstruction of theology for the sake of saving theology" under the conditions created by the twentieth-century's wars. Nosthoff, "Beckett, Adorno, and the Hope," 50.
60. Beckett, "Endgame," 4. See also Georgiades, "Trauma, Company, and Witnessing," 99.
61. Beckett, "Endgame," 43.
62. Beckett, "Endgame," 69.

Nature and Nothingness

In its instability, in its resistance to chronology, Beckett's work offers testimony to the ways that trauma, through its own kind of complex of fragmentation, dispersal, and postponement, renders problematic the typical modes by which those in the West conceive and appraise cognition, making the experiences of trauma unspeakable.[63] This witness to fragmentation, to loss of plot, and to that of hope, is bound up with something even more basic—the sense of nature's unreliability, of nature's own abandonment of us: "Nature has forgotten us," says Hamm. To which Clov replies: "There's no more nature."[64] *Endgame*, by way of a kind of non-ridiculed Kierkegaardian parody, is an invitation to imagine—or to confess—a world unmarked by what was once marked with human hands; to imagine—or to confess—that some unnamed and perennial catastrophe, one achieved at human hands, has left nature itself extinguished, where nothing grows anymore:

> HAMM: Did your seeds come up?
>
> CLOV: No.
>
> HAMM: Did you scratch round them to see if they had sprouted?
>
> CLOV: They haven't sprouted.
>
> HAMM: Perhaps it's still too early.
>
> CLOV: If they were going to sprout they would have sprouted.
>
> (*Violently.*)
>
> They'll never sprout![65]

---

63. A notable exception to such modes is found in Polanyi's *Personal Knowledge* and *The Tacit Dimension*. Stanley Cavell describes the way that both couples in *Endgame* "have discovered the final plot: that there is no plot, that the truth has come out, that this is the end. But they would be mad to believe it and they cannot, being human, fully give up suspense. So they wait. Not for something, for they know there is nothing to wait for. So they try not to wait, but they do not know how to end." Cavell also suggests that "the confrontation with Christian writing would perhaps be the final test of the power of Beckett's sensibility." Cavell, "Ending the Waiting Game," 132, 161. A number of commentators, including Cavell, have argued that *Endgame* tells the story about the passion and resurrection—and about the end of Christianity, and that it is possibly the most unbroken portrait of Beckett's religious sensibilities. See Bryden, *Samuel Beckett and the Idea of God*, 144–45; Cohn, "*Endgame*," 40–52; Eisele, "The Apocalypse of Beckett's *Endgame*," 11–32; Sheedy, "The Comic Apocalypse of King Hamm," 310–18.

64. Beckett, "Endgame," 11.

65. Beckett, "Endgame," 13.

Scene from *Endgame*, directed by Dominic Hill. Featuring Peter Kelly as Nagg, David Neilson as Hamm, and Chris Gascoyne as Clov. Citizens Theatre, Glasgow, 2016. Photo by Tim Morozzo.

What Beckett teaches us is that to be human is, perhaps above all else, to wait, even if the object of that waiting is Friedrich Nietzsche's "nothingness."[66] Such waiting is characterized by one of two alternatives: "either nihilism or else the task of purposely undoing, re-evaluating all the purposes we have known, re-locating the gravity of purpose itself."[67] At one level, both alternatives—and they are real alternatives—look to be the same. Both are marked too by the danger that the end one seeks might in fact arrive. So Pozzo's confession in *Waiting for Godot*: "I don't seem to be able . . . (*long hesitation*) . . . to depart."[68] Or that of Estragon, in the same play: "Nothing happens, nobody comes, nobody goes, it's awful!,"[69] words that

---

66. So Nietzsche, *On the Genealogy of Morality*, 120: "[Humanity] still prefers to *will nothingness*, than *not* will." Stephen Levine notes: "It is no accident that during the siege of Sarajevo in the 1990s, Susan Sontag came to the Bosnian city to stage *Waiting for Godot*. The play was a repetition (*mimesis*) of the experience of the inhabitants: to wait, to be disappointed, to wait again, finally to realize that the one who is waited for will never arrive, to go on living while recognizing one's plight." Levine, *Trauma, Tragedy, Therapy*, 146.

67. Cavell, "Ending the Waiting Game," 150.

68. Beckett, *Waiting for Godot*, 31.

69. Beckett, *Waiting for Godot*, 28.

could easily have been attributed to Qoheleth, the pseudonymous author of the biblical book of Ecclesiastes. And that of Hamm (in *Endgame*): "It all happened without me. I don't know what's happened."[70] And then.

In a review entitled "The Uneventful Event," the Irish literary critic Vivien Mercier famously described *Waiting for Godot* as "a play in which nothing happens, *twice*."[71] And in Text 8 of *Texts for Nothing*, Beckett offers a lengthy description of how such going on, such *not* happening, is experienced:

> Time has turned into space and there will be no more time, till I get out of here. Yes, my past has thrown me out, its gates have slammed behind me, or I burrowed my way out alone, to linger a moment free in a dream of days and nights, dreaming of me moving, season after season, towards the last, like the living, till suddenly I was here, all memory gone. Ever since nothing but fantasies and hope of a story for me somehow, of having come from somewhere and of being able to go back, or on, somehow, some day, or without hope. Without what hope, haven't I just said, of seeing me alive, not merely inside an imaginary head, but a pebble sand to be, under a restless sky, restless on its shore, faint stirs day and night, as if to grow less could help, ever less and less and never quite be gone. No truly, no matter what, I say no matter what, hoping to wear out a voice, to wear out a head, or without hope, without reason, no matter what, without reason. But it will end, a desinence will come, or the breath fail better still, I'll be silence, I'll know I'm silence, no, in the silence you can't know, I'll never know anything. But at least get out of here, at least that, no? I don't know. And time begin again, the steps on the earth, the night the fool implores at morning and the morning he begs at evening not to dawn. I don't know, I don't know what all that means, day and night, earth and sky, begging and imploring.[72]

On one reading, this may be an example of the effects of *Nachträglichkeit* (afterwardness, deferred action) of which Freud spoke, and which Jacques Lacan revived in his use of the word *après-coup*, to describe the way

---

70. Beckett, "Endgame," 74.

71. Mercier, "The Uneventful Event," 6. See also Mercier, *Beckett/Beckett*, 74. Another critic, Kenneth Tynan, called *Waiting for Godot* a "dramatic vacuum." It has "no plot, no climax, no *dénouement*; no beginning, no middle, no end." Tynan, "New Writing," 11.

72. Beckett, *Texts for Nothing*, chap. 8.

that a repressed memory "only become[s] a trauma by *deferred action*,"[73] after the event. Here, lived time comes to a standstill and the traumatized subject is placed, trapped, in an inescapable "feedback loop that initiates a temporal stasis."[74] We see something similar expressed by Mouth in *Not I*:

> straining to hear . . . make something of it . . . and her own thoughts . . . make something of them . . . all– . . . what? . . . the buzzing? . . . yes . . . all the time the buzzing . . . [. . .] and the whole brain begging . . . something begging in the brain . . . begging the mouth to stop [. . .] like maddened . . . all that together . . . straining to hear . . . piece it together . . . and the brain . . . raving away on its own . . . trying to make sense of it . . . or make it stop . . . or in the past . . . dragging up the past . . . flashes from all over . . .[75]

Beckett's work, here and elsewhere, is certainly concerned with what Cathy Caruth describes as "a break in the mind's experience of time,"[76] the kind of disruption that is basic to accounts of trauma. So too Roger Luckhurst: "No narrative of trauma can be told in a linear way: it has a time signature that must fracture conventional causality."[77] That "buzzing," and those short phrases punctuated by pauses, denote and underscore an incapacity to make stable the present. And yet reading Beckett's text as a description of the effects of trauma—as witness to *Nachträglichkeit*—is not straightforward, for the narrator speaks too of the loss of all memory—"all memory gone." We know that one of the realities of trauma is that while some memories are (graciously) locked away, others are continually present, haunting survivors. It is one's inability to relate these memories to other memories that makes trauma trauma. This means that one "must be willing to read the narrator's condition as being one that displays the symptomology of trauma without being able to determine or name the etiology of that trauma."[78] This reading is at least plausible if one follows Caruth's defining trauma as the paradox that occurs when "the most direct seeing of a violent event . . . occur[s] as an absolute inability to know it."[79] And yet even still,

---

73. Freud, "Project for a Scientific Psychology," 356.

74. Boulter, "Does Mourning Require a Subject?" 340.

75. Beckett, "Not I," 220. Nico Muhly's recording *Mothertongue* appears to be a musical version of Beckett's *Not I*. See Muhl, *Mothertongue*.

76. Caruth, *Unclaimed Experience*, 61.

77. Luckhurst, *The Trauma Question*, 9.

78. Boulter, "Does Mourning Require a Subject?" 340; cf. Tranter, *Beckett's Late Stage*, 111–12.

79. Caruth, *Unclaimed Experience*, 91–92.

this does not account for the subject's claim to be robbed of all memory. "There is," as Boulter has noted, "a difference between not being able to recognize the past as your own and not having a past at all: 'My past has thrown me out.'"[80] He continues:

> By severing the narrator from his past, Beckett radicalizes the Freudian notion of *Nachträglichkeit*: memories may still be introjected into the narrator's present, but there is no hope of establishing a link between his own present condition and the trauma that is its precondition. Instead of having a story seemingly given to him unawares—as in the case of the victim of trauma who cannot recognize his past as his own—the Beckettian narrator can only hope (without hope, I suggest) for a story that will reconnect his present atemporal (nontemporal) condition to his past.[81]

Scene from *Happy Days*, directed by Yuta Hagiwara. Featuring Honami Shimizu as Winnie and Shin Ito as Willie. Keio University, Tokyo, 2018. Photo by Rakutaro Ogiwara.

80. Boulter, "Does Mourning Require a Subject?" 340.
81. Boulter, "Does Mourning Require a Subject?" 340–41.

To repeat the narrator's words in *Texts for Nothing*: "Ever since nothing but fantasies and hope of a story for me somehow, of having come from somewhere and of being able to go back, or on, somehow, some day, or without hope."[82] Boulter suggests that this line represents "a hope for a narrative that can only be a narrative of trauma, a hope for a memory that will clarify how the present condition came about . . . a desire for a kind of nostalgic return, perhaps an understanding that mourning is a kind of return in order to forget. But," he continues, "this can only be an aporetic hope."[83]

What Beckett represents in *Happy Days*, as in a number of other plays, "is the endless repetition of dying moments rather than death itself."[84] His characters desire life's end, but their desires remain unfulfilled as proximity to that end is dammed by the slowing down of the clock. As Richard Frank observes:

> The end of conventional tragedy usually coincides with the death of the protagonist. Beckett's protagonist never dies at the end of the action. Nor does his world end once and for all. His tragedy is not of death but of the impossibility of death. The final destination for man after a lifetime of learning is death. Knowledge brings no solution to the existential problem. Habit is not potent enough to keep the void at bay forever. No matter how effectively she tries to extend the length of time for each habit, Winnie [in *Happy Days*] does not succeed in filling her day with the habits she mobilizes. Time still remains, leaving her without any more resources. Beckett's character is bound to be exhausted, and language, her instrument, is not something that lasts forever either. It too runs out. When she dreams of being 'sucked up' into the air, she is in fact sinking deeper and deeper. When the tension between her aspiration and gravity reaches the maximum point, her parasol catches on fire. As she says: 'Ah earth you old extinguisher,' Winnie ultimately gives in. The earth will ultimately devour her and leave nothing.[85]

So Winnie, the play's main character:

> There always remains something. (*Pause.*) Of everything. (*Pause.*) Some remains. (*Pause.*) If the mind were to go. (*Pause.*) It won't of course. (*Pause.*) Not quite. (*Pause.*) Not mine. (*Smile.*) Not now. (*Smile broader.*) No no. (*Smile off.*

---

82. Beckett, *Texts for Nothing*, chap. 8.
83. Boulter, "Does Mourning Require a Subject?" 341.
84. Frank, "The Concept of Time and Space," para. 57.
85. Frank, "The Concept of Time and Space," para. 66.

Long pause.) It might be the eternal cold. (*Pause.*) Everlasting perishing cold. (*Pause.*)[86]

Scene from *Happy Days*, directed by Caitríona McLaughlin. Featuring Siobhán McSweeney as Winnie and Marty Rea as Willie. Olympia Theatre, Dublin, 2021. Produced by Landmark Productions. Photo by Patrick Redmond.

"Not quite." Here, as elsewhere in Beckett's work, we are exposed to the possibility of being haunted by memories that are nonexistent, that are ghosts and traces of ghosts. Traces that are like what "air leaves among the leaves, among the grass, among the sand . . . the air quite still that trembled once an instant, the tiny flurry of dust quite settled."[87] Here, trauma finds expression in mourning. Mourning is a kind of "working-through" (in the Freudian sense) but one that, in trauma, reaches no satisfying end but rather leaves one alone with "nothing but fantasies and hope of a story"[88] birthed of a nugatory desire to be a narrated and narratable self. Such desire finds expression in the incapacity to move past one's own voice, and in an ache that finds its end—for those who take the risk of living, of going on—in lamentation, in wondering "what pity is doing here and if it's not

86. Beckett, *Happy Days*, 52.
87. Beckett, *Texts for Nothing*, chap. 13.
88. Beckett, *Texts for Nothing*, chap. 13.

hope gleaming, another expression, evilly among the imaginary ashes, the faint hope of a faint being after all, human in kind."[89] And then beyond that to another possibility:

> Last everlasting questions, infant languors in the end sheets, last images, end of dream, of being past, passing and to be, end of lie. Is it possible, is that the possible thing at last, the extinction of this black nothing and its impossible shades, the end of the farce of making and the silencing of silence, it wonders, that voice which is silence, or it's me, there's no telling, it's all the same dream, the same silence, it and me, it and him, him and me, and all our train, and all theirs, and all theirs, but whose, whose dream, whose silence, old questions, last questions, ours who are dream and silence, but it's ended, we're ended who never were, soon there will be nothing where there was never anything, last images.[90]

Tricks Memories Play

Little wonder then that in a letter sent to his confident, Tom MacGreevy, Beckett writes: "Putting down old memories is enough to make anyone crack."[91] Or, as he articulated it in *The Expelled*:

> Memories are killing. So you must not think of certain things, of those that are dear to you, or rather you must think of them, for if you don't there is the danger of finding them, in your mind, little by little. That is to say, you must think of them for a while, a good while, every day several times a day, until they sink forever in the mud.[92]

And yet. Time and memory. These are, for Beckett, the modes that make self-recognition possible at all, however brief. His one-act play *That Time* explores this possibility, however difficult and knotty. It examines something like pure subjectivity in a play on time itself—an anniversary that is, as is the nature of the case, both exactly on time and always belated. Here the original event is marked in the loop of anniversary making,

89. Beckett, *Texts for Nothing*, chap. 13.
90. Beckett, *Texts for Nothing*, chap. 13.
91. Samuel Beckett to Tom MacGreevy, handwritten correspondence dated April 6, 1965, Archives of Trinity College, Dublin. Cited in Brown, "Yesterday's Deformities," 199. For more on how memory functions in Beckett's work, see Olney, *Memory and Narrative*; Kozdon, *Memory in Samuel Beckett's Plays*.
92. Beckett, "The Expelled," 32.

thereby unveiling the "impossibility of recalling or representing any single, specific historical moment in its completeness."[93] Beckett's characters do not suffer from amnesia, as some have suggested,[94] but rather from the burden of memories that refuse narration. They are continually trying to push away such memories. And they continually fail in doing so.

Scene from *Happy Days*, directed by Michael Hurst. Featuring Robyn Malcolm as Winnie and Cameron Rhodes as Willie. Silo Theatre, Auckland, 2010. Photo by Andrew Malmo.

In both *The Expelled* and *That Time*, Beckett achieves attention to the experiences of mourning and trauma through the trope of failure—to "sink and vanish without your having stirred any more than the two knobs on a dumbbell."[95] Indeed, Beckett's work is haunted by failure—presented, paradoxically, as the struggle of being itself, of continuing to cease. In *Texts for Nothing*, we read: "Suddenly, no, at last, long last, I couldn't any more, I couldn't go on."[96] And in *The Unnamable*: "I don't know, I'll never know, in

---

93. Tranter, *Beckett's Late Stage*, 163.

94. See, for example, Kennedy, "Action and Theatricality," 21; Carter, "Estragon's Ancient Wound," 130.

95. Beckett, "That Time," 232.

96. Beckett, *Texts for Nothing*, chap. 1.

the silence you don't know, you must go on, I can't go on, I'll go on."[97] This is what remembering, repeating, and trying to work-through is like:

> Where would I go, if I could go, who would I be, if I could be, what would I say, if I had a voice, who says this, saying it's me? Answer simply, someone answer simply. It's the same old stranger as ever, for whom alone accusative I exist, in the pit of my inexistence, of his, of ours, there's a simple answer.[98]

> I've been away, done something, been in a hole, I've just crawled out, perhaps I went silent, no, I say that in order to say something, in order to go on a little more, you must go on a little more, you must go on a long time more, you must go on evermore, if I could remember what I have said I could repeat it, if I could learn something by heart I'd be saved, I have to keep on saying the same thing and each time it's an effort, the seconds must be alike and each one is infernal, what am I saying now, I'm saying I wish I knew.[99]

In *Waiting for Godot* also we are confronted with a further vision of traumatic memory. Vladimir's monologue, for example, depicts his inability to integrate past events into a meaningful life narrative. Like Hamm's attempts to chronicle the past in *Endgame*, Vladimir's recollections are marked by incoherence, unfinishedness, absence, helplessness, immunity to "the vicissitudes of time,"[100] emotional paralysis, "accursed time."[101] When something is evoked, it is quickly dismissed: "That's all dead and buried. . . . There's no good harking back on that. Come on."[102] Both are also victims of their own past. So Hamm: "(*Violently*.) Use your head, can't you, use your head, you're on earth, there's no cure for that!"[103] And Estragon, in *Godot*'s opening line: "(*giving up again*). Nothing to be done."[104] One further way that Beckett's work witnesses to traumatic memory is by having Vladimir refer to the past through a series of questions, thus throwing into doubt memory's function in the aftermath of a traumatizing event because

---

97. Beckett, *The Unnamable*, chap. 1.
98. Beckett, *Texts for Nothing*, chap. 4.
99. Beckett, *The Unnamable*, chap. 1.
100. So Langer, *Holocaust Testimonies*, 112: "Trauma stops the chronological clock and fixes the moment permanently in memory and imagination, immune to the vicissitudes of time."
101. Beckett, *Waiting for Godot*, 58. Cf. Beckett, "Endgame," 36.
102. Beckett, *Waiting for Godot*, 35.
103. Beckett, "Endgame," 53.
104. Beckett, *Waiting for Godot*, 7.

memory no longer serves to link the past to the present. "Will night never come?"[105] "Extraordinary the tricks that memory plays!"[106]

To be honest is to see all in "failing light, at some little distance."[107] But in Beckett, who consistently repudiates the "craze for explicitation,"[108] even this is not always possible. In "Act without Words I,"[109] for example, the subject, who is himself thrown (the Heideggerian *Geworfenheit*) into the barren world, hears the call, the whistle that breaks the silences, but cannot respond in ways that build any meaning. Meaning, and even the possibility of meaning, remains elusive, refusing the subject the desperate possibility of escape, promising and then stealing away hope, exposing reality itself to be a mirage, his context a lie, his being resistant to being made sense of. In "A Piece of Monologue," the Speaker "stands stock still staring out. Into black vast. Nothing there. Nothing stirring. That he can see. Hear. Dwells thus as if unable to move again. Or no will left to move again. Not enough will left to move again."[110] But unlike in "An Act without Words I," here there is a turn, however brief, as the subject "turns in the end and gropes to where he knows the lamp is standing":

> Stands there staring beyond. Nothing. Empty dark. Till first word always the same. Night after night the same. Birth. Then slow fade up of a faint form. Out of the dark. A window. Looking west. Sun long sunk behind the larches. Light dying. Soon none left to die. No. No such thing as no light. Starless moonless heaven. Dies on to dawn and never dies. There in the dark that window. Night slowly falling.[111]

That groping appears again in "Act without Words II," which I interpret as an example of modernity's futile attempt to break free from humanity's primal needs—for example, friendship, clothing, food, rest, transcendence.

---

105. Beckett, *Waiting for Godot*, 24.
106. Beckett, *Waiting for Godot*, 33.
107. Beckett, *Watt*, 3.
108. Beckett, "Catastrophe," 299.
109. Beckett, "Act without Words I," 41–46.
110. Beckett, "A Piece of Monologue," 267.
111. Beckett, "A Piece of Monologue," 267.

Reading Beckett

Reading[112] Beckett is not easy.[113] For one, his work confronts us with difficult truths about the nature of things most of us spend a lifetime, and considerable resources, avoiding. It invites us to stay with such difficulties, and with the possibility of their being unresolved. But there is also something else: what can we make of texts that appear to have already read themselves? What is left for the reader to do? Reading Beckett to better understand trauma is equally difficult because he appears to make it impossible to speak of trauma as *trauma*. Indeed, he appears to use the concept of trauma against itself, and as a way of interrogating how Freudian psychoanalysis, for example, has approached the subject. For Beckett, trauma's traces play out only against the noise of a more encompassing architecture of ideas whose permissibility exists now mostly, or only, as an object of historical curiosity. His work pushes against the (Freudian and other) calls to work-through trauma by undertaking the painful odyssey backwards into history in order to resuscitate the past and thereby attempt to construct a meaningful narrative. It resists such a confident, and somewhat nostalgic, return on grounds that the kinds of coherence sought thereby remain, in short, impossible. (A play such as *That Time*, for example, shows just how complicated our relationship to history is.)

It is this, I suggest, that makes reading Beckett in order to better understand trauma—and trauma's paradoxes—so worthwhile. The value of his work lies exactly in the ways it donates itself unceasingly as a difficult deviation from more fashionable and admissible orthodoxies by which trauma is typically understood in modernity, and invites a re-examination of the underlying assumptions of narrative and interpretive agency. As Tranter noted, "the promise of 'inevitable outcome' is perpetually deferred and complicated" in Beckett's work, attesting to the fragility, instability, and "ceaseless transition from meaning to meaning"[114] associated with the experience of trauma itself. If Caruth is right to suggest that trauma is "marked, not by a simple knowledge, but by the ways it simultaneously defies and demands our witness,"[115] then Beckett's work both demonstrates

---

112. Here I use the word "reading" as a catch-all for all that is communicated to the senses in Beckett's work, and in the performances of such.

113. And yet, it is made more difficult than it might be when read in such a way as to support "impositions from an impression of fashionable philosophy." Cavell, "Ending the Waiting Game," 115. Cavell suggests that we should take Beckett's language far more literally and plainly than most commentators, and particularly contemporary analytical philosophers, are wont to do.

114. Tranter, *Beckett's Late Stage*, 30, 31.

115. Caruth, *Unclaimed Experience*, 5.

and exposes the ways that trauma itself both resists and problematizes Western epistemologies—including theological ones—through fragmenting, dispersing, and deferring the kinds of logic the Western canon has come to demand. In Beckett's work, trauma's realities are made most explicit precisely by "remaining inexplicit,"[116] and by refusing attempts to "harmoniously restore the past to the present" by "preserving the possibility of impossibility, silence, and darkness."[117]

Scene from *Krapp's Last Tape*, directed by Patty Gallagher. Featuring Paul Whitworth as Krapp. Jewel Theatre Company, Santa Cruz, 2011. Photo by Steve DiBartolomeo.

Beckett's plays also disrupt and challenge the usual modes that theatre typically assumes. While the vocabulary frequently recalls a cultural and artistic location, his plays are, by and large, geographically, historically, and relationally dislocated, without, or with very little, reference apart from his own *oeuvre*. They take place nowhere, and everywhere, witnessing, it seems, to a universal temporality. They are texts that witness to life lived always in the traumatized logic of travail, "continually moving from

116. Kennedy, "Introduction," 5.
117. Tranter, *Beckett's Late Stage*, 33.

one place to another, transgressing boundaries of here and there, past and present," resisting the temptation to witness to life—even post-apocalyptic life—as anything other than "a process of continual and partial transmission from one site to another, a series of discontinuous echoes and fragments that undermine the security of a final resting place,"[118] resisting the "unfortunate privilege"[119] of having the last word. They are concerned with that which "remains when the thematics [are] exhausted."[120] They play with elements of reality but refuse to take a position. They are, both literally and figuratively, as stark as they are quotidian. In most cases, the plays' characters evidence very little known history or pre-established relationships. "His 'homeless' people have simply been thrown into a strange land without any preliminary explanation about their situation. They hardly recognize each other as members of the same community, nor know what to do with each other or the time given them."[121]

Adorno suggests that by so hiding its face, Beckett's work "participates in the absurd."[122] Dennis Potter, a reviewer in London's *Sunday Times*, sourly identified Beckett's work with the same mode of depravity that birthed Nazi concentration camps and Stalin's gulags: "Would Solzhenitsyn have understood [Beckett's work]? Would the Jews on the way to the gas chamber? Question: Is this the art which is the response to the despair and pity of our age, or is it made of the kind of futility which helped such desecrations of the spirit, such filth of ideologies come into being?"[123] On one level, these are odd words to level against someone who had joined the French Resistance movement against the Nazis, work for which he was awarded the Croix de Guerre, and who, indeed, produced some of his most prolific and best-known work during this "siege in the room" period.[124] On another level, they evidence a misreading, I think, of Beckett's relationship with nihilism, seeing in his work a cooperation with the kind of being thrown towards death that birthed the great horrors of the twentieth century and that characterizes the human condition under the aegis of modernity rather than holding up a mirror to them. But Beckett's work does what modernity won't do—give the dead a voice. By doing

118. Tranter, *Beckett's Late Stage*, 40, 41.

119. Blanchot, *The Infinite Conversation*, 326.

120. Derrida, *Acts of Literature*, 61.

121. Frank, "The Concept of Time and Space," para. 37; cf. Georgiades, "Trauma, Company, and Witnessing," 9.

122. Adorno, "Trying to Understand *Endgame*," 126.

123. Dennis Potter, *Sunday Times*, April 24, 1977. Cited in Knowlson, *Damned to Fame*, chap. 24.

124. See Bair, *Samuel Beckett*, 346–80.

so, it evinces both compassion towards and complicity in the experience of trauma in ways that can both give broader significance and upraise further obstructions for how trauma is understood.

I do not know if the Japan Society for the Promotion of Science ever discovered through reading Beckett's work a way to "overcome" trauma, as they had hoped. But it seems impossible to imagine that their engagement with his work would not have assisted its members to at least better understand the complexities of trauma. While Beckett's work stubbornly eludes any single definitive interpretation—whether about trauma or anything else—and there is the ever-present danger, and temptation, of reading too much, or too little, into his work, there is therein, deliberately so, "a form," as Beckett puts it, "that accommodates the mess"[125] that is the twentieth century, and, so far, the twenty-first century, and that resists the lie that "the Transcendent will save us,"[126] whether that which is dressed up in the vestments of ethical and political commitments, or those of religion.

Bibliography

Adorno, Theodor W. "Trying to Understand *Endgame*." *New German Critique* 26 (1982) 119–50.

Améry, Jean. *At the Mind's Limits: Contemplations by a Survivor on Auschwitz and Its Realities*. Translated by Sidney Rosenfeld and Stella P. Rosenfeld. Bloomington: Indiana University Press, 1980.

Bair, Deirdre. *Samuel Beckett: A Biography*. London: Cape, 1978.

Beckett, Samuel. "A Piece of Monologue." In *Collected Shorter Plays*, 263–69. New York: Grove, 1984.

———. "Act without Words I." In *Collected Shorter Plays*, 41–46. New York: Grove, 1984.

———. "Catastrophe." In *Collected Shorter Plays*, 295–301. New York: Grove, 1984.

———. "Come and Go." In *Collected Shorter Plays*, 191–97. New York: Grove, 1984.

———. *Echo's Bones and Other Precipitates*. Paris: Europa, 1935.

———. "Endgame: A Play in One Act." In *Endgame: A Play in One Act; Followed by Act without Words: A Mime for One Player*, v–84. New York: Grove, 1958.

---

125. Samuel Beckett, as cited in Driver, "Beckett by the Madeleine," 23.

126. Deleuze and Guattari, *What is Philosophy?* 47. Levine suggests: "If to live in hope is to die in despair, then perhaps to live in despair is to die in hope. By abandoning the myth of salvation, without surrendering the pathos of the infinite, we are given the divine gift of laughter by means of which we can witness our own condition. This is the message of Beckett's art of despair." Levine, *Trauma, Tragedy, Therapy*, 151.

———. "The Expelled." In *First Love and Other Novellas*, 32–46. London: Penguin, 2000.
———. *Happy Days*. New York: Grove, 1961.
———. "Krapp's Last Tape." In *Krapp's Last Tape, and Other Dramatic Pieces*, 7–28. New York: Grove, 1960.
———. *Malone Dies*. Translated by Samuel Beckett. New York: Grove, 1956.
———. "Not I." In *Collected Shorter Plays*, 213–23. New York: Grove, 1984.
———. "Ohio Impromptu." In *Collected Shorter Plays*, 283–88. New York: Grove, 1984.
———. *Proust*. New York: Grove, 1978.
———. "Rough for Theatre I." In *Collected Shorter Plays*, 65–73. New York: Grove, 1984.
———. *Texts for Nothing and Other Shorter Prose, 1950–1976*. Edited by Mark Nixon. London: Faber and Faber, 2010. ePub.
———. "That Time." In *Collected Shorter Plays*, 225–35. New York: Grove, 1984.
———. *The Unnamable*. Edited by Steven Connor. London: Faber and Faber, 2010. ePub.
———. *Waiting for Godot: Tragicomedy in 2 Acts*. New York: Grove, 1954.
———. *Watt*. Edited by C. J. Ackerley. London: Faber and Faber, 2009.
Blanchot, Maurice. *The Infinite Conversation*. Translated by Susan Hanson. Minneapolis: University of Minnesota Press, 1993.
Boulter, Jonathan. "Does Mourning Require a Subject? Samuel Beckett's *Texts for Nothing*." MFS 50.2 (2004) 332–50.
Boxall, Peter. *Since Beckett: Contemporary Writing in the Wake of Modernism*. London: Continuum, 2009.
Brown, Laura S. "Not outside the Range: One Feminist Perspective on Psychic Trauma." In *Trauma: Explorations in Memory*, edited by Cathy Caruth, 100–112. Baltimore: Johns Hopkins University Press, 1995.
Brown, Verna J. M. "Yesterday's Deformities: A Discussion of the Role of Memory and Discourse in the Plays of Samuel Beckett." DLitt et Phil diss., University of South Africa, 2005.
Bryden, Mary. *Samuel Beckett and the Idea of God*. London: Macmillan, 1998.
Butler, Judith. *Bodies That Matter: On the Discursive Limits of "Sex."* New York: Routledge, 1993.
Carter, Steven. "Estragon's Ancient Wound: A Note on *Waiting for Godot*." *Journal of Beckett Studies* 6.1 (1996) 125–34.
Caruth, Cathy. "An Interview with Robert Jay Lifton." In *Trauma: Explorations in Memory*, edited by Cathy Caruth, 128–47. Baltimore: Johns Hopkins University Press, 1995.
———. "II. Recapturing the Past: Introduction." In *Trauma: Explorations in Memory*, edited by Cathy Caruth, 151–57. Baltimore: Johns Hopkins University Press, 1995.
———. *Unclaimed Experience: Trauma, Narrative, and History*. Baltimore: Johns Hopkins University Press, 1996.
Carville, Conor. "Smiling Tigers: Trauma, Sexuality, and Creaturely Life in *Echo's Bones*." In *Samuel Beckett and Trauma*, edited by Mariko Hori Tanaka et al., 155–72. Manchester: Manchester University Press, 2018.
Cavell, Stanley. "Ending the Waiting Game: A Reading of Beckett's *Endgame*." In *Must We Mean What We Say? A Book of Essays*, 115–62. Cambridge: Cambridge University Press, 1976.

Chim↑Pom. "Level 7 feat. 'Myth of Tomorrow.'" http://chimpom.jp/project/real-times.html#lev7.

Cohn, Ruby. "*Endgame*." In *Twentieth Century Interpretations of Endgame: A Collection of Critical Essays*, edited by Bell G. Chevigny, 40–52. Englewood Cliffs: Prentice-Hall, 1969.

Deleuze, Gilles, and Félix Guattari. *What Is Philosophy?* Translated by Hugh Tomlinson and Graham Burchell. New York: Columbia University Press, 1994.

Derrida, Jacques. *Acts of Literature*. Edited by Derek Attridge. New York: Routledge, 1992.

Driver, Tom F. "Beckett by the Madeleine." *Columbia University Forum* 4.3 (1961) 21–25.

Eisele, Thomas D. "The Apocalypse of Beckett's *Endgame*." *Cross Currents* 26.1 (1976) 11–32.

Frank, Richard. "The Concept of Time and Space in Beckett's Dramas *Happy Days* and *Waiting for Godot*." https://blesok.mk/en/blesok-editions/blesok-no-25/the-concept-of-time-and-space-25/.

Freud, Sigmund. *Beyond the Pleasure Principle*. Translated by James Strachey. New York: Norton, 1961.

———. "Heredity and the Aetiology of the Neuroses (1896)." In *The Standard Edition of the Complete Psychological Works of Sigmund Freud, Volume III (1893–1899): Early Psycho-Analytic Publications*, edited by James Strachey et al. 141–56. London: Hogarth, 1962.

———. *Inhibitions, Symptoms, and Anxiety*. Translated by Alix Strachey. London: Hogarth, 1936.

———. "Project for a Scientific Psychology (1950 [1895])." In *The Standard Edition of the Complete Psychological Works of Sigmund Freud, Volume I (1886–1899): Pre-Psycho-Analytic Publications and Unpublished Drafts*, edited by James Strachey et al., 281–391. London: Hogarth, 1966.

———. "Remembering, Repeating, and Working-Through (Further Recommendations on the Technique of Psycho-Analysis II) (1914)." In *The Standard Edition of the Complete Psychological Works of Sigmund Freud, Volume XII (1911–1913): The Case of Schreber, Papers on Technique and Other Works*, edited by James Strachey et al., 145–56. London: Hogarth, 1958.

Garrison, Alysia E. "'Faintly Struggling Things': Trauma, Testimony, and the Inscrutable Life in Beckett's *The Unnamable*." In *Samuel Beckett: History, Memory, Archive*, edited by Seán Kennedy and Katherine Weiss, 89–109. Basingstoke: Palgrave Macmillan, 2009.

Georgiades, Electra. "Trauma, Company and Witnessing in Samuel Beckett's Post-War Drama, 1952–61." PhD diss., University of Manchester, 2014.

Gibson, Andrew. *Samuel Beckett*. London: Reaktion, 2010.

Gontarski, Stanley E. "The Body in the Body of Beckett's Theatre." *Samuel Beckett Today/Aujourd'hui* 11 (2001) 169–77.

———. "An Interview with Director Makoto Sato." *Journal of Beckett Studies* 15.1–2 (2005) 186–94.

Goroncy, Jason A. "The Catholicity of Time in the Work of George Mackay Brown." *Pacifica* 29.1 (2016) 22–44.

———. "'Live Bread for the Starved Folk': Some Perspectives on Holy Communion." *Ecclesiology* 18.1 (2022) 57–77.

Herman, Judith L. *Trauma and Recovery: The Aftermath of Violence—From Domestic Abuse to Political Terror*. New York: Basic, 2015.

Jones, David H. "*Insignificant Residues*: Trauma, Face and *Figure* in Samuel Beckett." In *Samuel Beckett and Trauma*, edited by Mariko Hori Tanaka et al., 71–93. Manchester: Manchester University Press, 2018.

———. *Samuel Beckett and Testimony*. London: Palgrave Macmillan, 2011.

———. "Strange Pain: Archive, Trauma, and Testimony in Samuel Beckett and Christian Boltanski." In *Samuel Beckett and Pain*, edited by Mariko Hori Tanaka et al., 135–50. Amsterdam: Rodopi, 2012.

Kataoka, Noboru. "Structure of Images in Samuel Beckett's *. . . but the clouds . . .*" *Theatre Studies: Journal of the Japanese Society for Theatre Research* 51 (2010) 19–37.

Kennedy, Andrew K. "Action and Theatricality in *Waiting for Godot*." In *Waiting for Godot and Endgame*, edited by Steven Connor, 16–26. Basingstoke: Macmillan, 1992.

Kennedy, Seán. "Introduction: Beckett in History, Memory, Archive." In *Samuel Beckett: History, Memory, Archive*, edited by Seán Kennedy and Katherine Weiss, 1–10. London: Palgrave Macmillan, 2009.

Knowlson, James. *Damned to Fame: The Life of Samuel Beckett*. London: Bloomsbury, 2014. ePub.

Kozdon, Sabine. *Memory in Samuel Beckett's Plays: A Psychological Approach*. Münster: LIT, 2005.

Kyong, Youngsuk. "A Portrait of the Writer in Beckett's *Ohio Impromptu*: The Fictitious 'Other' Created by the Hands of the Blind." *Theatre Studies: Journal of the Japanese Society for Theatre Research* 46 (2008) 147–64.

Laing, Ronald D. *The Divided Self: An Existential Study in Sanity and Madness*. London: Penguin, 1990.

Langer, Lawrence L. *Holocaust Testimonies: The Ruins of Memory*. New Haven: Yale University Press, 1991.

Langlois, Christopher. *Samuel Beckett and the Terror of Literature*. Edinburgh: Edinburgh University Press, 2019.

Laub, Dori. "An Event without a Witness: Truth, Testimony and Survival." In *Testimony: Crises of Witnessing in Literature, Psychoanalysis, and History*, edited by Shoshana Felman and Dori Laub, 75–92. New York: Routledge, 1992.

Levine, Stephen K. *Trauma, Tragedy, Therapy: The Arts and Human Suffering*. London: Kingsley, 2009.

Luckhurst, Roger. *The Trauma Question*. London: Routledge, 2008.

McMullan, Audrey. "The Eye of Judgement: Samuel Beckett's Later Drama." In *The Death of the Playwright? Modern British Drama and Literary Theory*, edited by Adrian Page, 82–96. Basingstoke: Macmillan, 1992.

Melville, Herman. *Moby Dick*. Edited by Tony Tanner. Oxford: Oxford University Press, 2008.

Mercier, Vivian. *Beckett/Beckett*. New York: Oxford University Press, 1977.

———. "The Uneventful Event." *The Irish Times*, February 18, 1956.

Moody, Alys. "The *Non-Lieu* of Hunger: Post-war Beckett and the Genealogies of Starvation." *Samuel Beckett Today/Aujourd'hui* 24 (2012) 261–74.

Moorjani, Angela. *The Aesthetics of Loss and Lessness*. New York: St. Martin's, 1992.

Muhl, Nico. *Mothertongue*. Bedroom Community HVALUR 5CD, 2008, compact disc.

Nietzsche, Friedrich. *On the Genealogy of Morality*. Edited by Keith Ansell-Pearson. Translated by Carol Diethe. Cambridge: Cambridge University Press, 2007.

Nosthoff, Anna-Verena. "Beckett, Adorno, and the Hope for Nothingness as Something: Meditations on Theology in the Age of Its Impossibility." *Critical Research on Religion* 6.1 (2018) 35–53.

Okamuro, Minako. "'Make Sense Who May': The Influence of Samuel Beckett on Betsuyaku Minoru's Dramaturgy." *Theatre Studies: Journal of the Japanese Society for Theatre Research* 41 (2003) 21–40.

Olney, James. *Memory and Narrative: The Weave of Life-Writing*. Chicago: University of Chicago Press, 1998.

Polanyi, Michael. *Personal Knowledge: Towards a Post-critical Philosophy*. New York: Routledge & Kegan Paul, 1962.

———. *The Tacit Dimension*. Chicago: University of Chicago Press, 1966.

Rabillard, Sheila. "The Body in Beckett: *Dénégation* and the Critique of a Depoliticized Theatre." *Criticism* 34.1 (1992) 99–118.

Rada, Michelle. "Boring Holes: The Crystalline Body of Beckett's *The Lost Ones*." *Journal of Beckett Studies* 27.1 (2018) 22–39.

Rank, Otto. *Das Trauma der Geburt: und seine Bedeutung für die Psychoanalyse*. Leipzig: Internationaler Psychoanalytischer, 1924.

Sheedy, John J. "The Comic Apocalypse of King Hamm." *Modern Drama* 9 (1966) 310–18.

Sigg, Anna. "Bodily Object Voices in *Embers*." In *Samuel Beckett and Trauma*, edited by Mariko Hori Tanaka, Yoshiki Tajiri, and Michiko Tsushima, 116–31. Manchester: Manchester University Press, 2018.

Tanaka, Mariko Hori. "The Global Trauma of the Nuclear Age in Beckett's Post-war Plays." In *Samuel Beckett and Trauma*, edited by Mariko Hori Tanaka et al., 173–93. Manchester: Manchester University Press, 2018.

Tanaka, Mariko Hori, et al. "Acknowledgements." In *Samuel Beckett and Trauma*, edited by Mariko Hori Tanaka et al., xi. Manchester: Manchester University Press, 2018.

———. "Introduction." In *Samuel Beckett and Trauma*, edited by Mariko Hori Tanaka et al., 1–19. Manchester: Manchester University Press, 2018.

———, eds. *Samuel Beckett and Pain*. Amsterdam: Rodopi, 2012.

Tonning, Erik. "*Not I* and the Trauma of Birth." *Journal of Beckett Studies* 15.1–2 (2005) 21–34.

Tsushima, Michiko. "'The Skin of Words': Trauma and Skin in *Watt*." In *Samuel Beckett and Trauma*, edited by Mariko Hori Tanaka et al., 94–115. Manchester: Manchester University Press, 2018.

Tranter, Rhys. *Beckett's Late Stage: Trauma, Language, and Subjectivity*. Stuttgart: Ibidem, 2018.

———. "'Without Solution of Continuity': Beckett's *That Time* and Trauma Memoir." *Samuel Beckett Today/Aujourd'hui* 27 (2015) 115–28.

Tynan, Kenneth. "New Writing." *The Observer*, August 7, 1955.

Uchino, Tadashi. "After the Quake: Some Reflections on Immediate Performative Responses to <3.11.>." Paper presented at *Interweaving Performance Cultures*, International Research Center, Freie Universität Berlin, January 12, 2016.

Waxman, Zoë. "Rape and Sexual Abuse in Hiding." In *Sexual Violence against Jewish Women during the Holocaust*, edited by Sonja M. Hedgepeth and Rochelle G. Saidel, 124–35. Lebanon: Brandeis University Press, 2010.

Yoshiko, Takebe. "The Effect of Translated Plays: Samuel Beckett and Japanese Theatre." *Interpreting and Translation Studies* 11 (2011) 113–22.

22

Fellowship

Christian Wiman

Tragedy and Christianity are incommensurable,
he declared, which we'd have chalked to bluster
had he not, within the month, held a son
hot from the womb but cold to his kiss,
and over a coffin small as a toolbox wept
in the wrecked unreachable way that most resist,
and that all of us, where we are most ourselves,
turn away from.
                        Bonded and islanded
by the silence, we waited there,
desperate, with our own pains, to believe,
desperate, with our own pains, not to.

23

Do You Believe in God?

Pádraig Ó Tuama

My grandad came from Abbeydorney, near Tralee,
and so the Banna Strand was always in his memory.
When we—my dad, his dad, and me—visited
my great uncle, they discussed the land, and family;
debts due to the drink, and bitter neighbours. I threw myself
from dunes, believing I could fly.
I climbed up to the top of one and arched my back against its peak,
seeing only blue. The long drive home was famine
roads, laid by starving men whose grandchildren my grandfather knew.

When I was twenty-three, I stood beneath the statue on Bull Island's
stretch of beach. Mary far above me. Star of the Sea. I took off
all my clothes and shouted I Am Lonely at the water.
It was the middle of the night. There was the smell of oil
and rotting seaweed, the glow of factories: smoke catching
all the light from Dublin city.

My dad went fishing, climbing with his gear down the Old Head's
cliffs to the rocks right by the sea. Mackrel by dozen. Cast out.
Reeled in. Put the fresh meat inside the stripey plastic bag
he'd brought along. Then he saw the wave,
knew that it would take him, drag him, gash him,
tear him, kill him, drown him, neither care about nor notice him,
reduce him, toss him, fill him with its waters, pummel him till it
coughed him on some distant shore. He threw his things away
—his penknife and his favourite rod, the bag half filled with headless

fish, the hooks, their little feathers—he lay his body face down
on the jagged rocks and let that wave consume him. It scraped his skin away,
leaving bits of him on sharp and it almost took him to the deep.
He felt the sea attempt to take him to the sea. He couldn't even
scream—all under water. Somehow he held on, resisted,
rose, at some point, bloody, soaked and shaking.

24

Imagined Conversations and Real Letters during COVID-Times

Naomi Wolfe

We sat on the rocks of our favorite rockpool by the sea at Boat Harbour Beach in North West lutruwita (Tasmania) as we had done many times before in my life. The crisp squeaky sand had noisily yielded beneath our feet. It was one of those lazy summer afternoons, but a hint of cool air meant the abrupt departure of families who'd made our beach their home for the day. Dad put down his signature black coffee with three sugars and lit up a ciggie.

"Well kiddo, did you ever imagine such a thing happening? Perhaps we will see humanity remember that they are human and remember that they are connected to the rest of the bloody place, eh?" Dad drew hard on his ciggie with more waiting in his pack of 20s . . . because, you know, he was giving up.

"Dad, it's been too long, and so much has happened since you suddenly went. Did you know what was happening? Did you suffer? Did you want to leave us in this life? What about all the plans we made literally days before you went? I agreed to see Neil Diamond in Las Vegas, for goodness' sake!"

Words rushed out of me and tumbled across both of us as if escaping from my mouth and wanting desperately to get somewhere else. It was true, I had so many questions that had until this moment remained unanswered.

"C'mon, Dad! Did you see what was happening? Did it hurt? Did you know in advance? Was that why we went travelling around Preolenna and talking about the old people? Did you know and not tell me? I just can't even . . ."

I felt upset as when I first heard the news. It was like a rush of emotions all came back at once.

"Naya! Listen, stop talkin', and let me get a word in eh; always were a bloody talker. . . . Right from birth, I reckon. Always asking questions, wanting to know this and that. It got you into so much trouble at times. Do you remember that time you stood up to the religious studies woman and got kicked out? I laughed so hard when the principal rang. Your mother was as mad as a cut snake." Dad laughed and laughed, only stopping when he began to cough. It was an achingly familiar cough I'd heard all my life—one that long-term heavy smokers develop after several packets of ciggies every day for several decades.

"Oh yeah, Dad. I remember. She was right mad at me until she found out who Grandma was . . . then she settled. But she never let me back in her class again. Good thing too; the woman was stupid and nasty."

"Naya, now you know that people are what they are, and sometimes kiddo, you just gotta accept that. It'll make life easier for you when you realize that, truly it will. You are you, and they are themselves. You just got to accept it." Dad looked serious, and I wondered what else he was trying to say.

Boat Harbour Beach, December 2020. Photo by Naomi Wolfe.

"Dad, stop avoiding my questions, please. It's been really hard trying to sort through all of the emotions that come, especially with lockdown and not being able to get here. And now I have Ollie, and I wish you and Mum were still around to ask questions and help. Cliff and Tess are so far away, and I can't get there either."

I was frustrated and violently kicked the sand and seaweed in front of me, making such a mess that I thought that my mother would appear to castigate me and somehow make me clean it up. I gave a laugh.

"She's around too, you know. You'll speak with her soon enough. Stop kicking that sand. Let's walk and talk before the sun goes down. No floundering tonight,[1] got no gear anyway. I still remember your brother catching that big flounder and Uncle Johnny crackin' the shits because he didn't catch one that night. Memories."

Dad set off walking, and realizing I wasn't yet with him, he stopped and waited.

"Sometimes Nay, you just gotta let things go. It'll eat you up inside and kill you. You'll be alive but dead inside. So, learn to let things go! Just do as your mother and I raised you, as everyone raised you, as our family does. Just do the best you possibly can—even in difficult circumstances. Look at our ancestors—on all sides. They had little, and never ever give up. You need to do the same even though it's hard. There's probably a bible verse that talks about it, but you'd know better than me. You'd have to ask Jan about it."

We walk up to the surf life savers' café and kids' playground. Dad takes a seat on one of the swings. I join him, and we both stare out to sea.

"paywoota[2] . . . long time ago, such an interesting language our language.[3] Wish we'd all been able to learn it. I did learn more and more about stuff after I moved home but I'm sorry I didn't get a chance to tell you before I went. Sorry for the shock, kiddo."

Dad continued to stare out at the sea as if looking for something. I wasn't concerned with the sea. I wanted to look at Dad. He looked exactly the same as I had seen him in the days before his death. Yet, there was a difference, a lightness, a presence that I'd never seen before. It was intriguing and intoxicating, but frightening too.

---

1. Floundering, in this context, is going fishing with homemade or bought spears and collecting flounder, a fish commonly found in Tasmania and eaten by many. The turning of the tide is the best time to go floundering. It is a family and community activity with lots of fun and laughter. If floundering at night, then some will hold torches and others will spear the flounder.

2. "paywoota" means "long time ago" in palawa kani, which doesn't have capitalization.

3. Many Aboriginal people, including Tasmanian Aboriginals, were denied their cultural languages. Thankfully, many communities can revive them. It is a mistake to say that languages are dead—as not only humans speak our languages. A better way is to say that those languages not spoken by humans are sleeping or resting languages. See Marks, "Channelling Mannalargenna," 174–92.

Dad cleared his throat and started to speak, making sounds but stopping as if he was trying to think and speak at the same time. He beamed his cheeky smile. I smiled back too.

"I have always been proud of you and your brother. Really, bloody proud. I may not always understand you and what you do but I am so proud. And I love you all so much, and never left. I am here; you just gotta take time to see me. You're going on about pandemics and hard stuff . . . that's life, kiddo, but you've forgotten that there is more than this life. You are here *now* on the beach with me. Look around you. You can hear and see reminders even back in Melbourne—you just have to slow down and breathe. Just take some time out and come walking. Even God took Sunday off, kiddo. You need to do it for Ollie, but you need to do it for yourself too. You're the one now. You got things to do . . . places to go. This virus thing can be positive, not the people suffering and dying, but look at what good is being done. Rise to the occasion. Be brave. I wasn't brave enough at times and it was a regret. Not now though. All that has passed. It's time to rest."

Dad closed his eyes, still sitting on the swing next to me. His face so peaceful and glowing a look so different than the last time I'd seen his face at the funeral parlor. I had to ask them to give Dad a shave, so he didn't look untidy. He would've hated being untidy at a formal occasion like a funeral. I could see the sun starting to set.

"There goes the sun, Dad. Resting up for another day. It's really good to be home and to see you. I reckon I bring Ollie next time if I can. I've missed you so much and I noticed you still haven't really answered my questions . . . cheeky aye. But I feel better, Dad. I feel like I can get through this somehow." I wanted to say more, but it suddenly didn't feel that important anymore to talk. I could feel the wind and smell the seaweed so acutely that I closed my eyes and drew in a deep breath.

"There you go, kiddo. It's not so hard after all. You just gotta listen to your dear old Dad sometimes."[4]

Dear Reader,

In Aboriginal families, indeed in most families, there is a strong desire to seek comfort and solace from our parents and other Elders when confronted

---

4. Our Dad died suddenly in June 2019 at home in lutruwita (Tasmania). Despite being told by health professionals that he was "fine" literally the day before he died, he had a massive embolism caused by metastatic cancer. His death brought much shock, many challenges, and a renewed energy to fight for health justice.

with life's challenges. I was already feeling very fragile when 2020 came around as we had lost our father suddenly and we were awaiting news of the coronial investigation. It had been hard living on the mainland and going home every chance I got to try and sort out Dad's possessions and to try to make sense of how Dad came to die when he believed he was well (as did his GP and his extended family.) Ollie, my sister's[5] eldest son, unexpectedly came to live with me and my then housemate. It became clear that the living situation we had needed to change, and so my housemate of over a decade moved out. I had major surgery on my leg just before the pandemic struck the state where I live, and so life had really become quite uncertain. In many ways, life felt quite fragile. I was physically limited, and COVID-19 further impacted upon life for not only me, or for our house, but for the whole world. I was incredibly homesick, and after our planned trip home for firecracker night[6] on my Uncle and Aunt's farm[7] had to be cancelled, I felt even more homesick. The firecracker night was a night that was dedicated in honor of our cousin Graeme (who had committed suicide ten months before Dad's passing) and our Dad. Both of them loved firecrackers and big country bonfires, and I was keen to take Ollie home to meet more family and walk the land. It was not to be, so we started exploring country and waterways via things we could access here in Naarm.[8] We would bring out old cards and photos—telling the stories of who was who and what the event might have been. We went online and watched Vimeo and YouTube clips showing all over the state. For some time, it helped. Luckily for Ollie, he wasn't fixated on going home; unluckily for me, I was.

 I also took solace in re-reading lives of different saints, and of their journeys that often took them far from home. I also connected with another aspect of my family story—the Jewish–German side of my paternal grandfather's family. I read the stories of those who perished and of those who survived the Sho'ah, as well as the stories of those who tried to save Jews and others from evil racist laws and deeds. I marveled and wept at the strength of those fighting and those who were lost in the Sho'ah.

 I wondered what my Dad would've made of the whole COVID-19 situation. Would he have taken it in his stride and waited it all out? Or

---

 5. Ollie's mum is, in European terms, my first cousin.

 6. Every year, Tasmania celebrates firecracker night where locals can obtain permits and legally purchase fireworks. Most are held on country properties with bonfires and celebrations. It is a chance for the community to gather before winter sets in. Many people use it as a reason to journey home from the mainland.

 7. David and Janice Smith, of Boat Harbour, give us so much love and provide a home for us. I can write and work because of their love and prayers.

 8. Naarm is the Kulin word for Melbourne.

would he have succumbed to it like so many others from my district did in March 2020? March 27, 2020 saw Tasmanian Premier Peter Gutwein announce the temporary closure of the North West Regional Hospital, and its collocation with the North West Private Hospital at Burnie, due to a COVID-19 outbreak.[9] The outbreak, traced back to the Ruby Princess cruise ship,[10] would see many lives lost, including many my family personally knew. Other relatives were forced into mandatory isolation as all health professionals and workers at the hospitals were also quarantined with the Australian Defence Forces arriving to run the hospitals, look after existing patients, and oversee a deep clean of facilities.[11]

As a coping mechanism, I started to have conversations and spiritual journeys with significant people in my life, including my parents and others who I'd never ever met or could have met in this western oriented linear life. But my faith and culture, and my hope for better days, allowed me to walk beyond the linear constraints and enter ancestral time—God's time and space. It allowed me to see, hear, and feel what I desperately needed, and to maintain some level of hope when the external world was fast losing it. So, journey with me in my imagined conversations, and may you gain some moment of respite from your weariness as you enter my world for a time.

"You're not doing it properly! Naomi, wake up! You need to listen to me. I know what I am talking about. Get up, let me show you. Come on, Naomi Cathyrn, I have other things to do, you know."

I had been sleeping, and I think was quite enjoying being asleep. I was with one of my best friends, Margaret, and we were back in Natovi, Fiji, where we had a teaching immersion experience back in 1997.[12] I could feel the warm breeze and hear the laughter of our school children as Miss Margaret attempted to play cricket.

"She's not the reason Australia just won the Ashes, is she?" laughed Mr. Ceri Ceri, the principal. I laughed along too, knowing that my history at cricket was equally funny . . . well when I wasn't smacking the ball into windows,

---

9. See Tasmanian Government Gazette, "COVID-19 Disease Emergency."

10. See Campbell, "The Carnival Cruise Ship."

11. See Wahlquist, "We Can Save Lives."

12. My dear friend Margaret Canny and I travelled along with some other teaching students to Fiji to experience life at the Catholic Teacher's College in Suva, and to experience teaching in a Fijian village. Our assigned village was Natovi, about two-hours bus ride, give or take stops, from Suva. We were welcomed in by the community of St. John the Apostle Catholic parish.

that is. It was a lovely dream; I could feel it and smell it as if I was really there instead of in my rather messy bedroom on Wurundjeri Country.

The sudden shaking, and my mother's voice, was an untimely interruption, and one I wasn't too keen upon. I was fed up: fed up with lockdowns; fed up with meltdowns of a nephew unable to cope with remote schooling; fed up with worrying about family here and overseas and whether this new virus would be their end; fed up adulting and life getting in the way of plans to travel and see the world with my partner, Stephen. My nightly escape into dreaming was my refuge, a refuge I counted down the hours to, a place where I could breathe, and a place with no masks!

"Come on, Naomi! I'm really getting quite cross."

I opened my eyes and there she was, not like the last time I had sighted her, but in all her Sandra glory, her face fully made up, her hair immaculately coiffed, wearing a dress that was part Marilyn Monroe and part renaissance angel.[13]

"Mum, what are you doin'? What's the hurry?" I crankily responded as I wanted to be back in Fiji rather than in my room in Melbourne.

Mum had only visited me once before, and that was to let me know that I needed to be prepared. I was half asleep at the time and I gave it little thought until Dad died. Ah, I thought in the quiet moments of the first night, that's what she meant. Typical mum, always the flair for drama and mystery.

She repeated the words: "You're not doing it properly," stamping her foot as she did when she was getting frustrated. It was a sign that us kids had better pull up because her temper was about to blow. Quite frankly, I had enough problems without Mum losing her cool at me. I already had a cranky nephew having daily tantrums because of stress and trauma, and then lockdown. I did not need yet another cranky relative in my ears and in my face.

"Okay Mum, I am sorry. I am awake and listening now." I hope that might calm her down and I was getting more and more awake, so I was becoming more and more intrigued about what I wasn't doing properly.

"You aren't doing life right. I thought we'd had this conversation and you were clear. Life is for living, not just for existing and for making do. I am so angry with you right now. You can't be wasting time. I wasted too much time doing what I had to do, and not what I wanted to do. And look where

---

13. My mother, Sandra, was a hairdresser and a beautician. She had a very keen interest for fashion which wasn't always appreciated by those around her. Her daughter was the complete opposite, which was an interesting challenge for both. One of the biggest challenges for her with cancer was the loss of her hair and her energy.

it got me. Nowhere. I told you before: spend less time being Martha, and more time being Mary."

Mum got up from the edge of my bed where she had been sitting, and walked across the room, navigating my work bag and the chair with the ever-growing (where the heck does it all come from?) pile of clean laundry that needed sorting and folding. She ran her fingers across one of the shelves of my bookcases. Oh Lord, I thought as I watched her, have mercy, I have no patience for Chaucer this evening. Mum loved Chaucer, and I have not so fond memories of *The Canterbury Tales*. It wasn't the middle English that was a problem; it just wasn't my choice of book.

"Here it is. Right, now listen."

I couldn't yet see the book, but I sat up in my bed and made myself comfortable—well, as comfortable as I could with Mum in my room, and not a cup of coffee in sight. I resigned myself to hearing Chaucer . . . again.

Mum was flipping through the book until she came to the page that she wanted. I could now see it was one of the bibles I have. It was one that I used back in the days when I taught primary school education. Now, this was a surprise (and a relief) but I was also tired, so tired. COVID had me sleeping less restfully.

"Mum, do we really need to do this now? It's 4 a.m. and it's cold, and I have to get up in a few hours to get things ready. Dekan[14] is going to take Ollie out for a walk while I take my first class online,[15] but I have lots to do, and I need sleep."

Don't get me wrong, I love reading the texts in the bible, particularly the Hebrew Scriptures, but not usually at that hour, and never without my coffee.

Mum began to read, and I could hear quite clearly: "Now as they went on their way, he entered a certain village, where a woman named Martha welcomed him into her home. She had a sister named Mary, who sat at the Lord's feet and listened to what he was saying. But Martha was distracted by her many tasks; so, she came to him and asked, 'Lord, do you not care that my sister has left me to do all the work by myself? Tell her then to help me.' But the Lord answered her, 'Martha, Martha, you are worried and distracted

---

14. Dekan is my eldest nephew, and he lived with Ollie and I after I had some leg surgery. As the COVID-19 pandemic struck, he was unable to get back to his home in the Swan Valley, in Western Australia. He was a great help to us, especially with looking after my younger nephew Ollie, who has come to stay with me permanently.

15. Throughout the pandemic I have been supervising my nephew with remote schooling, as well as teaching across several institutions, including in the NAIITS Indigenous theological education programs.

by many things; there is need of only one thing. Mary has chosen the better part, which will not be taken away from her.'"[16]

I went to open my mouth and tell her that I understood, so that I could get back to sleep. Mum and I had a contentious relationship, but we had mended our relationship as best we could. I closed my mouth, as I knew that it would not end well, and, frankly, I was too tired from worrying about other arguments.[17]

"So, listen to me when I tell you that you can't just exist. Housework will never end, nor will caring for others within the family and community; but you must be less like Martha and allow them to distract you from what you need and want to do." She had on her no-nonsense serious face, her eyes blazing with fervor. For some reason, it made me want to giggle. My mother the former Sunday School teacher[18] standing before me, all dressed to the nines, with one of my bibles, looking like she was about to give Billy Graham a run for his money.

I laughed and said: "Hey Mum, what's with the theology blitz? What are they putting in your coffee these days?"

Mum's fervor dimmed as if my words had been quick scissors that cut the wick of a burning candle. She seemed older, and sadder. There was a noise, a vibrating frequency that was not frightening but was disconcerting. I couldn't quite work out exactly what it was, but I knew one thing for sure: it made me desperately uncomfortable and desperately sad.

"You remember that conversation we had? The one in my room at your place when I called you in to look at the wattle shrikes in the back courtyard? Do you remember?"

I did remember that day. It was a very busy day when I was trying to mark papers written by undergraduate students who all wanted sympathy for their work but extended no sympathy to my situation. Mum and I had never really seen eye to eye or been close. It was a fraught relationship that others, both within and outside the family, sought to have opinions on, but none really understood, except us. We both agreed on the word "hurdy-gurdy" to describe it. Months before that day, I had a strange occasion where I got a spiritual warning that something important (usually negative) was about to happen or was happening. Within an hour, I would

---

16. Luke 10:38–42.

17. Issues such as family harmony, money, health, and wellbeing have become flashpoints for so many during the COVID-19 pandemic. See Ruppanner et al., "Emotional and Financial Health during COVID-19"; Evans et al., "From 'It Has Stopped Our Lives.'"

18. My mum taught Sunday School for a time at St. Stephen's, and she was known for being kind but serious in her lessons.

be making plans to fly back home because Mum had collapsed, and it was not looking good. Mum and I had barely talked in the years prior. But I was waiting for some random doctor to ring me and let me know which airport I was to fly to, as her condition deteriorated. All the doctors could say was that it was bad, quite bad. Mum would eventually end up in ICU and I would take an unexpected business seat flight to nipaluna.[19] Mum would learn that she had advanced-stage lymphoma.[20]

I realized that I had drifted away from Mum's attention and I mentally shook off those memories to concentrate on what she was saying to me.

"You must not forget that life is short and that one day you are going to be robbed of it. You have to prioritize things that matter—not just the domestic stuff, the taking care of stuff. You need to be happy when the time comes. I was angry. I had so many things planned, and yet not many of them came to fruition. I spent years being unhappy, very unhappy. And a lot of it was socialization from family, from society, from the bloody church. Women always have to put their needs last . . . and it gets us nowhere. Don't fall for that mistake. It will cost you your life."

I sat back and I saw that the fire had returned to her eyes as she spoke, and I wondered how she thought I was any different given that she had pretty much socialized me the same way. I had always struggled with seeing how she suffered when I was growing up. I was under no illusions about how unhappy she was because she told me on a regular basis about how she'd made sacrifices, how she had lost opportunities. I struggled to see her so unhappy, believing that I was a contributing factor to that unhappiness. I looked around and saw other women throughout the family, our parish, the community, and wider society, and saw the daily sacrifices that they consistently made. I saw the devaluing of their contributions, their hard work and sacrifice, and the lack of recognition of the difference it made to society, to church. I heard sermons that exhorted turning the other cheek and walking the extra mile, and I saw how that was used as a weapon against women, against Aboriginal peoples, and against other marginalized groups. Was this one of the reasons I was so drawn to understanding the context and original meanings of the texts as I studied theology? Was it to satisfy or make sense of how those texts came to be used against women rather than to support and empower women? It's something I didn't have an answer to.

Mum was moved by her deep emotion and, uncharacteristically, she came forward and wiped my cheek of tears; I had not realized I was even

---

19. nipaluna is the palawa kani name for Hobart, the capital city of the state of Tasmania (lutruwita).

20. Lymphoma is a form of blood cancer. Our mother had a rare type of blood cancer which remains hard to beat.

crying. She hugged me and said in a quiet but fierce voice: "You will remember that not all sacrifices are needed or even asked for, and making yourself small and allowing your dreams to die will make you unhappy. It will not make you a better mother, a better aunty, a better partner, a better sister. It will eat away at your soul. And when that day comes, you will be as mad as hell, with no one but yourself to blame. Be brave. Go and do what you need to do, not what you or others think that you should."

And in typical Sandra style, she smiled, gave a triumphant yet graceful flounce, and was gone.[21]

Dear Reader,

My mother was a fiercely independent woman, a woman of contrasts. We didn't always see eye to eye. She loved makeup and dressing up and public attention, whereas I most certainly do not. She was an incredibly talented artist as well—another talent that I did not receive from either of my parents. I am lucky to have several of her artworks now that I can look at each day.

Mum and I clashed often because some of the fundamental things that were incredibly important to her were the polar opposite for me. I had hoped we would iron out more of our issues before her death, but cancer robs people of opportunities, and of life itself. It is a particularly cruel disease that robs people of their hair and their physical attributes, which is especially hard for those whose identity is intimately tied to them. As David Morgan reminds us, "Life is unpredictable, riddled by randomness, menaced by powers and events beyond human control."[22]

We also clashed because her theological stances were more conservative than are mine. To be fair, she actually didn't see that the churches would change to accommodate difference so she thought it was silly to spend too much time on fighting battles that would be ultimately futile. I didn't agree, and I would often use her reluctance and apathy as a sounding board before attempting to take my arguments to places such as a Parish Council or Youth Synod. When as a late teenager I became involved in the Movement for the Ordination of Women, my mum did support me in practical ways, however—such as allowing me to borrow the car, even if she did think it was

---

21. Our mother fought lymphoma long and hard after nearly dying in ICU several times. She outlasted the original time allocation that oncologists gave her, but finally she made her peace and passed away in the company of her children and their father, and some of her favourite aunts. Cancer did not beat her; she triumphantly left it behind.

22. Morgan, *The Forge of Vision*, 71.

all in vain. The night before the youth groups in our parish travelled four hours to St. David's Cathedral to see the first women ordained in the Diocese of Tasmania, she pressed into my hand a $50 note saying, "Don't tell your father!" As I got into the youth group minibus, Dad pulled me aside and gave me $20 saying, "Don't tell your mother!" Both wanted us (that is, the senior youth group) to celebrate the occasion with some style.

My mother was as mad as hell during her cancer diagnosis and journey. She had so much planned and yet was being robbed of any opportunity. She wanted to go travelling and made a list—she refused to call it a "bucket list," preferring to invoke the BBC comedy *Keeping up Appearances* and declared instead that she had a "Bouquet List."[23] I made her a promise to keep her bouquet list because she could not. One of the things on the list was to visit the collections of Renaissance and Impressionist art works. Artwork remains a way that I connect with my mother now that she has gone. I often hear her voice talking about techniques and likes and dislikes while looking at art or watching art documentaries. Artwork is such a big part of Aboriginal and Torres Strait Islander life,[24] and it always has a spiritual dimension, so I don't feel too weird about hearing Mum while looking at art. I know that other cultures and artists are remembering the spiritual in art too.[25]

After travelling back and forth from nipaluna, Mum got a medical transfer from the Royal Hobart Hospital to The Royal Melbourne Hospital, which is ten minutes' drive from my home. She wasn't supposed to, but her oncologist had a best friend at the RMH, so it became possible. Mum would move in with me and my housemate, and we began the journey back and forth between home, the RMH, and the Peter MacCallum Cancer Centre. It was exhausting for Mum as she dealt with intense chemotherapy and radiation, plus the ever-growing kooky "alternative" ideas for treatment that others foisted upon her. I too was tired. I was continuing to work full time to pay the bills both here and at home at Mum's place. I went through various emotional stages, usually by myself as I wanted to keep Mum's spirits up.[26]

---

23. *Keeping up Appearances* was an English comedy show commissioned by the BBC, and which gained popularity worldwide. The main character is a woman named Hyacinth Bucket (pronounced "bouquet") who is determined that all should know her status within the community, no matter how aspirational. See Gymnich, "The Lady of the House Speaking," 240–53.

24. See Grieves, *Aboriginal Spirituality*; Gough, "Tayenebe / Exchange," 83–85.

25. See Arya, *Contemplations of the Spiritual in Art*.

26. Much is written about the emotional effects of cancer, including those on care givers. See, for example, Grbich et al., "The Emotions and Coping Strategies of Caregivers," 30–36.

I have some art books here in Naarm with me that were Mum's books, her art treasures. They have given me immense comfort during numerous COVID-19 lockdowns. They allow me to enter another world where I am free of the current constraints, and where western linear time is suspended, and I can meet and greet loved ones once more. I knew that I needed to keep strong during COVID-19 (some days are stronger than others!) because I had others that depended on me; but, equally important, it became clear that my conversations with my Dad and my Mum were reminding me that my needs, my dreams, my hopes were also as important.

COVID-19 lockdowns remain hard each time, and the stress builds and builds. At these times, I try to remind myself that I can escape into my other world through looking at my mum's artworks, or her favorite books, or through imagined (and yet real) conversations with loved ones. And it has reignited some connection for me with organized institutional religion, albeit in a very random and ad hoc way.[27] I am quite enjoying choosing random religious services and events freely available online through social media platforms and discovered through digital word of mouth. I once ended up watching a service at an Italian cathedral because I was following an artistic rabbit hole prompted by one of my mother's books. The comfort in hearing and seeing the familiar online without the transmission risk posed by COVID-19 has also been an unexpected delight.[28] I know that others struggle with online presence, but I have not.

I have begun to re-engage across all levels with my, so far, unfinished Master of Philosophy thesis. I've begun to imagine a world where I can be responsible and yet creative. I am giving myself permission to engage my imagination with my culture, my faith, and my intellect. Doing so brings me closer to God, to my Ancestors, and to loved ones. And it gives me strength, release, and renewal in times of struggle . . . including in COVID times.

Dear Reader, may you discover (dare I say re-discover?) your imaginings in these uncertain times and return ever more hopeful in the days to come.

---

27. Apparently, I am not alone here. See Halafoff et al., "Worldviews Complexity in COVID-19 Times," 682.

28. I have particularly enjoyed local experiences online, including services from the Welsh Church in Melbourne, and St. Andrew's Anglican Parish Aberfeldie, plus live-streamed Mass from Melbourne's St. Patrick's Cathedral.

Bibliography

Arya, Rina, ed. *Contemplations of the Spiritual in Art*. Oxford: Lang, 2013.

Campbell, Matthew. "The Carnival Cruise Ship That Spread Coronavirus around the World." *Bloomberg*, September 15, 2020. https://www.bloomberg.com/news/features/2020-09-15/carnival-s-ruby-princess-cruise-ship-spread-coronavirus-around-the-world.

Evans, Subhadra, et al. "From '*It Has Stopped Our Lives*' to '*Spending More Time Together Has Strengthened Bonds*': The Varied Experiences of Australian Families during COVID-19." *Frontiers in Psychology* 11.588667 (2020). https://doi.org/10.3389/fpsyg.2020.588667.

Gough, Julie. "Tayenebe / Exchange: Tasmanian Aboriginal Women and Fibre Work." *Artlink* 30.1 (2010) 83–85.

Grbich, Carol, et al. "The Emotions and Coping Strategies of Caregivers of Family Members with a Terminal Cancer." *Journal of Palliative Care* 17.1 (2001) 30–36.

Grieves, Vicki. *Aboriginal Spirituality: Aboriginal Philosophy, the Basis of Aboriginal Social and Emotional Wellbeing*. Casuarina: Cooperative Research Centre for Aboriginal Health, 2009.

Gymnich, Marion. "'The Lady of the House Speaking': The Conservative Portrayal of English Class Stereotypes in *Keeping up Appearances*." In *British TV Comedies: Cultural Concepts, Contexts, and Controversies*, edited by Jürgen Kamm and Birgit Neumann, 240–53. Basingstoke: Palgrave Macmillan 2016.

Halafoff, Anna, et al. "Worldviews Complexity in COVID-19 Times: Australian Media Representations of Religion, Spirituality, and Non-religion in 2020." *Religions* 12.9 (2021) 682.

Marks, Kathy. "Channelling Mannalargenna: Surviving, Belonging, Challenging, Enduring." *Griffith Review* 39 (2012) 174–92.

Morgan, David. *The Forge of Vision: A Visual History of Modern Christianity*. Berkeley: University of California Press, 2015.

Ruppanner, Leah, et al. "Emotional and Financial Health during COVID-19: The Role of Housework, Employment, and Childcare in Australia and the United States." *Gender, Work, and Organization* 28.5 (2021) 1937–55.

Tasmanian Government Gazette. "COVID-19 Disease Emergency." http://www.gazette.tas.gov.au/__data/assets/pdf_file/0009/573651/22073-_-Special_1_April.pdf.

Wahlquist, Calla. "'We Can Save Lives': Tasmania's Isolated North-West Succumbs to Australia's Strictest Coronavirus Rules." *The Guardian*, April 13, 2020. https://www.theguardian.com/world/2020/apr/13/we-can-save-lives-tasmanias-isolated-north-west-succumbs-to-australias-strictest-coronavirus-rules.

25

Circular Repetition

Karly Michelle Edgar

I WAS DIAGNOSED WITH fibromyalgia the year after I returned to Melbourne, after living in Sydney for three years while studying theatre. It was a diagnosis that gave a name to my condition but provided very little assistance with regards to actual treatment. My life quickly stopped as I resigned from work due to the immense pain and my quickly diminishing energy. My life shrunk to the size of the house I was living in and my day-to-day activities were dictated by the amount of pain I had. I was just trying to survive each day. Even so, it wasn't long before I realized that even though being unwell is exhausting and time consuming, I still needed something I could do, at home, that was enjoyable and easily accessible in those rare moments when I had the energy. I began experimenting with a bit of jewelry making, paper collage, and other forms of visual art.

Right from the start there was tension, as fibromyalgia is a condition where I must be careful with repetition, due to the pain I quickly feel in my hands, arms, neck, and back. With the type of fibromyalgia that I have, there is no physical injury, but pain and inflammation can occur in any of these locations for any, or in fact, for no reason at all, as my body tries to protect itself from some unknown threat. It also effects my head, and there have been long periods of time when I have felt as though I have lost all my words, an experience dubbed "fibro fog." My daily allocation of words was small and quickly used up, so I rationed them, hording them away for what was most important. The sum of my life consisted of short walks, attempting to sleep with insomnia, very minimal attempts at housework, occasionally making something creative, and resting, always trying to rest.

The physicality of creating was, and still can be, a painful activity and I have to constantly monitor the repetition, pace, and length of time I spend on any single activity. Even so, making things became one of the only enjoyable activities I could engage in, when I had the energy. At some point, I remember seeing a short video on breath and line drawing and I was inspired to experiment with circles.

I sat at home simply trying to survive each day. I began to draw circles and wait. I was waiting to feel better or, waiting until I had to stop drawing because everything hurt. I was waiting to understand what was happening to me; waiting until I had the energy to do something; waiting for the words to come and thoughts to form; waiting to hear God; waiting to see if I got better; waiting for some certainty; waiting to figure out how to live with it; waiting to work out what I felt, what I thought. Just waiting.

The process of drawing circles was (and still is) both distraction and contemplation, as needed: meditative, quiet, reflective, with no words required. A blank page but with defined edges that I can slowly fill with tiny circles. Particularly in the early days, it was a form of stress release, focus, distraction, occupation, preparation for sleep, self-administered therapy, and a brief moment of pseudo-achievement in a world where my other daily, maybe weekly, significant achievement may have consisted of putting out the washing. The circles slowly began to form themselves into a practice that merged the boundaries of creativity and spiritual discipline, inviting me to combine them into just *practice*.

Over time, my health has ebbed and flowed, increased and decreased, and is currently following a surprising, but gratefully accepted, process of steady improvement; or, at least, of stability. For now. But, even within this period of stability, earlier this year I returned to a deliberate circle drawing practice first established during uncertainty. This was because, for better or worse, in early 2020 I re-entered the world of full-time research towards a PhD. It was something I really wanted to do, but I was also un-practiced at the vast number of words required. I returned to a circle practice almost without realizing what I was doing as I tried to come to grips with the number of words such researched entailed. The space of the circle became preventative and an opportunity for a different focus to the word-saturated world of research, as words once again began to fill my life in a way that I had thought might not ever again be possible.

It was an instinctual choice that perhaps demonstrates that after fifteen years of ill health, I am finally learning to recognize and respect the integration of myself: words and silence, action and stillness, thought and feeling, physical and spiritual, all working together. The ideas that were slowly forming about how I would engage with circles this time around were accelerated by what turned out to be only the first of the Melbourne lockdowns due to the COVID-19 pandemic. My panic buying consisted of paper in a variety of sizes and new packets of pens.

Even though I had always planned to study from home, and I was aware that I would need to develop an intense awareness of the interplay between activity and resting during my research, learning how to do this within the restrictions of a lockdown was different to what I had expected. I was fortunate: I didn't lose my job; I live in a nice suburban house with a garden; I live within a household but still have my own living space, and a garden gate that leads directly to a beautiful walking trail. Even so, the weirdness of lockdown was different to my past experience of being at home, as were my circumstances. Sometimes I thought I was going to get through this easily; other times I wondered why I wasn't able to deal with this all better given my experience. Time appeared to move differently. Some days there was the fear that *this will never end* while then struggling to remember how I had spent my days—*where did that time go?* All that could be done was to do the right thing and stay home. To keep reading, researching. To keep on walking, eating, and sleeping. To keep on drawing and creating while we waited to see what happened—while we relied on others to discover a cure and to create a vaccine, and hoped that by staying home the prevalence of the virus in our society might diminish.

Even though I knew that surviving this period would be about finding a routine, it took a while to find one that helped rather than hindered. I had to re-learn the tension between following routine strictly and allowing for flexibility. Slowly, I became more practiced at it and settled into an enclosed rhythm. While I kept researching, reading, and writing, an important part of this routine included significant time spent on circle drawing and other creative pursuits. When sitting with the circle drawing it was as though my body began to recognize the feeling of waiting within uncertainty and a life I could not control. Waiting, isolated at home, and drawing circles: but also, not completely alone this time, but with Melbourne, the world even.

Within the quiet and space of lockdown, I began to notice that I was feeling a little differently about the circle drawing, even though it took me a while to figure out what it was. I eventually realized I had been feeling self-consciousness about the simplicity of the circle. I think it was brought on by the contrast with the complexity of the PhD process and of witnessing all the amazing academic researchers I met virtually in workshops and seminars. The contrast was too apparent, too wide.

I wonder now if this is why I choose a large paper size as I rushed out to shop prior to lockdown. I purchased A2 size paper and began the largest circle design I had ever attempted. Was I trying to legitimize a process I was, unconsciously, beginning to question, yet still determined to practice? The simplicity of the circle seemed to reflect too significantly on my (perhaps lacking) creative abilities. The simplicity of the circle made more sense when I was very unwell, as it reflected back to me the barrenness of a life of pain and fibro fog that engulfed my brain and subtracted my thoughts. Why did I continue it still?

Karly Michelle Edgar, *Repetition 1*, 2020. Ink pen on paper, 76 x 56 cm. Artist's collection.

These past few years, I have been trying to deliberately practice speaking to myself the way I might speak to a student or friend, and in this situation I knew I would encourage someone else to continue in their drawing even if they felt this way, and so I did. In some way though, it barely mattered; I had to continue. It was a practice my body and my mind needed. Needs.

So, I sat and circled and listened to the silence, or sometimes to a podcast or a TV series; but mostly I just listened to the silence. Each time I sat down I practiced re-acclimatizing physically and mentally to the process: loosening my fingers on the pen, finding a comfortable posture, gradually encouraging my thoughts to weave their way around whatever was on my mind, and become a little more still.

I sat and I circled, and I realized that in this stillness and silence, the words and the worry and the weirdness of the year gently moved to one side: just for a moment. Not gone, just placed to the side, and perhaps seen a little more clearly for what they were. I sat and I circled, and in these moments of stillness and silence I began to realize that the circles were not about a lack of something but were rather about gaining something.

I sat and I circled, not because it was all I could do but because of what this process gave me. Repetition, circles, were not *all* I had, but rather is *what* I have. It is not a last resort or *all* I can do in these times, but is rather *what I can do*. I *have* repetition. It slows me down. It focuses me. It reminds me to breathe. It gives me a single, simple process to follow, freedom within a defined space. It helps me to pray, to focus, to feel, to be, to rest a moment. It helps me to sit within what is happening around me, the things I cannot control—the health that is uncertain, the life that is so different to what I imagined years ago. Not everything can be anticipated, or entirely planned for. In moments of sensory overstimulation, it allows the tingling of the blood in my veins to flow out of my fingers and into the black ink. It allows me, as I re-find myself, to not think so much, and then, to begin to think again. But mostly it helps me to feel. It reminds me that if I am prepared to really listen to myself, and feel what I am feeling, then I may be all the more able to hear God. It reminds me that things do not have to be fancy or difficult to be complex and interesting. It gently fills me back up. The repetition becomes what I am.

Creating during the period of lockdown came from a desire to sit within a quiet, still, adaptive space rather than from the need to complete anything. I am surprised, though, by how much I did actually make over these past nine months, and I wonder how I was able to complete the vast number of drawings and artworks I now have stacked up in my studio space. But then I recall the many evenings spent sitting and waiting, the shorter moments during the day when I'd sit at the page in between other parts of my day as circle drawing is something that can be easily done in short spaces of time. Then there were the Friday night catch ups on Zoom as I chatted to friends. We quickly realized that given the significant number of hours we already spent at our computer screens during the week, if we had to socialize on Zoom as well, it was time best spent also doing something creative. So each time we met up online we picked up knitting needle, coloring pencil, watercolor brush, pastel, or pen as we caught up on the weird lives we were living in lockdown. It was a wonderful time of connection, and grounding, within an experience we had never imagined would be necessary.

It has been the year of repetition and of monotony and of drawing circle after circle, and of covering page after page with pastel layer upon pastel layer, and of walking the same paths each day, and of living and working and being in the same space day after day. But all of this has somehow shown me the beauty, and the peace, and the rest, that *may* be found within repetition and routine, and even within uncertainty. I was fortunate, and I recognize that the lockdown was not this type of space for everyone, but it was an opportunity found within my experience. Even when frustrated, or bored, or anxious, about the routine and life, all of which did happen often, eventually I returned and re-found it. I am constantly reminded that day becomes night becomes day, and while each season is different, they always cycle back around.

Now in Melbourne many of the restrictions have been lifted. We are, thankfully, beginning to see and feel the end of this period of what for many has been a long, dark time of uncertainty and fear. Overall, the lockdown has greatly benefitted us as a community, even though it was difficult and long, and certainly not perfectly executed. We now must figure out how to live a bit longer in a less anxious but still uncertain place of what "COVID normal" means, until a vaccine is available to all. Or, if things go badly, a repeated experience of lockdown. But even with the community re-opening, it took me a while to re-enter. I found myself continuing in my routine—being at home (happily), reading and researching, walking the same trails, and starting up a new circle drawing before cautiously trying out what it was like out in the world again.

Maybe this means that, slowly, finally, I am learning a way of living within some form of uncertainty, and of appreciating the repetitive cycle of routine. Maybe I am learning that life, spirituality, and creativity, are carefully built upon repetitious practices that reflect a continual but active form of waiting, as skills are developed, and God is slowly revealed, and as I become more aware of my own self.

It's a practice that I both already know, and continually need to learn, until the practice of repetition and active waiting is embedded deeply within myself and imprinted upon every thought and action, and seep out of every pore. I am a creature of habit, of routine, of ritual. There's a natural preference, certainly, but it is also something I am learning to appreciate even more. At least, it is a realization I am continually learning and re-learning. It takes practice.

26

Ida Nangala Granites

Steve Bevis

Ida Nangala Granites is a senior Warlpiri woman and a respected artist painting in the style of the Western desert art movement.[1] Ida has been painting for many years and her artworks have been hung at galleries and exhibitions across the country. For most of the year, she resides in Mparntwe, Alice Springs, the well-known outback town that is a hub and service provider for remote communities across Central Australia. While Ida's time is largely spent living in a town camp on the fringes of Alice, she regularly returns to Yuendumu, the main remote community in the Tanami Desert. It is there, in the vast expanse of the Tanami's landscape that Ida is really at home—on "country"—on her *ngura*. Caught between the two worlds of desert community and life in Alice Springs, the practice of painting has become a significant aspect of Ida's spiritual and emotional connection to her country. Painting is important to Ida, and the practice of putting acrylic on canvas provides a "new" medium with which Ida enacts an age-old-yet-living-connection to her country, ancestors, and *Jukurrpa*, her Dreaming.

Ida can often be found sitting in the shade of her home, trailing dots of paint across a canvas. Series of parallel dots sweep across the canvas, like the falling of rain on desert sands. Dots coalesce and seem to move like waves across the canvas. Everything is at rest and in motion, the whole canvas is one trembling vista. When Ida paints dots on canvas—the medium that most *kardiya* (non-Indigenous people) around the globe now associate with Indigenous art—she does so to consciously create an object that can be viewed and appreciated by others. The objects she creates are beautiful and widely valued for their aesthetic power. And yet this reading of what is happening in her art practice can remain at the surface of things. Her paintings, like those of her family members, are resonant with many meanings. When Ida paints she is, in fact, intentionally re-enacting and

---

1. The story that follows is told with permission.

participating in her Dreaming, her "truth." This Dreaming is the story that she is a part of and which she is charged with living and protecting. She is not simply making an object which "represents" that Dreaming, although that is what the painting may become for her viewer and for her customer. In the act of painting she is also participating in a process of connection to the Dreaming itself. In producing what *kardiya* call "art," Ida is, within a Warlpiri worldview, also giving expression to her oneness with her country and ancestors, to the truth of which they are both an expression: the all-encompassing reality of the Dreaming.

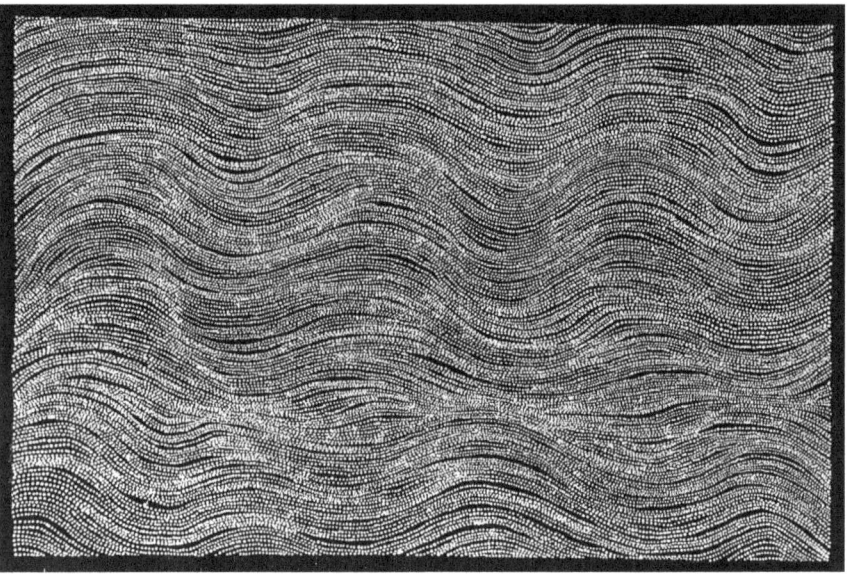

Ida Nangala Granites, *Mina Mina*, 2020. Acrylic on canvas, 105 x 70 cm. The Binet Collection.

When Ida paints her family's Dreamings she is at one with the same reality as her ancestors. The trails of dots she applies to the canvas are variations on the motif of the Mina Mina Dreaming. This Dreaming story tells of how the ancestral women moved across the landscape with their digging sticks, and as they dug they created the important sites that are essential to Warlpiri life—the soakages, waterholes, and other sacred sites. In the process of painting, Ida enacts and lives this same reality: she inhabits this story and makes it manifest. She also participates in the place that this Dreaming narrates and shares in its ongoing creation. This is a key source of strength in a world that is in crisis—the ability to connect to creation and to participate in re-creation and renewal.

Of course, the need to recreate in a time of crisis is precarious. In a Warlpiri worldview, these works of "art" need to be accompanied with the songs, dances, and oral stories of which they are a part. Removed from this wider cultural-system they risk becoming objectified. This is not necessarily a problem for those of us who are outsiders, for the objects are intrinsically beautiful, and they successfully make their way through the wider world to inspire and enlarge our collective sense of vision and possibility. Nevertheless, the potentially-objectifying gaze of the outsider towards them points us to broader issues within which Warlpiri artists like Ida have to live.

Ida herself is no stranger to objectification. For her, the crisis in her life emerges from her peoples' displacement from country, and from the poverty and racism that has undermined her family. Making art is literally an answer to this crisis: for it is a means by which she might make enough money to pay for food, or reach a doorway to the resources with which to visit children who have been sent interstate for schooling. Practicing art in the form of painting her *Jukurrpa* keeps Ida's cultural connection strong for both herself and her family, as well as replaces broken washing machines.

But even this artistic practice, which so aids that connection, is itself bound up in the difficulties that undermine cultural life and well-being for those, like Ida, who reside in Alice Springs. For example, in Alice Springs there is no Aboriginal arts center to assist someone like Ida. Even more devastatingly, as a member of an economically-marginalized family and community, and as a widow, she often cannot afford art supplies, and can often go for many months without the means to paint.

Ida's work is produced in a time of crisis, and through her imagination she helps others see in new ways and grow in understanding of country and the place of First Peoples within it. Particularly for those who are part of faith-traditions in Australia, her works have been instrumental in helping others imagine their way into a sense of connection with country, and into being a reconciled nation. Despite loss, grief, and struggle, Ida points above and says, "I'm OK as long as this one is with me." In her soul, she has found a way to reconcile the heavens and the earth, the past and the present; and, in her art, she helps those of us who view it to enter a wider, more hopeful future.

27

George Gittoes

The Artist as Prophet and Mystic

Rod Pattenden

The development of contemporary art in the twentieth century has been largely shaped by cultural frames based in modernity and the apparent assuredness of progress. In many ways, artworks themselves became a grand gesture of modernism as they filled the vestibules of increasingly high skyscrapers, and acted as a sign for progress and the triumph of the human spirit. It was not until the late 1980s, in the context of increasing uncertainty and political change, that things began to shake the seamless belief in the progress of art, and in the art of progress. Robert Hughes, then art critic for *The New York Times*, voiced his concern for this loss of belief on the basis that art had become subsumed into market forces as a commodity of status and wealth: "The idea of social renewal by cultural challenge had lasted a hundred years, and its vanishing marked the end of an eagerly sought, if unconsummated, vision of art's relation to life."[1] Hughes's comments were intended to announce the end of the "avant-garde," the possibility that art might make a difference in society as a force for change and renewal. Art, in Hughes's terms, had arrived at a point where it become an endless pursuit of what might be considered to be fashionable.

Behind such pronouncements about the death of art lies a more complex story about the spiritual intent of art, as both a point of inspiration for the individual artist and as an energizing sense of aspiration for shared social meaning. One of the often-repressed aspects of modern art that championed a sense of progress towards a secular future was its dalliance with things spiritual, and the possibility that the role of the artist could fulfil the aspirations of prophet, seer, and harbinger of future utopian ideals. Wassily Kandinsky's meditations on the spiritual in art, written at the beginning

---

1. Hughes, *The Shock of the New*, 365.

of the century, remained influential for artists in exploring beyond surface representation to garner the winds of change and cultural formation, giving such ideas visuality, allure, and social context: "We have before us the age of conscious creation, and this new spirit in painting is going hand in hand with the spirit of thought towards an epoch of great spiritual leaders."[2] The groundbreaking exhibition curated by Maurice Tuchman—"The Spiritual in Art: Abstract Painting 1890–1985"—sought to uncover the many ongoing influences, ranging from religious traditions to esoteric practices, that have continued to fund ideas about the social role of the artist and the impact of their works on forming human futures.[3]

Since the turn of this century, religion and spirituality have returned to the vocabulary of the contemporary arts, and critics and audiences are re-engaging with the role of the arts in forming the cultural imagination and human horizons.[4] In place of a general belief in increasing secularization, spirituality now proliferates as part of the postmodern and culturally diverse contexts of arts' production and its engagement with audiences. A major 2008 survey of contemporary art practice, undertaken by the critic Eleanor Heartney, identifies a re-emergence of an interest in spiritual and religious themes for contemporary artists: "Artists have continued to draw on religious sources and spiritual beliefs in the face of indifference and even resistance from the art establishment for reasons that take us back to the traditional relationship between art and religion. . . . It has served to articulate the ultimate questions. . . . These questions are too powerful to be abandoned by contemporary art."[5]

Part of the shift in understanding the role of art in society has been a return of an interest in ethics, and whether human society can act creatively in the face of such issues as climate change and terrorism. This invites questions about whether art can renew the human imagination, offer warnings, create possibilities, and reimagine a future worth inhabiting. Modernism had cultured the value of art for art's sake in an effort to keep art pure from politics and partisanship. In this century, human futures are no longer secure and artists now ask whether art can make a difference to what many consider to be an imperiled future.

This development towards a greater sense of social and ethical responsibility within arts practice has been spurred on by the increasing rise of global terrorism, funded in part by religious and cultural conflicts.

2. Kandinsky, *Concerning the Spiritual in Art*, 57.
3. See Tuchman, *The Spiritual in Art*.
4. See De Loisy, *Traces du Sacré*.
5. Heartney, *Art & Today*, 266.

Acts of terrorism are purposively conducted in highly visual forms and are ready for consumption through news media. Such visual terror is designed to impact on viewers and to unsettle their sense of safety. This opens up questions for artists about the reception of their work in a visual field that is being marked by images that resemble the genre of horror and the grotesque. These violent images disrupt the everyday, where ordinary existence is impacted by the conventions found in films that explore horror or extra-terrestrial encounters. Making art as if life mattered has found a new urgency, which has only increased as the effects of climate change has disturbed the confidence of human ordering.

Bernadette Buckley describes the shift that has occurred as contemporary art has moved outside a focus with individual identity towards more fundamental concerns about the nature of the human in the face of disintegrative forces: "By stepping into the no-man's land between 'ethical' and the 'aesthetical,' the fate of art in an 'age of terrorism' is therefore to cast art out of the relative isolation of the art world and subject it to all kinds of intellectual, political and aesthetic scrutiny—to enact, in other words, a syncopation between the 'ethical' and the 'aesthetical' realms."[6]

The question that arises in this development is whether art can provide a form of social renewal, sponsor justice making, convey dreams and visions, and whether artists can fulfil the role of prophet or seer within a postmodern cultural context. This is a pressing question about the function of art and the role of the artist in the face of the current forces of globalism that tolerates international conflict and, in turn, manages the current health pandemic.

In seeking to explore the possibility that art might provide a social resource for renewing the human imagination, I would like offer the following analysis of the Australian artist and filmmaker George Gittoes (1949–). Gittoes's work assumes that as an artist he can create awareness and compassion in his audience towards the key issues that shape our global future. He believes in a role for art as prophecy, a form of scrutinizing false beliefs that allows for the shock of the new, a reimagining of the future based in hope and compassion. Gittoes's work contributes to a renewal of the social imagination that also values the role of religion as a cultural resource.

George Gittoes in Context

I have had a long working relationship with Gittoes, having first met him when I judged the 1992 Blake Prize for Religious Art. I have written regularly

---

6. Buckley, "Terrible Beauties," 28.

about his work since that time, and I have curated several exhibitions of his work, the most extensive being a survey show in 2014 at Hazelhurst Regional Gallery in Sydney.[7] Most recently, I developed an exhibition addressing the manner in which he works in conflict zones, how he survives and draws out artistic responses, and how he collaborates with local people impacted by conflict—drawing them into his creative projects, such as painting, drama, and film making.[8] These projects have given me wide access to his studio archives and, more importantly, to his visual diaries that demonstrate his working methods and exploratory visual processes.[9]

Gittoes has placed himself in the most unlikely of places, having traded the comfort of an art studio in Sydney for a life in places where global conflict erupts into violence. For over fifty years he has made the world his studio, with current history being the subject. His work is sometimes startling, and always deeply engaging. It is emotionally charged, and unflinching in its efforts to witness to the impact of war on the human person. Since the 1970s, Gittoes has worked in such places as Nicaragua, the Philippines, the Middle East, Sudan, South Africa, Rwanda, Cambodia, and, in 2022, in Ukraine. He has sought to give witness to human suffering and the capacity for survival through a string of major exhibitions, and, in more recent years, a series of documentary films that give insight into the lives of people in Iraq, Pakistan, and Afghanistan. Gittoes's work as an artist and humanitarian has been recognized by a number of awards, including the prestigious 2015 Sydney Peace Prize.[10] Gittoes summarizes his motivation: "I feel privileged to have been able to spend so much of my life creating beauty in the face of the destruction of war. I have been waging a personal war against war with art. I believe in art so much that I am prepared to risk my life to do it."[11]

Critical discussion of Gittoes's work has understandably focused on his role as a war artist, which has, however, served to overlook the wider frame of his interests and, in particular, the manner in which he engages the complex nature of his subject matter.[12] Bernard Smith has linked Gittoes to the work of German Expressionists such as Max Beckman, who explored the social conditions in the period after the First World War.[13] US critic Daniel Herwitz links Gittoes's approach to that of humanitarianism

7. See Pattenden, "George Gittoes: I Witness."
8. See Pattenden, *George Gittoes: On Being There*.
9. See Denoon, "War Diaries of George Gittoes."
10. See ABC News, "George Gittoes."
11. George Gittoes, interview with the author, January 15, 1997.
12. See Hart, *The Realism of Peace*.
13. See Smith, *Modernism's History*, 144–46.

where scrutiny is given to human crises as a result of natural disaster or conflict. Herwitz helpfully highlights Gittoes's role as a witness who draws in the viewer to grasp an immediacy of experience that invites compassion and action: "It is only because he starts from the position of witness that the power of his art can unfold as it does. For his work presents the viewer with a way of grasping the formless, contingent power of events at their horrifying sources, and retaining that in all that follows.... We too become witnesses, confronting his victims as he does."[14]

Darren Jorgensen has focused on the manner in which Gittoes deals with the technology of war in a post-heroic context, highlighting the alienating experiences of wars that are increasingly conducted with advanced visual technologies.[15] His analysis draws attention to the manner in which Gittoes investigates the nature of visuality in human situations of conflict and violence, in particular, in his documentary films. Gittoes has received international recognition for his documentary films, as they find part of their context in the visual conventions found alongside media stories that are shaped to support a particular political perspective. Gittoes is interested in an ethics of seeing that implicates the viewer in the origins of the image-making process. Joanna Bourke's survey of war art recognizes that we are all consumers of images of horror through the media, and that this works to limit any sense of active response from the viewer: "Consuming war art might simply lead to declarations of horror, rather than any deeper political response."[16] Gittoes's work does not provide spaces for abstraction or detachment, but is concerned to draw the viewer into a proximity with the stark realism of the work. Appreciation of Gittoes's work has tended to focus on this context of danger and violence. In a recent summary interview, US critic David Levi Strauss highlighted this focus on war, to which Gittoes responded: "I can tell you, and I think, I hope, that my work is finally about that light within people."[17]

A more adequate understanding of Gittoes's work is provided through an awareness of his use of religion as a cultural resource, and, in turn, an examination of his work as an artist through roles that draw on the social role of religion, such as being a seer, mystic, or prophet. Within his overall artistic output there is a continued interest in religious and mystical ideas. He studied Islamic art while at high school, an influence that is evidenced in the visual and performance work he did as part of The Yellow House arts

---

14. Herwitz, *Aesthetics, Arts, and Politics*, 164.
15. See Jorgensen, "George Gittoes," 54.
16. Bourke, *War and Art*, 33.
17. Gittoes and Strauss, "George Gittoes."

community at the beginning of his career.[18] This sensitivity has also enabled him to work in Iraq, Pakistan, and, more recently, Afghanistan and Ukraine, having respect and interest in local cultures and forms of behavior, and in finding points of contact and collaboration with creative communities. Gittoes is sensitive to the manner in which narrative and story work within communities, and to the role of the imagination as form of social cohesion and community change. There is, in his work in these communities, an understanding of the role of art as a form of ritual hope and social reimagining that seems to energize his ability to build creative communities that echo his early experience at the Yellow House in Sydney in 1970. This aspect of his work as a social art form is generally overlooked and is better understood through his interest in the spiritual imagination.[19]

At the beginning of his autobiographical book of stories and art works, *Blood Mystic*, published in 2016, Gittoes explains the choice of the title through recounting a conversation with a monk at Mount Sinai in Egypt in 1994. The term "blood mystic," as explained by the monk, describes the role of a person who would enter places of conflict without weapons and tend to the soldiers, particularly the sick and wounded, and listen to their needs. "Blood mystics were able to do this because they had certain knowledge of the eternal and indestructible nature of the human soul. Their mystical experiences of life beyond their physical bodies took away all fear of their own death."[20] In highlighting such an observation, I want to be clear that I am not endorsing Gittoes as being part of a certain religious tradition or ideology. Artists are generally hesitant to commit themselves publicly to a particular tradition or practice in case they are misunderstood to then support the whole of that ideology. Given that the public role of religion in secular society has often alternated between defensive gestures and rhetorical attacks on moral matters, many artists choose not to align themselves with institutional forms of religion. James Elkins points out that when religion has appeared as a subject in contemporary art it has been generally received with skepticism, or at best embarrassment, rather than with any sense of sympathy or respect.[21]

In the following analysis, I draw on insights about the social role of religion and its capacity to nurture a cultural imagination that sustains human community with values of justice and inclusion, and that works towards the common good. An understanding of the social role of the

18. See Mendelssohn, *The Yellow House*.
19. See Pattenden, *George Gittoes: On Being There*.
20. Gittoes, *Blood Mystic*, 15.
21. See Elkins, *On the Strange Place of Religion in Contemporary Art*.

artist is not well understood within models that are sustained by economic or instrumental parameters. The intentions of the artist as prophet and mystic provide an understanding of the role of the artist that values actions towards provoking awareness, creating change, and offering hope in social contexts. It moves the role of the artist from the modern concept of an individual innovative genius towards a model that takes account of cultural formation and social settings. It gives art a role in forming the ethical and moral basis for choices, for celebrating what it is to be human in society, of negotiating difference, and of building community.

Artist as Witness

One key work that illuminates Gittoes's approach to religion is found in his winning entry for the 1995 Blake Prize for Religious Art, entitled *The Preacher*.[22] This work is rendered in expressive thick oil paint, and depicts a young man in a yellow coat holding up his two hands in resignation, one of them holding a bible. Gittoes had come across this man in the frightened crowd at Kibeho, Rwanda. This crowd had gathered on the one-year anniversary of the end of the Rwandan Civil War (1990–94) and were seeking the protection of the United Nations' peacekeeping forces. This man was paying attention to some of the isolated younger children, giving them comfort. Gittoes had heard his voice speaking in French and recognized words that were familiar:

> This afternoon . . . I came into a group who were calm, tough bursts of machine gun fire surrounded them—continually getting closer with terrifying inevitability—they remained a solid congregation—bound together not by walls, but by prayer. A solitary preacher read to them from a ragged bible. He was a tall man in a yellowish coat sitting high on a sack of grain. He spoke in French with a thick dialect—his voice hoarse and broken—but I could recognize the Sermon on the Mount: "Blessed are the pure in heaven, for they shall see God."[23]

---

22. See Crumlin, *The Blake Book*, 142.
23. Gittoes, cited in Bennie, "Preacher Takes the Prize," 14.

George Gittoes, *The Preacher*, 1995. Oil on linen, 181 x 250 cm. Collection of National Gallery of Australia, Canberra, Australia.

Gittoes had been in Kibeho documenting the work of Australian peacekeeping soldiers and medical staff working with the UN when violence broke out, and the local military starting attacking the crowd that had gathered hoping that the UN peacekeepers would keep them safe.[24] Gittoes and his fellow Australians were constrained as non-combatants. Gittoes got his cameras out and started filming. These photographs would eventually find their way to a war crimes tribunal, and also into a series of paintings and drawings that remain some of his most powerful work.

Gittoes's *The Preacher* addresses the viewer with its subject's arms outstretched. He is a human person, a victim, vulnerable and defenseless, inviting our compassion and drawing us into this difficult situation that matches powerlessness with implied power of those who threaten his life. Gittoes offered this response to winning the Blake Prize: "*The Preacher* represents

24. See Fry, *Rwanda*.

what I think religion should be, raise people up, make people feel human and spiritually alive and give them courage and faith. When I returned home, I was carrying this terrible imagery in my head. I have a wife and two children. I didn't want to go straight into the studio and start painting dead children. And the one powerful positive image I had was the preacher. I could see him in his yellow coat and I could feel his courage."[25]

This was the second time that Gittoes had won the Blake Prize, and his subject again linked the experience of faith and religious belief with current political realities faced by real human beings, drawing in the viewer, inviting their compassion. Here the artist has developed a role as witness that in turn invites viewers to experience the complex emotions and awareness that Gittoes himself evidences in shocking and confronting situations. This is a form of realism that evokes moral and ethical relations, and that demolishes the safe distance that looking usually implies. The artist as witness invites the viewer to enter the world that Gittoes re-creates, and to experience its destabilizing effects and its disturbing ethical implications, as a prompt to action.

Given that contemporary social experience is marked by rich visuality and that it is socially ordered by unending practices of surveillance, the role of the artist as witness takes on a complex sophistication. This is an underlying element of Gittoes's work that is overlooked in the face of the initial reactions or disgust or horror at the subject matter, and its painterly visceral presentation.

Gittoes's awareness of the processes of visualization and hierarchies of looking engender his work with visual power and effect. Herwitz draws attention to the manner in which Gittoes's work is a kind of performance—from drawing to painting, and then drawn into the worlds of the viewer who recognize the categories of heightened emotion and threat to the ordered social imagination: "It is well known that in any traumatic moment, time always flows too fast and too slow, and the instant remains strange, distant, foreign, horrifying, unreal—a point of amnesia and perpetual memory, over in an instant and never over."[26] In evoking such visual strategies, Gittoes is tampering with the underlying order of image reception that encultures the eye into seeing a coherent form of reality. These strategies are further illuminated by the manner in which Gittoes uses the camera in the field, turning the views around and putting it in the hands of victims, or observing the manner in which young street kids in Chicago document their lives on their mobile phones. Jorgensen notes that Gittoes provides a "nuanced picture of

---

25. Gittoes, cited in Bennie, "Preacher Takes the Prize," 14.
26. Herwitz, *Aesthetics, Arts, and Politics*, 170.

the way in which people within war zones are not only victims but are also witnesses to their own circumstances."[27]

The role of artist as witness examples the manner in which Gittoes uses and makes plain the technologies and power structures at work in the visual field of human relations, a space with potential for conflict or collaboration, for surveillance or for the democratization of power relations. It is from within this field Gittoes intends to operate as an active element, rather than a dispassionate observer, a position that is impossible to maintain in the face of injustice or inequity. Gittoes's motivation is clear—he believes that in making art, he is making a difference:

> If you can create in a war zone, then you're doing that in the face of all this destruction. It is a really important gesture of creating in the midst of this intensively destructive atmosphere. I have discovered from all these conflicts that I have covered that violence only leads to more violence. Human beings are creative. All these international situations need love, consideration and creativity. . . . I want to spend the rest of my career doing creative work in the face of all these violent forces. We are creative beings and we don't have to be destructive.[28]

A related aspect to this role of witness is Gittoes's capacity as a storyteller, an important but often overlooked part of his creative expression. This highlights the underlying performative context to his work, which moves from the context of its creation to its presentation to an audience. The artist is actively involved in illuminating, expanding, re-phrasing through words and images, narrative and story, thereby stretching time and creating a performative moment that collapses real time into an aesthetic event. The work is never finished, as its interpretation is ongoing. Any fuller understanding of his work requires this expanded concept of performance, as it holds together his storytelling, the making of images in the field, his use of texts on drawings, his photography and film, and the large scale of his works, often making best sense when they come together in immersive exhibition environments that link the various visual forms. Gittoes uses every skill at his disposal to draw the viewer into his own timeframe. In some ways, this acts like ritual space, where one becomes a participant in a reality that has otherwise gone unnoticed; such spaces as those that are sacred, holy, or even dark and undisclosed. In discussing the nature of time in religious ritual and myth, David Chidester comments: "Sharing sacred time . . . is sharing

---

27. Jorgensen, "George Gittoes," 66.
28. George Gittoes, interview with the author, July 24, 2003.

social cohesion."[29] Gittoes's regular return to making large puppet heads of imagined creatures is evidence of a theatrical impulse that seeks to create a stage for performance in ritual time, seeking to re-enact the meanings of the work with participants rather than audiences.

Gittoes is a witness to the creativity that lies at the heart of what it is to be human. Even in the most difficult situations, people are creating, improvising, making music, imagining things to be different, and generating reasons to hope. Gittoes sees that his role as an artist is to assist in the activation of the cultural resources found in local communities through the arts. This kind of role steps well outside the usual parameters for art production in a consumer driven arts industry. Gittoes's collaboration with local artists and filmmakers dismantles the usual confines of individual authorship and copyright boundaries, and locates his practice within social relationships and shared cultural outcomes. These social outcomes are part of the work, and contribute to an expanded understanding for the role of the artist in society. Art makes worlds.

Prophetic Criticism

To understand the role that Gittoes has forged and, in particular, the valuing of social outcomes as being part of the work, I would like to draw on Deborah Haynes's analysis of the vocation of the artist. Haynes explores the various ways in which religious traditions have helped to form a social understanding of the role of the artist and to, in turn, form the reception given to such work within cultural contexts. Haynes reviews the manner in which the work of artists has been shaped by a variety of expectations that impact their social reception. She borrows the term "vocation" from the context of a calling to religious ministry and uses it as a means of describing the function for an artist who might critically stand outside the current social structures shaped by consumerism, so as to contribute to hopeful human futures. She reviews the manner in which artists have been sustained through their role in historical cultures ranging from "craftsperson," "romantic creator," "avant-garde prophet," and "postmodern bricoleur." Haynes is aware of the many layers of association with the term "prophecy," but centers in on the notion of prophetic criticism as an urgent and necessary role for the arts within contemporary culture: "The artist as prophetic critic attends to what is wrong in the present situation, relating the present to the past and future. The artist

---

29. Chidester, *Religion*, 48.

as visionary attempts to envision possible futures. This is what it means to say that the vocation of the artist is the reclamation of the future."[30]

Alongside the commitment that Gittoes has made to being an artist who is a witness, there is a body of his work where he turns his attention more directly to what Haynes considers as prophetic criticism, where he sharpens his image-making skills on current history, using a variety of forms ranging from parody, irony, and the horror of the grotesque, that serves to critique and dismantle the glossy images that seek to shape contemporary cultural formation for those in power. Gittoes is a sharp critic of the smooth image-making of politics and global power, and this is where he engages the grotesque vocabulary of the apocalyptic imagination. The apocalyptic imagination in the west derives from such biblical texts as the Book of Revelation, and is fuelled by historical uncertainty and the fear of chaos and death. It includes speculations about the end of history, judgment for evil ones, and glory for those chosen, and has impacted on understandings of contemporary moments in history for the last two thousand years. In this light, current history is always being shadowed by an impending future, which is clear if you can read the signs! This is true not only for those who work within a theological paradigm, because these ideas have spilled out through western culture and echoed through political manifestos and popular imagination.[31]

Eleanor Heartney's study of the apocalyptic imagination within contemporary art practice finds ample evidence of its lively impact as a way of understanding current events and a form of mediating anxiety about the future. She points to this as a resource to assist in gestating the impact of current events and to purchase some sense of choice and action in the face of possible futures: "It may not be enough simply to understand the influence of the apocalyptic imagination. We need to know, as well, how to break its fatal attraction. We find the instruments for this in the imaginations of contemporary artists."[32] The future is not simply an overwhelming inevitability, as humans have choice, and implicit in the apocalyptic world is a sense of purchase towards more hopeful options for human existence. Tina Pippin highlights this ethical aspect when she states: "The edge of apocalypse is the edge of ethical, a possible journey into a destructive future."[33] And this is where Gittoes inhabits a position on the edge of destruction or renewal

---

30. Haynes, *The Vocation of the Artist*, 227–28.
31. See O'Hear and O'Hear, *Picturing the Apocalypse*.
32. Heartney, *Doomsday Dreams*, 11.
33. Pippin, *Apocalyptic Bodies*, 26.

as a holder of signs and warnings about the nature of our choices today in creating tomorrow's possible habitation.

George Gittoes, *Security*, 2020. Oil on linen, 168 x 244 cm. Artist's collection.

During the period of COVID-related physical confinement in early 2020, Gittoes developed a large body of work that served as a summary series of images to express the state of the world and current global conflicts. As he has done previously, he turned to the vocabulary of the grotesque, and populated the scenarios with creatures, or human figures, undergoing stress and transformation due to the pressures they were enduring. Gittoes sought to encapsulate the dying days of the Trump Presidency, ongoing global conflict, the COVID pandemic, and the impact of climate change on the environment. These works were exhibited in Brisbane during March 2021.[34] It is a series of works with the apocalyptic elements writ large, a key work being *Security* (2020), which explores the situation of national security in the face of both internal and external threats to stable society. This large-scale work in oils provides a visceral response to the nature of surveillance and the technologies of control as they are imagined through large and malevolent creatures.

34. See Mitchell Fine Art, "Augustus Tower."

In a large-scale mural format, a striking human hybrid insect figure holds the central position of surveillance over a cityscape. Other stick figures also patrol the city with guns and night-vision goggles. Religious references are scattered around the composition, and a blond blue-eyed Christ figure rides the abdomen of the central protagonist, while drones populate the air. A figure on the roof of a building is about to be crushed by the boot of this malignant stick figure, while another figure is falling to their death. The city has become its own captive enemy, and the need for safety has been turned into a form of control. Technologies like facial recognition, credit cards, mobile phones, security cameras, drones, and robots are all part of an increasing concern to maintain security while personal freedoms are eroded and conformity is celebrated. Through this grotesque and forbidding scenario, Gittoes is offering both critique and a warning, painting possible futures, provoking viewers to choose and act. An apocalyptic imagination sees tomorrow as a shadow on the choices that are required today.

Facing Death

Gittoes acts like a prophet—critiquing the present, offering warnings about the future, and prompting hopeful action. But alongside this, he is also deeply concerned with the inner meanings of life. In this regard, he could also be considered to operate like a mystic who is managing the intense impact of inner experiences that are a counterpoint to the challenges of the external world. These concern the sharp boundaries of personal extinguishment and death. The mystic is the one who has transcended the fear of death, and has their eye on another future. Their life is no longer defined by the end supplied by physical death. This term is helpful in explaining the lack of fear that Gittoes exhibits while working in war zones or places of heightened danger. Gittoes has a personal relationship with death and it is not a source of fear. This is illuminated in a diary entry over two large pages, from his time in Kabul, Afghanistan, in 2010. Here is a personal reflective note, with a short-written text and the drawing of a curious embryonic form: "People always ask me about how I can keep facing and witnessing war and death. I've come up with hundreds of answers—all with some truth—but really it is because of my certainty that death is just a transition and not the end."[35] These words accompany a drawing of what appears to be a delicate embryo figure that is growing and spiraling out into the space. It is Gittoes's affirmation of life, after life, a kind of daring inner belief in the

---

35. Gittoes, Art Diary, entry for May 30, 2011, Kabul, Afghanistan. Unpublished personal diary.

survival of some sense of self, against the backdrop of war, violence, and chaos. It appears like an exclamation mark against the terrible darkness of a history that he has witnessed, over and over again.

George Gittoes, Diary entry, May 30, 2011. Kabul, Afghanistan.

Every viewer of Gittoes's work, every visitor to his exhibitions, every member of the audience at his presentations, and every critic, art historian, and commentator, all hover in some way around this question—how does one keep facing and witnessing war and death? It is a question that doesn't belong in the canon of behavior on how an artist works and behaves. Why does Gittoes choose to live out this role of an artist, working in the face of chaos, violence, and nihilism? Why does he put himself at such personal risk? How does he survive in such places that are marked by overwhelmingly heightened emotional impact? The answers lie in his generally positive framework, that he keeps focused on where he can make a difference. He remembers the more than a dozen people who are alive today because of his direct intervention, and the many others whose lives have improved after their involvement in projects involving his work. But at the heart of it, Gittoes is comfortable with the nearness of death in a manner that allows him to make good choices and create hope.

Searching for Gittoes's own relationship with death goes back to one of the most profound experiences of his youth. In the midst of the creative excitement of the Yellow House experience at the age of twenty-one, Gittoes had to face the repercussions of the death by suicide of his girlfriend Marie. While this period was one of great creativity and a blossoming role as an artist, it was also a period of stress in making a living and building a life and a relationship. On being given the news of Marie's death, the police requested Gittoes to come to the morgue and identify her body. When they arrived, her body was unceremoniously pulled out of a metal drawer. Gittoes saw the marks of agony and suffering due to an overdose of sleeping pills. "All the dead bodies I have witnessed since are eclipsed by Marie's dead eyes—her face has made the realm of death my alternative home."[36]

In the face of fear and death, Gittoes continues to create, and finds in creating over and over again the ability to transcend the dread associated with the end. There is something like a spiritual discipline of creativity that involves the process of improvisation and letting go in the face of new and emerging needs. Past attachments are let go of, as creativity requires a total concentration on the current moment. Gittoes does not dwell on failure, as his life practice is founded in the capacity for invention to find new solutions. Roles like witness, ritual performer, prophet, or mystic, are useful because they stand outside the commercial parameters of the arts industry. They are also useful because they are porous, relational, ethical, and communal. They deal with meanings and imagination rather than with function and instrumentality. They incorporate the work as well as the maker, the context of their origins, and the trajectory of the community that is drawn in as audience. Such roles allow for love, sacrifice, pain, and ecstasy to be part of the materiality in forming what it is to be human, where art and life become inseparable: "There is no greater test in this life than to face death. Survive and you will move to another level. . . . My life has been threatened in many wars and I've seen more pain and death than anyone should. But I still describe myself as an optimist. Wherever there is war, there need to be artists willing to create in the face of it—the ultimate act of resistance to the destroyers."[37]

George Gittoes is not an artist centrally concerned with war and conflict. He actively eschews descriptions of his role that liken him to a journalistic adventurer who lives off the adrenaline of war. In contrast, his mode of operation moves outside the normal structures of the arts industry to develop a role as a conjurer of hope, healer, humanitarian, circus director, teacher, and community builder. This is celebrated most clearly in the film *Love City, Jalalabad* (2013), which tells a narrative of his involvement in regenerating the film industry in the city of Jalalabad in Afghanistan through

36. Gittoes, *Blood Mystic*, 87.
37. Gittoes, *Blood Mystic*, 18.

activating a community of actors and technicians.[38] This joyful and yet dangerous narrative pitches the generative capacity of art-making in community against the destructive forces of war and conflict. This social dimension of Gittoes's work as a collaborator and instigator calls for an analysis from the perspective of roles found in lived forms of religion that seek to energize a community through activating the resources of the cultural and religious imagination found in the creative arts. Witness, ritual performer, prophet, and mystic, are words borrowed to take account of an individual who is re-imagining the future from contexts that are among some of the most difficult, dangerous, and, therefore, unlikely places on earth. The mystic knows that light will shine its brightest in the dark.

Bibliography

ABC News (Australia). "George Gittoes, War Artist and Filmmaker, wins Sydney Peace Prize." *YouTube*, November 9, 2015. https://www.youtube.com/watch?v=_9ZefIzyZ2c.

Bennie, Angela. "Preacher Takes the Prize." *Sydney Morning Herald*, December 15, 1995, 14.

Bourke, Joanna. *War and Art: A Visual History of Modern Conflict*. London: Reaktion, 2017.

Buckley, Bernadette. "Terrible Beauties." In *Art in the Age of Terrorism*, edited by Graham Coulter-Smith and Maurice Owen, 11–33. London: Holberton, 2005.

Chidester, David. *Religion: Material Dynamics*. Oakland: University of California Press, 2018.

Crumlin, Rosemary. *The Blake Book: Art, Religion, and Spirituality in Australia: Celebrating 60 Years of the Blake Prize*. Melbourne: Macmillan, 2011.

De Loisy, Jean. *Traces du Sacré: Visitations*. Paris: Centre Pompidou, 2008.

Denoon, Louise. "War Diaries of George Gittoes." https://www.sl.nsw.gov.au/stories/war-diaries-george-gittoes.

Elkins, James. *On the Strange Place of Religion in Contemporary Art*. New York: Routledge, 2004.

Fry, Gavin. *Rwanda: The Australian Contingent, 1994–1995*, Canberra: Australian Army, 1996.

Gittoes, George. *Blood Mystic*. Sydney: Pan Macmillan Australia, 2016.

Gittoes, George, and David Levi Strauss. "George Gittoes with David Levi Strauss." https://brooklynrail.org/2010/07/art/george-gittoes-with-david-levi-strauss.

Hart, Deborah. *The Realism of Peace: George Gittoes*. Darwin: Museum and Art Gallery of the Northern Territory, 1995.

Haynes, Deborah J. *The Vocation of the Artist*. Cambridge: Cambridge University Press, 1997.

Heartney, Eleanor. *Art & Today*. London: Phaidon, 2008.

———. *Doomsday Dreams: The Apocalyptic Imagination in Contemporary Art*. New York: Silver Hollow, 2019.

38. See Pattenden, "Love City Jalalabad."

Herwitz, Daniel. *Aesthetics, Arts, and Politics in a Global World*. London: Bloomsbury Academic, 2017.

Hughes, Robert. *The Shock of the New: Art and the Century of Change*. London: Thames & Hudson, 1991.

Jorgensen, Darren. "George Gittoes in an Era of Post-Heroic, Hyper-Real Warfare." *Australian and New Zealand Journal of Art* 20.1 (2020) 54–67.

Kandinsky, Wassily. *Concerning the Spiritual in Art*. Translated by M. T. H. Sadler. New York: Dover, 1977.

Mendelssohn, Joanna. *The Yellow House: 1970–1972*. Sydney: Art Gallery of New South Wales, 1990.

Mitchell Fine Art. "Augustus Tower: George Gittoes." https://www.mitchellfineartgallery.com/art-exhibitions/previous-exhibitions/george-gittoes-2021-exhibition.

O'Hear, Natasha, and Anthony O'Hear. *Picturing the Apocalypse: The Book of Revelation in the Arts over Two Millennia*. Oxford: Oxford University Press, 2015.

Pattenden, Rod. "George Gittoes: I Witness." In *George Gittoes: I Witness*, edited by Claire Armstrong, 17–23. Gymea: Hazelhurst Regional Gallery, 2014.

———. *George Gittoes: On Being There*. Newcastle: Newcastle Art Gallery, 2020.

———. "Love City Jalalabad: George Gittoes in Afghanistan." *Art Monthly* 266 (2013) 23–26.

Pippin, Tina. *Apocalyptic Bodies: The Biblical End of the World in Text and Image*. New York: Routledge, 1999.

Smith, Bernard. *Modernism's History: A Study in Twentieth-Century Art and Ideas*. Sydney: University of New South Wales Press, 1998.

Tuchman, Maurice, ed. *The Spiritual in Art: Abstract Painting 1890–1985*. New York: Abbeville, 1986.

28

The Portable Church

John Foulcher

Sunday. We sit to watch church in its absence, here in our church, where we've come to live. Above us, that which was the choir loft sings of our bed. A kitchen huddles off to the side of the nave. The bathroom is a baptistry, and our small study has the intimacy of a confessional, just about. On the television, we are glimpsing a distant paradise. There, the priest is alone with the sacraments, in all his tumbling robes. I'm wondering where God is. You can't help but think. Clouds part, and the sky falls on the floor from the sharp, arched window, here in our church. It lies there, and makes the floor shine, though it's not like the window itself, which is a hull of shimmering blue day. And the window is not like the sky, which goes on and on, out into the stars, while the tiny televised liturgy, here in our church, is beginning its end.

29

Who Is an Artist, and Who Cares Anyway?

Libby Byrne

"Our lives are made of stories—some of them big, some small, some complex and convoluted, some simple. Some we may keep to ourselves and some we share with others."[1] When I introduce myself by saying, "I am an artist," I begin sharing a complex story that is shaped and re-shaped in the experience of the telling. There is nothing fixed about living into my identity as an artist. The context in which I choose to share this story shapes and re-shapes the way I perceive my identity as an artist, and I often find myself communicating from a strange "state of self-negotiation."[2] There are times when claiming to be an artist leaves me feeling unnecessarily isolated from others, and in the loneliness of this place I begin to wonder how and why I have come to think of myself in this way. More broadly, I wonder how it is that some people find the wherewithal to identify and live as an artist, while others seem to persistently negotiate complex experiences of desire and resistance, before ultimately rejecting the idea of being an artist in the world. In this essay, I will work towards understanding the experience of this conundrum by employing art materials to examine layers of experience with art and people.

The ideas and perceptions that have imprinted and seeped through my consciousness from one layer of coherence into the next reveal what it is like for me to draw near with faith, and. "*Draw Near in Faith, and . . .*" is indeed the title of a work of mine embedded in a small A5 sketchbook that now resides in the Brooklyn Art Library (BAL).[3] This artefact has awakened me to think more deeply about what it means for me to be an artist in the experience of *making*, exhibiting, and *being with* other people as together

---

1. Lawson, "Using Narrative and Story Telling in Research," 183.
2. Luger, "But I'm Just an Artist?" 1329.
3. Byrne, "Draw Near in Faith, and . . ."

we care enough to see and to respond to the call of desire that resides and resounds in the world through the presence of art.

Being an Exhibiting Artist

In my practice in the studio, I am seeking to discover ideas and images that extend the way I think and perceive through material, imaginative, and co-operative knowing about existential questions that provoke and sustain my attention. Over time, I have learned to trust in the experience of mutuality that seems to exist for me within the practice of making and seeing art. Sometimes I release into the world art that I have made, and as it resides in galleries and public settings it finds ways of being with people who are open to seeing the work in unexpected ways; thereby, art in the world extends my practice. When I give myself over to the time it takes to be with art, art becomes something of an event—a liminal space where memory is awakened and welcomed into the present. I have learned over time that in the liminal space of exhibiting art, transformation is possible. My desire to be transformed and to imagine new possibilities provokes me to insert different ways of exhibiting into the perpetual practice of making art.

While art galleries come in many shapes and sizes, the BAL is home to the world's largest collection of artist sketchbooks. Founded in 2006, Steven Peterman began the library with the goal of creating a small community art space. Fifteen years later, The Sketchbook Project connects and inspires creatives as it cares for and creates a home for fifty thousand sketchbooks from thirty thousand different people. The BAL claims to be more than a project: "We are a slice of global creativity. We are an inside look at what people are thinking. We are an archive, a library, a source for endless inspiration."[4] The invitation issued by the BAL is for all—artists and those who do not think of themselves as artists—to stretch their imaginations into and beyond the themes offered by the library as starting points by contributing to a collective and growing narrative about what it is like to be here; what it is like to be living in the world in the twenty-first century.

In allowing anyone who cares to be involved and to exhibit their work for a nominal fee, this not-for-profit organization moves toward democratizing the work of the artist. As an artist who does regularly exhibit finished artworks in public settings, for the purpose of sales, public comment, and critique, there is something extraordinarily challenging about submitting what is essentially an unfinished work in progress to this international art library. As I sent the original sketchbook to the collection without any idea

---

4. Brooklyn Art Library, "Our Mission."

of the impact or level of engagement that might result, my identity as an exhibiting artist prompted me to pay the small extra fee ensuring that my work would be photographed and added to the Digital Library.

The philosophical and theoretical constructs that inform our thinking about the question of who an artist is profoundly shape our capacity to respond to the desire we might experience to be seen and known in this way. In Western philosophy and tradition, there has been a considerable change in the last five hundred years regarding the way we have understood the work and calling of the artist. During the Middle Ages and the early period of the Renaissance, artisans belonged to guilds and were apprenticed to a workshop where they trained under a master, contributing to the completion of commissioned projects. The role of the classic artisan "was to confront chaos and creatively organize raw and untamed matter to generate a stable relationship between form and content."[5] As the Enlightenment dawned, however, the identity of the artisan was transformed, and the artists who emerged in this time were seen as romantic and beautiful souls, set aside to be "the privileged mediator of Nature (the Earth); the genius artist was to produce the infinite and continuous variations of form, the privilege of *adding* to Nature."[6] Whilst the artisan had learned and practised a valuable trade in the service of others, the aspirational power that was afforded to the artist as genius meant that this way of working became a way of identifying as special, and even set apart, in some way.

By the late-nineteenth century, there was an emerging concern that people valued the sacredness of the work of art over the sacredness of everyday work. In 1886, concerned with the social and economic implications of treating the artist as special, Lewis F. Day warned young artists of the danger they faced in over-estimating their own value and usefulness in a working society: "There is something too conscious about our consciousness of the artist in us. If we are artists, that will appear; we need not pose superior to the workman."[7] Day was concerned people valued the sacredness perceived in the work of art above the sacredness of the work-a-day world—"this new doctrine of its divinity appears to imply that we should be everlastingly singing its praises, magnifying ourselves through it, and thanking God that we are not as other men."[8] Modernism, therefore, ushered in a time when artists discovered the value of art more broadly in society, using imagery, materials, and techniques to

---

5. Jagodzinski, "From the Artist to the Cosmic Artisan," 88.
6. Jagodzinski, "From the Artist to the Cosmic Artisan," 88.
7. Day, "Artist and Artisan," 294.
8. Day, "Artist and Artisan," 295.

create works that reflected the realities, thoughts, and hopes burgeoning in ordinary people at the dawning of a new century.

Throughout the twentieth century, the work of art became increasingly open to a plurality of possible interpretations. In his treatise, *The Phenomenology of Aesthetic Experience*, Mikel Dufrenne submitted that the work of art is grasped in the aesthetic experience, and in these moments of apprehending the work the viewer confers particular significance and meaning upon the work itself.[9] Dufrenne considered the viewer's experience to be an important contribution to the development of the work of art.

In the postmodern era, artists began the work of challenging, reconstructing, and reinterpreting social theory. The extent of their revisions and reconstructions have enabled contemporary artists, working now, arguably, from a meta-modern perspective, to continue to challenge ideas about the nature, purpose, and form of art in different layers of society. The formation of the artist's identity has been described as a "flashpoint," as "an experience that makes one aware of oneself as an artist and how this intersects with other aspects of identity, such as race, ethnicity, religion, class, gender, and/or sexuality."[10] Indeed, the idea of intersectionality has offered a frame to "reconceptualize the artist as a relationally connected set of constantly shifting identities rather than an assumed category, as sometimes portrayed."[11]

The empty sketchbook destined for Volume 16 of the BAL Sketchbook Project became an invitation to explore the constantly shifting experience of identity as an artist, mapping what it is like to be a body alongside other bodies, in public worship. Over several months, I made marks in the sketchbook as a reminder of my experience of being in worship each week. As the work now resides in the BAL Digital Library, it welcomes the stories of others, who were not there when it was made, through the experience of seeing and of being with the artefact. As I sat with the sketchbook in worship, I drew on my capacity for relaxed awareness of the self, while being present and attuned to the colors, lines, and emerging shapes. This dynamic and reflexive experience required me to trust in the process of improvisation. Taking the time to hold space for and to care for the vulnerability of an emergent work of art is a process that shapes my identity as an artist. In taking care of the sketchbook as I worked on it over weeks, I was also caring for and liberating my imagination, looking for new ways of being with and alongside other people in the world.

9. Dufrenne, *The Phenomenology of Aesthetic Experience*, 3.
10. Travis, "Flashpoints of Artist Identity Formation," 18.
11. Luger, "But I'm Just an Artist?" 1329.

Being an Artist With and Alongside Other People

As an artist, I often find myself invited to speak with people who are fascinated by what I do, and who wonder what it would be like to be an artist. I have found that identifying as an artist can be intimidating for people. I was once told: "Well, if you are an artist, that means I can't be." If I choose to protect the vulnerability of my story by blocking the challenge, I will shrink back from the possibility of a conversation and live into the fear of scarcity. If, however, I risk extending my vulnerability toward the other, I am offering more than my own story. I am also offering to hear the stories of others. If we both lean into the vulnerability of an honest conversation, there is freedom, inclusiveness, responsibility, and the possibility of abundance. Artists care about stories other than their own and they respond with loving attention that "assumes suffering . . . (knowing) that there is no way truly to apprehend the other without being grieved by the other's complexity, or their difference, or their imperfections, or their loss, or all four."[12]

When I took my A5 sketchbook to the post office to send it to the BAL, the woman behind the counter weighed the package and asked me what I was sending. I found myself explaining the forthcoming pilgrimage to Brooklyn, and as I spoke she listened and expressed amazement that the BAL exists. Then she asked if I was an artist. I thought quickly and said, "Yes, but this project is for anyone who cares to be involved." She expressed her wonder and desire to find the website with its digital collection of works in the library. As the transaction progressed, she wondered aloud if I had ever been to the library in Brooklyn. When she heard that I had never been there, she blessed me with the gift of imagination, saying, "Wouldn't it be good if, one day, you could go there and see your book in this library?" Yes, it really would be good.

In an age of crisis, when seemingly insoluble and global problems require immanent solutions, it is possible to justify investing in the slow and careful cultivation of imagination as a response to the urgent call for action. In the CARE Project,[13] Jacqueline Millner called upon artists throughout Australia to explore, interpret, and enact their practices of care as a means of privileging time and attention, and holding space as a form of political practice.[14] In taking up this challenge, the choice to identify, live, and work as an artist redefines how we care to live, by engaging and sustaining our collective imagination to address the global challenges of our time.

---

12. Wells, *A Nazareth Manifesto*, 127.
13. Contemporary Art and Feminism, "CARE."
14. See Millner, "Caring through Art," 163–74.

If we consider the work of the artist to be a discursive practice, then we might well ask if the artist is also a storyteller. Robyne Latham is a contemporary Indigenous Australian artist whose active engagement with art promotes "consciousness raising" and inclusion. Latham's work "Empty Coolamons" awakened many Australians to the lived experience of absence and desire for the Stolen Generations, revealing layers of grief, loss, and stories that belong to them.[15] In 2015, Latham performed her work "The Aborigine is Present" at the Koorie Heritage Trust in Melbourne.[16] The work was inspired and endorsed by Marina Abramovic who produced *The Artist is Present*, a seminal work where the artist sits silently at a table and a queue of strangers take turns sitting opposite her and hold her gaze in silence for five minutes. Latham adapted this work by inviting different indigenous people to take turns sitting in silence and holding the gaze of a non-indigenous person, again for five minutes. Each person who sat at the table had an experience of seeing and of being seen, while a crowd gathered around holding the space, and observing individuals watching one another.

Not only did the performance reduce the perceived difference between indigenous and non-indigenous people, but Latham also described the way the public who engaged with this work began to find ways to live *beyond* the weight of history that hangs in the space between us. Through her work, Latham has found ways to engage our cultural silence and to give voice to those who were taken from the places where they belonged. By inviting people to participate in the process of meaning-making, Latham invites us also to see the world and the "other" who is alongside us, as if for the first time. Latham's work shifts the power dynamic in the work of art, ensuring that the artist and the viewer are engaged in the work of art alongside one another in a particular way that acknowledges the gift of presence that each person brings to the work. The success of "The Aborigine is Present" event was a result of her own commitment to the vision, and of the courageous vulnerability expressed by those who took up the invitation to see and be seen in the work of art. The boundaries between the artist and the viewer were dissolved and the unique qualities of each person were amplified as they found a place in something larger than themselves.

Anthropologist Ellen Dissanayake has argued that along with food, warmth, and shelter, making art is central to the adaptation and survival of human beings, and so all people have an innate aesthetic capacity. The experience of making and seeing art reduces the damage of psychological and

---

15. Latham, "Empty Coolamons."
16. Latham, "The Aborigine Is Present."

physical stress, and instils "collective emotions of trust and belongingness."[17] The stories of experience that reside in art become an invitation for those who care to see, and who care to reconstruct their perceptions, ideas, and ways of being in relation to self, others, and the natural world. It is the possibility of transformation that inspires me as an artist to work for the good of the thing being made, which includes both the artwork itself and the community who eventually receives the work.[18]

Figure 1: Libby Byrne, *Draw Near in Faith, and …* , 2020. 19 pages. Graphite, gouache, and oil pastel on paper, 48 x 21 cm. Brooklyn Art Library, New York, USA.

The images in my sketchbook (Fig. 1) are the result of chance as much as they have been determined by intention. So it is also with worship. Memories of scripture, people, and places inform the ways in which worshippers hear and see themselves in the story being improvised each week in public worship. When I handed the sketchbook over in the post office, there was a sense in which the sketchbook encountered an audience for the first time, and in doing so issued an invitation for others to participate. I entered the conversation that followed with what Samuel Wells

---

17. Dissanayake, "A Bona Fide Ethological View of Art," 52.
18. See Dissanayake, *What Is Art For?*

describes as an *overacceptance* of vulnerability and possibility,[19] a stance that sustains me in the practices of faith and art.

Being With the Unfinished Practice

In the practice of making art, I am often called to the practice of overaccepting unexpected possibilities, and this requires a willingness to improvise. When I made art in worship, I practiced the overacceptance of unexpected possibilities with faith, improvising what it is like *being for* and *being with* God. Along with shape and color, there were moments when text became important, particularly as I ruminated on the work over the following days. As pencil and oil pastel interacted, I accidentally began a process of imprinting layers of text and imagery onto the different pages of the journal (see Fig. 2), and this resonated strongly with my experience of being with the practice of faith and making art. The question "Who cares anyway?" is embedded through the work. Having surfaced on the fifth page of the sketchbook, this text imprinted itself upon the image from the page before, and on the page that was still to come. The question spread insidiously through the sketchbook, resonating with the continual doubt I experience being an artist who practices faith in worship.

The question can be read with the weight of cynicism, or as a search for others who care with me about deepening relationships with art. "Put down the weight of your aloneness and ease into the conversation."[20] David Whyte's words accompanied me from the first pages of this sketchbook, and eventually challenged the cynicism I was tempted to hear in asking this question. In putting down the weight of my aloneness as an artist, I am open to the discovery of wisdom shared by Whyte in the poem "Working Together": "We shape ourselves to fit this world and by the world are shaped again."[21] As they are imprinted upon one another, images and text are working together, shaping and reshaping the other over time. To continue to work with these materials week after week, I needed to either accept or block the images and ideas that emerged in the art. As I practiced the discipline of being with and overaccepting the sketches, I discovered an emerging narrative of abundance and possibility in being an artist who is shaped and reshaped through the improvisation of the practice of art and faith.

19. See Wells, *Improvisation*, 109.
20. Whyte, "Everything Is Waiting for You," 6.
21. Whyte, "Working Together," 356.

Figure 2: Libby Byrne, "Who is an artist, and who cares anyway?" in *Draw Near in Faith, and ...*, 2020, 2–7. Graphite, gouache, and oil pastel on paper, 48 x 21 cm. Brooklyn Art Library, New York, USA.

The first page of this book began with a simple response to words I heard in worship—"Draw Near with Faith, and . . ." This phrase called my attention, and as I stopped listening for words I began looking for the shape and texture of the invitation, tracing around a holding cross with graphite pencil. The embodied practice of tracing and then re-placing the cross on different pages allowed me to improvise with different possibilities for the relational patterns I experienced in working together with materials and people in faith. Half-way through the sketchbook, I found myself living in isolation, due to the COVID-19 global pandemic. Sunday morning worship was improvised via ZOOM, and I realized I was simply watching someone else perform. I stopped tracing complex graphite patterns and began employing water-based graphite, making marks that became pools of dissolving color. I had surrendered into the call to improvise. Possibility in the form of blue and green splotches awaited me on the pages that lay ahead, and, over time, became scaffolding for marks inscribing and re-membering what it was like being with and in worship. As I practiced the overacceptance of splotches of color, the work took on the form of a map, grounding and guiding me in the process of being with, for, and in worship throughout our isolation.

At the midway point of the work, the language I employed shifted and I found myself writing "Draw near *in* faith" rather than "Draw near *with* faith." The shift in language signified a shift in my thinking about being in worship *in* faith, rather than *with* faith. To draw near *with* faith requires me to draw on my capacity for *doing* worship; I need to summon the wherewithal to bring faith with me into worship. To draw near *in* faith, however, speaks of what it might be like simply *being with and in* the gift of faith that surrounds me. There are days when I sit in worship and cannot summon the faith required to draw any nearer. When I improvise what it might be like being *in* faith and with other people in worship, I am reminded that everything is waiting for me and that nothing is fixed. Just as the shape of one drawing fits with and re-shapes another, faith is formed and re-formed through memories that are imprinted from the experience of being in worship alongside others. "The visible and the invisible, (are) working together in common cause."[22] When I am present with the material embrace of making art in worship, I am able to be with other people in the experience of faith.

Wells argues that *being with* is the mode of engagement that God has modelled through the incarnation. Practicing the art of *being with* rather than of *working for* God in worship is, therefore, a fruitful frame of reference for considering all that happens as an improvisation. As we practice the art of *doing* less and *being* more, we actively rest into the reality of Jesus's definitive doing, and this becomes an invitation to participate in God's mysterious being through our own attentive presence and creative response. There is an active quality to the mode of *being with* that releases us from the need to be still, or even to be original in worship. As I improvised and overaccepted the art of being with God by drawing near in faith, the invisible power of faith shaped and re-membered my invisible presence in a material and visible way.

Being With and *For* the Calling of Art

In choosing to live and work as an artist, I have responded to a sense of calling in the way of Isaiah 6: "Then I heard the voice of the Lord saying, 'Whom shall I send? And who will go for us?' And I said, 'Here am I. Send me!'" (Isa 6:6–8). Being with and for this calling is the result of invocation and blessing. However, this calling is to tell the story with both power and powerlessness, clarity and mystery: "Go and tell this people. Be ever hearing, but never understanding; be ever seeing, but never perceiving" (Isa 6:9). While the artist cares how God's story is shared, they are not responsible for perceiving and for understanding meaning. All that is asked of the artist is to be with the story and be for the making, as the invisible becomes visible in and through the work of art. When we are free to improvise the practice of faith and art, particularly in worship, the way in which we care and are cared for becomes increasingly democratized. Those who care to take up the call to live and work together in this way participate in the flourishing of a collective imagination, which is foundational for living well in an age of crisis.

The moment when a work of art emerges is often shaped by vulnerability and surprising recognition—as the artist sees the art as if looking in a mirror, receiving a new awareness of the story being carried. In this

---

22. Whyte, "Working Together," 356.

fresh moment of really seeing, the artist receives with care the story being told, and considers if it is revealing something that needs to be seen by and shared with others. The decision to choose to share an intimate experience of seeing can be a challenging struggle, and so artmaking can be lonely work. "Jacob was left alone; and a man wrestled with him until daybreak. When the man saw that he did not prevail against Jacob, he struck him on the hip socket; and Jacob's hip was put out of joint as he wrestled with him. Then he said, 'Let me go, for the day is breaking.' But Jacob said, 'I will not let you go, unless you bless me'" (Gen 32:24–26).

As an expression of care for the story being shaped, I have a habit of asking an image emerging on the canvas: "What do you want me to do for you?" Trusting in this process requires the courage to be disciplined and attentive to my own vulnerability. I can find myself wrestling with my desire to reveal a real and uncomplicated statement of truth while holding space for the possibility that it is me who needs to be shaped and reshaped by the work of art. Though wounded by the struggle, Jacob did not let go, and he was reshaped by desire through his commitment to improvisation and the overacceptance of being with the struggle, and of living for the blessing. When the human imagination is formed and sustained within a framework of care, the experience of being with the struggle and being for the blessing means that the choice to live as an artist also reshapes the way we care to live in the world.

So, Are You an Artist?

I call myself a painter but I think that's more about the way I think than anything else. As the BAL extends a call for artists to locate their stories in a growing narrative about what it is like to be here, it is the art itself that is called into the world. It is the art that finds a place and resides in the collection over time. The invitation to the artist is simply to care enough to attend through the labor and delivery of the artefact. Those who care to see the art, either in person or through the Digital Library, are also invited to caretake the story as it is revealed in and through their aesthetic experience. To care with and for the stories that are revealed in the work of seeing art is to live in the way an artist lives.

If making art is a form of paying attention, then choosing to live as an artist means taking the time to care about the work of being through layers of embodied experience. This is not an endless flow of making; rather, it is a commitment to time spent caring about the relational, participatory, and risky process of gathering in and of opening up toward the everyday "wound of wonder."[23] Listening for stories as they take shape on the canvas requires the solitude of the studio and the quiet companionship of others who care about the work of art. Marks made in this sketchbook awakened me to the ways in which I was actively shaping the image while being shaped within the work of art that calls me to be still, to watch, and to wait for all that is still becoming.

There is a sense in which our response to the question of whether one finds the wherewithal to think and live as an artist is really a choice about how we choose to be with and to participate in the human experience of complexity and difference. Working with a posture that is open in this way leads to seeing and hearing stories of scarcity and suffering that are entwined with one another through the quality of desire, which in turn brings hope for healing and for the possibility of abundance. This is the way into mystery, and the essence of wonder. We each bring different and vital qualities to the world because "we are not part of some grander plan: we are the plan."[24]

Artists are people who care about and attend to the presence of art in and from the midst of our collective chaos. Being an artist, therefore, requires a willingness to care for and to be with the unfinished calling of the work of art in the world. As artists are drawn to express and experience care in this material way, they improvise new ways of being with other people while overaccepting the relational risks that are bound up with our personal vulnerabilities and our shared liberation. Choosing to live and work in this way will grow and expand our personal and collective imagination in such a way that when faced with a time of crisis we will be ready and able to see and to attest to the need for art, asking anyone who seems to care, "Are you an artist?"—because if you are, we care, just like you.

Bibliography

Brooklyn Art Library. "Our Mission." https://brooklynartlibrary.org/mission.
Byrne, Libby. "Draw Near in Faith, and . . ." https://www.sketchbookproject.com/library/S304519.
Contemporary Art and Feminism. "CARE—Feminism, Art, and Ethics in Neo-Liberal Times." https://contemporaryartandfeminism.com/care.
Day, Lewis F. "Artist and Artisan." *Magazine of Art* 9 (1886) 294–95.
Dissanayake, Ellen. "A Bona Fide Ethological View of Art: The Artification Hypothesis." In *Art as Behaviour: An Ethological Approach to Visual and Verbal Art, Music, and Architecture*, edited by Christa Sütterlin et al., 43–62. Oldenburg: BIS, 2014.

---

23. Rubenstein, *Strange Wonder*, 7.
24. Wells, *A Nazareth Manifesto*, 140.

———. *What Is Art For?* Seattle: University of Washington Press, 1988.
Dufrenne, Mikel. *The Phenomenology of Aesthetic Experience*. Translated by Albert A. Anderson et al. Evanston: Northwestern University Press, 1973.
Jagodzinski, Jan. "From the Artist to the Cosmic Artisan: The Educational Task for Art in Anthropogenic Times." In *Art, Artists, and Pedagogy: Philosophy and the Arts in Education*, edited by Christopher Naughton et al., 83–95. London: Routledge, 2018.
Latham, Robyne. "The Aborigine Is Present." http://robynelatham.net/home.
———. "The Empty Coolamons: In Memorium to the Stolen Generations." http://robynelatham.net/ritual-gallery.
Lawson, Alison. "Using Narrative and Story Telling in Research." In *Alternative Market Research Methods: Market Sensing*, edited by David Longbottom and Alison Lawson, 182–204. New York: Routledge, 2017.
Luger, Jason D. "But I'm Just an Artist? Intersections, Identity, Meaning, and Context." *Antipode* 49.5 (2017) 1329–48.
Millner, Jacqueline. "Caring through Art: Reimagining Value as Political Practice." *Art & the Public Sphere* 8.2 (2019) 163–74.
Rubenstein, Mary-Jane. *Strange Wonder: The Closure of Metaphysics and the Opening of Awe*. New York: Columbia University Press, 2008.
Travis, Sarah. "Flashpoints of Artist Identity Formation." *Art Education* 73.5 (2020) 16–25.
Wells, Samuel. *Improvisation: The Drama of Christian Ethics*. Grand Rapids: Brazos, 2004.
———. *A Nazareth Manifesto: Being with God*. Chichester: Wiley-Blackwell, 2015.
Whyte, David. "Everything Is Waiting for You." In *Everything Is Waiting for You*, 6. Langley: Many Rivers, 2003.
———. "Working Together." In *River Flow: New & Selected Poems*, 356. Langley: Many Rivers, 2007.

30

Compelling Stories

Glenn Loughrey

My paintings use beautiful colors that tell compelling and sometimes disturbing stories. I suspect it is easier to approach difficult subjects if you are, at least, put at ease by the beauty of the piece. In much of my work, small dots accentuate the scale of the landscape in front of you. We often see the scale of the Australian landscape and see it as all being the same. It is certainly not. It is a diverse pattern of connected ecosystems changing many times in one's field of view. Understanding this is key to traditional burning and land management for Aboriginal people. The dots indicate the diversity, depth, and expanse of the kinship connections we embrace on country.[1]

Western perspectives are primarily linear and encompass linear distance and spatial distancing. Perspective in mine and more traditional indigenous art is all about connections and relationships. It can alternate from a form of mapping (looking down on the landscape), to placing one in the more accepted view of looking on the same level as or from a particular place—generally in front of and at a distance from such. This perspective is about our sense of place and our relationship to the place of others; sometimes that is about the various ecosystems/people identified by dots and symbols present in the work. Instead of being an outside observer, we are drawn into and become an integral element of the landscape—we see it as we are one with it.

---

1. Country refers to the particular place that gives each Indigenous nation its identity.

Glenn Loughrey, *Kurrajong Dreaming*, 2020. Acrylic on canvas, 122 x 182 cm. Collection of The Community of the Holy Name, Melbourne, Australia.

Lines in my work act in a similar manner as do the dots. They usually begin as almost straight and then gradually take on a form of their own. By so doing, they create unique patterns depicting various images and ideas independently. These patterns develop organically as part of the conversation with canvas, paint, and mark. There are no straight lines in our culture because one simply cannot walk in a straight line. In walking our songlines,[2] we move around creating the patterns explaining our own lives and the life of our people.

Much of my art relies on light, not for shadow or highlighting, but rather for illuminating the landscape from behind, accentuating the scale and individual elements of the landscape. White or black backgrounds do this equally as well as each other. White reminds us the light comes from behind the object we are looking at to reveal it to us. The light comes from within the landscape, not as a reflection of the external light, but rather, in a sense, as its source. In our thought, the country or landscape holds all the wisdom, knowledge, and experience we need for our lives. It is the light source for our journey. The darker the background, the deeper

---

2. Songlines refer to the connected places that make up the Indigenous knowledge systems. They can be particular to a Nation, or universal and shared by all Nations.

the light. In other words, what is there is so bright we only see what the landscape is if held by darkness.

The background is often heavily textured to allow another story to appear. I use old unclean rollers covered in the remainder of previous stories to get the texture required, thereby giving a rough natural surface, creating texture and character. The truth is that the canvas, the various layers of paints, and the random marks have their own particular story to tell as part of the final piece. I rarely correct drips, blobs, and other errors. It is what it is in this conversation with the various elements making up the finished or almost-finished piece. I allow parts of the underpainting to peer through and regularly leave bits unpainted as doorways to the Dreaming beyond the Dreaming.[3]

---

3. The Dreaming refers to the everywhere, when of existence. In other words, it is the past, present, and future all here now, in this place and people.

31

Figure Held in Water

Michael Symmons Roberts

Like those people in Bill Viola's films,
slowed to within an inch of their lives,
absolutely caught in it,

or maybe by it, but that's immaterial,
either way it's constant, attendant
at your making and at your undoing,

at the first bath that sent you all howl,
when a haul of arms lowered you,
a tepid dip not what you needed then,

arched plucked bird you, skinned fish,
it held you then and still,
or it's falling and you honour the fall,

halt your sprint for shelter,
stand in a rinsed-out city square
head back, fighting to keep your eyes open,

waiters and cooks from the cafes
step out to watch the deluge too,
beckoning you from under awnings,

taxis swerve to miss you,
statue you, head back to let it gather you,
alone you in the heart of your city,

just you and an old bronze king on a horse,
who is melting on the cobbles
in spite of his pomp, and if you

had clothes on now their colours
would be running, or not a fall but
a weight of it, the sea, a sea, or back up

the throat of an estuary, a choked spring
waits for you to break the dam of it,
to prise away what stems it,

lie down on its stony bed to prove it,
let it swarm you, or just your hands
turn in it, over and over until stunned by cold,

or times you thought you did the holding,
a pin-head-studded tumbler of it
left by your bed but untouched,

stubbed when you reached in the night,
shattered and woke the whole Hotel Splendide
where you take a box-room each winter

pay the rent by washing-up while you
draw up a ledger of your losses,
your near misses, earn scraps from the kitchen

in exchange for personalised verses of love,
or a drop from the blank blue on
the rick of your neck in a summer drought,

the electric shock of it, threatening monsoon
or a midday heart attack,
but comes to nothing but the one,

or the bay in a storm on New Year's Eve,
gales too stiff to stand against,
and a couple shouting from a lit boat

too far out, or the thirst for it,
the walking miles to find it, then not sure
if you can trust it when you do, the overwhelm,

floating cars, house roofs as refuge,
each room an aquarium, horrible
unwitting beauty of the mirrored sun on it

even as it bears away, ungovernable,
frontierless, ground-seeker, spirit-leveller,
giver of everything up to an ocean,

to any sea it meets, diviner of the flaws
in hulls, hairlines, bringer of angler-fish,
sea-snails to rusted containers

stacked with undelivered gifts,
or the times you turned it down for something
stronger, the fact that it's the most of

what you're made of, that and carbon,
a pencil and a drink is you, head down in
a sink so many miles from

home, slow-hearted, how you long
to hold it there, and hold
and hold until your face dissolves,

or the salt bite of it, the boil of it,
how you, in it, lose all the weight you
couldn't shift, or falling overboard, the gasp,

a startle-reflex, trying not to thrash,
willing to believe that effortful stilled limbs
will save you if you don't give in,

or the lift of it, what you take from it unthinking,
the rush of calm when all is fury,
respite with no prospect of a cure,

or outside the infirmary, patients on drips
wheeled out to take the air,
or in the visiting hours

the sips you take from a baby's beaker
held by your daughter or your son
as you did for them,

now you are too frail to lift it,
and all you can say is how fine it is,
how cold and rare and in that moment

how it brings you back to your attention,
or the sluice-down hose on the slab
where you were lain

in search of causes, reasons,
though by then you were far gone, far out
to sea yourself, heartless now

but more loved than ever and still loving,
or the wade-in, not through,
the fear of what might be in it,

a good fearing, a chest-high walk in it,
or what might rise up in the current,
brush against your back,

the lack of clarity, its limpid gift to us
rendered lethal by this murk,
this ever-teeming other state,

never been to the fishhouses you,
to take a swig of it, to know
what it was she saw and tasted fierce there,

or you, stepping out of your grave-pit
coughing up roots, longing for nothing more
than to stride out through a downpour,

or trying to join the dots you,
reading words off floating crates and tins
to form a line you could live by.

32

"Goin' to the City"

African American Folk Ritual for Communal Healing

Amina McIntyre

Introduction

OFTEN WHEN ASKED ABOUT religion, the focus is on ritual and worship within a physical edifice, the building, that is "the church." The elements are around the preacher, the full liturgical experience, the assistants (both lay and clergy), and concern how a specific event on a "Sabbath" makes way for spiritual healing, emotional support, and the inspiration to fight another day. Within African American religious traditions, there are also ongoing conversations around religion, specifically outside of the church. From a christocentric perspective, there are often a mélange of liturgical, ritual, and lived practices that are frequently connected to healing in "secular space," often derived from African traditional religious traditions. What could be learned by taking a look into such lived, folk religions? What examples in the African American cultural experience show the merger as part of the culture? Are there any implications for current movements, or for visioning their usage for the future? In what follows, I argue that Black folk religious rituals can work to heal and transform communities through memory, culture, and imagination, as is evidenced in the City of Bones scene in August Wilson's *Gem of the Ocean*.[1]

As a United States-born, Southern Black woman ordained in the Christian Methodist Episcopal Church (Black Methodist), who also understands the institutional liturgy, I see the intersections of African American folk religion and their influence within the arts, especially theatre, as a rich resource. Studying a variety of traditions interwoven in southern culture

---

1. See Wilson, *Gem of the Ocean*, 64–73.

has amplified my craft as an artist, minister, and scholar. This experience also attunes my ear to the tension between institutional and folk religious practices. This recognition, additionally, heightens my sensitivity to instances where folk religion is operating in lived, everyday life and how it is used, especially in literature like Wilson's *Gem of the Ocean*. Admittedly, this particular play is my favorite of Wilson's work because of its account of the journey to the City of Bones. I have seen, read, and even directed the play, for the Marietta Theatre in the Square in Marietta, Georgia. This places me close to the text.

In this essay, I employ literary analysis to survey folk religion to interpret and assess the category of African American folk religion. I ground my work in defining terms and then show how they can be used to reveal the intent and impact of the work. Finally, I use Victor Turner's understanding of rites of passage to analyze and discuss how the ritual of the City of Bones could be used for a wider community. At its center, through the journey to the City of Bones, *Gem of the Ocean* shows ritual[23] in everyday life, the ways we often seek *rites of passage* after a traumatic event, and how such can offer a sense of care from our own cultural orientation, oral history, and empowerment for Black people to live whole lives. This story is embodied in Aunt Ester, the play's 285-year-old fiery matriarch and former slave whose name is sometimes considered to be a play on the word "ancestor." She is a soul cleanser,[4] a keeper of the tradition, a conjure woman and spiritual guide, and a preacher in her own right, ordained in the tradition of folk religion.

Gathering the Elements

Folk religion is the ritual, practice, belief, and value considered sacred within home and community. Sometimes called "lived religion,"[5] it often uplifts and legitimizes natural remedies, traditional habits, and oral history passed down by both griots and grandparents. In literature and the arts, it readily functions in storytelling and embodiment of myths, stories, and rites of passages that consecrate celebrations and movements.

---

2. Harry Elam explains the ritual nature of traveling to the City of Bones. Much like the function of hush harbors, the City of Bones engages the psychological and spiritual needs of Citizen Barlow. See Elam, "*Gem of the Ocean* and the Redemptive Power of History," 75–76.

3. Wardi, *Water and African American Memory*, 24.

4. Citizen Barlow specifically mentions coming to Aunt Ester because she washes souls: "They say you wash people's souls." Wilson, *Gem of the Ocean*, 20.

5. See McGuire, *Lived Religion*.

This essay grounds the study of folk religion in memory, culture, and imagination. According to Astrid Erll: "Memory is the umbrella term for all those processes of biological, medical, or social nature which relate past and present (and future) in social cultural contexts."[6] Erll discusses the varieties and categories of memory and how they are impacted by the environment. Houston Baker too is interested in critical memory: "I believe critical memory compels the Black intellectual such as [Richard] Wright to keep before his eyes (and the eyes of the United States) a history that is embarrassing, macabre, and always bizarre with respect to race."[7] Memory is always colored and shaped by the experiences of the individual, the community, and the wider society. Memory can also frame rituals and use the collective to establish cultural memories. Lisa Thompson recalls the importance of memory for preachers and congregational environments: "Preachers rely heavily on the community's language and memory, whether by recalling the collective experiences and language of the community or by creating common points of experiences around which the community can engage."[8] Communal cultural memory and imagination can also lead to reimagining rituals. For the purposes of this essay, "memory" is the collective knowledge obtained by rituals and cultural experiences that have the potential to establish and lead to a group's healing.

Memory can also preserve culture, bringing dignity to its hybrid character. Dale Andrews defines African American folk religion as a hybrid of West African traditional religious influences, Christianity, and the birth of African American culture from Middle Passage and beyond.[9] African American folk religion also values "hush harbors," Black denominations, and ritual and conjure in culture. "Hush Harbors" are brush arbor religious experiences that involve gathering in secret, often at the risk of punishment. They are where traditions are observed, and where new rituals and observations are created. African American folk religion also integrates the mélange of these elements into every day lived experiences.

I define "imagination" as the way of seeing possibilities that are not there—the bringing in of a future, the writing oneself into existence. Imagination also recalls the possibilities of customization, the belief in myth and resistance. I argue that imagination allows for ritual customization, the idea that communal familiarity/memory is altered to accommodate the needs of persons, seasons, and contemporary events that may impact a community.

6. Erll, *Memory in Culture*, 7.
7. Baker, *Critical Memory*, 10.
8. Thompson, *Ingenuity*, 52.
9. See Andrews, *Practical Theology for Black Churches*.

One space where imagination and African American folk religion exist together is in literature, specifically poetry, novels, and theatre. Langston Hughes's poem "The Negro Speaks of Rivers," Toni Morrison's novel *Beloved*, and Ntozake Shange's choreopoem *For Colored Girls Who Have Considered Suicide/When the Rainbow Is Enuf* are examples of this.[10]

Surveying the Quilt: A Conversation on Folk Religion

The juxtaposition of African American folk religion with institutional religion is an argument about legitimacy, respectability, and receptibility. Issues of race, class, and gender in a changing society provide further locations for this argument. African diasporic practices are considered "primitive," and (women) practitioners and preservers of these practices are typically not considered equal to those associated with Christianity, Islam, and Judaism. Practicing folk religion is also a sign of poverty; when freedom and class become inhibiting factors, folk traditions are put away. Scholars such as Zora Neale Hurston and Dale Andrews seek to observe, celebrate, and elevate the conversation around folk religion. Hurston captures the church, hoodoo, voodun, and conjure spells, and her books *Mules and Men* (1935), *Tell My Horse: Voodoo Life in Haiti and Jamaica* (1938), and *The Sanctified Church* (1981) offer anthropological accounts—specifically, interviews about worship, lived encounters, and beliefs.[11] Her work is significant because she records via video and field notes (following the new Franz Boas ethnographic methodology), and interviews a variety of former slaves and participants of religious practices. She pushes against W. E. B. Du Bois's highlighting of "highly arranged spirituals,"[12] which Hurston argues are not representative of the practices of the people. Emphasizing the role of folk practices within religion becomes an ongoing discussion among scholars and parishioners.

Dale Andrews develops the conversation around African American practical theology by emphasizing the connection between Black liberation theology and folk religion. His remedy is to focus on ecclesiology to see where religion should consider both liturgy and live experiences. He argues that practical theology can be the place to engage the intersection of areas of religious interest and the elements that divide them, including gender and

---

10. Hughes, "The Negro Speaks of Rivers"; Morrison, *Beloved*; Shange, *For Colored Girls Who Have Considered Suicide*.

11. See Hurston, *Mules and Men*; Hurston, *Tell My Horse*; Hurston, *The Sanctified Church*.

12. Hurston, *Dust Tracks on a Road*, 215. See Du Bois, *The Souls of Black Folk*.

class. Such concerns, I argue, have been best addressed in literature, such as the journey to The City of Bones in Wilson's *Gem of the Ocean*.

The City of Bones ritual in *Gem of the Ocean* provides a case study for the survey of African American practical theology and African American folk religion. Harry Elam writes: "Wilson delves into and rewrites the African American past, addressing and righting the wrongs of historical amnesia and social oppression, ritualistically reconnecting African Americans to the blood memories and cultural rights of the African past."[13] Memory, culture, and imagination are here engaged within Wilson's story, where the nuances of gender and class are prevalent in intracommunal healing.

Getting the Boat: A Case Study of *Gem of the Ocean*

August Wilson (1945–2005) was an American Pulitzer Prize-winning playwright. He is considered one of the most produced African American playwrights.[14] Born in Pittsburg, Wilson attended several high schools before dropping out to work "menial jobs that exposed him to a wide variety of people,"[15] and he left town and developed most of his work and career in Minnesota. He went on to develop theatre companies that became home to his own and other work by African American writers before receiving Broadway debuts. His plays include *Fences* (1984), *Ma Rainey's Black Bottom* (1984), and *The Piano Lesson* (1987). *Gem of the Ocean* is the first installment of his ten-play The Pittsburgh Cycle, which dramatizes, by decade, the African American experience in the northeastern United States in the twentieth century.

Gem of the Ocean was first performed at the Goodman Theatre in Chicago in 2004. It went on to open at the Walter Kerr Theatre (now the Gen Taper) in Los Angeles, and was nominated for a Tony Award for Best Play. The play is actually the ninth in the series, after *King Hedley II*, the play that announced Aunt Ester's death, and before *Radio Golf*, the final play in the series. While *Gem of the Ocean* is the first in The Pittsburg Cycle, it was written much later than were the other plays. It is also the first one where Aunt Ester, the muse for many of Wilson's plays, shows up in person and has a role.

The play takes place in 1904, in Aunt Ester's home at 1839 Wylie Avenue, Pittsburgh. Citizen Barlow, a young man from Alabama, comes seeking Aunt Ester's services as a "soul cleanser" after stealing a bucket of nails from

---

13. Elam, "*Gem of the Ocean* and the Redemptive Power of History," 76.
14. See engagement with his work in Nadel, *August Wilson*.
15. Bogumil, *Understanding August Wilson*, 2.

his factory, an action that leads to the death of another Black male worker. Barlow steals the nails because he feels the factory is working under sharecropping-like conditions. Another factory worker, Garret Brown, hops into a river and refuses to come out even though he was innocent. This weighs heavily on Citizen. Amid growing strikes, riots, and a subsequent burning of the factory, Aunt Ester's house becomes a hush harbor environment, a safe place to freely be and to hide from the concerns of the outside. To get his soul cleansed, Citizen must travel to the City of Bones.

Gem of the Ocean introduces characters such as Black Mary Wilks, Ester's housekeeper, and her brother Caesar, a constable. We also meet Solly Two Kings, Aunt Ester's suitor and a former Underground Railroad conductor, and Eli, Aunt Ester's caretaker, as well as Rutherford Selig, a finder who also sells dog excrement, otherwise known as "pure," for manure. All but Caesar and Selig are involved in the trip to the City of Bones. Aunt Ester, Solly Two Kings, and Eli have been to the City of Bones before.

Aunt Ester is a mythical woman who spans the majority of Wilson's ten-play cycle. She is referred to in eight of the plays (all but *Radio Golf* and *Ma Rainey's Black Bottom*), but is seen only in *Gem of the Ocean*. Her legacy is that she is as old as the number of years since slavery began in the colonies (1619) that later formed the United States, and she operates in ways akin to Yoruba orisha Yemanjá, responsible for water, birth, and cleansing children of sorrow, and Marie LaVeau, the renowned practitioner of Voodoo and midwifery in New Orleans who was recruited, taught the style, rituals, and work, and then recruits another to pass down the persona. Aunt Ester is in many ways the practitioner Michel de Certeau describes: "mak[ing] use of spaces that cannot be seen; their knowledge of them is as blind as that of lovers in each other's arms."[16] Aunt Ester only dies when there is someone else to take her place.

In *Gem of the Ocean*, the audience meets Aunt Ester as an older woman who is apprenticing a young woman, Black Mary, to take up her role. The audience also meets Citizen Barlow. Aunt Ester gets to know Citizen, and then decides to take him to the City of Bones, a ritual space that is imagined earlier but only becomes real in act 2, scene 3. The City of Bones is "a half mile by a half mile" city at the bottom of the Atlantic Ocean, and is considered the place where those tossed overboard during the middle passage live.[17] It is also the place to visit when one is confronting one's own life, fears, and concerns.

---

16. Certeau, *The Practice of Everyday Life*, 93.

17. Wilson, *Gem of the Ocean*, 54. See also Elam, "*Gem of the Ocean* and the Redemptive Power of History," 75–88.

Aunt Ester draws on a blend of hoodoo and Christianity to interfuse the space. Her work as a ritualist is in fact a hybrid of Christianity and West African traditional water rituals.[18] As a character, she is the living embodiment of Jason Young's Kongo women[19] who integrated Christianity and traditional religions to become a spiritual leader, a "soul cleanser." She is also the kind of woman written about by Yvonne Chireau and Marla Frederick, who both embrace the traditional religions as part of their lives.[20] The ritual begins with Aunt Ester asking Citizen if he wants to go to the City of Bones. She asks him to find two pennies—"They got to be lying side by side. You can't find one on one street and another on another street. They got to be lying side by side"[21]—and she gives instructions to get clean and dress nice for the journey.

Before taking the journey, several items must be gathered over the course of the play. In addition to the two pennies, there is also a paper boat, which was made by Aunt Ester; a quilt, which must stay in the house and which signifies an unspoken communal memory of significance through the Underground Railroad; a map to the City of Bones, which also holds the story of the journey and how the city was made; and a piece of metal, Solly's metal chain from his time as an enslaved person, which is given at the last moment. There is, in fact, a final item, which is a spoken confession, a desire to travel to the City of Bones and then to complete the return journey. Only after this confession does Aunt Ester determine that all items are in place for the journey.

Before announcing they are going on a journey, Aunt Ester passes Citizen the boat, telling him not to drop it no matter how hard it gets. She then begins a song of call and response, which the entire group sings, and opens her storytelling of the journey, which is infused with pre-slavery and mid-slavery narratives. As Aunt Ester guides, it is critical that Citizen buys into the journey to the City of Bones—by feeling the boat move, the turbulence, the reenactment of being captured by the enslavers, of being beaten and thrown into the hull of the ship.[22] Citizen begins to direct his own path, fighting to make it to the City of Bones, seeing the city itself, and facing the gate keeper, Garret Brown. Brown will not accept the pennies, but only Citizen's confession. The City of Bones ritual ends after this

---

18. See Wardi, *Water and African American Memory*.
19. See Young, *Rituals of Resistance*.
20. See Chireau, *Black Magic*; Frederick, *Between Sundays*.
21. Wilson, *Gem of the Ocean*, 48.
22. See Wardi, *Water and African American Memory*; Elam, "*Gem of the Ocean* and the Redemptive Power of History," 75–88.

confession, and with being granted entry into the City. The ritual ends the way it begins, with a song.

A Chain Link: Memory as Liturgical Narrative

Gem of the Ocean recalls the memory that considers physical, spiritual, and emotional elements that are inescapably part of all religion, including folk religion. Memory is truly hypersensory.[23] In act 1, scene 3, Aunt Ester discusses how knowledge was passed down to her; specifically, how she forgoes her own name in order to put on this persona. She carries within herself the memories from the Middle Passage, her tie to the birth of African American culture.[24] What Baker refers to as "critical memory" was also necessary to remind Citizen of who he was and is, lest he be defined by his labor as a factory worker. Such memories are recalled for the journey. Before the ritual, Aunt Ester and Citizen have the following exchange while studying the history of the City of Bones on the quilt:

AUNT ESTER   You see that, Mr. Citizen. That's a boat. You gonna take a ride on that boat.

(She hands it to him.)

   Do you believe you can take a ride on that old boat, Mr. Citizen?

CITIZEN   This is a piece of paper.

AUNT ESTER   That not what you call your ordinary boat. Look at that boat, Mr. Citizen. That's a magic boat. There's a lot of power in that boat. Power is something. It's hard to control but it's hard to stand in the way of it. God sweep the stars aside, Mr. Citizen. He don't let nothing stand in his way. God don't know nothing but the truth. That boat can take you to that city, Mr. Citizen. Do you believe it can take you to that city?

CITIZEN   I don't know, Miss Tyler.

AUNT ESTER   If you believe it can take you. God got room for everybody. I don't know if you ever seen

---

23. See Bada and Pagnoulle, "August Wilson's *Gem of the Ocean*."
24. See Pittman, "Voicing the 'Law of the Sea,'" 19–36.

> him but God wear all different kinds of clothes. He got all kinds of faces and he got a sword. It's a big sword. The Bible say it's a mean and terrible swift sword. And when he get to waving that sword around he can do anything. I can take you to that city, but you got to want to go. Do you want to go, Mr. Citizen? Do you want to get your soul washed?[25]

Reminiscent of Albert Raboteau's method,[26] this dialogue infuses the Middle Passage as a text with biblical content. It is later revealed to the audience (although it is earlier revealed to the reader in the stage directions) that the boat itself is folded out of Aunt Ester's Bill of Sale, her purchase price into slavery, and is named the *Gem of the Ocean*. Getting on the boat for the Bill of Sale is a confession of belief in a higher power, similar to an invitation to follow Christ. That is also the significance of a later instruction to not let go of the boat, as in the memory of the enslaved getting caught without having papers on them, as a way of protection. While in 1904 there was no longer any requirement to carry papers of identification (the Thirteenth Amendment to the United States Constitution had been passed), the practice was still recent—only thirty-nine years had passed—in communal history.

Another element of communal memory is the call and response of the songs. The ritual of going to the City of Bones employs a number of songs, including "Oh what a Day," "I got a Home in the Graveyard," an African lullaby,[27] and "Twelve Gates to the City." Each song recounts a spiritual narrative. "Oh What a Day" is reprised as a celebration for safe return; it is also the only original song. Each of the others are spirituals that would have been created by the slaves and carried into current knowledge via oral tradition, finding function *with* and *as* ritual. These rely on what Thompson refers to as "communal choreography."[28] Black Mary, unlike Eli and Solly Two Kings, knows these songs and so is able to participate in their movement through time. Although she has not in fact been to the City of Bones in person, the reality of prior collective memory means that she is able to lead, as a solo, the song "Twelve Gates to the City." "This holy truth is only clarified as it is named and recognized as such by the entire community, while everybody contributes to arranging a choreography

---

25. Wilson, *Gem of the Ocean*, 56.
26. See Raboteau, *Slave Religion*.
27. In the stage directions, this song, performed by Citizen, is not designated. It only reads "an African lullaby." Wilson, *Gem of the Ocean*, 70.
28. Thompson, *Ingenuity*, 35.

that responds to inspiration."²⁹ The living room in Aunt Ester's house is then transformed because of this memory, and all who live in and visit the home are invested in the communal memory it carries.

Cleaning the Soul: Culture in the Ritual

One specific area that recurs in memory, and which is highlighted especially within the City of Bones ritual, is the presence of culture. There is in this scene also what we might refer to as "liturgical representation." Prior to this ritual, Aunt Ester is considered a "soul cleanser," but it is also evident that she has some kind of ordination into a religious position. At the close of act 2, scene 2, Aunt Ester is careful to go away and prepare herself in her room. She makes certain Citizen is prepared for the journey, and she is responsible for him and his soul returning to the room. She begins her homily, asking: "You ever seen a boat, Mr. Citizen?"³⁰ Because Citizen is from the middle of Alabama, it was likely that he had not in fact encountered a boat before. So she guides him until he feels the boat:

> AUNT ESTER   A boat is made out of a lot of things. Wood and rope. The sails look like bedsheets blowing in the wind. They make a snap when the winds catch them. Wood and rope and iron. The workmen with their hammers ringing. A boat is something. It takes a lot of men to make a boat. And it takes a lot of men to sail a boat. Them was some brave men. They left their family and didn't know if they was ever gonna see them again. They got on that boat and went out into the world. The world's a dangerous place, Mr. Citizen. It's got all kinds of harms in it. It take God to master the world. The world is a rough place. But there's gold out there in the world. There's good luck out there in the world. Them brave men went looking for it. Remember I told you you could take a ride on that boat? The wind catch up in them sails and you be off across the ocean. The wind will take you every which way. You need a strong arm to steer that boat. Don't you feel it, Mr. Citizen?

---

29. Thompson, *Ingenuity*, 36.
30. Wilson, *Gem of the Ocean*, 66.

> Don't you feel that boat rocking? Just a rocking and a rocking. The wind blowing. . . . Just a rocking and a rocking. The wind blowing and the birds following behind that boat. They follow whenever it go. What is they following for, Mr. Citizen? The wind snapping them sails and the birds following. The birds following and singing and the fish swimming and the wind blowing—

(Citizen gets up and makes a sudden move to balance himself.)

CITIZEN   It's moving! The boat's moving! I feel it moving! The land . . . it's moving away.[31]

Citizen's excitement soon subsides as the cultural reality of what happened to Black bodies like his on a boat becomes realized. By Aunt Ester's walk through cultural knowledge, Citizen is suddenly chained to the boat, placed there by white men, played by Solly and Eli wearing European masks.

The stage directions at this point in the script also detail cultural and historical knowledge:

> *(Citizen struggles against the storm to reach the boat. Masked Solly and masked Eli seize him before he reaches it. They symbolically brand and symbolically whip Citizen, then throw him into the hull of the boat. The hatch slams shut. Citizen finds himself alone.)*[32]

The aloneness, acting within this trauma as an individual and not as a community, is what causes people not to survive. Culture is created by how the environment shifts and changes people, raising questions, even in the midst of violence, about what future possibilities there might be for fragmented communities able to hold past this moment.

City of Bones is a metaphor for a heaven of sorts. There is a level of mythology, such as stories of Igbo landing and of people flying. Based on real life experiences, it has been reworked and reconsidered for the purpose of living on. For the ritual to work, for the City of Bones to come alive, the group, and not just the preacher, must journey with the narrative. So Aunt Ester:

> Them people you seen got some powerful gods, Mr. Citizen. But they ain't on the boat with them. They don't know to call him on their own. God don't answer to no one man. God answer to the

---

31. Wilson, *Gem of the Ocean*, 66–67.
32. Wilson, *Gem of the Ocean*, 70.

all. All the people. They need all the people. Them people you see is without God. When we get to the City of Bones I'm gonna show you what happen when all the people call on God with the one voice. God got beautiful splendors.[33]

This is an example of Raboteau's insights about the "death of the gods."[34] Yet, Aunt Ester offers assurance that there is still a place for those who call out. She guides Citizen through a rite of passage that encompasses memory, culture, and imagination, but also the group. Even before this journey, Citizen talks about what it would be like to see the place:

CITIZEN	There it is! It's made of bones! All the buildings and everything. Head bones and leg bones and rib bones. The streets look like silver. The trees are made of bones. The trees and everything made of bone.[35]

Citizen's selfishness, an individual choice, triggers the larger chain of calamitous events. But his ability to imagine a solution is what makes the journey towards healing possible. Seeing the City of Bones reveals what can be possible when a community can unify. During the City of Bones ritual he feels more connection, more part of the community, and more aware of the consequences that one single action might have on the community. Aunt Ester has helped to impact a community, as the work Citizen does after this transformation will become communal work. Aunt Ester has taken Citizen through a transition, a rite of passage, that allows him to become a better person, more confident and equipped to work for his culture.

Twelve Gates to the City: A Discussion

Drawing on Arnold van Gennep's seminal *Les rites de passage*, first published in French in 1909,[36] Turner describes three stages of transition—separation, margin, and reaggregation. He writes: "During the intervening liminal period, the state of the ritual subject (the 'passenger') is ambiguous; he passes through a realm that has few or none of the attributes of the past or coming state."[37] As a site of resistance, we might interpret the journey to the City of Bones along such lines: The navigator commands

33. Wilson, *Gem of the Ocean*, 69.
34. See Raboteau, *Slave Religion*, 43–92.
35. Wilson, *Gem of the Ocean*, 71.
36. See Gennep, *The Rites of Passage*.
37. Turner, *The Forest of Symbols*, 94.

the journey and the passengers must be ready to embark upon the journey by themselves. The navigator, Aunt Ester, is the keeper of the rules of a history and place. The navigator can only walk Citizen to and guide him through his matriculation. This is evident in the way that Aunt Ester asks: "What do you see?" and "What are you meeting?" Citizen must undergo a transformation to clean his spirit, but it is Aunt Ester's memory and folk cultural knowledge that guides him to that end.

In traveling to the City of Bones, Citizen, who has learned to take responsibility for his actions, comes to be at peace with himself. His peace also impacts other members of the house. He is given the courage and confidence to go to the community and complete his work, now with a cleansed spirit. What is also beautiful about the City of Bones is a temporary brush arbor/hush harbor. The story is one thing all must buy into, audience included. The stage must be transformed and come alive in order for the story to work. Imagining the hurt of the Middle Passage, the place with African American culture, in the womb of the ship, allows Citizen—and indeed the audience—to walk through private traumas and move to other beginnings.

Using a Black woman's folk religious practices as a framework—in this case, a womanist reading of a Black spiritual figure at the turn of the twentieth century—we might ask how Black culture can be celebrated and used to assist in healing. Is it unavoidably retraumatizing to bring up concerns of generational memory and folk rituals? How can Black culture be important in meaning-making? African American culture is a hybrid of what was brought over from Africa, what has to be used in the present, and what might still be used in the future for Black people. Once created, a culture, including its self-understanding and memory, can be protected, can even become naturalized. This is where, again, Thompson's communal choreography comes into play. The communal suggests a shared culture, history, and knowledge. There is no community without culture. Turner's use of the category of liminal space can also be utilized here, particularly as such space concerns relationships between culture's orientation, disorientation, and reorientation. Between the orientation and disorientation there is liminal space. This space is generative for the formation of culture, and that in ways akin to how the Middle Passage and the institution of slavery are liminal in creating the lives of Africans in transit. The memory of this origin story can also provide a foundation for imagining future possibilities.

Memory in the City of Bones ritual is necessary for the narrative. "Every story is a travel story—a spatial practice,"[38] and when the City of Bones begins to occupy space, memories are opened. Even before this part

---

38. Certeau, *The Practice of Everyday Life*, 115.

of the play, Solly and Eli recount experiences with the City of Bones. Solly specifically talks of wanting to be buried there upon his death. While not a written liturgy, The City of Bones ritual is chronicled in the elements—the metal, the quilt, the boat, the masks, and the griot-style story. Present also in the memory of this scene are the spirituals and, most notably, the oral history of the journey to the City of Bones. The communal choreography requires characters assisting Black Mary to help guide Citizen through, as well as Solly and Eli enacting the enslavers and the gate people. Participation in the City of Bones ritual signifies the community being necessary for every person's healing.

Learning this knowledge is crucial to cleansing Citizen's own memory. He watched a young man die from an offense Citizen committed. His memories are dominated by the scene, which is reminiscent of a lynching scene, with a mob crowded to hold this man accountable. These memories threaten to cripple him in the same way as do his Southern memories. Ironically, it is communal urging and Southern memory that sent him to get his soul cleansed to begin with, and that by a woman who practices folk religion rather than who is an established pastor.

The City of Bones ritual requires a willingness and capacity to understand the past and to imagine the possibility of creating a future that is finally undetermined by the horrors of that past. The ability to so imagine is evidence of faith, which Aunt Ester has but cannot give to Citizen. It is also lived religion, and so always requiring translation into and beyond current contexts. In Wilson's work, imagination means developing something new and then having the sense enough into protect it. There is a sacred imagination here in the shared experience.

Do You Want to Ride on the Boat? A Conclusion

The novelty of the City of Bones ritual in *Gem of the Ocean* is the practical application of Black folk religion for the healing of persons and communities. It relies on a method of caring for a person by helping them to develop their own tools associated with memory, culture, and imagination. Those researching trauma describe how experiences are forever etched not only in memory, but also physically.[39] And because trauma's impacts are communal as well as individual, the tools for recovery, in this case African American folk religion, must be so too. Are there not valuable insights and implications here for African American Christian worship as well?

---

39. See, for example, Van der Kolk, *The Body Keeps the Score*.

Prompted by the inhumane killing of Michael Brown, an innocent Black man from St. Louis, the founders of the Black Lives Matter movement—the Black women Alicia Garza, Patrisse Cullors, Opal Tometi, two of whom identify as queer, and others—guided a community through a journey to face the wrongs committed, and to demand change. While there are some modern differences, these founders, alongside mothers whose children have been violently taken become Aunt Ester figures, keepers of history and encouragers of change.

Similarly, when Ahmaud Arbery, George Floyd, and Breonna Taylor were killed, and protests were organized to scream their pain, many leaders spoke not only of empowering people with jobs in institutions, but also of bringing people into mutual connection for Black joy. Here, women, again, were at the forefront of recovering community, with the mothers of the slain victims running for political office to change the laws that prevented those who slaughtered their loved ones from being justly prosecuted. Their stories, coupled with horrors of the past and present, can help write a new future. "The hermeneutical process for personal wholeness is a communal process of mutual storytelling. This reflexive process includes interpretation and reinterpretation between individual experiences and those experiences common to the culture or faith community itself."[40] This is the work too of African American folk religion, and rituals such as the City of Bones scene in Wilson's *Gem of the Ocean*, as they begin to show how such work might be undertaken today, and so how wholeness might be realized.

Bibliography

Andrews, Dale P. *Practical Theology for Black Churches: Bridging Black Theology and African American Folk Religion*. Louisville: Westminster John Knox, 2002.

Bada, Valérie, and Christine Pagnoulle. "August Wilson's *Gem of the Ocean*: Translating Multilayered Sensory Experience." *Palimpsestes. Revue de traduction* 29 (2016). https://doi.org/10.4000/palimpsestes.2294.

Baker, Houston A., Jr. *Critical Memory: Public Spheres, African American Writing, and Black Fathers and Sons in America*. Athens: University of Georgia Press, 2001.

Bogumil, Mary L. *Understanding August Wilson*. Columbia: University of South Carolina Press, 1999.

Certeau, Michel de. *The Practice of Everyday Life*. Translated by Steven Rendall. Berkeley: University of California Press, 1984.

Chireau, Yvonne Patricia. *Black Magic: Religion and the African American Conjuring Tradition*. Berkeley: University of California Press, 2006.

Du Bois, W. E. B. *The Souls of Black Folk*. Edited by Brent H. Edwards. New York: Oxford University Press, 2007.

---

40. Andrews, *Practical Theology for Black Churches*, 25.

Elam, Harry J., Jr. "*Gem of the Ocean* and the Redemptive Power of History." In *The Cambridge Companion to August Wilson*, edited by Christopher Bigsby, 75–88. Cambridge: Cambridge University Press, 2007.

Erll, Astrid. *Memory in Culture*. Translated by Sara B. Young. Basingstoke: Palgrave Macmillan, 2011.

Frederick, Marla F. *Between Sundays: Black Women and Everyday Struggles of Faith*. Berkeley: University of California Press, 2003.

Gennep, Arnold van, *The Rites of Passage*. Translated by Monika B. Vizedom and Gabrielle L. Caffee. London: Routledge, 1960.

Hughes, Langston. "The Negro Speaks of Rivers." In *The Collected Works of Langston Hughes, Volume 1: The Poems, 1921–1940*, edited by Arnold Rampersad, 36. Columbia: University of Missouri Press, 2001.

Hurston, Zora N. *Dust Tracks on a Road*. New York: Arno, 1969.

———. *Mules and Men*. Philadelphia: Lippincott, 1935.

———. *Tell My Horse: Voodoo Life in Haiti and Jamaica*. Philadelphia: Lippincott, 1938.

———. *The Sanctified Church*. Berkeley: Turtle Island, 1981.

McGuire, Meredith B. *Lived Religion: Faith and Practice in Everyday Life*. Oxford: Oxford University Press, 2008.

Morrison, Toni. *Beloved*. New York: Knopf, 1987.

Nadel, Alan, ed. *August Wilson: Completing the Twentieth-Century Cycle*. Iowa City: University of Iowa Press, 2010.

Pittman, Elizabeth. "Voicing the 'Law of the Sea': Commemoration and Cultural Nationalism in August Wilson's *Gem of the Ocean*." *Culture, Theory, and Critique* 54.1 (2013) 19–36.

Raboteau, Albert J. *Slave Religion: The "Invisible Institution" in the Antebellum South*. Updated ed. Oxford: Oxford University Press, 2004.

Shange, Ntozake. *For Colored Girls Who Have Considered Suicide/When the Rainbow Is Enuf*. San Lorenzo: Shameless Hussy, 1975.

Thompson, Lisa L. *Ingenuity: Preaching as an Outsider*. Nashville: Abingdon, 2018.

Turner, Victor W. *The Forest of Symbols: Aspects of Ndembu Ritual*. Ithaca: Cornell University Press, 1967.

Van der Kolk, Bessel A. *The Body Keeps the Score: Mind, Brain, and Body in the Transformation of Trauma*. London: Penguin, 2015.

Wardi, Anissa Janine. *Water and African American Memory: An Ecocritical Perspective*. Gainesville: University Press of Florida, 2016.

Wilson, August. *Gem of the Ocean*. New York: Theatre Communications Group, 2006.

Young, Jason R. *Rituals of Resistance: African Atlantic Religion in Kongo and the Lowcountry South in the Era of Slavery*. Baton Rouge: Louisiana State University Press, 2007.

33

What to Make of This, What to Make

Scott Cairns

—*Isaak's epistle*
Isaak, dim and grinning servant, sometime
scribe, to the scattered, blinking latecomers
just now waking to our long, common slog
through meandering marshlands, deserts, right
chafing storms of circumstance: Yo! Condolences.

The challenge may appear uncommonly
arduous of late, but the challenge has
always been thus: a strenuous matter
demanding we apply every scrap of wit,
hope, our senses of humor, and creative ken—

all of these brought to bear as tools to tweak
the mess extending far as we can see
and—from what we might gather—a good bit
farther. The challenge and the endless chore
remains that we must each make something new of all

that lay before us, all that lay behind.
Imagination, duly understood,
proves yet to be the key, and yet our most
revealing due inheritance, owned by
our having been created in His Image. Lo.

So, yes, the challenges ahead lie fraught
with new demands yet mixed with prior sins,
and these have caused a clamor, deafening
the ears of those who might have rectified
the past, who must yet listen more attentively.

The sighs, the tears, the angry cries arising
provoked by generations unconcerned,
denying all conviction—that's the mess
each soul is now obliged to mitigate,
the new construction to which all must lend a hand.

I'm in. In His Image, each is vastly
well endowed to turn the heart, the mind, all
noetic agency to this endless
task—imagining the road ahead, there-
after setting out to build it as we go. Yes.

Index

Page numbers in italics refer to illustrations/photos.

Aboriginal, 18–19, 21–22, 30–43, 87, 174, 189–93, 198–215, 254–66, 275–77, 310–12
    art, 18–19, 21, 30–43, 87n9, 198–215, 275–77, 302, 310–12
    dreaming, 31–33, 36–37, 211, 275–76, *311*, 312
    songlines, 311
Aboriginal Memorial, The, 199–201, *199*
Adnyamathanha, 21, 200n4, 209–13
Adorno, Theodor, 6–9, 13n53, 15n61, 228n37, 229, 230n47, 231n59, 245
Ai, Dan, 152
Ai, Lao, 158, 163
Ai, Qing, 149–50
Ai, Weiwei, 20, 148–69
    biography, 149–52, 158
    Chinese Government, and, 158, 160–62
    internet, and, 152–53
    Little Girl's Cheeks, 153
    Remembering, 155
    response to Sichuan earthquake, 148–49, *149*
    response to Tiananmen Square, 151
    societal indifference, 164
    Straight, 159–60, *159*
    Sunflower Seeds, 156, *157*
Albrecht, Glenn, 96
Ali, Tariq, 111
Andre, Carl, 159

Andrews, Dale, 22, 320–21
anthropocene, 16, 94, 96
Antigone, 99
Antiochus Epiphanes IV, 75
apocalypse, apocalyptic, 1, 20, 94, 96, 109–11, 119, 121–22, 245, 289–91
    entertainment, and, 111
    hope, and, 76
    imagination in art, and, 289–91
    poetry, and, 95–96
Arbery, Ahmaud, 22, 332
Arendt, Hannah, 13–14
armageddon, 94–96
Armstrong, Louis, 78
art,
    complicity, and, 3, 4, 277–78
    confronting falsity, and, 170
    connection, and, 265, 275–76
    contemplation, and, 68, 69, 269, *270*
    discursive practice, and, 302
    drawing, 151, 160, *177*, 269–70, 271, 272–73, 285, 287, 291, 292, 297–308, *303*, *305*
    engagement, as, 70
    envisioning uncertainty, as, 269
    exhibitions, 4, 22, 154–60, 298–300
    experience, as, 159
    expression of country, as, 310–12, *311*
    film, 21, 198–215, *201*, *205*, *210*, *212*
    identity, and, 301

art *(continued)*,
  indulgence, as, 49
  literature (fiction), 11, 174–93, 223, 319, 321–22
  music, 20, 78–80, 127–44, 288
  oppression, and, 80–81, 164
  painting, 12, 18, 31, 32, 34, 35, 36, 44–46, *44*, 68–70, *69*, 72, *73*, 81, 83–84, 109, *110*, 170–72, *171*, *173*, 275–77, *276*, 279, 281, 284, *285*, 286, *290*, 291, 310–12, *311*
  photography, 151–52, 154, 285, 287
  poetry, xxvii, 6, 14n57, 19, 28–29, 49, 51, 68, 85–103, 174, 183, 197, 321
  prophetic, as, 13, 166–67, 280, 289
  reenactment, as, 276, *276*
  remembrance, as, 160, 162
  response to current problems, as, 2
  risk, as, 16–18, 47, 68
  sacrament, and, 91, 276
  salvation, and, 2–3
  sculpture, 72, *74*, 154–60, *157*, *159*, *199*, 217–19, *218*
  self-definition, and, 272–74
  self-identification, and, 297
  social transgression, and, 153–54, 165
  spiritual intent, and, 276–77
  theatre, 21, 220–46, *221*, *224*, *227*, *233*, *236*, *238*, *240*, *244*, 318–32
  time, and, 110, 153
  truth, and, 3, 10–11, 45, 163
  unfinished, as, 308
artist, artists, 2–5, 8, 10–12, 14n57, 17, 45–46, 49, 53, 74, 150–52, 155, 164, 199, 221, 278–80, 283–84, 286–89, 292–93, 297–308
  faith, and, 303–04, *303*, *305*
  identifying through work style, 298–300
  improvisation, and, 305–06
  mystic, as, 22, 282–84, 291, 293–94
  prophet, as, 20, 22, 148–67, 278, 280, 282, 284, 288–91, 293–94
  vocation of, 4, 10, 288–89
  vulnerability, and, 307–08
Auden, W. H., xxvii, 10–11

Ault, Henri, 83n1
awareness, 3, 15, 46, 53, 70, 140, 280, 284, 300, 306, 329

Bacon, Francis, 177
Baker, Houston, 320, 325
balance, 107–08
Bauckham, Richard, 62n24, 62n25, 64n30
beauty, xxviin8, 2, 12, 13n53, 55, 68, 273, 281, 315, 329
Beckett, Samuel, 3, 21, 220–50
  Come and Go, 227, *227*
  connections, impossibility of, 238–39
  Endgame, 232, *233*, 234
  Happy Days, 236–38, *236*, *238*, *240*
  haunted bodies, and, 222–23
  Krapp's Last Tape, 223, *224*, 227, 230, *244*
  managing trauma, and, 243–44
  Not I, 228–29
  presence, and, 231, 235, 237
  Waiting for Godot, 220–21, 233n66, 234, 241
Beckman, Max, 281
Beesley, Luke, 93
belief, 1n5, 46–47, 55, 90, 93–98, 140, 144, 164, 175, 180, 189–90, 210, 251–52, 278–79, 281, 286, 291–92, 320–21
  hope, and, 285–86
  imagination, and, 66
Bellows, Nathaniel, 94
Bennett, Jane, 86n7
Berger, John, 11n45
Bloch, Ernst, 15n61, 15n64, 64, 65n34
Boas, Franz, 321
Bonhoeffer, Dietrich, 3n13, 4n16
Boulter, Jonathan, 228–29, 231, 235–37
Bourgeault, Cynthia, 133n4
Bourke, Joanna, 282
Brecht, Bertolt, 5n18
Brexit, 111
Brooklyn Art Library (BAL), 297–98, 300, 307
Brown, Laura, 226n29
Brown, Michael, 332

Brown, Verna, 239n91
Brown, Wendy, 114
Buckley, Bernadette, 280

Cambodia Sings, 127, 129–30
Camus, Albert, 15n62
capitalism, 2–3, 5, 7, 18, 20, 112–13, 115, 151, 163
Carson, Anne, 19, 102–3
Caruth, Cathy, 222n7, 222n9, 226n29, 235, 243
Cave, Nick, 5, 6n19, 8, 176–77, 183
Cavell, Stanley, 232n63, 233n67, 243n113
ceremony, 31, 35, 38–39, 42, 128, 206–07, 211
Champion, Denise, 21, 202, 209–11, 213–15
chaos, 6, 180, 289, 292, 299, 308
Chidester, David, 287–88
Chim↑Pom, 220n2
chronic illness/pain, 268–74
church, 41, 46–47, 66, 86, 101, 229, 263–64, 296, 318, 332
    colonialism, and, 45, 202, 204
    failings of, 47, 86
    reflection on, 296
    society, and, 283
Clark, Manning, 179
climate change, 18, 60, 85, 92, 96, 131, 164, 279–80, 290
Clothier, Kim, 206
colonialism, colonization, 1, 4, 7, 18–21, 31, 38, 39n14, 45, 85, 109–10, 115, 116n11, 122, 163, 174, 191, 198, 200–04, 208–11, 213–15
    capitalism, and, 116–19
    dispossession, and, 109
    Indigenous Australia, and, 198, *199*
    New Zealand, and, 116–22
compassion, 98, 182, 246, 280, 282, 285–86
contiguity, 138
COVID-19 pandemic, xxvii, 1, 4–5, 7, 8n33, 18, 21, 30n1, 45, 68–70, 69, 85, 111, 131, 170, 219, 220n2, 254, 257–59, 261, 262n17, 266, 269, 273, 280, 290, 305
Crawford, Anwen, 5n18
creation, creative, 5, 7, 10n38, 11n43, 15n62, 19, 21–22, 33, 37, 49, 53, 55, 59–60, 64, 92, 94, 133–34, 137, 144, 172, 180, 202, 208–09, 211, 214, 268, 273, 276, 279, 287–88, 290, 293, 298, 306, 311–12
crisis, crises, 5, 8, 19, 48–51, 59–61, 64, 131–32, 149, 221, 276–77, 301, 306, 308
Cronin, M. T. C., 19, 85, 87, 92–98, 101, 103
    God Is Waiting in the World's Yard, 85, 87, 92–93, 96–97
Cullors, Patrisse, 332
culture, cultural, 1n5, 6–8, 18, 21–22, 37, 40–42, 48, 57, 80–81, 86n8, 92, 95–96, 111, 116, 128, 139, 150, 152, 157, 166, 174, 184, 191–92, 198, 200–205, 207, 210, 213, 222, 224, 244, 256n3, 259, 265–66, 277–80, 282–84, 286, 288–89, 294, 302, 311, 318–20, 322, 325, 327–32

Daniel, Book of, 72–81
Daniel, Prophet, 72, 75, 77
Dante, 63
Davis, Megan, 203
Day, Lewis, 299
Daylight, Teagan Bennett, 188–90
death, 7, 9n38, 13n53, 14, 19, 21, 52, 65, 70, 72–74, 93–94, 97, 116, 118–21, 133, 139, 181, 186–87, 206, 229–30, 237, 245, 251, 254–66, 283, 289, 291–94
De Boever, Arne, 3n10
De Gruchy, John, 9n38, 10n38
Deloria, Vine, 90
De Maistre, Roy, 177
democracy, 2, 112–13, 151–52
Democritus, 51
Derrida, Jacques, 93–94, 245n120

340　INDEX

desire, 17, 61, 63–64, 117, 132–33, 142–43, 180, 182, 192, 237–38, 297–99, 307–08
despair, 4, 9, 52, 63, 111–12, 245, 246n126
Dhamarrandji, Maratja, 30n2, 31n4, 32, 32, 34, 34, 35–36, 36, 38, 43
   Coat of Arm, and, 33–35, 34
   Contextual readings, and, 35, 36
Diamond, Neil, 254
Didi-Huberman, Georges, 17
discrimination, 2, 40–41, 77
disruption
   art as, 2, 10
   exposure of, 10–11
   loss, and, 257–58
   responses to, 6, 9
   revelation, and, 2
Dissanayake, Ellen, 302–3
Djigirr, Peter, 203–4
Donne, John, 93
Dostoyevsky, Fyodor, 92n23
Du Bois, W. E. B., 321
Duchamp, Marcel, 151, 159
Duduk, Debra, 206
Dufrenne, Mikel, 300
Dupain, Max, 197
Dux, Monica, 86n8

Eagleton, Terry, 49, 62–64
ecology, ecological, 85–86, 94, 96
economic ideologies, 112–15
Edwards, Denis, 85n3
Einstein, Albert, vi
Elam, Harry, 319n2, 322
Eliot, T. S., 13, 231
engagement
   apophatic, 28–29
   art, with, 27–29
   contextuality, and, 36–37
   entry to, 32–35
   limited, 31
   relational, 56
   wholistic, 30–32, 43
Erll, Astrid, 320
eschatology, eschatological, 10n38, 14, 94, 96
existential meaning
   assumed, 50
   created, 51
   imagination as, 56
   trauma, and, 221–24
Eyre, Edward, 178

faith
   connections, 277
   nihilism, and, 51
   practice, and, 120–23
   redemption, and, 47
   secular, 175
   shaping discourse, and, 116
Flaubert, Gustave, 66
Floyd, George, 22, 332
Forsyth, Peter Taylor, 3n11, 66n37
Frank, Richard, 237
Frederick, Marla, 22, 324
freedom, 3, 8, 10–12, 45, 64, 77, 115–16, 122, 151, 153, 163–65, 213–14, 242, 272, 291, 301, 306, 321, 323
Freud, Sigmund, 222, 225, 228, 230, 234–36, 238, 243
Frye, Northrop, 13n53
Fukushima
   Waiting for Godot, and, 220, 221
Fukuyama, Francis, 112–15

Gallagher, Michael Paul, 170
Gandhi, Mohandas, 122
Garibay, Emmanuel, 44–47
   Selda, 44
Garner, Helen, 21, 174n1, 176, 185, 187–91, 193
Garza, Alicia, 332
Gaskin, Claire, 19, 98–101, 103
Gennep, Arnold van, 329
Gittoes, George, 22, 280–94
   Love City, Jalalabad, 293–94
   religion, and, 286, 288
   Security, 290–91, 290
   theatres of conflict, and, 281–82
   The Preacher, 284–86, 285
   witness, as, 284, 287
globalization, 20, 111, 114–15, 280
Gore, Al, 111
Goroncy, Jason, xxvii
Gould, Glenn, 8
government, 45, 112, 118–20, 122, 148, 151–55, 158, 161–62, 192

Grady, Constance, 1n1
Graham, Billy, 262
Granites, Ida Nangala, 275–77
　Mina Mina, 276
Green, Garrett, 15n65
Greene, Graham, 53
Gukuk, 30n2, 32, 33, 35, 38–39
Gulpilil, David, 21, 198, 200–205, *201*,
　208–9, *210*, *212*, 214–15
Gurala Binyanbi, 32n6, 34, 36
Gutiérrez, Gustavo, 43
Gutwein, Peter, 259

Hagiwara, Yuta, 220–21
　Waiting for Godot in Fukushima,
　220–21, *221*
Hart, Deborah, 281n12
Hart, Trevor, 2n6, 15n64, 16n67, 19,
　57n18, 62n24–n25, 64n30
Havel, Václav, 16–17
Haynes, Deborah, 288–89
Heartney, Eleanor, 279, 289
Hecq, Dominique, 99–101
Heer, Rolf de, 21, 198, 200–204, *201*,
　208n20, 212, 213n28, 214–15
　Ten Canoes, 200, 203, 205–9, *205*,
　214–15
　The Tracker, 201, 209, *210*, 212
Hegel, G. W. F., 6n20, 113
hermeneutics, 15n65, 19, 40–43, 58,
　228, 332
Herwitz, Daniel, 281–82, 286,
Hiebert, Theodore, 89
history, 5–6, 10n38, 21, 40–41, 46–47,
　62, 65–66, 80–81, 112–15, 121–
　23, 192, 214–15, 227, 229–31,
　243, 289, 292, 302, 330–31
Hitler, Adolf, 155
Holloway, Richard, 51–52, 54, 62
hope, 1–2, 9, 14–19, 47, 50–52, 63–66,
　77, 96, 101, 110–12, 115, 117,
　122–23, 130, 141–42, 166, 188,
　191–92, 197–98, 213–14, 223,
　232, 234, 236–39, 242, 246n126,
　259, 266, 280, 283–84, 288–89,
　291–93, 300, 308, 334
　artificial, 65
　deliverance, and, 76–77
　engagement, and, 111–12, 115

　human identity, and, 65–66
　humility of god, and, 122–23
　imagination, and, 16–18, 47, 63–65
　offering possibilities, 101
　reinventing the past, and, 75–80
　within the world, 92, 96
Horkheimer, Max, 7n25
Hughes, Graham, 137n11
Hughes, Langston, 321
Hughes, Robert, 278
Hurston, Zora Neale, 321

icon, iconography, xxvii, 72, 75
imagination, 1–2, 4–5, 7n23, 9n38,
　10–11, 13–22, 45, 48–66, 90,
　112, 130–32, 134, 136–37, 139,
　144, 148, 155, 164–66, 174–77,
　179–87, 190, 193, 198, 202, 204,
　206, 214, 232, 241n100, 254,
　259, 266, 277, 279–80, 283, 286,
　288–91, 293–94, 298, 300–301,
　306–8, 318, 320–22, 329–31,
　334–35
　art, and, 4
　connection, and, 254–57
　creating meaning, and, 51–53,
　　56–57, 60
　discernment, and, 60
　engaging the other, and, 301
　frame of interpretation, and, 61–62
　grammar, and, 63–64
　healing, and, 257, 259
　hope, and, 16–18, 47, 63–65
　meaning, and, 181–82, 184
　misinterpretations of, 48–49
　moral compass, and, 50
　physicality of, 214–16
　physical presence, and, 186–87, 193
　rebuilding meaning, and, 132–33
　redemption, and, 112
　representation, and, 165
　responsibility to, 13–14
　risk, and, 15
　secularity, and, 174–77
　story, and, 254–66
　thinking modes, and, 58–59
Indigenous film, 198–215
　land, and, 212
　theology, and, 198

Infeld, Leopold, vi
Ismene, 99

Jackson, Andy, 19, 91, 98, 101, 103
Jacob, 307
Jennings, Willie James, 21, 202, 204, 206n13, 207–09
Jeremiah, Prophet, 166
Jesus Christ, 42, 47, 66, 72, 83–84, 95–96, 122, 132–34, 138–43, 165, 170, 179–80, 182, 211, 214, 291, 306
Johnson, Darlene, 203n6
Johnson, Mark, 58, 137n10
Jorgensen, Darren, 282, 286–87
Judd, Donald, 159
justice, injustice, xxvi, xxviii, 2, 4, 19, 45, 47, 75–77, 80–81, 110, 116, 162–64, 166, 175, 185, 187, 191–92, 198, 200, 203, 213–14, 257n4, 280, 283, 287, 332

Kākahi, Tohu, 115, 118
Kandinsky, Wassily, 278–79
Kant, Immanuel, 7, 15n64, 56
Kearney, Richard, 49
Keenan, Danny, 117, 119, 120n22
Keller, Catherine, 94n38, 96
Kim, Sharon, 190
King, Martin Luther, Jr., 76–77, 81, 122
Kojève, Alexandre, 113
Krugman, Paul, 7n30

Lacan, Jacques, 234
land, 21, 30, 39, 109, 115–20, 122, 128, 177, 180–81, 183, 191–93, 199, 200–202, 204–5, 208–15, 258, 275–77, 310–12
Langer, Lawrence, 241n100
Langlois, Christopher, 222n9
Lascaris, Manoly, 177
Latham, Robyne, 302
Laub, Dori, 225n24, 226n28, 226n29
LaVeau, Marie, 323
Leane, Jeanine, 87n9
Le Guin, Ursula, 10n40
Leichardt, Ludwig, 178
Levine, Stephen, 233n66, 246n126

Lewis, C. S., 4n15, 55–58
liberalism, 112–15
liberation, xxvii, 77, 133, 308
Lodish, Emily, 166n67, 166n68
Lord, Audre, 68
Lucas, Rose, 19, 87–90, 101
Luckhurst, Roger, 235
Lynch, William, 64n31, 65

Macfarlane, Robert, 217
MacGimsey, Robert, 78
MacGreevy, Tom, 239
MacKinnon, Donald, 11
Macron, Emmanuel, 146
Malouf, David, 176
Maniopoto, Rewi, 117–18
Manson, Mark, 51–52, 54, 62
Mao, Zedong, 149–50, 156
Maōri, 109–22
Marlow, Tim, 148n1, 160n37, 164n57, 165n61, 166n66
martyrdom, 19, 75–77, 98, 165, 180
Marx, Karl, 113
McCahon, Colin, 109–10
    Parihaka Triptych, 109–10, *110*
McCallum, Christina, 102
McCredden, Lyn, 90
McGilchrist, Iain, 58
McLean, Donald, 117
McLeish, Tom, 60n21
McMullan, Audrey, 228n36
meaning, 139, 146, 239
Melville, Herman, 230
memory, memories, 21–22, 81, 128, 155, 162, 166, 180, 199–200, 211, 217, 222–23, 226n29, 228–29, 231, 234–42, 252, 256, 261, 263, 286, 298, 303, 306, 318, 320, 322, 324–27, 329–31
    inability to express, 240–41
    network, 320
    severed from present, 236, 239
    trauma, and, 243–44
Mercier, Vivien, 234
Merrill, Robert, 78
Messiaen, Olivier, 20, 132–34, 139, 142
    Praise to the Immortality of Jesus, 132–44

INDEX

score signing, 142–44
militarism, 2, 18, 45, 85, 285
Millner, Jacqueline, 301
Milton, John, 50
Miró, Joan, 3
Modernity, Modernism, 1, 15n65, 48, 62, 151, 155, 162, 177, 179, 228, 242–43, 245, 278–79, 284, 299–300
Morrison, Toni, 321
mourning, 111–12, 229–31, 237–38, 240
Mundine, Djon, 199–200
Murdoch, Iris, 15n62, 53, 60
museums, 4, 81
mystery, 9n38, 12, 14, 52, 68, 83, 143, 306, 308

Nabi, Haji-Daoud, 123
nationalism, 1, 80–81, 114
natural disasters, 1
nature, 7n25, 13n53, 55, 65–66, 299
Nebuchadnezzar II, 72, 74–76, 79
neoliberalism, 2, 111
Nietzsche, Frederick, 93n28, 233
nihilism, 50–52, 233, 245, 292
    George Gittoes, and, 292
    hope, and, 97
    meaning, and, 50–53
    Samuel Beckett, and, 233–34
Nolan, Sidney, 177
Nosthoff, Anna-Verena, 228, 231n59

Obama, Barack, 111
oppression
    art, and, 80–81
    destruction of identity, and, 128
    life, and, 12–13
optimism, 16, 61–62, 64, 122

pākehā, 109–10, 115–18, 121
pandemics, xxvii, 1, 4–5, 7, 13, 18, 21, 45, 68–70, 85, 95, 101, 131, 170, 220n2, 257–58, 261n14, 262n17, 269, 280, 290, 305,
Parihaka, 20, 109–10, 115–18, 120–22
Parris, Robert, 116–17
Pascoe, Bruce, 199
patriotism, 81, 119, 161

Paul, Saint, xxvi, 59, 185, 187
Péguy, Charles, 16
Peirce, Charles, 20, 134–37
Peterman, Steven, 298
philosophy, 6, 9, 11, 28, 46, 53, 58, 159, 243n113, 299
Picasso, Pablo, 3n12
Pippin, Tina, 289
Plato, 6n20, 14n57
Polanyi, Michael, 232n63
politics, political, xxvii, 1–2, 5, 10, 14–15, 18, 20, 45, 53, 57, 81, 92, 96, 111–12, 114–15, 117, 132, 149, 151–52, 155, 161, 163, 177, 180, 192, 200, 246, 278–80, 282, 286, 289, 301, 332
Pollock, Jackson, 3
Pot, Pol, 128
Potter, Dennis, 245
protest, 9, 80–81, 122, 332

Qoheleth, 234

Raboteau, Albert, 22, 326, 329
race, racism, 4, 7n23, 45, 81, 122, 184, 277, 300, 320–21
Rae, Murray, 8n34
Rank, Otto, 230
Rasmussen, Erica, 107–08
Raypirri', 35n10
reason, 7, 9n38, 17, 19, 48, 54–62, 64–65, 134, 137–38, 234, 316
    failures of, 28–29
    fallacy of, 58
    hope, and, 64
    imagination, and, 55–57
    intelligent reflection, and, 62
    limits of, 51–52, 56
    networks, 38
    truth, and, 57
redemption
    art, and, 11, 47
    broken, 99–101
    conflict, and, 179–83
    protest, and, 9
religion, folk, 22, 318–32
repetition, 101, 143, 225, 231, 237, 268–74, *271*

resemblance, 136–38
responsibility
　art, and, 3, 7
　humanity, and, 6–7
　relationships, and, 13
resurrection, 94–95, 100–01, 116, 121–23, 170, 180, 232n63
revelation, 2, 7, 11, 164, 214
　art, and, 10–12, 27–29
Revelation, Book of, 76, 289
Reynolds, Molly, 204
Ricœur, Paul, 56–57
ritual, 18, 21–22, 31, 39, 42–43, 128, 139, 164–65, 182, 274, 283, 287–88, 293–94, 318–32
Roach, Archie, 213
Roberts, Michael Symmons, xxviii
Robeson, Paul, 77
Robson, Jon, 3n10
Rosbottom, Daniel, 165n60
Rose, Deborah Bird, 85n3, 97
Rothko, Mark, 12–13
Roy, Arundhati, 4–5
Royal Commission into Institutional Responses to Child Sexual Abuse, 86, 99–100
Rublev, Andrei, 101

Sacks, Jonathan, 9n36
sacrament, sacramentality, 86, 90, 101, 296
　art, and, 110
sacred, the, 87, 175
　absence, and, 187, 190
　breath, and, 88–89
　brokenness, and, 182–83, 190
　form, and, 90
　land as, 209–11
　modern Australian literature, and, 176–77
　natural world, and, 92, 95
　secularism, and, 184–86
　wound, and, 91
sacred texts, 39–40, 42–43
Sagan, Carl, 62
Santner, Eric, 92n24
Schleiermacher, Friedrich, xxv–xxvi
science, 6n22, 28, 53, 58, 62, 221n5,

Scorsese, Martin, 180
Scott, Dick, 116–21
Scott, Kim, 21, 176, 190–93
scripture, scriptures, 18–19, 30–43, 303
Sebald, W. G., 11
semiotics, 134–36
sexual abuse, 85–86, 100–101
Shakespeare, Nicholas, 179–80
Shakespeare, William, 11
Shange, Ntozake, 321
singing
　healing, and, 129
　hope, and, 130
Smailović, Vedran, 9
Smith, Bernard, 281
Smith, James K. A., 131n1
Snake, Reuben, 15n59
Snider, Sarah Kirkland, 94
Sophocles, 11, 99
sovereignty, 20, 112–17, 123
spirituality, 86, 144, 189, 207, 273, 279
Steinbeck, John, 15
Steiner, George, vi, 3n12, 15n64, 63, 65
Stevenson, Leslie, 54–55
story, stories, 15, 18–19, 30n2, 31, 33, 39, 51–52, 54, 128, 142, 189, 198, 206, 211–12, 214, 258, 277, 297, 300–303, 307–8, 310, 319, 332
　community identity, and, 283
Strauss, David Levi, 282
structural bias, 4
　colonialism, and, 31, 39, 41
　power, and, 46
　racism, and, 41
　religion, and, 47
suffering, 13, 19, 52, 75, 77, 92, 134
symbols, 31, 37, 45, 70, 75, 77, 80–81, 112–13, 155–56, 174, 179, 181, 199, 310
Szymborska, Wisława, vi

Tajiri, Yoshiki, 221–22
Tanaka, Mariko Hori, 221–22
Tancock, John, 165
Taylor, Breonna, 22, 332
Taylor, Charles, 53–54, 62, 131n1

technology, 2, 46, 53, 62, 161, 282, 287, 290–91
terrorism, 128, 220, 222n9, 279–80
Te Tiriti o Waitangi, 115, 118, 121
Te Whiti-o-Rongomai III, 109–10, 115–22
theology, xxv–xxvii, 9–10, 19–21, 43, 46–48, 77n2, 86, 92, 95–96, 101, 111–12, 117, 132, 134–44, 179–80, 190, 195–98, 202, 204, 208–9, 211, 215, 228, 230, 231n59, 244, 262–64, 289, 321–22
Thomas, Saint, 95
Thompson, Lisa, 320, 330
time, xxvii, 1, 3–5, 8, 13, 14n57, 16, 21, 27, 29, 31, 35, 39–40, 48–49, 55, 62–63, 86, 94–96, 114, 133, 141–42, 185, 217, 219, 226–31, 234–35, 239, 241, 254–66, 270, 286–88, 307, 326
Tometi, Opal, 332
Tomlinson, Rob, 182
tragedy, 15, 92, 99, 148, 155, 176, 228, 237, 251
Tranter, Rhys, 222n7, 222n8, 223n13, 224–25, 226n30, 227–29, 240, 243–45
trauma, 6n20, 19, 21–22, 75, 85–90, 94, 96, 98–99, 101, 130, 165, 180, 191, 220–46, 260, 286, 319, 328, 330–31
    art, and, 286–87
Trump, Donald, 111, 114, 170, 290
truth, xxvi, 6n20, 6n22, 10, 17, 19, 21, 48–52, 54, 56–57, 59, 98–101, 166, 192, 213–15, 222n7, 228–29, 232n63, 276
Tsiolkas, Christos, 21, 176, 183–87, 191
Tsushima, Michiko, 221–22
Tuchman, Maurice, 279
Turner, Victor, 319, 329–30
Tynan, Kenneth, 234n71

Uhlmann, Anthony, 181–83, 190

Viola, Bill, 313
violence, 8–9, 18, 20, 39, 80, 85, 93, 98, 109–11, 115–19, 122–23, 199, 203, 222–23, 235, 280–82, 287, 292, 328

Wagner, Richard, 3, 13n53
waiting
    as being, 269
    repetition, and, 270, 272
Waŋarr, 33–34
war, 6, 8, 11, 42, 80, 107, 110–12, 115–16, 118, 120, 122, 128, 176–77, 180, 201, 223, 231n59, 281–82, 284–85, 287, 291–94
Ward, Russell, 175
Warhol, Andy, 151, 159
Warlpiri, 275–77
Watt, George, 179
Weil, Simone, 11n43, 112
Wells, Samuel, 303–4, 306
White, Patrick, 21, 176–85, 187, 190–91, 193
    Christ figures, and, 179–80
    outsiders, and, 176–77
    The Solid Mandala, 181–83
    Voss, 177–78, 177
Whitely, Brett, 177
Williams, Rowan, xxv–xxviii, 3n14
Wilson, August, 318–19, 322–32
    City of Bones, 319, 322–25, 329–31
    Gem of the Ocean, 319, 322–32
witness, 87, 110
Wolterstorff, Nicholas, 48n1
Woolf, Christopher, 81n4
Woolf, Virginia, 9
worship, 47, 74–76, 80–81, 131, 138, 300, 303–6, 331

Yeats, W. B., 1–2, 93
Yemanjá, 323
Yolŋu, 18–19, 30–43, 200–203, 205–7, 209, 214
Yothu-Yindi, 33, 37–40
Young, Jason, 324
Younn, Elain, 129
Yunupingu, Dhanggal, 207
Yunupingu, Djungadjunga, 207

Zabala, Santiago, 2–3

www.ingramcontent.com/pod-product-compliance
Lightning Source LLC
Chambersburg PA
CBHW062021290426
44108CB00024B/2727